Ethnomusicology and Cultural Diplomacy

The Lexington Series in Historical Ethnomusicology: Deep Soundings

Series Editors
David Hebert (Western Norway University of Applied Sciences)
Jonathan McCollum (Washington College, USA)

The Lexington Series in Historical Ethnomusicology: Deep Soundings is a series from Lexington Books envisioned to offer rigorous, cutting-edge research that probes music of the past and mechanisms of sociomusical change. We champion innovative approaches and diverse methodologies, ranging from archival and oral histories to syntheses of organological and music-archaeological findings, to computational studies of musical evolution across decades, as well as novel interpretations of non-Western music philosophy. The series also features original works that synthesize the oeuvre of influential scholars whose publications are primarily in languages other than English. Books in this series offer theoretically robust presentations of unique discoveries, written in lucid prose appropriate for liberal arts colleges and universities, as well as professional researchers.

Ethnomusicology and Cultural Diplomacy, edited by David Hebert and Jonathan McCollum

The Malay Nobat: A History of Power, Acculturation, and Sovereignty, by Raja Iskandar bin Raja Halid

Activism through Music during the Apartheid Era and Beyond: When Voices Meet, by Ambigay Yudkoff

Ethnomusicology and Cultural Diplomacy

Edited by David G. Hebert
and Jonathan McCollum

LEXINGTON BOOKS
Lanham • Boulder • New York • London

Published by Lexington Books
An imprint of The Rowman & Littlefield Publishing Group, Inc.
4501 Forbes Boulevard, Suite 200, Lanham, Maryland 20706
www.rowman.com

86-90 Paul Street, London EC2A 4NE, United Kingdom

Copyright © 2022 The Rowman & Littlefield Publishing Group, Inc.

All rights reserved. No part of this book may be reproduced in any form or by any electronic or mechanical means, including information storage and retrieval systems, without written permission from the publisher, except by a reviewer who may quote passages in a review.

British Library Cataloguing in Publication Information Available

Library of Congress Cataloging-in-Publication Data

Names: Hebert, David G., editor. | McCollum, Jonathan, editor.
Title: Ethnomusicology and cultural diplomacy / edited by David G. Hebert and Jonathan McCollum.
Description: Lanham : Lexington Books, 2022. | Series: The Lexington series in historical ethnomusicology: deep soundings | Includes bibliographical references and index. | Summary: "Music has long played a prominent role in cultural diplomacy, but until now no resource has comparatively examined policies that shape how non-western countries use music in international relations. Inspired by decolonization, this book describes policies and legal frameworks that impact music's role in cultural diplomacy worldwide"— Provided by publisher.
Identifiers: LCCN 2022001909 (print) | LCCN 2022001910 (ebook) | ISBN 9781793642912 (cloth) | ISBN 9781793642936 (paper) | ISBN 9781793642929 (ebook)
Subjects: LCSH: Music and diplomacy. | Cultural diplomacy. | Ethnomusicology.
Classification: LCC ML3916 .E75 2022 (print) | LCC ML3916 (ebook) | DDC 327.101—dc23
LC record available at https://lccn.loc.gov/2022001909
LC ebook record available at https://lccn.loc.gov/2022001910

To marginalized voices
that sing for reconciliation
even in the face of adversity,
twisted conspiracies,
and baseless "truths."

Contents

Preface: Why this Topic and these Authors ix
David G. Hebert

PART 1: INTRODUCTION TO MUSIC AND CULTURAL DIPLOMACY

1 Introduction: Ethnomusicology as a Resource for Cultural Diplomacy 3
David G. Hebert

2 International Soft Law and the Promotion of Musical Rights 21
Marja Heimonen and David G. Hebert

PART 2: MIDDLE EASTERN PERSPECTIVES

3 "Afghanistan is Not What You Think": Cultural Diplomacy through Music Education and Performance 49
Lauren Braithwaite

4 Music Festivals and Cultural Diplomacy in Uzbekistan 77
Elnora Mamadjanova and David G. Hebert

5 Sufi Voices: Music as a Unifying Pathway toward the Divine 93
Chaden Yafi

6 Soft War and Multilateral Musical Pathways in Iran 119
Nasim Niknafs

PART 3: EAST ASIAN VIEWS

7 Cultural Diplomacy in Collaborative Music Projects between
China and Europe 139
Marianne Løkke Jakobsen and David G. Hebert

8 A Gap in Cultural Policy: Non-Japanese Experiences of
Learning Japanese Music 157
Koji Matsunobu

9 Cultural Diplomacy and Transculturation through the History of
Vọng Cổ in Vietnam 181
Nguyễn Thanh Thủy and Stefan Östersjö

PART 4: AFRICAN INSIGHTS

10 Cultural Policies and Music Production across
Ethiopian Regimes: A Historical Study 209
Abraha Weldu and Jan Magne Steinhovden

11 Musical Activism from South Africa: The "Soft Power"
of Cultural Diplomacy 229
Ambigay Yudkoff

12 Intercultural Relations in Church Music of Nigeria
and South Africa 255
Rhoda Abiolu

PART 5 LEGAL PERSPECTIVES FROM ASIA

13 Cultural Heritage and Music Diplomacy: The Legal Framework
in India 277
Karan Choudhary

14 China's Legal Framework Supporting Protection and
Sustainability of Artistic Heritage 297
Juqian Li

PART 6: CONCLUSION: RETHINKING MUSIC HERITAGE AND CULTURAL DIPLOMACY

15 Toward Global Models and Benchmarks for Music Diplomacy 315
David G. Hebert and Jonathan McCollum

Index 335

About the Editors and Contributors 353

Preface
Why this Topic and these Authors
David G. Hebert

Music heritage and cultural diplomacy might seem to be an unusual topic for a book, but it is a theme that is close to our hearts as authors, something profoundly connected to personal experience, and about which there is valid reason to believe that—with the help of colleagues—it may be possible to offer some new insights. This theme has been at the center of much of my own work across recent decades, and many of the contributors to this book are musicians and scholars with whom I have collaborated on various projects. Reflecting on the background of this book, it becomes clear that like many other things in life, credit is owed to one's teachers. With some persistence, I was fortunate to be admitted for postgraduate studies in music at the University of Washington, Seattle, in the late 1990s. Master studies in ethnomusicology only made me more curious about the entire world, and upon advancing to PhD studies, I served as a teaching assistant for Patricia Shehan Campbell's course Ethnomusicology in the Schools, as well as for a summer course taught by the late Bruno Nettl. As part of the former course, we took students to the Yakima Indian Reservation to live for a week, where they learned from local people and taught music from around the world in a school that primarily served American Indians and Hispanic students. This eye-opening experience especially convinced me that music has a special power to transcend borders—for either good or ill—and educators have a solemn responsibility to determine how its power can be used in ethical ways (Hebert and Kertz-Welzel, 2016).

My PhD dissertation research, on Western music in Japan, was funded by Japan's ministry of education. The doctoral research period turned out to be quite formative as I got to know dozens of young researchers from across the world who lived in the same *Kokusai Kaikan* "International House" while studying Japanese language and culture together in Tokyo. From that point onward, I became even more curious about other cultures and was willing to apply for jobs in almost any country worldwide, which resulted in unexpected opportunities that demonstrate how academia itself can function as an institution of cultural diplomacy. In fact, I first met the accomplished scholar and shakuhachi player Koji Matsunobu, a contributor to this volume, while living in Tokyo at the Kokusai Kaikan. After working for a while as the only foreign employee in a Japanese music company in Tokyo (while still analyzing field notes from ethnographic and historical research for the dissertation), I departed in 2003 for a job in Russia—as a US citizen—to teach music courses at the Lomonosov Moscow State University through a "sister college" relationship that was in the process of being dissolved with the University of Colorado, Denver. I was the last American teacher to be sent as part of that joint program since there had been troubling issues with academic accountability at Russia's leading university. This complex experience certainly caused me to think about issues associated with international relations and diplomacy, all while I continued to record my findings regarding the process by which Western music came to Japan and was ultimately popularized there (Hebert, 2012). While in Moscow, I gave some recitals on trumpet and voice with a skilled Russian pianist, performing a program of music by American and Russian composers (from Barber and Gershwin to Rachmaninov and Prokofiev), as well as jazz standards, and performed free improvisation with the Tchaikovsky Conservatoire's experimental "Pan Asian Ensemble." The collaborating musicians in these contrasting situations sought to communicate musically across a cultural divide, but in quite different ways, which ultimately prompted me to reflect on how music itself becomes a vehicle for translated understandings (Hebert, 2018).

Soon after that experience, I moved to New Zealand to work for a few years as head of music for Maori college Te Wananga O Aotearoa (translated from Te Reo Maori as "University of New Zealand"), which at the time was considered the world's largest Indigenous people's college. "Te Wa" had many Maori students, but also Pacific Islanders from Samoa, Tonga, Fiji, Tuvalu, Tahiti, Rarotonga, and elsewhere. Perhaps it was during this time that I developed a more focused interest in music as cultural diplomacy, as I witnessed several formal diplomatic ceremonies between Maori, Samoan, and Tongan chieftains in which music played a major role. Three of my research projects from this period made headway in this direction, including a historical study of the Maori Ratana bands that uncovered fascinating examples of early exchange between Maori and Japanese musicians, already a century in the past (Hebert, 2008a). Another project from this time was an ethnographic study of a Tongan youth band that, despite featuring brass instruments, turned out to be an important vehicle for sustaining Tongan culture among the immigrant community in New Zealand (Hebert, 2008b). Finally, the topic of music as cultural diplomacy really came to the fore with the Thai-Maori Musical Exchange Project, a collaboration with Dr. "Ros" Pornprapit Phoasavadi at Chulalongkorn University in Thailand, who had been my Thai traditional music teacher when I studied in Seattle. Incredibly, Ros had managed to attain government funding to bring her entire Thai traditional music ensemble to New Zealand for a tour that was arranged through embassies. Since I was working for a Maori institution, the tour mostly benefitted Maori audiences, while the Thai musicians also enjoyed an opportunity to learn about Maori musical traditions and cultural practices. After teaching for Boston University for a few years, I was hired as a professor at the Sibelius Academy (now University of the Arts Helsinki) in Finland, where I first met music law scholar Marja Heimonen, who would become my coauthor for various projects, and is also a contributor to this book (Heimonen and Hebert, 2010). Since moving to Europe for long-term work, I have mostly taught in Scandinavia, but have enjoyed projects in Africa and the Middle East, as well as visiting research scholar positions funded by the governments of Japan, Brazil, and China, in addition to visiting professor positions in Sweden and China. There have also been fruitful opportunities in Poland, especially in collaboration with Mikolaj Rykowski (Hebert and Rykowski, 2018), who was recently promoted as vice rector of the music academy in Poznan. It has also been a pleasure to join Stefan Östersjö (2020) for his intercultural music projects in Vietnam in collaboration with Thanh Thùy Nguyễn (now a postdoctoral researcher with my research group in Bergen), who together wrote a chapter for this book.

In Norway, I have been teaching courses in global cultural policy and international higher education for PhD students from across the world at the Bergen Summer Research School (BSRS), and four of the contributors to this book—Rhoda Abiolu, Abraha Weldu, Karan Choudhary, and Marianne Jakobsen—were students in the BSRS courses, from Nigeria, Ethiopia, India, and Denmark, respectively. Across recent years I have also been teaching intensive summer courses in arts policy for China University of Political Science and Law, in Beijing, which is where I first met law professor Juqian Li, another contributor to the present book. Cultural diplomacy is also part of my work in managing the Nordic Network for Music Education, which has long-term Nordic government funding to coordinate teacher and student exchange and shared master courses for seventeen music teacher education institutions across the eight Nordic and Baltic countries (Hebert and Haugen, 2019). In 2021, I joined an EU Erasmus Plus-funded project for Norwegian collaboration with a youth education NGO in North Macedonia and the music academy and community music schools in Latvia, and also received funding to develop an online collaboration at the doctoral level between Norway and Hong Kong. Finally, I am now part of a research team that has funding from the Norwegian Ministry of International Affairs to develop PhD programs in Uganda (2021–2026). Much could be written about each of these music diplomacy projects, and it is difficult to succinctly summarize what can be learned from such practical experiences in the field of music heritage and cultural diplomacy, but they have inspired in me a firm conviction that a book is very much needed on this topic.

I share this background at some risk of appearing self-absorbed, but the intention is to introduce specific experiences that inform this book while illustrating the extent to which music can be part of cultural diplomacy projects across a few years of activity in the life of even a single scholar. Of course, although people usually focus on the positive side, there have been many struggles faced in such work as well. Only a few months after meeting Chaden Yafi (a contributor to this book) in Damascus—where we visited unique heritage sites and collaborated with musicians at the opera house and the National Institute of Music—Syria plunged into a horrific and long-lasting civil war. The situation caused Dr. Yafi to move to the United States. I also recall some excitement about my trip to Brazil in 2015, with support of the Brazilian government, where I eagerly anticipated developing fruitful collaborations with musicians and music researchers. Instead, I became quite ill on the airplane, barely able to breathe, and even suffered from pneumonia for about a month upon returning to Europe. There are certainly risks involved in international projects and sometimes despite our very best efforts to carefully plan, things do not work out quite as hoped.

For some years I have collaborated with Jonathan McCollum, who coedited this book and contributed as a coauthor for chapter 15, in which we aim to synthesize ideas and offer recommendations based on each of the cases presented here. Although neither of us works full time with a high-ranking research university, we have nevertheless managed together to nurture and shape the field of historical ethnomusicology. Jon and I have both served terms as leaders of the Historical Ethnomusicology SIG (and later, Section) of the Society for Ethnomusicology, which we established together from a preexisting special interest group (in collaboration with Ann Lucas and others), and we coauthored encyclopedia entries and research handbooks on the topic of historical ethnomusicology, a field that we sense offers unique insights into the mechanisms of music in cultural diplomacy. Jon's work has shown how even music notations can become negotiated systems of international understanding across historical time. In our previous coedited book, *Theory and Method in Historical Ethnomusicology*, Jon and I briefly considered the topic of diplomacy as we reflected on how digitization is profoundly impacting both music activity and its prospective historical traces (McCollum and Hebert, 2014). Together we developed the Deep Soundings series for Lexington Books, of which this book comprises volume 2, to bring a more historically and geographically informed perspective to important musical topics.

Ethnomusicology, as a field concerned with global music practices, has great potential to demonstrate music's role in cultural diplomacy, but we find it has not always lived up to its promise. While developing this book, I had the opportunity to talk with an ethnomusicologist in an Asian nation who had recently hosted a major international conference. I learned from the Asian scholar about the challenges of hosting European and American ethnomusicologists in a traditional country that has very different protocols associated with respect for royalty. It is worth noting here that the Society for Ethnomusicology, which often appears to its members to be an international organization, actually does not have conferences outside of North America, while the British Forum for Ethnomusicology, true to its name, only holds conferences in the United Kingdom. Other music organizations, such as the International Society for Music Education and the International Council for Traditional Music, schedule conferences in many locations worldwide. Even while hosted by countries that preserve ancient traditions, some ethnomusicologists from Europe and North America seem to sense a need to frequently make public statements concerning their views of equality, social justice, and human rights, and some actively object to holding conferences in nations that are politically different from what they regard as an appropriate form of governance. I have personally seen objections raised to holding conferences in Israel (due to its violent occupation of Palestinian territories), Russia (due to policies regarding homosexuals), Turkey (due to compromised elections), and so on. These are all legitimate concerns from a human rights perspective, but their relationship to a prospective music conference seems misguided, and arguably fails in certain ways to recognize ethnomusicology's potential role in cultural diplomacy. Indeed, scholars from Arab nations still routinely visit Israel, gay couples can certainly be found in Russia, and people of various political positions continue to be identifiable in Turkey, regardless of whether a music conference is hosted there. Meanwhile, from the opposite side, what we often do *not* encounter at European and North American conferences is special efforts to make non-Western delegates comfortable: vegan and halal meals, prayer rooms and breaks for prayer time, inclusive opportunities for leadership, etc. Compromises are often understood to be inevitable, yet international organizations are rarely as equitable as they aspire to be. These observations have made me realize that deeper awareness of cultural diplomacy may still be needed even in a field that, as this book demonstrates, has done so much to champion deeper international awareness through music.

One of the contributors to this book, Elnora Mamadjanova, has repeatedly hosted an international musicology symposium in Samarkand, Uzbekistan, affiliated with the enormous Sharq Taronalari music festival, for which both coeditor Jonathan McCollum and I have served as keynote speakers. Some readers will surely be familiar with Uzbekistan's reputation in terms of democracy and human rights. We found the conference to be quite successful, with an incredibly diverse group of scholars (diverse in terms of almost *every* demographic) from across the world, including many people who we otherwise *never* had the opportunity to meet at conferences hosted by Western countries. Surprisingly, we find a relatively more interesting mix of people tend to participate in international conferences held in Asia, the Middle East, Africa, and Latin America. It is partly from this kind of experience that it became clear a book on this topic—comprised mainly of writers from outside Europe and North America, including law experts—might have the potential to be especially insightful, particularly during times in which there is growing interest in the theme of decolonization.

Like all books, it seems, the production of this one was a unique adventure. While the global COVID-19 pandemic has surely affected us all, some of the contributing authors to this book especially experienced challenging conditions. Karan Choudhary, an Indian judge, completed much of his chapter on a day in which India was facing a horrific health crisis, with four hundred thousand new COVID-19 cases per day (and upward of four thousand deaths per day) while hospitals were overwhelmed by insufficient oxygen supplies. Meanwhile, in Ethiopia, Abraha Weldu would travel one hundred miles for internet access in order to email files of his chapter because the internet was completely blocked in Tigray, where civil war had broken out. As we were still editing his chapters, the situation there became increasingly difficult, with the UN's World Food Programme reporting that 90 percent of Tigray's inhabitants were in desperate need of food aid. Schools were reportedly used as bunkers by the warring parties in Ethiopia, and there were even widespread accusations of mass execution of civilians and other atrocities in the vicinity of Weldu's institution, Mekelle University. As this book neared publication, we were completely unable to reach Abraha by telephone or email for months due to what the international press called a "total communications blackout." Another contributor, Koji Matsunobu, a Japanese scholar living in Hong Kong, has faced the complicated circumstances of enormous street protests and police responses that have repeatedly shut down entire transportation systems, as well as difficulties in returning home to see family due to the pandemic conditions. Yet another contributor, law professor Juqian

Li, finished his chapter while quarantined in a hotel room due to pandemic-related mandates. For Lauren Braithwaite, the final stage of this book was an unsettling period in which her research participants in Afghanistan, to whom she had devoted three years of her life, faced chaotic turmoil due to the rapid withdrawal of US forces from an occupation of more than twenty years, while the Taliban seized control of the entire country. Indeed, recent years have been a challenge for many of us, which is why I am so grateful for the efforts devoted to completing this book. I thank all the authors and my coeditor Jonathan for their determination to complete this project, and I hope readers will find some useful ideas in it.

REFERENCES

Hebert, David G. 2008a. "Music Transculturation and Identity in a Maori Brass Band Tradition." *Alta Musica* 26, edited by Raul F. Camus and Bernhard Habla, 173–200. Tutzing: Schneider.
———. 2008b. "Music Transmission in an Auckland Tongan Community Youth Band." *International Journal of Community Music,* 1, no. 2: 169–88.
———. 2012. *Wind Bands and Cultural Identity in Japanese Schools*. New York: Springer.
———. 2018. "Cultural Translation and Musical Innovation: A Theoretical Model with Examples from Japan." In *International Perspectives on Translation, Education and Innovation in Japanese and Korean Societies*, edited by David G. Hebert, 309–31. New York: Springer.
Hebert, David G. and Torunn B. Haugen, eds. 2019. *Advancing Music Education in Northern Europe*. London: Routledge.
Hebert, David G. and Alexandra Kertz-Welzel, eds. 2016. *Patriotism and Nationalism in Music Education*. London: Routledge.
Hebert, David G. and Mikolaj Rykowski, eds. 2018. *Music Glocalization: Heritage and Innovation in a Digital Age*. Newcastle: Cambridge Scholars.
Heimonen, Marja and Herbert, David G. 2010. "Pluralism and Minority Rights in Music Education: Implications of the Legal and Social Philosophical Dimensions." *Visions of Research in Music Education,* 15.
McCollum, Jonathan and David G. Hebert, eds. 2014. *Theory and Method in Historical Ethnomusicology*. Lanham, MD: Lexington Books.
Östersjö, Stefan. 2020. *Listening to the Other*. Leuven: Leuven University Press.

1

INTRODUCTION TO MUSIC AND CULTURAL DIPLOMACY

Chapter One

Introduction

Ethnomusicology as a Resource for Cultural Diplomacy

David G. Hebert

In 1642, when Dutch explorer Abel Tasman navigated the first known European ships to New Zealand, local Maori warriors approached on canoes from which they played tones on conch shells, prompting the sailors to respond on trumpets (Hebert, 2008). Even earlier, in Jean de Léry's *Histoire d'un voyage faict en la terre du Bresil* from 1585—the first eyewitness account of a European in South America—the musical activities of local people were described in great detail by an author whose responsibilities were the contemporary equivalent of a diplomatic mission (Harrison, 1973). These colonial examples might seem like long ago, but the sixteenth and seventeenth centuries are relatively recent against the long span of time in which music has been a prominent part of diplomatic history. Indeed, Enheduanna (c. 2300 BCE), an Akkadian princess credited as the "first named author in the history of the world," composed many hymns in the ancient Sumerian language, and her ritual performances are credited as helping to strategically "underpin political unity in Sargon's empire," which had expanded in Mesopotamia (Holmes, 2018, 208). Even the biblical David (c. 1040–970 BCE), who first entered the ancient Hebrew court as a lyre player brought to soothe the troubled King Saul with songs, would later himself become king, capture the city of Jerusalem, and lead a musical procession of a thousand people—with singing, dancing, and instruments—to bring the Ark of the Covenant to its new home. From ancient times, music has served as a prominent symbol of political power and a tool of diplomacy (Fletcher, 2001), which continues across many centuries to the present day (Spitzer, 2021). Indeed, scientists continue to argue that among the most plausible evolutionary explanations for the origins of musical behavior are the needs to signal group strength (Mehr et al., 2020) and to facilitate social bonding (Savage et al., 2020), but such theorizing must be interpreted with cautious recognition of its inherent limitations (Merker, Morley, and Zuidema, 2015).

Today, music is frequently encountered as a mode of mediation across national borders, institutionalized in the ritual use of national anthems in diplomatic and sporting events (Kelen, 2014), even while varying emphases on national identity shape the distinctive ways that music is taught in schools (Hebert and Kertz-Welzel, 2016). Moreover, diplomatic ministries and global philanthropic foundations continue to incorporate music in a diverse array of international and cross-cultural activities. But what exactly is cultural diplomacy and how is music connected to it? Cultural diplomacy has been defined in various ways, but it generally entails the use of diverse forms of *intercultural exchange*—including projects in traditional and contemporary arts—for the purpose of fostering enhanced mutual understanding, respect, and reconciliation. Cultural diplomacy is facilitated in many ways, including through embassies and formal government institutions (such as the United Kingdom's British Council and Germany's Goethe-Institut), exchange programs (such as the Fulbright Commission and Japan Foundation), and an array of private sector and non-governmental organization projects affiliated with foundations, religious organizations, and corporate entities. Cultural diplomacy most often features international projects, but the concept may also apply to programs that seek to inspire a broader appreciation of the heritage of Indigenous peoples and ethnic minorities within a single nation-state.

Cultural diplomacy is influenced by *cultural policy*, or a state's legal frameworks concerning arts and culture that, among other things, directly impact how artistic traditions are recognized and sustained, through commissions, curation, and lifelong education initiatives. According to Kevin Mulcahy, "Public culture is strongly associated with identity and heritage, and how people define their communities and see themselves in the world and in history. Consequently, a cultural policy would support a broad array of activities that could promote a sense of communal continuity and distinctiveness without a determinate cost-benefit cultural analysis" (2017, xxvi). Therefore, to understand how cultural diplomacy functions in international relations it is necessary to examine how relevant laws and cultural policies impact local traditions in diverse locations.

CULTURE IN PUBLIC DIPLOMACY, SOFT POWER, AND NATION BRANDING

Before proceeding further, it is useful to briefly reflect on some key concepts. The term "cultural diplomacy" indicates a particular form of *diplomacy*, and its very existence suggests that some diplomatic activities are more or less explicitly *cultural* in nature. Diplomacy typically involves relationships between different nation-states, so it may be difficult to imagine how diplomacy could ever *not* be in some sense "cultural." However, in the context of diplomacy, "cultural" is commonly understood in terms of its connection to traditional arts and heritage rather than in its more abstract sense, as in the general concept "cultural differences." Cultural diplomacy is often seen as closely related to *public diplomacy*, but there are also some important distinctions between these interrelated spheres, as well as concerning such notions as "soft power" and "nation branding." Unlike diplomacy in general (which is typically concerned with strategic negotiations behind closed doors), *public diplomacy* focuses on how media and discourse shape how a nation comes to be perceived, so it is more concerned with public attitudes than the arguments, strategies, and actions of individual leaders.

Joseph Nye is especially well-known for popularizing the notion of *soft power*, which may be understood as the ability to "shape the preferences of others" and thereby to achieve political objectives "through attraction rather than coercion or payments" (Nye, 2004, x)—an endeavor at the very core of *public* diplomacy (Nye, 2019). *Nation branding*, one component of public diplomacy, has a more precise definition, namely the use of "marketing communications techniques to promote a nation's image," which research suggests can be significantly influenced by arts and cultural policy (Ahn and Wu, 2015). Still, *cultural diplomacy* is understood as much more than merely *nation branding through the arts as a form of public diplomacy*. Goff notes that although public diplomacy and cultural diplomacy both target "audiences beyond diplomatic circles" there are some important distinctions, including that unlike public diplomacy's "outward projection of one's message," cultural diplomacy maintains an emphasis on mutual recognition toward finding a common ground of equality and reciprocity (2013, 421). Another major figure in this field, Nick Cull, defines public diplomacy similarly as "working to develop a relationship of mutual understanding" (2019, 23), so distinctions between these fields remain to some extent open to debate, but generally discussions of *cultural* diplomacy emphasize learning and sharing through mutual appreciation of heritage, while *public* diplomacy is concerned with shaping public opinion, so the latter is thereby more closely related to media public relations strategies and even propaganda. Nye links the two in a way that offers yet another view: "Cultural diplomacy is one of the public diplomacy instruments that governments use to mobilize these resources to produce attraction by communicating with the public rather than merely the governments of other countries. If the content of a country's culture, values and practices are not attractive, public diplomacy that 'broadcasts' them cannot produce soft power. It may produce just the opposite" (2010, 120). Cultural diplomacy, therefore, seeks to make use of the heritage and creative work of a nation-state's people that, irrespective of any general political differences or specific policies, may help inspire mutual appreciation and respect. It follows that music is a robust and meaningful form of heritage that lends itself particularly well to the aims of cultural diplomacy.

How, then, is cultural diplomacy relevant to ethnomusicology? The field's largest scholarly organization, the Society for Ethnomusicology (SEM), currently defines the field in this way on its website: "Ethnomusicology is the study of music in its social and cultural contexts. Ethnomusicologists examine music as a social process in order to understand not only what music is but what it means to its practitioners and audiences" (SEM, 2020). Research conducted by ethnomusicologists produces knowledge that is potentially of great value when applied in cultural diplomacy, and this book is founded on the premise that professionals associated with these two fields have much to gain from enhanced mutual understanding and strategic cooperation. To be even more specific, this book is concerned with developing and sharing essential ideas at the nexus of *music diplomacy* (music-related initiatives within the broader field of cultural diplomacy) and *applied ethnomusicology* (the branch of this field concerned with how musical knowledge can be used for practical purposes). Applied ethnomusicology is often intertwined with intercultural learning initiatives, so lifelong *music education* also has an important stake in music diplomacy. It follows that this book will address questions related to how cultural policies in different nation-states impact the forms of intercultural exchange seen in the music performance and education fields. Its purpose is not only to document music diplomacy initiatives but to offer comparative analysis and devise recommendations of relevance to philanthropy, governance, education, and other sectors.

Background and Rationale

Across recent decades, several books have helped pioneer the growing field in which this book seeks to make its unique contribution. Specifically, three books examine how music has played a role across the history of cultural diplomacy in European nations and North America (Ahrendt, Ferraguto, and Mahiet 2014; Ramel and Prevost-Thomas, 2018), one of which emphasizes popular music (Dunkel and Nitzsche, 2018). Additionally, previous studies have demonstrated specific cases of musical diplomacy projects implemented by the US government (Fosler-Lussier, 2015; Katz, 2020). With only a few exceptions, these five books emphasize the ways that Western nations use music in cultural diplomacy outside their borders, and these appear to be the only books to date—in English language on major academic presses—that explicitly examine the topic of *music diplomacy*.

Three other books offer a more *ethnomusicological* perspective, with substantial discussion of global relations and cultural policies outside of non-Western states, albeit with an emphasis on *cultural heritage* rather than an explicit focus on *diplomacy*. Namely, one book has considered ways that music may be reconceptualized as cultural heritage in the digital age, and how both local and international ("glocal") forces intersect to impact musical traditions and practices (Hebert and Rykowski, 2018). Then, two other books have provided great insights into how musical heritage is sustained within specific nation-states, particularly in Asia (Howard, 2016; Norton and Matsumoto, 2018). Each of these three books is concerned with how musical traditions may qualify as heritage, which might at first seem to be only a historical concern, but the significance of this issue in relation to the present may be understood as follows: "Is, then, the concern with heritage only or principally backward-looking? No, because we are dealing with a past—a certain past—whose visible embodiment is important for the present" (Hartog, 2015, 152). As a whole, the aforementioned eight books demonstrate a growing and sustained interest in topics related to this book's central theme of *ethnomusicology and cultural diplomacy*, but some brief discussion of each previous book will reveal more clearly how the present book builds upon their important contributions while also offering entirely new insights of its own.

Ahrendt, Ferraguto, and Mahiet's volume (2014) entitled *Music and Diplomacy: From the Early Modern Era to the Present* is especially useful for its historical insights, revealing how the notion of music as diplomacy emerged across time in Europe and North America. Each of its chapters demonstrates how either a European or North American nation (e.g., the United States in China and Morocco) has developed projects that apply musical diplomacy as a form of "soft power."

The volume by Ramel and Prevost-Thomas (2018) entitled *International Relations, Music and Diplomacy: Sounds and Voices on the International Stage* also emphasizes European relations, with historical and contemporary studies across an array of European states. Additionally, the book includes a few chapters concerned with the diplomacy of nations outside of Europe, such as the cases of Argentinian pianist Miguel Ángel Estrella and Russian diplomacy in the Baltic states.

Eurovision and Cold War diplomacy feature prominently in *Popular Music and Public Diplomacy: Transnational and Transdisciplinary Perspectives* (Dunkel and Nitzsche, 2018). Although its emphasis on popular music enables this volume to offer a slightly different angle than that of the previous two books, its approach otherwise resembles the others in terms of its focus on European and US cultural policy initiatives in relation to other states.

One book that addresses American government approaches to music diplomacy during a particularly complicated period is *Music in America's Cold War Diplomacy* (Fosler-Lussier, 2015). Its author demonstrates in rich detail how both the distinctive advantages of classical music (an art form shared with Soviet states) and jazz (an American idiom) were strategically used for performances during the Cold War as effective forms of "soft power." Across recent decades, diplomatic strategies shifted toward an embrace of more popular culture, including hip-hop music and dance, as documented in *Build: The Power of Hip Hop Diplomacy in a Divided World* (Katz, 2020).

Ethnomusicological studies of how notions of heritage are changing, due to intensified global interaction, are also highly relevant to the present book. *Music Glocalization: Heritage and Innovation in a Digital Age* is a volume edited by Hebert and Rykowski (2018) that includes studies from many parts of the world, unified by the theme of "glocalization," or how global forces are refracted in local interpretations. Several chapters in this book demonstrate how social forces and policies impact contemporary composers—from Northern Ireland to Estonia to Uzbekistan—as well as the emergence of global fusion genres (in rural Indonesia and among urban street musicians), and how local instruments (such as the Australian didgeridoo) and specialized music professions (as seen in opera) circulate globally.

Howard's volume *Music as Intangible Cultural Heritage: Policy, Ideology, and Practice in the Preservation of East Asian Traditions* is a groundbreaking work with broad and enduring resonance, as the first notable ethnomusicology book to directly address the role of governments in recognition of musical heritage, with a geographic focus on East Asia (Howard, 2016). Another book entitled *Music as Heritage: Historical and Ethnographic Perspectives* (Norton and Matsumoto, 2018), offers insights into how music is sustained in particular nations, again mostly limited to Asia, and might best be understood as a companion volume to Howard's book.

This brief review—limited to English language books on major presses—has demonstrated growing interest in the present book's theme of *ethnomusicology and cultural diplomacy*, and how important strides have been made across recent decades, yet it should be clear that major gaps in knowledge remain. For instance, the five books that explicitly discuss musical diplomacy clearly emphasize how *Western* states use music in their relations with each other and the rest of the world (rather than vice versa). This begs an essential question: *What about cultural policies in China, Japan, Vietnam, India, even the Middle East, and the African continent—an array of non-Western nations and regions that use music in their own distinctive forms of cultural diplomacy?* This is exactly how we recognized a need for the present volume. With a unique perspective, its purpose is to examine such questions from the opposite angle, considering cultural policies from outside "the West" and how they contribute to musical relations with Europe and North America. This is also why an ethnomusicological and historical perspective is so essential to the present book (McCollum and Hebert, 2014), and why we have indicated the relevance of previous studies of musical *heritage*. In our view, apprehension of music's status as an evolving form of heritage requires recognition of history as "successive but not cumulative" in its purview (Egan, 2021, 493).

Decolonizing Ethnomusicology

The perspective offered in the present book seems especially relevant and timely in light of recent developments in the field of ethnomusicology. There are strong indications that the issues of colonialism and racism have become more prominent than ever before in ethnomusicology during the past two years as this book was under development. Discussions arising from a recent SEM conference ultimately led to the removal of its president, alongside online debate of an open letter by Danielle Brown that argued racism is an enduring problem in ethnomusicology. Brown's letter was endorsed by many scholars affiliated with online groups Project Spectrum and "The Scare Quotes," the latter of which describes itself as "a coalition of BIPOC and queer ethnomusicologists." Ten former SEM presidents responded with their "Open Letter from SEM Past Presidents on Racism" on August 20, 2020 (SEM, 2020), in which they wrote the following:

> We, the undersigned past presidents of the Society for Ethnomusicology (SEM), publicly support the views Dr. Danielle Brown expressed in her "Open Letter on Racism in Music Studies" and those of the marginalized scholars who have raised their voices in protest before and since that letter appeared. Deep-seated white supremacy and colonialism shape SEM, and SEM is a site in which these systems of power are produced and reproduced. This situation demands a strong and proactive response. We offer our time, energy, and commitment to the SEM Board, the SEM Council, and the SEM membership to work on initiatives that will address this reality.

In the United Kingdom, an issue in the journal *Ethnomusicology Forum* argued that Brown's letter in the United States "exposed the long-unsaid but widely-known reality: that systemic racism is embedded within the field in small and large degrees; that academia itself (including ethnomusicology) remains a neo-colonial enterprise—by dint of its default setup of (often, BIPOC/ Black & Global Majority [henceforth BGM]) research informants as secondary inputs to the careers of (often, tenured, elite and white) scholars in established institutions" (Tan, 2021, 4). Moreover, the SEM-affiliated journal *Ethnomusicology*, which has typically followed a rather traditional academic article format across sixty-five years, published an issue in 2021 featuring a multilingual poem of fourteen stanzas by Ama Oforiwaa Aduonum, for which the author wrote, "In the Spirit of My Nananom, Ngũgĩ wa Thiong'o, and decolonization, I offer no translations for Akan, Ewe, Ga, Igbo, Kiembu, Swahili, and Zulu texts" (Aduonum, 2021, 220). While Aduonum's poem might be interpreted in various ways, the author is clearly responsive to concerns regarding the impact of racism and colonialism in ethnomusicology, explicitly noting that in response to Brown's letter, "Some SEM members wrote and signed letters of support and endorsement; others responded in self-justifying and belligerent tones" (Aduonum, 2021, 220). Still, in *Ethnomusicology Forum*, Tan cautioned readers to also consider "how can these conversations take place without degenerating into unhelpful binaries of Culture Wars-led identity politics?" (2021, 5). Moreover, Tan warned of the risks of "'friendly fire' upon colleagues we respect" and of "bringing unintended parties into collateral damage" (Tan, 2021, 6–7). Despite ongoing debates in this field, we remain optimistic regarding the future of musicology. The present book was designed with a diverse team of authors long before these developments in ethnomusicology organizations, but recent events have only inspired us with greater confidence in the timeliness and potential value of our project, which was conceived in a way that endorsed the notion of decolonization from its very inception.

Music and Peace Studies

Beyond ethnomusicology, an interdisciplinary field that might best be called *music in peace and conflict studies* also calls for some discussion due to its relevance to the present book. Representative scholars of this field include Olivier Urbain (2007), Arild Bergh (see Bergh and Sloboda, 2010), as well as some applied ethnomusicologists, such as John Morgan O'Connell and Salwa El-Shawan Castelo-Branco (2010). Urbain is a humanities scholar with degrees in literature and peace studies who directs research programs affiliated with Soka Gakkai, a lay Buddhist organization in Japan. Arild Bergh is a researcher with the Norwegian Defence Research Establishment who studied sociology under Tia DeNora and writes about music in conflict transformation. Urbain and Bergh take rather contrasting approaches—each valuable in its own way—with Urbain showing more interest in broadly philosophical (and even spiritual) issues while Bergh is focused more on scientifically verifiable claims, and neither may be properly understood as an ethnomusicologist although their work is highly relevant to the field. John Morgan O'Connell (Cardiff University) and Salwa El-Shawan Castelo-Branco (Nova University Lisbon) are ethnomusicologists who explore various ways that music participation may contribute to alleviation of conflict. While neither O'Connell nor Castelo-Branco explicitly examine "cultural diplomacy," the fundamental concerns as well as specific issues considered in their work are highly relevant (O'Connell and Castelo-Branco, 2010). The differences between *peace and conflict studies* and *cultural diplomacy* approaches are subtle but significant and worth at least brief consideration. Peace and conflict studies is a holistic field conceptually rooted in humanities disciplines, such as philosophy and history, and its most prominent scholar is social theorist Johan Galtung from Norway. Cultural diplomacy, on the other hand, is both a professional and applied field concerned with the practical effectiveness of specific intercultural projects, and which generally takes a social science orientation toward problem-solving. Although the two fields often share similar aims, we detect little cross-referencing between them. Still, alleviation of conflict—as well as improvement of intercultural understanding and other goals—tends to be among the main objectives typically pursued by collaborators in cultural diplomacy projects. Research in *music psychology* and other fields also increasingly show an array of "real-world case studies in which music has been used for preventative or restorative peace-building efforts in a variety of conflict, post-conflict and politically contentious settings" (Dieckmann and Davidson, 2018, 40). It follows that the interdisciplinary theme of peace and conflict will be a recurring topic across the present book, one to which we will return in chapter 15, where we reflect on general recommendations for music diplomacy.

A Distinctive Purpose

In this book, we seek to bridge the gap our review has identified between (1) ethnomusicological studies of local music heritage in non-Western nations, and (2) studies of music in cultural diplomacy that have hitherto tended to emphasize the policies and projects of Western nations. Our focus is, rather, on *cultural policies and arts diplomacy outside Europe and the United States*, since non-Western nations have developed their own approaches to the use of music in cultural diplomacy. Another distinctive feature of this book is its inclusion of *law* scholars, and it thereby seeks to offer a more thorough exploration of the *legal bases* for cultural policy in general, and music diplomacy in particular, in terms of Asian legal theory. Because cultural diplomacy often entails educational initiatives, we have also included scholars with deep knowledge in the field of music education. Moreover, we include examples from a broad range of countries that are not represented in any of the aforementioned books on music diplomacy, including nations with a history of complex relationships to Europe and the United States, such as Afghanistan, Iran, Vietnam, Uzbekistan, Syria, Ethiopia, Nigeria, South Africa, Japan, and India, as well as two chapters on China due to its rapidly expanding global prominence in the sphere of "soft power."

Decolonization of knowledge is an essential concept that has shaped the foundations and design of this book. We find that the global movement to "decolonize" academic subjects—irrespective of whatever frustrations it might sometimes provoke—is based on legitimate concerns regarding curricular balance, since philosophy and social theory have even in the twenty-first century tended to convey an undeniably Eurocentric orientation (Hebert, 2021). Across an array of academic fields, scholars from the continents of Asia (Elliott, Katagiri, and Sawai, 2013; Qi, 2014), Africa (Fomunyam and Khoza, 2021), Latin America (Quijiano, 2000), and Oceania (Smith, 2012) have increasingly identified what they see as an unbalanced representation of knowledge due to a perceived incompatibility between Eurocentric theoretical bases and non-Western orientations. As we have explained elsewhere, "Decolonizing methodologies, as an approach, is especially relevant to ethnomusicologists from indigenous backgrounds with an interest in studying the history of their own people's music" (Hebert and McCollum, 2014, 134). It follows that with few exceptions, the contributors to this book describe music from the vantage point of a cultural insider who seeks to share new insights with readers from elsewhere. Our position is not so much that cross-cultural research—especially in the rich ethnographic tradition—is somehow inadequate, but rather that there can also be unique advantages to indigenous scholarship that emphasizes a decidedly introspective orientation, particularly when it comes to discussions of such complex topics as music-related policy and law. While not every chapter in this book will directly address a specific international cultural diplomacy initiative, perceptive readers will recognize how each author's discussions offer relevant insights into this mulitfaceted field in which music can play an important role. Due to our inclusion of writers from unusually diverse academic backgrounds, readers should not be surprised to encounter a broad range of tones, approaches, and styles across the volume. The book includes not only ethnomusicologists, but also scholars of law, music education, history, and music performance. We have aimed to produce a book that is relevant to such fields as ethnomusicology, musicology, cultural policy, public diplomacy, and law, and have sought to guide authors toward a cohesive collection that nevertheless preserves their individual voices to the extent possible.

Overview of Chapters

This chapter, authored by editor David G. Hebert, offers a general introduction to the book's topic and key concepts—including cultural diplomacy, cultural policy, and applied ethnomusicology—as well as the purpose and formal structure of the entire book.

Chapter 2, "International Soft Law and the Promotion of Musical Rights," extends the introductory section of this book by offering an overview of basic concepts from a legal perspective. Marja Heimonen (in partnership with Hebert) interrogates the notion of music rights in the context of international "soft law" initiatives, and how related agreements and regulations impact the use of music in intercultural and international diplomacy. Heimonen is widely recognized as a leading expert on the legal bases of music education, and the authors have collaborated on several previous publications that consider music in relation to legal frameworks and policies.

Next, we launch into part 2, "Middle Eastern Perspectives," which begins with chapter 3, "'Afghanistan is Not What You Think': Cultural Diplomacy through Music Education and Performance," by Lauren Braithwaite of Oxford University. Braithwaite provides a detailed account of a case that is especially relevant to the theme of this book, demonstrating the complex array of diplomatic challenges associated with Afghanistan's first all-female orchestra. Affiliated with the Afghanistan National Institute of Music in Kabul, the ensemble emerged from the struggles of a war-torn country and has increasingly attracted international attention while seeking to convey a positive image of Afghan cultural traditions.

In chapter 4, "Music Festivals and Cultural Diplomacy in Uzbekistan," Elnora Mamadjanova (in partnership with Hebert) offers a detailed description of the enormous Sharq Taronalari festival as well as the younger International Maqom Festival. They note that since 1991, a new era developed for the Uzbek people, with a desire to emphasize their historical belonging to a great civilization, and a gradual opening to the world to display their cultural values and achievements. This is facilitated by the hosting in Uzbekistan of various international music festivals, symposia, and conferences, as well as the active participation of musical representatives of Uzbekistan in prestigious forums around the world. The first of such international music festivals was held on the art of maqom in Shakhrisabz, the art of bakhshi in Termez, and the folklore festival in Margilan. The Sharq Taronalari International Music Festival, sponsored by UNESCO, has been especially notable and since 1997, the geographic impact of the festival and music conference is very extensive, with scholars from thirteen countries taking part in its activities at World Heritage Sites in Samarkand.

In chapter 5, "Sufi Voices: Music as a Unifying Pathway toward the Divine," Chaden Yafi offers a deeply personal account of intellectual and music life in Syria, as well as her reflections on how Western musicians may benefit from knowledge of Sufi philosophical thought. Intending to improve intercultural understanding between the Middle East and other parts of the world, Yafi's chapter provides a historical overview of Arabic contributions to "Western music," while describing the enduring relevance of medieval Arab and Muslim scholarship for musicians today.

In chapter 6, "Soft War and Multilateral Musical Pathways in Iran," Nasim Niknafs offers new insights into the situation for cultural policy in Iran, and how music culture has played a role in international relations. Niknafs describes how Iran has endured the challenging conditions of strict international economic sanctions that were only exacerbated by the global COVID-19 pandemic. When the US government stepped away from the Iran nuclear deal in 2018, with no actionable opposition from the EU and other involved countries, the Iranian government faced tremendous pressure both from within and outside to respond to a stifling economic situation in what has come to be called *mobârezeh bâ jang-e narm* or "fighting against soft war" through its changing rhetoric. This chapter explores ways in which the Iranian government put cultural policies in such fields as education, music, and media at the forefront of this conversation and how musicians have creatively navigated the changing landscape.

Part 3, "East Asian Views" begins with chapter 7, "Cultural Diplomacy in Collaborative Music Projects between China and Europe." Here, Marianne Løkke Jakobsen (in partnership with Hebert) presents insights from innovative collaborations between China and Europe developed through her directorship of the Music Confucius Institute in Copenhagen. This chapter demonstrates how traditional Chinese music has been strategically used as a means by which to generate positive interest in Chinese culture, and that Europeans have responded variously, with both enthusiasm and skepticism. The chapter vividly illustrates some of the complex challenges associated with managing major intercultural initiatives.

Next is chapter 8, "A Gap in Cultural Policy: Non-Japanese Experiences of Learning Japanese Music," by prolific scholar and shakuhachi player Koji Matsunobu. In this chapter, Matsunobu reflects on how Japanese music has come to be more widely practiced outside Japan across recent decades. Matsunobu notes how the spiritual connotations of the music are often misunderstood, and impact perceptions of what it means to fully understand foreign music cultures. He also notes some revealing gaps between the underlying intentions of the Japanese government's cultural policies and the views of shakuhachi players from outside Japan.

In chapter 9, "Cultural Diplomacy and Transculturation through the History of *Vọng Cổ* in Vietnam," Nguyễn Thanh Thủy and Stefan Östersjö describe a multiyear music research and development project in Vietnam that received Swedish funding. Vietnam may be understood as the southernmost country of East Asia, and from the early twentieth century has maintained a complex relationship with such East Asian neighbors as China and Japan, as well as the former colonizers (France) and the United States. This chapter demonstrates how cultural diplomacy can be examined through cases of intercultural collaboration in music ensembles that contribute to music hybridity and ultimately transculturation. The chapter focuses on a well-known piece called *Vọng Cổ* in southern Vietnam, to understand how this music was created and altered across time. Through use of stimulated recall interviews, the experience of each participating artist is considered in an analysis that discusses the nature of such intercultural diplomacy across musical cultures.

Part 4, "African Insights," includes three chapters from the East, West, and South of the continent. It begins with chapter 10, "Cultural Policies and Music Production across Ethiopian Regimes: A Historical Study," which offers Abraha Weldu and Jan Magne Steinhovden's perspectives on how music and arts policies have shifted across recent generations of Ethiopian political history. Weldu is a cultural historian affiliated with Mekelle University in the Tigray region of Ethiopia, where war was ongoing during the production of this book. Steinhovden is a Norwegian ethnomusicologist who collaborated with Weldu in order to integrate a musicological perspective into the topic. Together, they trace the history of music research in Ethiopia and note that although Ethiopia is home to a multicultural society, cultural policy has only been introduced in recent decades, but serves to mediate cultural diplomacy across the disparate nations that comprise the state of Ethiopia. Cultural rights and their contribution to sustainable development have tended to receive little attention from the rulers of Ethiopia. Rather, regimes have utilized culture to inculcate their moral and political values in Ethiopia across the Imperial, the Derg, and the incumbent Federal Democratic Republic of Ethiopia governments. The authors pay due attention to the influence and ideology of each regime on the development of culture for sustainable development.

Chapter 11, "Musical Activism from South Africa: The 'Soft Power' of Cultural Diplomacy," is a contribution by Ambigay Yudkoff that considers the cases of four prominent South African musicians: Hugh Masekela, Miriam Makeba, Johnny Clegg, and Sharon Katz. Yufkoff demonstrates how each musician's story illustrates processes in musical activism that constitute various approaches to cultural diplomacy.

In chapter 12, "Intercultural Relations in Church Music of Nigeria and South Africa," Rhoda Abiolu examines how Christian music on the African continent is used for intercultural exchange, with cases in Nigeria and South Africa. The chapter examines prominent choral groups, such as the Soweto Gospel Choir in South Africa, and the Lagos City Chorale in Nigeria, examples selected due to the dominance of each group within the cultural and musical landscapes of their countries of origin. These cases from the west and south of the African continent illustrate how music contributes to cultural diplomacy through religious organizations.

Finally, we reach part 5, "Legal Perspectives from Asia," which offers the views of legal experts—an active judge and a prominent law professor—regarding music's conditions in the cultural policies of the world's most populous countries, China and India. Previous ethnomusicological research has established the relevance and need for further studies of music law in these countries (Booth, 2015; Harris, 2005; Rees, 2003). Rather than directly addressing specific *diplomacy* initiatives, these law scholars explain the legal foundations for music and cultural policy in nations that are likely to be of sustained interest to ethnomusicologists in the future. This part begins with chapter 13, "Cultural Heritage and Music Diplomacy: The Legal Framework in India," by the Honorable Karan Choudhary. Dr. Choudhary explains legal structures in India that support the sustainability of musical heritage. According to Judge Choudhary, management of cultural diversity is a profoundly important responsibility, and nation-states have developed diverse approaches to the conservation and protection of their cultural heritage (in all its varied expressions). Choudhary argues that "with the recognition of culture as a strategic dimension of sustainable development there is an urgent need to assess and comprehend national responses in terms of law and policy designs—whether such designs construct a sustainable, informed, transparent and participative system of governance for culture" (277). In this chapter, he offers an overview of the legal framework pertaining to culture in India, noting that the choice of policy design and national responses to culture (both its conservation and protection) directly inform work in the field of arts diplomacy.

Chapter 14, "China's Legal Framework Supporting Protection and Sustainability of Artistic Heritage," is by Chinese comparative law scholar Juqian Li, who describes the legal frameworks supporting music and arts-related policies in China as well as initiatives to promote Chinese culture both internally and abroad. Li is a professor with China's leading law school, China University of Political Science and Law, and has actively participated in major international negotiations, particularly in the field of space law. Li demonstrates how artistic heritage is an important component of cultural heritage, which is protected by law in different ways. China has fifty-six ethnic minorities living across a vast geographic area. The diversity of ethnic groups and geographic locations make the protection and sustainability of cultural heritage challenging for both national and local governments. The legal framework in this area is composed of international treaties and both national and local laws, which are outlined in the chapter and illustrated through specific examples of case law.

The book concludes with chapter 15, "Toward Global Models and Benchmarks for Music Diplomacy," in which editors David G. Hebert and Jonathan McCollum offer a general synthesis, various kinds of analyses, and both theoretical and practical recommendations based on findings from all the book's chapters. This includes suggestions for public education and lifelong learning initiatives that most stand to benefit from new approaches to music diplomacy.

REFERENCES

Aduonum, Ama Oforiwaa. 2021. "Ethnomusicology, Ayɛ Kradow?" *Ethnomusicology* 65, no. 2: 203–20.

Ahn, Michael J. and Hsin-Ching Wu. 2015. "The Art of Nation Branding: National Branding Value and the Role of Government and the Arts and Culture sector." *Public Organization Review* 15, no. 1: 157–73.

Ahrendt, Rebekah, Mark Ferraguto, and Damien Mahiet, eds. 2014. *Music and Diplomacy: From the Early Modern Era to the Present*. New York: Palgrave Macmillan.

Bergh, Arild and John Sloboda. 2010. "Music and Art in Conflict Transformation: A Review." *Music and Arts in Action* 2: 2–18.

Booth, Gregory. 2015. "Copyright Law and the Changing Economic Value of Popular Music in India." *Ethnomusicology* 59, no. 2: 262–87.

Cull, Nicholas J. 2019. *Public Diplomacy: Foundations for Global Engagement in the Digital Age*. Cambridge: Polity.

Dieckmann, Samantha and Jane W. Davidson. 2018. "Emotions." *Music and Arts in Action* 6, no. 2: 29–44.

Dunkel, Mario and Sina A. Nitzsche, eds. 2018. *Popular Music and Public Diplomacy: Transnational and Transdisciplinary Perspectives*. Bielefeld: Transcript.

Egan, Patrick. 2021. "Insider or Outsider?: Exploring Some Digital Challenges in Ethnomusicology." *Interdisciplinary Science Reviews* 46, no. 4: 477–500.

Elliott, Anthony, Masataka Katagiri, and Atsushi Sawai, eds. 2013. *Routledge Companion to Contemporary Japanese Social Theory: From Individualization to Globalization in Japan Today*. New York: Routledge.

Fletcher, Peter. 2001. *World Musics in Context: A Comprehensive Survey of the World's Major Musical Cultures*. New York: Oxford.

Fomunyam, Kehdinga G. and Simon B. Khoza, eds. 2021. *Curriculum Theory, Curriculum Theorising, and the Theoriser: The African Theorising Perspective*. Leiden: Brill.

Fosler-Lussier, Danielle. 2015. *Music in America's Cold War Diplomacy*. Berkeley: University of California Press.

Goff, Patricia M. 2013. "Cultural Diplomacy." In *The Oxford Handbook of Modern Diplomacy*, edited by Andrew F. Cooper, Jorge Heine, and Ramesh Thakur, 419–35. Oxford: Oxford University Press.

Hartog, François. 2015. *Regimes of Historicity: Presentism and Experiences of Time*. New York: Columbia University Press.

Harris, Rachel. 2005. Wang Luobin: Folk Song King of the Northwest or Song Thief?: Copyright, Representation, and Chinese Folk Songs. *Modern China* 31, no. 3: 381–408.

Harrison, Frank. 1973. *Time, Place and Music: An Anthology of Ethnomusicological Observation, c.1550 to c.1800*. Amsterdam: Fritz Knuf.

Hebert, David G. 2008. "Music Transculturation and Identity in a Maori Brass Band Tradition." *Alta Musica* 26, edited by Raul F. Camus and Bernhard Habla, 173–200. Tutzing: Schneider.

———. 2021. "Editorial Introduction: Global Competence, Decolonization, and Asian Educational Philosophies." *Nordic Journal of Comparative and International Education (NJCIE)* 5, no. 2: 1–7.

Hebert, David G. and Alexandra Kertz-Welzel, eds. 2016. *Patriotism and Nationalism in Music Education*. New York: Routledge.

Hebert, David G. and Jonathan McCollum. 2014. "Philosophy of History and Theory in Historical Ethnomusicology." In *Theory and Method in Historical Ethnomusicology*, edited by Jonathan McCollum and David G. Hebert, 85–147. Lanham, MD: Lexington Books.

Hebert, David G. and Mikolaj Rykowski, eds. 2018. *Music Glocalization: Heritage and Innovation in a Digital Age*. Newcastle: Cambridge Scholars.

Holmes, Lewis M. 2018. *The Mystery of Music: An Exploration Centered on the Lives of Thirty Ancient Musicians*. Burlington, VT: CEK Publishing.

Howard, Keith, ed. 2016. *Music as Intangible Cultural Heritage: Policy, Ideology, and Practice in the Preservation of East Asian Traditions*. New York: Routledge.

Katz, Mark. 2020. *Build: The Power of Hip Hop Diplomacy in a Divided World*. New York: Oxford University Press.

Kelen, Christopher. 2014. *Anthem Quality: National Songs-A Theoretical Survey*. Bristol: Intellect.

McCollum, Jonathan and David G. Hebert, eds. 2014. *Theory and Method in Historical Ethnomusicology*. Lanham, MD: Lexington Books.

Mehr, Samuel A., Max M. Krasnow, Gregory A. Bryant, and Edward H. Hagen. 2020. "Origins of Music in Credible Signaling." *Behavioral and Brain Sciences*, 1–41. doi:10.1017/S0140525X20000345.

Merker, Bjorn, Iain Morley, and Willem Zuidema. 2015. "Five Fundamental Constraints on Theories of the Origins of Music." *Philosophical Transactions of the Royal Society B 370*. http://dx.doi.org/10.1098/rstb.2014.0095.

Mulcahy, Kevin V. 2017. *Public Culture, Cultural Identity, Cultural Policy: Comparative Perspectives*. New York: Palgrave Macmillan.

Norton, Barley and Naomi Matsumoto, eds. 2018. *Music as Heritage: Historical and Ethnographic Perspectives*. New York: Routledge.

Nye, Joseph S., Jr. 2004. *Soft Power: The Means to Success in World Politics*. New York: Public Affairs.

———. 2010. "Soft Power and Cultural Diplomacy." *Public Diplomacy* (winter): 120–24.

———. 2019. "Soft Power and Public Diplomacy Revisited." *The Hague Journal of Diplomacy* 14, nos. 1–2: 7–20.

O'Connell, John M. and Salwa E. Castelo-Branco, eds. 2010. *Music and Conflict*. Urbana: University of Illinois Press.

Qi, Xiaoying. 2014. *Globalized Knowledge Flows and Chinese Social Theory*. London: Routledge.

Quijano, Anibal. 2000. "Coloniality of Power and Eurocentrism in Latin America." *International Sociology* 15, no. 2: 215–32.

Ramel, Frédéric and Cécil Prevost-Thomas, eds. 2018. *International Relations, Music and Diplomacy: Sounds and Voices on the International Stage*. Cham: Palgrave Macmillan.

Rees, Helen. 2003. The Age of Consent: Traditional Music, Intellectual Property, and Changing Attitudes in the People's Republic of China. *British Journal of Ethnomusicology* 12, no. 1: 137–71.

Savage, Patrick E., Psyche Loui, Bronwyn Tarr, Adena Schachner, Luke Glowacki, Steven Mithen, and W. Tecumseh Fitch. 2020. "Music as a Coevolved System for Social Bonding." *Behavioral and Brain Sciences*, 1–36. doi:10.1017/S0140525X20000333.

SEM. 2020. Open Letter from SEM Past Presidents on Racism. Society for Ethnomusicology. http//www.ethnomusicology.org

Smith, Linda Tuhiwai. 2012. *Decolonizing Methodologies: Research and Indigenous Peoples*. London: Zed Books.

Spitzer, Michael. 2021. *The Musical Human: A History of Life on Earth*. London: Bloomsbury.

Tan, Shzr Ee. 2021. "Special Issue: Decolonising Music and Music Studies." *Ethnomusicology Forum* 30, no. 1: 4–8.

Urbain, Oliver, ed. 2015. *Music and Conflict Transformation: Harmonies and Dissonances in Geopolitics*. London: I. B. Tauris.

Chapter Two

International Soft Law and the Promotion of Musical Rights

Marja Heimonen and David G. Hebert

This chapter explores the relationship between international soft law and musical rights. Our concerns are both how music is legally protected and promoted within countries *and* how it is used across borders, and ultimately, our objective is to determine what is needed for the future to have improved music rights and conscientious uses of music in diplomacy. Our principal concern is whether, and how, international soft law can promote music rights. Our perspective is based on the capabilities approach, which is closely linked with human rights (Nussbaum, 2011). We also draw upon the arguments of Martti Koskenniemi, who suggests that "soft law is no law at all" (2006, 193), since rules must be created by objective criteria to be binding. After discussing ethnomusicological views on this topic we propose new visions for the future of international music rights.

To many musicians, musicologists, and audiophiles, the field of law may seem quite removed from their principal interests. Copyright has relevance that is evident to most any composer or songwriter, but most other forms of legal theory may appear rather distant to concerns about musical sound and its production. However, we seek to demonstrate how, just as such fields as psychology and sociology can offer findings of value to musicians, *law* also offers unique insights to support the endeavors of musicians. The breadth of conceivable legal applications to music is profound, from questions about how copyrighted works can be acceptably shared in teaching and quoted in derivative works, to the rights of musicians to carry their instruments personally onto airplanes, to the rights of Indigenous peoples to maintain some control over their musical heritage.

How is this discussion of international "soft law" relevant to mechanisms of cultural diplomacy? As Kevin Mulcahy observed, "The basic distinction between traditional diplomacy and cultural diplomacy is clear: the former concerns interactions between or among national actors in the international system where the latter seeks to influence foreign public, often through non-official organizations of scholars, artists, intellectuals, and journalists. Essentially, public diplomacy should not be seen as merely an instrument of international politics" (2017, 35). Cultural diplomacy has been defined as "the exchange of ideas, information, art, and other aspects of culture among nations and their peoples in order to foster mutual understanding" (Cummings, 2009), but some authors question "how can cultural diplomacy be *both* in the national interest *and* go beyond the national interest?" (Ang, Isar, and Mar, 2016, 6). The same dilemma applies to the field of law, which traditionally seeks to influence behaviors according to national systems, yet increasingly in ways that aim to have global applicability.

"Soft law" is a growing corpus of conventions intended to serve as a universally applicable and unifying legal framework, as the basic foundation of international law. As we seek to better understand how music is used worldwide as a form of cultural diplomacy, it is necessary to understand both the international legal system in which such diplomacy occurs, as well as the different kinds of cultural orientations and state systems that shape diplomacy. Indeed, William Logan has argued that "Asian ways of dealing with rights—human rights, both individual and collective, as well as concepts of cultural and heritage rights—are likely to acquire greater importance within the international discourse" (2016, 180). The same claim might be made of "African ways" or any number of other "ways" to the extent that it is even meaningful to suggest the existence of general orientations associated with diverse continents. The point here is that an understanding of music in cultural diplomacy requires recognition of diplomacy in multiple directions, not only how European and North American states use music to relate with other parts of the world, but also vice versa, how other countries use music as part of their outreach to "the West" as well as in international relations that do not directly involve Western countries, such as between Ethiopia and China, for instance. In some cases, such musical exchange can be traced even to ancient times (Ranade, 2006). Music is often perceived as situated at the very heart of heritage and identity, inextricably connected with other arts, and emblematic of all that can be either good or ill in intercultural relations. The centrality of music as heritage is affirmed in a memorable passage of Helle Porsdam's book *The Transforming Power of Cultural Rights: A Promising Law and Humanities Approach*: "First the Taliban took our music, then our Buddhas, then our history" (2019, 72).

We begin this chapter by exploring the principal terms and discussing the relationships between international soft law and cultural rights. Next, we focus on music rights and specific issues in soft law. Then, we concentrate on determining what an ethnomusicological perspective on cultural policies entails. Finally, we conclude with rethinking the notion of music rights, with the aim of developing new visions for conceiving a global view of this field in the future.

CURRENT ISSUES IN MUSICAL RIGHTS

Several contemporary issues of relevance to musical concerns are related to international soft law, such as climate change, sustainability, Arctic questions, global health coordination, and international commercial arbitration. "The basic feature of arbitral proceedings is flexibility," states Hrncirikova (2016, 104), a principle that also applies to the global challenges mentioned above. Climate change is a severe global problem closely connected with Arctic questions, for instance, and impacts the musical life of communities in the far North, such as the Sámi and Inuits. Global health, especially during the COVID-19 pandemic, is a matter of concern to all nations around the world, and research demonstrates how music participation plays an important role in community health and well-being (Bonde and Theorell, 2018; Fancourt and Finn, 2019). Human beings are dependent on how these issues are dealt with globally; thus there is a need to develop flexible international instruments to solve these contemporary challenges. Law has unique power as one such instrument connected to governance and ultimately, social change.

Contemporary global challenges impinge on the lives and activities of musicians. In ethnomusicology, Indigenous peoples' rights to cultural heritage, including their music, have been compared with rights to their own languages around the world (Grant, 2014; Heimonen and Hebert, 2010). Musical rights of Indigenous peoples, such as Sámi children, for instance, have been studied (Kallio and Heimonen, 2019; Kallio and Länsman, 2018), and the results that are *joiked* by Hildá Länsman show how dissonances may express the pain of exclusion experienced by Sámi artists, musicians, and educators.

The right to free expression is one of the most fundamental rights claimed by musicians and other artists, and is even promoted by such organizations as the International Music Council (IMC) in its Five Music Rights (discussed below). Copyright of digital products is included in global intellectual property conventions, raising issues that are closely connected with musicians' rights and the rights of producers. The right of musicians to obtain fair compensation for their work may be governed by excessively restrictive versus excessively loose regulations within nation-states, whereas music technology and the global music business continuously and rapidly expand beyond borders with minimal regulation. International soft law, such as copyright treaties, has promoted the rights of weaker parties, that is, artists, whose interests sometimes contradict those of a powerful music industry. Intellectual property is a crucial concern, especially when it comes to Indigenous peoples' rights. How best to support Indigenous innovation and promote collaboration is arguably a more essential question than trying to define the traditional concepts of Indigenous peoples or knowledge that ought to be protected (Frankel, 2018, 790).

INTERNATIONAL SOFT LAW AND CULTURAL RIGHTS

Understanding International Soft Law

Soft law has been conceptualized in many ways. According to the European Center for Constitutional and Human Rights (ECCHR), it is used to "denote agreements, principles, and declarations that are not legally binding" (ECCHR, 2020). This kind of nonbinding law may be both national and international. As Goldmann states, "Non-binding international rules, generically referred to as 'soft law,' refer to formation of customary law, guide the interpretation of treaties, authorize action by international organizations, and give rise to duties of good faith such as a duty to consider" (2012, 336). Hard law is generally understood as the inverse to international soft law, and Goldmann notes that "soft law does not entail the same legal consequences as violations of binding international law, commonly referred to as 'hard law'" (2012, 336). Binding law, to the contrary, is connected with legal enforcement by a court (ECCHR, 2020). Still, soft law is usually observed de facto although not juridically binding, and this kind of law may ultimately have a great effect on activities in practice (Heimonen, 2002, 168).

The term "soft law" originates in international law and its instruments are mostly international in scope (ECCHR, 2020) although the term can be used with respect to some national laws as well (Heimonen, 2002, 168; D'Rosario and Zeleznikow, 2018). Typical examples of international soft law are declarations and resolutions by the United Nations. In addition, agreements are regarded as part of soft law, and so are principles when they are not legally binding (ECCHR, 2020; Heimonen, 2002, 168). Soft law has also been seen to cover standards and ethical guidelines (Pohjolainen, 1998, 442) such as the ethical principles and values of professions, for instance, the Comedius Oath for teachers.

Close to international soft law is *soft power*. Sarasola (2020) takes the arts and especially movies as examples of soft power, for example, *Schindler's List* and its influence on making the suffering of Jews during the Nazi era and the braveness of Schindler well-known all over the world. Thus, movies, and other arts as well, may promote human rights and make the world a better place to live. However, Sarasola (2020) also notes the limitations of movies since they do not recognize the rights of *all* minorities and thus some movies may even emphasize the status quo of the society comprising injustice and inequality. This phenomenon of soft power could be applied to other arts as well. Soft power is connected with *cultural diplomacy* according to which "culture and education can draw people closer" (Goff, 2013). Educational exchange programs, including those for music teachers, can be taken as examples (Hebert and Hauge, 2019). Moreover, musicians arranging joint workshops and orchestras for Israeli and Syrian children are seen to promote mutual understanding and respect between young people from politically hostile countries (Barenboim and Said, 2004). In the politically divided Nicosia of Cypros, a community music project named Long Distance Call offered a forum for Turkish and Greek Cypriots to play together in a musical performance (van den Hoogen and Boele, 2018). In other words, official diplomatic relations are not enough and sometimes not even possible when conflicts run deep.

There is frequent disagreement regarding the ultimate foundations and sources of soft law. Martti Koskenniemi (2006, 190) states that although there is "constant disagreement about the correct sources—the more positivistically oriented lawyer emphasizing treaties and custom, the more naturalistically inclined lawyer stressing general principles, systemic values etc.—only the former may be used as rules in the above, source-related sense." In short, Koskenniemi believes that only hard rules are legal rules. Legal and political procedures are distinct concepts. Objectivity is focal in juridical processes; thus, "soft law is no law at all" (Koskenniemi, 2006,193) since rules must be created by objective criteria to be binding. Soft law inherently lacks normativity because it is not created in a formal process governing the enactment of laws.

Koskenniemi's (2006) utopian vision, according to which ethics, rather than law, guides the social life of human beings in society is presented at the end of his *From Apology to Utopia*: "as society becomes more integrated, the (artificial) egoism of individual actors cedes more room to their (natural) altruism so that the need of law diminishes until at some imaginary point ethics and natural love allow the (now fully integrated) community to govern itself without formalism" (599). As an active and critical participant in public discussions on human rights, Koskenniemi (interviewed by Onninen in 2017/2020) sees human rights as neither stable nor above politics; they are inside and interwoven with politics. He also points to how an individual's rights have to be balanced with the rights of others if justice is to be attained. Juridification of human rights—implementing these notions into enforceable law—is not endorsed by Koskenniemi even if it is popular in present societies. Contrary to Dworkin (1977), he finds that political movements, such as taking rights seriously, tend to use their claims merely as slogans. Koskenniemi argues how human rights secured in the United Nations conventions are not always realized in practice and takes the restrictions in different societies in response to the worldwide COVID-19 pandemic as an example. Koskenniemi's critical view is a reminder of the paradox when human rights and international laws are viewed as an apolitical form of universal justice: even if these rights are included in international declarations and conventions, they are still realized—or not—via political actions.

CULTURAL RIGHTS

The book *Negotiating Cultural Rights*, edited by law professors Lucky Belder (from Utrecht University) and Helle Porsdam (from the University of Copenhagen), examines the field through discussion of reports on cultural rights by UN special rapporteur Faridah Shaheed (2017), including on such critical topics as artistic freedom and intellectual property (Belder and Porsdam, 2017; Porsdam, 2019). This extends on ideas developed in various earlier publications (e.g., Borelli and Lenzerini, 2012), and indeed the rapidly developing field of *cultural rights* is still rather young, enabling a book from as recent as 2009 to stake a claim as "the first publication to address the notions of cultural diversity, cultural heritage and human rights in one volume" (Langfield, Logan, and Craith, 2009). The field rests on foundations that are subject to complex debates. Indeed, Laurajane Smith in her book *Uses of Heritage* (2006) introduces the notion of "authorized heritage discourse," which in her conceptualization enables empowered authorities to view heritage as "fragile, finite, and nonrenewable," when in Smith's view heritage is performative, connected to power, and open to interpretation. Such views of heritage can work either for or against those who seek to argue for cultural rights, and the same goes for interpretations of other major concepts such as artistic rights and intellectual property.

Cultural Rights and the UN Human Rights Council

Cultural rights are increasingly recognized as a growing domain of international law, particularly through the establishment of a UN special rapporteur in the field of cultural rights within the UN High Commission for Human Rights (created by Human Rights Council Resolution 19/6 of 2012). The first special rapporteur to be established in this field was Ms. Farida Shaheed, who held the position from 2012 to 2015, following some years as an UN-recognized independent expert for cultural rights (2009–2012). The second and current special rapporteur for cultural rights is Ms. Karima Bennoune (2015–present). Shaheed is a Pakistani sociologist who has held various positions with the government of Pakistan and now works as the executive director of Shirkat Gah-Women's Resource Centre in that country. Bennoune grew up in Algeria and the United States and currently works as an endowed professor of law at the University of California, Davis. Both Shaheed and Bennoune have developed international law through their role as UN special rapporteur with implications for several topics of relevance to music, so it is useful here to examine some of the positions taken and issues explored through their office of special rapporteur for cultural rights with the UN High Commission for Human Rights.

Since its establishment (2012) the special rapporteur for cultural rights has had a six-point mandate (United Nations Human Rights Council, "Information on the Mandate" accessed September 12, 2021) follows:

- Identify best practices of promoting and protecting cultural rights at local, national, regional, and international levels;
- Identify obstacles to the promotion and protection of cultural rights, and submit recommendations to the Council on ways to overcome them;
- Work with States to foster the adoption of measures—at local, national, regional, and international levels—to promote and safeguard cultural rights, and make concrete proposals to enhance cooperation at all levels in that regard;
- Collaborate closely with States and other relevant actors like the United Nations Educational, Scientific and Cultural Organization, to study the relationship between cultural rights and cultural diversity, with the aim of further promoting cultural rights;
- Integrate a gender and a disability perspective into this work;
- Coordinate with intergovernmental and non-governmental organizations, other special procedures, the Committee on Economic, Social and Cultural Rights, the United Nations Educational, Scientific and Cultural Organization, and relevant actors, representing the broadest possible range of interests and experiences, including by attending relevant conferences and events.

Cultural Rights as Defined by UN Special Rapporteur

How exactly are "cultural rights" defined in this framework? Here is how the special rapporteur defines this field:

> Cultural rights protect the rights for each person, individually and in community with others, as well as groups of people, *to develop and express their humanity, their world view and the meanings they give to their existence and their development* through, inter alia, values, beliefs, convictions, languages, knowledge and the arts, institutions and ways of life. Cultural rights also protect access to heritage and resources that allow such identification and development processes to take place. (Shaheed 2010)

The mandate on cultural rights does not aim to protect culture or cultural heritage per se, but to promote the conditions allowing all people without discrimination to access, participate, and contribute to all aspects of cultural life in a continuously developing manner. Therefore, the focus of special rapporteur's thematic studies and country visits is not on cultural sites and institutions per se, but rather on considering how particular policies, legal frameworks relating to such sites and institutions, as well as other aspects of heritage, science, creativity, and discrimination contribute to the realization of cultural rights and respect for diversity on the ground (United Nations Human Rights Council, "Mapping Cultural Rights: Nature, Issues at Stake and Challenges" accessed September 12, 2021).

Initiatives of UN Special Rapporteur

In June 2010, in Shaheed's first thematic report to the Human Rights Council, "Cultural Rights: Conceptual and Legal Framework," even before becoming special rapporteur, sought to define how cultural concerns could best be conceptualized within a human rights legal framework, and these arguments served as a foundation for the establishment of the special rapporteur position (Shaheed, 2010). Shaheed's 2010 report notes that "many explicit and implicit references to cultural rights can be found in international instruments and the practice of human rights mechanisms" (6) and offers "a first working definition of cultural rights and develops her initial thoughts on the interaction among the principle of universality of human rights, the recognition and implementation of cultural rights and the need to respect cultural diversity" (1). As the first special rapporteur in this field, Shaheed issued important reports on such topics as cultural heritage, artistic freedom, and intellectual property, among others.

Importantly, *artistic freedom* is here defined in this way: "The right to freedom of artistic expression is a fundamental aspect of cultural rights. It includes the freedom to seek, receive and impart information and ideas of all kinds 'in the form of art,' the right 'to enjoy the arts,' and the creativity of others, as well as obligations from States to 'respect the freedom indispensable for . . . creative activity'" (United Nations Human Rights Council, "Artistic Freedom" 12).

In Shaheed's report, "The Right to Freedom of Artistic Expression and Creation," (2013) the special rapporteur affirmed "the right to freedom of artistic expression and creation, which includes the right of all persons to freely experience and contribute to artistic expressions and creations, through individual or joint practice, to have access to and enjoy the arts, and to disseminate their expressions and creations" (18). This trajectory was extended further in a report to the Human Rights Council by Karima Bennoune, "Report of the Special Rapporteur in the Field of Cultural Rights" (2018), in which the special rapporteur noted how "the field of culture can open a space in which individuals and groups can reflect upon their society, confront and modify their perception of one another, express their fears and grievances in a non-violent manner, develop resilience after violent or traumatic experiences, including human rights violations, and imagine the future they want for themselves and how to better realize human rights in the society they live in" (1).

Among the new themes introduced since 2015 by special rapporteur Karima Bennoune are cultural rights defenders, the intentional destruction of cultural heritage, as well as further developments related to copyright and patent policy. The first of these new themes was explored in her report "Cultural Rights Defenders" (2020), whom she defined as those who "pursue the elimination of violations of cultural rights and promote respect for and protection and fulfillment of these rights" (2). She also explicitly notes a connection with the UN's Sustainable Development Goals: "Defending cultural rights not only contributes to the protection and promotion of all interdependent and interrelated human rights, but also the realization of the sustainable development agenda" (United Nations Human Rights Council, "Cultural Rights Defenders," accessed September 12, 2021). The report outlines an international legal framework supporting the protection of cultural rights defenders.

Perhaps the work of the special rapporteur that is most likely to have deep and enduring relevance to the field of music is that concerned with copyright issues. Two reports from 2015 contain important arguments. The first, "Copyright Policy and the Right to Science and Culture" seeks to identify ways "to expand copyright exceptions and limitations to empower new creativity, increase educational opportunities, preserve space for non-commercial culture and promote inclusion and access to cultural works" (Shaheed, 2014, 1) The second, "Patent Policy and the Right to Science and Culture," stresses that "the right to the protection of the moral and material interests of authors does not necessarily coincide with the prevailing approach to intellectual property law. There is no human right to patent protection. The right to protection of moral and material interests cannot be used to defend patent laws that inadequately impact the right to participate in cultural life . . . and the rights of Indigenous peoples and local communities" (Shaheed, 2015, 2). It also affirms that "the human rights perspective demands that patents do not extend so far as to interfere with individuals' dignity and well-being. Where patent rights and human rights are in conflict, human rights must prevail" (United Nations Human Rights Council, "The Impact of Intellectual Property Regimes on the Enjoyment of Right to Science and Culture," accessed September 12, 2021).

CULTURAL RIGHTS AND CAPABILITIES

Culture is usually defined as encompassing worldviews and norms of social behavior, a living process of collective meaning-making that relates to the past, present, and future, and includes such expressions as music and dance. A dynamic interpretation of culture as a way of life has been endorsed in many cases. Reindeer hunting and music performances count both as culture (Donders, 2020). Cultural rights are most important, especially for minorities but for everyone, and thus secured both by international soft law, such as UN Conventions, and hard law, as seen in national constitutions and legislation. There has been much discussion of whether cultural rights are better understood from the perspective of individual versus collective (e.g., Porsdam Mann, Porsdam, and Donder, 2020, 343), and Donders (2020) argues that they are mostly collective, that is, rights of groups. These kinds of rights have strengthened when sustainable future, green movements, arctic concerns, and ethnic minorities have become issues of current political debates. However, in many conventions individual rights are still dominant although these rights have a collective dimension (Donders, 2020).

Especially in Western countries, rights have generally been individual-centered whereas in many non-Western cultures collective rights receive relatively greater emphasis (Donders, 2020). The influence of local communities is of great importance for an individual's life and well-being in Asia, Africa, and in many groups within Western societies, as well. As an example, collective rights have been connected especially with the rights of Indigenous peoples: the rights to their land, languages, and cultures as part of their living and existence, such as the Sámi in the Nordic countries. One way to promote these rights, which today especially include participation rights, is to ratify international soft law such as UN Conventions on a national level (Aikio, 2012, 4–5, 9).

A global view of rights undergirds the capabilities approach (Nussbaum, 2011), according to which welfare consists of each one's capabilities to live a meaningful and flourishing life in society. Nussbaum emphasizes a humanistic view of well-being rather than economic values, which she emphasizes civic values. However, even if economic growth and well-being are not valued as "ends in themselves," they are seen as possible "means" for promoting capabilities (Robeyns, 2016). Nussbaum connects education in the arts with empathy formed through a capability to play with others and sees arts education as crucial for democracy. Nussbaum argues that Aristotle's view of a flourishing life is still relevant since it is holistic, including friendship, beauty, love, and wide conceptions of a flourishing life (Alhanen, 2004, 33). She emphasizes the importance of emotions, especially their cognitive roles, as guides for a good life but admits that emotions can sometimes be misleading and sees some risks to trusting their guidance (Nussbaum, 2001, xviii; Alhanen 2004, 34). Nussbaum's way of doing philosophy is pragmatic and concrete, in that she writes about ethical problems situated in real-life experiences (Alhanen, 2004, 37).

Both Nussbaum and Amartya Sen, the main theorists of the capabilities approach, emphasize "the close link between capabilities and human rights" (Nussbaum, 2011, 62) even if their views also differ from each other (Ylimaztekin, 2017). Moreover, Klisala Harrison (2020) argues that even if the capabilities presented by Nussbaum and Sen are not synonymous with human rights they could be interpreted as "specific human rights" (Harrison, 2020, 16). Based on ethnographic research on music interventions in poor urban areas in Canada, Harrison points critically that only some people may have the capabilities to exercise human rights (15). Capabilities and the human rights approaches argue fundamentally that "all people have some core entitlements just by virtue of their humanity" (Nussbaum, 2011, 62), and society must "respect and support" the aforementioned core entitlements (62). The list of capabilities by Nussbaum overlaps with human rights (62); her ten central capabilities 33–34) are as follows: (1) life, (2) bodily health, (3) bodily integrity, (4) senses, imagination, and thought, (5) emotions, (6) practical reason, (7) affiliation, (8) other species, (9) play, and (10) control over one's environment. Here we should also note that Nussbaum explicitly mentions *musical* aspects of capabilities when it comes to point four, "Being able to use imagination and thought in connection with experiencing and producing works and events of one's own choice, religious, literary, musical, and so forth," but it is also implied in points 4, 5, and 9 (33–34).

Capabilities belong first of all to individuals: each individual is seen as an end and no one should be used as a means to capabilities of others, with each human being worthy of equal respect. All central capabilities are to be secured by a nation (Nussbaum, 2011, 35), although the list "is a proposal" (36), not mandatory law. In a way, the list could be seen as a model for international soft law if interpreted broadly. Nussbaum (2001) argues that fundamental rights are only words if they are not made effective in practice; for example, by enacting laws that secure a living wage or education for all (65). She states that "negative liberty"—or libertarian politics of laissez-faire, with minimal state involvement (see for example, Nozick, 1974)—is not what she values or considers effective. The capabilities approach has increasingly become an important model for "soft law" development and is widely discussed in Nordic welfare states that aim to secure conditions and circumstances for a flourishing good life with equality and equity as central concepts in education, including in music (Heimonen and Hebert, 2019). Indeed, effective community music programs nurture capabilities by widening space for every individual and group's participation in meaningful, life-affirming experiences (e.g., van den Hoogen and Boele, 2018; Harrison, 2020).

MUSIC RIGHTS AND SPECIFIC ISSUES IN SOFT LAW

The IMC, founded in 1949 by UNESCO, is an organization that promotes access to music for everyone around the world. It formally endorses five "music rights" (International Music Council, 2021) that it regards as universally applicable:

> *All children and adults* have the right: (1) to express themselves musically in all freedom, (2) to learn musical languages and skills, (3) to have access to musical involvement through participation, listening, creation, and information, and *all music artists* have the right (4) to develop their artistry and communicate through all media, with proper facilities at their disposal, and (5) to obtain just recognition and fair remuneration for their work.

The European Music Council is a member of the aforementioned IMC, and national music councils such as the Finnish Music Council are members of the European regional group. In addition, IMC is connected with approximately one thousand organizations (including the International Council for Traditional Music and the International Society for Music Education), formally connected with two hundred million people in 150 countries. Relevant soft laws, such as position statements and professional recommendations, are created via such organizations. For instance, "Access to music is a human right" is stated in the European Agenda for Music: "Everyone, regardless of physical ability, gender, age, social, cultural or geographical origin, should be able to engage in music from childhood" (IMC, 2021) In Finland, the Finnish Music Council (FMC) translated the five music rights into Finnish, defined these rights in groups of representatives of music institutions and associations, and published a booklet, in which music rights were justified by brain research and the five music rights by IMC. In addition, the FMC organized a public panel with politicians representing different political parties close to elections for a new parliament. The FMC explained how the first three rights are based on freedom of expression and participation in music activities, and the last two with the rights and conditions for activities of music makers and performers. Music rights are usually based on the Universal Declaration of Human Rights (1948), the Foundation document of PEN (1948) promoting freedom of expression of authors, and the Convention on Children's rights (1989). A glocal dimension is also evident in these rights: the IMC acts on a global level, while national councils interpret locally. Soft law's closeness to politics is also relevant, as public discussions with politicians are used to increase awareness of music rights and to promote a favorable politician who supports music rights for election to Parliament.

In many countries, music rights are under threat. The IMC condemned the terrorist attack on a music club in Paris, for instance. The IMC also awards prizes to honor individuals and organizations in notable situations in which music rights have been successfully promoted. As an example, the Music Rights Award was given in 2015 to a choir in Lebanon based on its valuable work with Syrian children. Moreover, drawing international attention to musicians arrested for merely performing their songs is part of its mission. Even death penalties have been used against musicians in some countries that apply religious law and fail to honor freedom of expression. Freedom of artistic expression is meant to protect an individual, an artist, not a majority religious group, according to the United Nations (IMC, 2021).

Benefits of soft law instruments include their flexibility, but there are varying degrees of effectiveness (Ellis, 2012, 313). Moreover, because soft law effaces the border between law and politics, it may sometimes be seen as a threat to conventional law. Interpreted broadly, soft law is connected with the same kinds of instruments used in soft power and cultural diplomacy. Soft law may be seen as a continuum between fully binding treaties and political positions and is especially useful in changing circumstances (Guzman and Meyer, 2010, 171–73; Peters and Pagotto, 2006, 2).

AN ETHNOMUSICOLOGICAL PERSPECTIVE ON CULTURAL POLICIES

Ethnomusicologists, as interdisciplinary scholars, tend to take great interest in the sociopolitical contexts of music genres and practices. While a large part of social control tends to be informal and associated with tacit social forces, *law* entails an explicit discourse of governance that both supports and limits what is musically possible in any given society. General cultural policy studies and legal studies often examine practical concerns related to the resolution of specific cases, while in ethnomusicology, cross-cultural *understanding* is the primary objective, and the field is also naturally associated with a global concern for music sustainability and the survival of cultural diversity (Schippers and Grant, 2016). Nevertheless, applied ethnomusicology is a growing field and general ethnomusicological knowledge can be of great value for fields with more of an "applied" orientation due to its potential role in shaping cultural policies, which ultimately bolster cultural diplomacy. This is particularly evident in such fields as cultural heritage law (Donders, 2020), as well as cultural rights and Indigenous heritage (Jakubowski, 2020).

One of the few previous discussions of law and ethnomusicology, which focused on issues concerning music recordings, decried the "lack of legal protection for non-Western music" (Mills, 1996, 59). Another study noted that ethical concerns regarding intellectual property have been rapidly transforming, and called for ethnomusicologists to pay closer attention to the changing landscape (Seeger, 1996). Cultural rights have also increasingly become an issue for schools, where "there is a sobering tendency for national systems of music education to not fully recognize or support the musical practices of ethnic minorities, particularly Indigenous and immigrant populations, despite ethical and even legal obligations to protect the cultural rights of all peoples" (Hebert and Kertz-Welzel, 2016, 175).

One musical right that frequently appears in ethnomusicological accounts is the right to access diverse forms of music as a consumer (Weintraub and Yung, 2009). Some countries, such as Iran and Saudi Arabia, control the extent to which Western popular culture is permitted on their airwaves (via radio or television). In many parts of the world, music is now primarily consumed via the internet, and a few countries (most notably, China) place strict controls on internet access. Questions of censorship in terms of both traditional media and internet control are relevant to almost every society, and norms can differ widely regarding what kinds of material are considered acceptable for the general public, and children in particular. Censorship is sometimes based on political concerns, but it can also derive from genuine concern for the welfare of the citizenry, and the line between politicized and welfare-oriented motivations is often open to debate due to general differences in cultural norms.

Rather than maintaining an absolutist position regarding the value of "freedom and openness" as a matter of cultural diplomacy, it may be beneficial for those from liberal democratic nations to frankly acknowledge that some commercialized forms (including certain high-profile US popular culture exports) are not necessarily relevant and beneficial to all societies, particularly when it comes to vulnerable individuals, whether children, the cognitively impaired, or those suffering mental health challenges. Consider, for instance, some Hollywood films in action, romance, and comedy categories that arguably may instill destructive attitudes (e.g., inevitability and normalcy of vigilante gun violence, female need for male heroism, racial and sexual stereotypes, anti-intellectualism, American exceptionalism, etc.). Other examples include the oeuvre of major media entertainment stars, from Joe Exotic to Alex Jones, or popular music stars such as Cardi B. and Megan Thee Stallion (known for award-winning hit song "WAP"). It is difficult to convincingly argue that the products associated with such performers elicit responses that are more beneficial than harmful to society, yet they are firmly entrenched with institutional recognition in Western markets. While it is inevitable that any appeals to "common sense" or "public decency" can be dismissed as merely cultural constructions (which they are), there may still be valid reasons for maintaining some sense of boundaries, irrespective of the strength of democratic principles. The case for "freedom and openness" would surely be strengthened if the West could *both* endorse freedom of expression *and* maintain higher standards of quality in its own media institutions, rather than bestowing awards in an ever-escalating competition for shock value that implies any notions of public decency inevitably derived from oppressive conservatism. Particularly when it comes to cultural diplomacy, formal recognition of products that promote unhealthy behaviors and lack evidence of substantive artistry (via Academy Awards, Grammy Awards, etc.) may inadvertently lead to a propensity to ban entire genres in conservative societies due to the difficulties of sorting out which cultural imports are relatively acceptable to local audiences. Heritage claims, albeit never free from politics (Smith, 2006), may still legitimately play some role in the process of determining which forms merit institutional recognition and public funding.

Another important topic for ethnomusicologists has been the musical implications of laws concerning intangible cultural heritage (Konach, 2015), particularly the UNESCO system for recognition of cultural heritage and various debates associated with its actual implementation (Howard, 2018; Keough, 2011). Political forces appear to have sometimes played a detrimental role in UNESCO's formal designation of tangible heritage sites (such as the case of a relatively insignificant mining town in Japan), and there are similar debates when it comes to musical genres and rituals that have (or have not) gained official UNESCO acknowledgment as significant intangible heritage.

Ethnomusicologist Greg Booth (2015) has demonstrated how the notion of music copyright has tended to be viewed rather differently in India, yet the situation has also continued to evolve as the nation becomes more economically interconnected with the West (see chapter 13). Similarly, research by Helen Rees (2003) has documented the changing views and practices concerning music as intellectual property in China, identifying trajectories that have developed further in more recent times as trade in cultural products intensified with Western nations (Chen, 2021; also see chapter 14). Moreover, in her study of Wang Luobin, Rachel Harris (2005) shows how in China's Xinjiang Province, home to the Uyghur people, attitudes have varied regarding ownership of folk songs. While ethnomusicologists have helpfully examined intellectual property concerns in relation to specific nations and regions, there appears to still be a dearth of scholarship concerned with the global picture of how soft law and intellectual property conventions are impacting music worldwide.

CONCLUSION: RETHINKING MUSIC RIGHTS WITH NEW VISIONS

In our final section of this chapter, we will first draw conclusions based on the research described above, then discuss our findings and propose visions for future research.

The Cultural Appropriation versus Cultural Approbation Debate

"Appropriate" is a term with multiple meanings in English, whether as a verb or adjective, but the notion of *cultural appropriation* is understood as the taking of something without permission to benefit oneself, while *approbation* contrarily means to offer approval or praise for something. Artists who borrow ideas and practices from another culture can do so in either a scavenger-like way that disregards the views of local people, or in a respectful way that benefits local traditions by appropriately giving credit where credit is due and drawing new attention to cherished features of heritage. In music, there is a long history of both positive and negative examples, both helpful *approbation* and regrettable *appropriation*, and it increasingly seems important for musicians to carefully reflect on such concerns as part of their professional education. While on the one hand, it is important to uphold the value of artistic freedom, there is also a strong argument for giving due consideration to any obligations to the milieu from which cultural heritage originates, and the values associated with these two objectives can easily come into conflict in intercultural music projects.

A Middle Ground Between Legal Traditions

Another important ideal to strive for is that of seeking a mutually acceptable compromise between contrasting legal traditions (Chen, 2021). While some practicing attorneys find the very notion of acknowledging non-Western and Indigenous legal traditions to seem hopelessly impractical—particularly within nation-states in which a colonizing power's system claims legal jurisdiction—sometimes the most ethically sound and admirable position is one that seeks to respectfully acknowledge other ways of thinking about laws and regulations (Jakubowski, 2020). This seems particularly relevant when it comes to disputes regarding the musical heritage of Indigenous and minority peoples, and there are indeed many circumstances in which music is very much intertwined with concern for Indigenous sovereignty. Even when attorneys sense that other systems have no standing relative to the colonizer's system in which they principally operate, conscientious musicians will empathetically seek to find a middle ground, and this principle can even be codified through the position statements of music organizations, musician unions, and educational institutions.

Acknowledging Evolution for Sustainability

In cultural heritage fields, as a matter of practicality, there is inevitably a tendency to think of any traditional practice as primarily a stable entity when in fact it is constantly evolving, even during periods when the changes are so subtle as to be almost imperceptible. Researchers have frequently found that evolving musical practices, along with other cultural forms, have gained "popular acceptance as 'traditional' because they contributed to an identity that was reinforced by festivals and public rituals" (Cusack, 2017, vi). Such phenomena have often been explained with reference to the "invention of tradition" theory (Hobsbawm and Ranger, 1983), which has maintained its relevance for nearly forty years despite some efforts to challenge aspects of its application (Babadzan, 2000; Boschung, Busch, and Versluys, 2015; Briggs, 1996; Plant, 2008).

The ability to digitally record audio and video files of performances, and to 3-D map musical instruments, promises to permanently change what is possible in terms of heritage documentation, analysis, and preservation, and when it comes to the field of intangible heritage we can see a chasm between the predigital and digital eras, although this is an oversimplification since many archives contain materials that first were recorded on other technologies, from wax cylinders to audiotapes. Still, one must recognize that prior to the late nineteenth century it was not possible to record sounds nor moving images. Film also arose in the early twentieth century, and now as so many historical collections have been digitized, and thereby made instantly available, a sharp division has arisen between the recent era for which sound and video recordings exist and all the earlier periods of human history (Hebert,

2018). Theoretically, such recordings could ensure that any cultural practice from recent eras that have died out could potentially be revived (Bithell and Hill, 2014), while for earlier eras there is a profound paucity of rich evidence.

Participatory Rights in Relation to Music

One important dimension in the current discourse on musical and other cultural rights is the question of participatory rights, that is, how to secure, for example, the participation of Indigenous peoples in decision-making in society, especially whenever issues relevant to their culture are discussed and decided. National ratification of UN conventions in national laws may offer a secure basis for these rights, although legal instruments are often insufficient in practice to promote the rights of Indigenous musicians. Interpretation and application of legal texts are needed in a way that encourages the citizenry to actively discuss and participate, and thereby to ultimately gain confidence in trusting the authorities. A formal right to participation, to ask local peoples but not to take into account their views and replies, is too often used when these rights are in question. However, music interventions, outreach projects, information campaigns, and public debates may be effective ways to realize participatory rights and empower authorities and the citizenry to recognize and value diverse forms of musical heritage, not in a static way but with an approach that enhances public understanding of the power of music.

Interpretations of Law versus. Cultural Rights

When it comes to cultural rights of Indigenous peoples, trust in judicial authorities who interpret national law and international treaties has often been broken, including in the arctic region. Cultural sensitivity and insider knowledge are needed in courts that decide cases related to the cultural rights of the Sami, for instance. The black letters of the law—as Justice Holmes describes it, "law in books"—often do not help to protect minorities or Indigenous peoples if the power to interpret resides in courts consisting of human beings unable to fully understand the law and that culture matters (or should matter). Even today, there is a difference between rights on paper and those realized in practice, argues Aili Keskitalo, the Sami president, with a critical view of how Norwegian courts have begun the year 2021 (Ravna, 2021). Thus, even "hard law" may fail as an effective instrument in promoting musical and other cultural rights if it is not interpreted and applied into practice in a culturally sensitive way. Education and information, and active participation in cultural projects to learn via experiences are promising ways to enhance mutual understanding between "those in power" and Indigenous peoples.

CONCLUDING REMARKS

As we have noted, there are at least five pressing issues that call for deeper consideration in relation to international soft law and music rights: (1) the cultural appropriation versus cultural approbation debate, (2) finding a middle ground between legal traditions, (3) acknowledging the evolution and sustainability of musical practices, (4) participatory rights concerning music, and (5) interpretations of law versus cultural rights. There are no easy solutions for these kinds of complex issues, but we hope our discussion is useful in terms of describing the main conceptual bases and long-term concerns in this field.

Music is important partly because it communicates in profound ways that are deeply visceral and connected to emotions. It entails emotional expression on the part of the performer, which may be interpreted differently by diverse listeners, but any listener may ultimately sense across time that a song has become "my music," something with which they identify that has become an important part of their life. This makes notions of ownership and rights rather complicated to sort out due to all the variables of human life. Moreover, it is of critical importance that scholars, educators, and artists recognize musical traditions—like other forms of cultural heritage—are living rather than static, therefore the very notion of authenticity is very much open to interpretation, since artists inevitably tend to modify traditional musics and mix genres. All the aforementioned conclusions and visions offer a foundation for future research on musical and cultural rights, diverse legal traditions, and international soft law. Tensions between local and global, universal and particular, are always present and part of the power structure of our world, and will be in the future as well. These issues are multidimensional and require cross-disciplinary studies, and creative artists and researchers, who envision futures collaboratively for a global musical ecosystem, a world of challenging questions, demands, and hopes.

REFERENCES

Aikio, Pekka. 2012. "Johdanto ja historia" ("Introduction and History"). In *YK:n julistus alkuperäiskansojen oikeuksista ja ILO:n yleissopimus nro 169 (UN Declaration on the Rights of Indigenous Peoples and Indigenous and Tribal Peoples Convention No 169)*, 3–17. Helsinki: Suomen YK-liitto (UN Association of Finland).

Alhanen, Kai. 2004. "Filosofia ja ihmiselämän haavoittuvuus - Martha Nussbaumin haastattelu" ("Philosophy and Fragility of Human Life – Interview of Martha Nussbaum"). *niin & näin* 4: 33–7.

Ang, Ien, Raj Isar Yudhishthir, and Phillip Mar, eds. 2016. *Cultural Diplomacy: Beyond the National Interest?* New York: Routledge.

Babadzan, Alain. 2000. "Anthropology, Nationalism and 'the Invention of Tradition.'" *Anthopology Forum* 10, 131–55.

Barenboim, Daniel and Edward W. Said. 2004/2002. *Parallels and Paradoxes. Explorations in Music and Society.* Edited and with a Preface by Ara Guzelimian. London: Bloomsbury.

Belder, Lucky and Helle Porsdam, eds. 2017. *Negotiating Cultural Rights.* Cheltenham, UK: Edward Elgar Publishing.

Bennoune, Karima. 2018. "Report of the Special Rapporteur in the Field of Cultural Rights." 37th Session of the United Nations Human Rights Council, Agenda numbers 2 and 3: Annual Report of the United Nations High Commissioner for Human Rights and Reports of the Office of the High Commissioner and the Secretary-General Promotion and Protection of All Human Rights, Civil, Political, Economic, Social and Cultural Rights, Including the Right to Development. January 4. https://undocs.org/en/A/HRC/37/55.

———. 2020. "Cultural Rights Defenders: Report of the Special Rapporteur in the Field of Cultural Rights." 43rd Session of the United Nations Human Rights Council, Agenda Item 3: Promotion and Protection of All Human Rights, Civil, Political, Economic, Social and Cultural Rights, Including the Right to Development. January 20. https://undocs.org/en/A/HRC/43/50.

Bithell, Caroline and Juniper Hill, eds. 2014. *Oxford Handbook of Music Revival.* New York: Oxford University Press.

Bonde, Lars Ole and Tores Theorell, eds. 2018. *Music and Public Health: A Nordic Perspective.* Cham: Springer.

Booth, Gregory. 2015. "Copyright Law and the Changing Economic Value of Popular Music in India." *Ethnomusicology* 59, no 2: 262–87.

Borelli, Silvia and Federico Lenzerini, eds. 2012. *Cultural Heritage, Cultural Rights, Cultural Diversity: New Developments in International Law.* Leiden: Brill.

Boschung, Dietrich, Alexandra W. Busch, and Miguel John Versluys, eds. 2015. *Reinventing 'The Invention of Tradition'? Indigenous Pasts and the Roman Present.* Paderborn: Wilhelm Fink.

Briggs, Charles L. 1996. "The Politics of Discursive Authority in Research on the 'Invention of Tradition'." *Cultural Anthropology* 11: 435–69.

Cusack, Carole M. 2017. "Foreword." In *Invention of Tradition and Syncretism in Contemporary Religions*, edited by Stefania Palmisano and Nicola Pannofino, v–viii. Cham: Palgrave Macmillan.

Chen, Zen Troy. 2021. "Flying with Two Wings or Coming of Age Copyrightisation? A Historical and Socio-legal Analysis of Copyright and Business Model Developments in the Chinese Music Industry." *Global Media and China* 20, 1–16.

Cummings, Milton C. (2009). *Cultural Diplomacy and the United States Government: A Survey.* Americans for the Arts. http://www.AmericansForTheArts.org.

D'Rosario, Michael and John Zeleznikow. 2018. "Compliance with International Soft Law: Is the Adaptation of Soft Law Predictable?" *International Journal* of *Strategic Decision Sciences* 9, no 3 (July-September): 1–15. DOI: 10.4018/ IJSDS.2018070101.

Donders, Yvonne. 2020. "Cultural Heritage and Human Rights." In *The Oxford Handbook of International Cultural Heritage Law*, edited by Francesco Francioni and Ana Filipa Vrdoljak. New York: Oxford University Press. DOI: 10.1093/law/9780198859871.001.0001.

Dworkin, Ronald. 1977. *Taking Rights Seriously*. Cambridge, MA: Harvard University Press.

Ellis, Jaye. 2012. "Shades of Grey: Soft Law and the Validity of Public International Law." *Leiden Journal of International Law* 25: 313–34.

European Center for Constitutional and Human Rights (ECCHR). Accessed April 29, 2020. https://www.ecchr.eu/en/glossary/hard-law-soft-law/.

Fancourt, Daisy and Saoirse Finn. 2019. "What is the Evidence on the Role of the Arts in Improving Health and Well-being? A Scoping Review." *Health Evidence Network Synthesis Report 67*. World Health Organization (WHO), accessed March 25, 2021. https://apps.who.int/iris/bitstream/handle/10665/329834/9789289054553-eng.pdf.

Frankel, Susy. 2018. "Traditional Knowledge, Indigenous Peoples, and Local Communities." In *The Oxford Handbook of Intellectual Property Law*, edited by Rochelle Dreyfuss and Justine Pila. New York: Oxford University Press. DOI: 10.1093/oxfordhb/9780198758457.001.0001.

Goff, Patricia M. 2013. "Cultural Diplomacy." In *The Oxford Handbook of Modern Diplomacy*, edited by Andrew F. Cooper, Jorge Heine and Ramesh Thakur. New York: Oxford University Press. DOI: 10.1093/oxfordhb/9780199588862.001.0001.

Goldmann, Matthias. 2012. "We Need to Cut Off the Head of the King: Past, Present, and Future Approaches to International Soft Law." *Leiden Journal of International Law* 25: 335–68.

Grant, Catherine. *Music Endangerment: How Language Maintenance Can Help*. New York: Oxford University Press, 2014.

Guzman, Andrew T. and Timothy L. Meyer. 2010. "International Soft Law." *Journal of Legal Analysis* 2, no 1: 171–225.

Harris, Rachel. 2005. "Wang Luobin: Folk Song King of the Northwest or Song Thief? Copyright, Representation, and Chinese Folk Songs." *Modern China* 31, no 3: 381–408.

Harrison, Klisala. 2020. *Music Downtown Eastside: Human Rights and Capability Development through Music in Urban Poverty*. New York: Oxford University Press.

Hebert, David G. 2018. "Music in the Conditions of Glocalization." In *Music Glocalization: Heritage and Innovation in a Digital Age*, edited by Mikolaj Rykowski and David G. Hebert, 1–19. Newcastle: Cambridge Scholars.

Hebert, David G. and Alexandra Kertz-Welzel, eds. 2016. *Patriotism and Nationalism in Music Education*. New York: Routledge.

Hebert, David G. and Torunn Bakken Hauge, eds. 2019. *Advancing Music Education in Northern Europe*. London: Routledge.

Heimonen, Marja. 2002. *Music Education & Law. Regulation as an Instrument.* Studia Musica 17. Helsinki: Sibelius Academy.
Heimonen, Marja and David G. Hebert. 2010. "Pluralism and Minority Rights in Music Education: Implications of the Legal and Social Philosophical Dimensions." *Visions of Research in Music Education* 15. Accessed August 22, 2021. http://www-usr.rider.edu/~vrme/v15n1/visions/Pluralism%20and%20Minority%20Rights%20in%20Music%20Education.Heimonen%20and%20Hebert.pdf.pdf.
———. 2019. "Advancing Music Education via Nordic Cooperation: Equality and Equity as Central Concepts in Finland." In *Advancing Music Education in Northern Europe*, edited by David G. Hebert and Torunn Bakken Hauge, 119–40. London: Routledge.
Hilder, Thomas R. 2014. *Sámi Musical Performance and the Politics of Indigeneity in Northern Europe.* Lanham, MD: Rowman and Littlefield.
Hobsbawm, Eric J., and Terence Ranger, eds. 1983. *The Invention of Tradition.* Cambridge: Cambridge University Press.
Howard, Keith. 2018. "The Life and Death of Music as East Asian Intangible Cultural Heritage." In *International Perspectives on Translation, Education, and Innovation in Japanese and Korean Societies*, edited by David G. Hebert, 35–55. Cham: Springer.
Hrncirikova, Miluše. 2016. "The Meaning of Soft Law in International Commercial Arbitration." *International and Comparative Law Review* 16, no. 1: 97–109.
International Music Council (IMC). Accessed February 2, 2021. https://www.imc-cim.org/.
Jakubowski, Andrzej. 2020. "Cultural Rights and Cultural Heritage as a Global Concern." In *The Oxford Handbook of Law and Anthropology,* edited by Marie-Claire Foblets, Mark Goodale, Maria Sapignoli, and Olaf Zenker. Oxford: Oxford University Press. DOI: 10.1093/oxfordhb/9780198840534.013.29
Kallio, Alexis Anja and Hildá Länsman. 2018. "Sami Re-imaginings of Equality in/through Extracurricular Arts Education in Finland." *International Journal of Education & the Arts* 19, no 7. Accessed Nov 14, 2020, http://www.ijea.org/v19n7/index.html.
———. 2019. "A Toothless Tiger? Capabilities for Indigenous Self-determination in and through Finland's Extra-curricular Music Education System." *Music Education Research* 21, no 2: 150–60.
Keough, Elizabeth Betsy. 2011. "Heritage in Peril: A Critique of UNESCO's World Heritage Program." *Washington University Global Studies Law Review* 10, no. 3, 593–615. https://openscholarship.wustl.edu/law_globalstudies/vol10/iss3/5/.
Konach, Teodora. 2015. "Legal Protection of Intangible Cultural Heritage: The Concept of the Safeguarding of Expressions of Folklore." In *Cultural Heritage: Management, Identity and Potential*, edited by Łukasz Gaweł and Ewa Kocój, 41–54. Krakow: Jagiellonian University Press.
Koskenniemi, Martti. 2006. *From Apology to Utopia. The Structure of International Legal Argument.* Cambridge: Cambridge University Press.

Langfield, Michele, William Logan, and Mairead Nic Craith, eds. 2009. *Cultural Diversity, Heritage, and Human Rights: Intersections in Theory and Practice.* New York: Routledge.

Logan, William. 2016. "Collective Cultural Rights in Asia: Recognition and Enforcement." In *Cultural Rights as Collective Rights: An International Law Perspective*, edited by Andrzej Jakubowski, 180–81. Leiden: Brill.

Mills, Sherylle. 1996. "Indigenous Music and the Law: An Analysis of National and International Legislation." *Yearbook for Traditional Music* 28, 57–86.

Mulcahy, Kevin V. 2017. *Public Culture, Cultural Identity, Cultural Policy: Comparative Perspectives.* New York: Palgrave Macmillan.

Nozick, Robert. 1974. *Anarchy, State, and Utopia.* Oxford: Blackwell.

Nussbaum, Martha C. 2001. *The Fragility of Goodness. Luck and Ethics in Greek Tragedy and Philosophy.* Cambridge: Cambridge University Press.

———. 2011. *Creating Capabilities. The Human Development Approach.* Cambridge, MA: Belknap Press of Harvard University Press.

Onninen, Oskari (2017/updated 2020). Ihmisoikeustaistelija Martti Koskenniemi: "Olen aina ollut ihmisoikeuksien kriitikko" (Human rights activist Martti Koskenniemi: "I have always been a human rights critic"). *Image*, May 17, 2017/updated March 17, 2020.

Peters, Anne and Isabella Pagotto. 2006. "Soft Law as a New Mode of Governance: A Legal Perspective." NewGov Project. Accessed June 30 , 2020. http://www.eu-newgov.org/database/DELIV/D04D11_Soft_Law_as_a_NMG-Legal_Perspective.pdf.

Plant, Byron King. 2008. "Secret, Powerful, and the Stuff of Legends: Revisiting Theories of Invented Tradition." *Canadian Journal of Native Studies* 28, 175–94.

Pohjolainen, Teuvo. 1998. "Soft Law in Public Law - Hard Regulation?" *JFT / Tidskrift utgiven av Juridiska Föreningen i Finland* Etthundratrettiofjärde årgången: 437–61.

Porsdam, Helle. 2019. *The Transforming Power of Cultural Rights: A Promising Law and Humanities Approach.* Cambridge: Cambridge University Press.

Porsdam Mann, Sebastian, Helle Porsdam, and Yvonne Donders. 2020. "'The Sleeping Beauty': The Right to Science as a Global Ethical Discourse." *Human Rights Quarterly* 42, no 2: 332–56.

Ranade, Ashok. 2006. "Performing Exchanges: A Conceptual Inquiry with Reference to Indo-Iranian Experience." *Journal of the Indian Musicological Society* 36/37: 173–207.

Ravna, Øyvind. 2021. "Indigenous Peoples' Rights and the Norwegian Courts Moving into 2021." *Arctic Review on Law and Politics* 12: 1–3.

Rees, Helen. 2003. "The Age of Consent: Traditional Music, Intellectual Property and Changing Attitudes in the People's Republic of China." *British Journal of Ethnomusicology* 12, no 1, 137–71.

Robeyns, Ingrid. 2016. "The Capability Approach." In *The Stanford Encyclopedia of Philosophy*, edited by Edward N. Zalta, (Winter). https://stanford.library.sydney.edu.au/archives/win2016/entries/capability-approach/ Read 29 June 2020.

Sarasola, Mikel Díez. 2020. "Hollywood, an American Factory of International Soft Law and Social Order." *International Journal for the Semiotics of Law* 34: 7–31. https://doi.org/10.1007/s11196-020-09757-y.

Schippers, Huib and Catherine Grant, eds. 2016. *Sustainable Futures for Music Cultures: An Ecological Perspective*. New York: Oxford University Press.

Seeger, Anthony. 1996. "Ethnomusicologists, Archives, Professional Organizations, and the Shifting Ethics of Intellectual Property." *Yearbook for Traditional Music* 28, 87–105.

Shaheed, Faridah. 2010. "Report of the Independent Expert in the Field of Cultural Rights." 14th Session of the United Nations Human Rights Council, Agenda number 3: Promotion and Protection of All Human Rights, Civil, Political, Economic, Social and Cultural Rights, Including the Right to Development. March 22. https://undocs.org/en/A/HRC/14/36.

———. 2013. "Report of the Special Rapporteur in the Field of Cultural Rights: The Right to Freedom of Artistic Expression and Creativity." 23rd Session of the United Nations Human Rights Council, Agenda number 3: Promotion and Protection of all Human Rights, Civil, Political, Economic, Social and Cultural rights, Including the Right to Development. March 14. https://undocs.org/en/A/HRC/23/34.

———. 2014. "Report of the Special Rapporteur in the Field of Cultural Rights: Copyright Policy and the Right to Science and Culture." 28th Session of the United Nations Human Rights Council, Agenda number 3: Promotion and Protection of all Human Rights, Civil, Political, Economic, Social and Cultural rights, Including the Right to Development. December 24. https://undocs.org/en/A/HRC/28/57.

———. 2015. "Report of the Special Rapporteur: Cultural Rights." 70th Session of the United Nations Human Rights Council, Item 73 (b) of the Provisional Agenda: Promotion and Protection of all Human Rights, Civil, Political, Economic, Social and Cultural rights, Including the Right to Development. August 4. https://undocs.org/A/70/279.

———. 2017. "The United Nations Cultural Rights Mandate: Reflections on the Significance and Challenges." In *Negotiating Cultural Rights: Issues at Stake, Challenges and Recommenations*, edited by Lucky Belder and Helle Porsdam, 21–36. Cheltenham, UK: Edward Elgar Publishing.

Smith, Laurajane. 2006. *Uses of Heritage*. London: Routledge.

United Nations Human Rights Council. "Artistic Freedom." OHCHR. Accessed September 12, 2021. https://www.ohchr.org/EN/Issues/CulturalRights/Pages/Artistic-Freedom.aspx.

———. "Cultural Rights Defenders." OHCHR. Accessed September 12, 2021. https://www.ohchr.org/EN/Issues/CulturalRights/Pages/CulturalRightsDefenders.aspx.

———. "Information on the Mandate." OHCHR. Accessed September 12, 2021. https://www.ohchr.org/EN/Issues/CulturalRights/Pages/MandateInfo.aspx.

——— "Mapping Cultural Rights: Nature, Issues at Stake and Challenges." OHCHR. Accessed September 12, 2021. https://www.ohchr.org/EN/Issues/CulturalRights/Pages/MappingCulturalRights.aspx.

———. "The Impact of Intellectual Property Regimes on the Enjoyment of Right to Science and Culture." OHCHR. Accessed September 12, 2021. https://www.ohchr.org/EN/Issues/CulturalRights/Pages/ImpactofIntellectualProperty.aspx.

Van den Hoogen, Quirijn Lennert, and Evert Bisschop Boele. 2018. "Community Music in Cultural Policy." In *The Oxford Handbook of Community Music*, edited by Brydie-Leigh Bartleet and Lee Higgins. Oxford University Press. DOI: 10.1093/oxfordhb/9780190219505.001.0001.

Weintraub, Andrew N. and Bell Yung, eds. 2009. *Music and Cultural Rights*. Urbana: University of Illinois Press.

Ylimaztekin, Hasan Kadir. 2017. "Rethinking Copyright from the 'Capabilities' Perspective in the Post-TRIPs Era: How Can Human Rights Enhance Cultural Participation?" PhD diss. Exeter, UK: University of Exeter.

2
MIDDLE EASTERN PERSPECTIVES

Chapter Three

"Afghanistan Is Not What You Think"

Cultural Diplomacy through Music Education and Performance

Lauren Braithwaite

On December 19, 2016, a lorry deliberately ploughed into visitors at a Christmas market outside the Gedächtniskirche (also known as the Kaiser Wilhelm Memorial Church) on Breitscheidplatz, Berlin, killing twelve people and injuring more than sixty others. The attacker was believed to be a "soldier of the Islamic State" who carried out the terror attack in response to calls from the extremist group to target "citizens of the Crusader coalition"[1] (Lui, Jenkins, and John, 2017). Six weeks later, the walls of the Gedächtniskirche resounded with the melody of Beethoven's famous "Ode to Joy" played by the thirty young women of Afghanistan's first all-female orchestra, Zohra (an ensemble of the Afghanistan National Institute of Music), and the young German musicians with whom they were collaborating. Although the words of Friedrich Schiller's poem, which call for unity and peace between all mankind, were absent in this rendition, the symbolism of the young women's performance was unambiguous. The earlier terror attack reinforced a binary of "Us" *and* "Them'" (i.e., the West and an unknown, threatening East), which was immediately reconfigured as "Us" *with* "Them" (that is, the West and a more familiar, unthreatening East) by the image of an orchestra of young Afghan and German musicians performing side by side on the same stage. At a time when Germany was experiencing increasing polarization over the recent influx of refugees to the country, and nationalism and Islamophobia were on the rise across Europe,[2] Zohra's performance offered a genuine cultural exchange across continents. For a short time at least, the young women's musical offering promised to supersede the previous month's message of terror with a message of peace, cooperation, and cross-cultural dialogue through music. The desire of Berliners to hear Zohra's performance and witness this alternative narrative was unprecedented, with more than 2,500 people turned away at the door once the church had reached capacity.

This opening vignette is an illustration of just one of the many possible ways in which music can be used as a vehicle or site for cultural diplomacy, or what is often described as "musical diplomacy." At its broadest, cultural diplomacy describes "the exchange of ideas, information, art and other aspects of culture among nations and their peoples to foster mutual understanding" (Cummings, 2003, 1). The central paradigm underpinning musical diplomacy is the contested notion of the universality of music as a language that can transcend cultural, linguistic, ethnic, political, religious, and even physical borders.[3] Musicologists and practitioners alike have cautioned against misleading assertions that music is a universal language and draw attention instead to the universal dimensions of musical experience and its culturally-specific manifestations (Campbell, 1997; Cohen, 2008; Letts, 1997). Indeed, while every culture on Earth has some form of music, not all music is universally *understood* (Campbell, 1997; Elliott, 1990). However, debates of universality aside, there is a strong acceptance that music affords a sense of shared human experience, can create solidarity across various physical and nonphysical divides, and is thus well positioned for intercultural work (Bergh and Sloboda, 2010; Higgins, 2012; Skyllstad, 2008; Small, 1998).

The divergent events that occurred in Berlin also introduce the central theme of this chapter; the way in which musical performances create a communicative space in and through which alternative images of places, nations, and peoples can be articulated. An important theme within ethnomusicology is the role of music in constructing, expressing, or symbolizing identity (Rice, 2017). Viewing Zohra's musical practices through the lens of cultural diplomacy elucidates the sociopolitical tenets underpinning such identities and clarifies why musical identities are expressed in particular ways at certain politically salient moments in history. As this chapter argues, Zohra's musical performances do not simply reflect Afghan identity but rather actively *construct* an alternative Afghan identity. In the context of Afghanistan's foreign-led reconstruction,[4] this identity necessarily negotiates between articulating local musical practices and embracing increasing global influences. Focusing on the Afghanistan National Institute of Music's (ANIM) ongoing engagement with cultural diplomacy, this chapter explores the ways in which music is used by actors as a medium for portraying "a different, positive image of Afghanistan" to the world and as a vehicle for engaging in cross-cultural dialogue, cultural exchange, people-to-people diplomacy, and developing mutual understanding across borders. In particular, I look at the musical activities of the Zohra Orchestra whose members are acutely aware of how Afghanistan and its citizens are represented in the West and the potential role their overseas performances and collaborations can have in changing global perceptions about their country. The orchestra joins a growing number of all-female music ensembles within the wider MENA (Middle East and North Africa) region that engage in musical diplomacy, including Tunisia's El 'Azifet ("The female instrumentalists") women's orchestra, which regularly collaborates with female musicians from other countries while touring internationally and engages in state-sponsored performances around the globe. Finally, using the relationship between ANIM and the US State Department as a case study, this chapter interrogates some of the more uncomfortable aspects of musical diplomacy including pressure from outside nation-states and the implications of international funding agreements on overseas activities.

This chapter broadens the scope for researching Afghan music within its social and cultural context beyond the work carried out by the "Golden Age"[5] ethnomusicologists from the late 1950s to late 1970s. Western academic interest in Afghanistan's musical landscape during this time resulted in a small but rich canon of literature documenting the country's diverse urban and regional musics (see Baily, 1979, 1988; Doubleday, 1988; Sakata, 1976, 1983; Slobin, 1976). Because of the increasing unrest in the country after the 1978 "'Saur Revolution,"[6] in-country ethnographic fieldwork dried up and academics shifted their focus toward music in and of the Afghan diaspora (Baily, 1999b, 2005, 2015). Recently, Afghan musics have (re) emerged within a diverse range of academic discourses that intersect, to varying degrees, with ethnomusicology, including community music (Howell, 2018), communication studies (Karimi, 2017), and sociology (Ghani and Fiske, 2020). Karimi's ethnography, for example, describes how, in response to ongoing political persecution and forced migration, Hazara *dambura*[7] music has become a powerful tactical medium of communication and is "serving as a crucial tool in political mobilization among this community" (2017, 732).

Ethnomusicology has become a conduit through which a more interdisciplinary approach to the study of music might be realized (Stobart, 2008, 1). As the following case study of the Zohra Orchestra demonstrates, there is much to be harvested at the intersection of ethnomusicology, cultural diplomacy, and music education. From the perspective of applied ethnomusicology, for example, Zohra's musical diplomacy practices offer a unique window into the complex local and global politics that shape musical exchanges and cross-cultural collaborations originating in non-Western contexts. Moreover, by looking at the cultural diplomacy activities of ANIM through the lens of ethnomusicology, we not only gain an understanding of music's place and function within contemporary Afghan society but can also shed light on the ways in which Afghanistan's cultural heritage is being preserved, revived, and transformed in response to "glocal" forces.

ZOHRA ORCHESTRA

The Zohra Orchestra—named after the Persian goddess of music[8]—is an educational initiative of ANIM[9] in Kabul, a coeducational vocational music school (grades 4–14). It was founded in 2010 by Ahmad Sarmast as part of Monash University's (Australia) "Revival of Afghan Music" project. In addition to Zohra, ANIM is home to the Afghan Youth Orchestra and the ANIM Symphony Orchestra. The school's ambitions to revive Afghan musical traditions while simultaneously transforming the lives of the country's most underprivileged groups through music resonate with characteristics of other contemporary ensembles and youth orchestra programs around the globe, including Uzbekistan's Omnibus Ensemble (Lisack, 2018) and Venezuela's El Sistema (Hallam, 2012; Tunstall and Booth, 2016),[10] respectively. Comprised of twenty-four Afghan girls and young women between the ages of fourteen and twenty-one (the majority of whom live in a local orphanage), Zohra boasts a unique combination of Afghan traditional, Hindustani classical, and Western classical instruments and plays a wide repertoire of music from traditional Afghan folk and popular songs to Western classical works. The initial idea to create an ensemble exclusively for girls came from a female trumpet student at the school and was quickly developed by the school's leadership. From a feminist perspective, the orchestra is breaking new ground in Afghanistan in three ways: it is the first all-female ensemble in the country's history; the first time Afghan women have stood on a conductor's podium; and many of its members are the first females in their families to have the opportunity to learn a musical instrument, either Afghan or otherwise.[11] As such, Zohra has become a symbol, both nationally and internationally, of women's rights, freedom, and gender equality in Afghanistan, which have been fiercely fought for since the official end of the Taliban regime and which are now again under threat amid the ongoing peace negotiations. The development of the Zohra Orchestra in Afghanistan bears striking similarities to the women's orchestra movement in the United States during the late nineteenth and early twentieth centuries (Neuls-Bates, 1986; Santella, 2012), a comparison that becomes more pertinent considering the United States' leading role in Afghanistan's reconstruction. In both cases, the establishment of orchestras exclusively for women was a direct response to the lack of public performance opportunities for women and an attempt to improve the status of women as orchestral musicians whose public presence on stage was seen as morally questionable. However, while women's orchestras in the United States continued to flourish into the twentieth century, creating further orchestral opportunities for women in Afghanistan is limited because ANIM is currently the only institution in the country that offers training in the majority of orchestral instruments.

MUSIC AND CULTURAL DIPLOMACY IN AFGHANISTAN

Music has been a vehicle for cultural diplomacy—in its broadest understanding—in Afghanistan for centuries. Beginning with the court patronage of north Indian musicians under Timur Shah Durrani (1772–1793) (Baily, 1988, 25; Sarmast, 2004, 172–73) and later Shah Amir Sher Ali Khan (1863–1866 and 1868–1879)[12] (Baily, 1999a; Sakata, 1985, 137, 2012, 3), Afghanistan's musical landscape has helped shape the country's overseas relationships, and vice versa. Throughout the twentieth century, Turkish, European, and Soviet musical advisors traveled to Afghanistan to assist a number of state institutions, including establishing the country's military brass bands and providing professional development for Radio Kabul's orchestral musicians (Sarmast, 2004). Arguably, this practice continues today with dozens of foreign music teachers settling temporarily in Afghanistan to work at ANIM and other educational institutions such as Kabul University.

At the intersection of music and education, Louise Pascale's Afghan Children's Songbook Project (Pascale, 2011, 2013) embodies the potential for igniting cross-cultural exchange and developing cultural understanding through music education, albeit in a one-directional way. Although the primary mission of the project is to revitalize children's music in Afghanistan (after the civil war and the Taliban's musical censorship) through the distribution of songbooks to schools across the country, Pascale realized that it also had the potential to challenge misconceptions and negative opinions about Afghanistan back home in the United States. When the Afghan Children's Songbook Project was adopted for a fundraiser—and, in the process raise cultural understanding—at a school in Colchester, Connecticut, students responded with comments such as "Don't we hate the Afghans? Aren't they our enemies?" (Pascale, 2013, 133). However, upon seeing the impact learning the Afghan songs and exploring Afghan culture had on the students, Pascale concluded that "the music provided an opening for an honest discussion to take place and for concerns and misconceptions to be addressed. As a result, perspectives could be shifted, views altered, barriers removed, and cross-cultural connections made" (133).

CULTURAL DIPLOMACY AT ANIM

As an institution, ANIM engages with cultural diplomacy in a number of ways, ranging from grassroots collaborative projects to state-organized overseas tours. The school's musical activities lie at the intersection of cultural *relations* and cultural *diplomacy* and illustrate the increasing blurring of boundaries between these two interrelated practices (see Ang, Isar, and Mar, 2015). The former, mostly practiced by nonstate actors, is driven by ideals and grows naturally and organically without government intervention, while the latter is motivated by national interests and takes place when formal diplomats try to shape and channel natural cultural flows to advance national interests (Arndt, 2006, xviii). On several occasions, ANIM ensembles have been officially engaged by Afghanistan's overseas diplomatic missions to celebrate and strengthen bilateral diplomatic relations. In September 2018, for example, the school's Chamber Orchestra was deployed to Islamabad, Pakistan, to mark the ninety-ninth anniversary of Afghanistan's independence and to provide a musical salve to the two countries' troubled relationship.[13] As ANIM's director explained, "We are using the healing power of music to look after the wounds of the Afghan people as well as the Pakistani people. We are here with the message of peace, brotherhood and freedom" (Gul, 2018). The event, held at the Pakistan-China Friendship Center, was particularly groundbreaking as it was the first official performance of Afghan musicians in Pakistan for more than forty years. The following year, the Zohra Orchestra traveled to Australia to commemorate fifty years of diplomatic relations between the two countries. Leading Afghan and Australian political figures hailed the tour as an opportunity to support "the development of people-to-people diplomacy and cultural links between Australia and Afghanistan" (H. E. Wahidullah Waissi, Afghan ambassador to Australia) and to "strengthen and celebrate relations between [the] two nations" (Hon. Gladys Berejiklian MP, premier of NSW).[14] Finally, although not solely an initiative of either the Afghan government or the US Department of State, ANIM's 2013 tour to the United States was framed by the media as a signal of "the growing potency of cultural diplomacy in Afghanistan amid ongoing negotiations over the United States' post-2014 role in the country" (Boyle, 2013).

Most of the time, however, ANIM's activities lack any top-down state intervention and are simply realizations of the school's vision to promote intercultural dialogue and people-to-people diplomacy through music. Since its inauguration in 2010, dozens of foreign ambassadors in Kabul have been invited to visit the school to strengthen the bond between Afghanistan and the international community. Technology and new media are also utilized by the school to engage in cultural relations, both transnationally and domestically. In 2018, ANIM installed a shared studios portal—an immersive, interconnected space that enables connection across distance and creates the sensation of truly being in the same room.[15] It enables staff and students to connect with other portals in Afghanistan and around the world to engage in shared music-making, workshops and performances, conversations around music and social change, instrumental and conducting lessons, and other multidisciplinary collaborations. Finally, during all of ANIM's international tours, the students collaborate with young musicians from the local area; the experience of rehearsing, performing, and sometimes touring multiple cities together is believed to foster deep interpersonal connection and understanding.

Zohra's musical diplomacy combines a form of nationalistic representation with a commitment to interpersonal dialogue and collaboration, the latter of which are not necessarily articulated in nationalistic terms. The ensemble's musical performances serve both as a site for cross-cultural encounters, as illustrated by the opening vignette, and as "stages of national self-representation" (Gienow-Hecht, 2012, 19). In the current context, the former describes the interactions between Zohra members and both their collaborating musicians and their foreign audiences, while the latter denotes the orchestra's particular portrayal of Afghanistan, which challenges hegemonic Western narratives. For Zohra's members, promoting a positive and beautiful image of Afghanistan to the world—what I will refer to as "cultural self-representation" (Ang, Iasr, and Mar, 2015)—is central to their paradigm of why the orchestra exists and what its role is within Afghanistan's present and future: "The main purpose of Zohra, I would say, is to show the positive side of Afghanistan to the world and that women can do all the good things that boys [can do]" (female student, interview, January 11, 2021). Building on the fundamental principle of symbolic representation, which underpins traditional diplomacy (Jönsson and Hall, 2005; Sharp, 2009), the Zohra Orchestra presents itself to the international community not only as a demonstration of the country's cultural beauty but also as a symbol of Afghanistan's achievements in the areas of women's rights and female empowerment over the past twenty years. The students have thoroughly internalized their role as musical ambassadors and feel a sense of duty to promote Afghanistan's beautiful side on the world stage: "We *need* to show other countries that Afghanistan also has a different side that is art, music, beautiful things like that, that it's not just only fighting and war here" (female student, interview, January 22, 2021). That Zohra is recognized as one of the country's valued exports is illustrated by the ArtLords'[16] mural—painted on a blast wall in downtown Kabul—of some of the ensemble's members that exclaims, in Pashto,[17] "Our heroes! Show Afghanistan's positive face to the world" (figure 3.1).

Among cultural diplomacy's many affordances is the ability to "tell another story about a country [and] offset negative, stereotypical, or overtly simplistic impressions" (Goff, 2013, 421). The practice of using music as a medium for challenging widespread stereotypes and misconceptions about a country is well established. In 1954 for example, the United States initiated an overseas cultural presentation program to counteract "the widespread European idea of

Figure 3.1. ArtLords mural of Zohra Orchestra members, Kabul, March 2018. Author's own photograph.

the United States as consumed by financial rather than intellectual endeavors" (Fosler-Lussier, 2014, 55). Dominant narratives of Afghanistan that circulate in the West characterize the country as a place of perpetual war, (gendered) violence, and conservative Islamic beliefs. By communicating an alternative image of their country through musical performance, the Zohra Orchestra attempts to expand the "accepted grid" (Said, 1978) through which knowledge of Afghanistan is filtered into Western consciousness. The following sections explore this process, situating it within a wider artistic movement that challenges misrepresentative dominant narratives, and offers a framework in which to understand the musical mediation of Zohra's positive image in a performance context.

THE "ACCEPTED GRID" AND ORIENTALIST NARRATIVES

For the "positive image of Afghanistan" embodied in and articulated by Zohra's performances to have an impact on their audiences and collaborators, it necessarily relies on the latter possessing a mental conception of its antithesis, the "negative image of Afghanistan." In 2014, the College of New Jersey held an exhibition entitled *Art Amongst War: Visual Culture in Afghanistan, 1979–2014*. Before inviting her students to view the works, the exhibit's curator, Dr. Deborah Hutton, asked them to write down the first five words associated with Afghanistan that came to their minds and asked the same of members of the public. Both groups' chosen words, such as Taliban, destruction, death, war, oppression of women, gave a snapshot of their negative and limited mental image of the country. It was this negative image of Afghanistan that the exhibition hoped to redefine (Meharry, 2014).

As most people in the West have never been to Afghanistan—or, in some cases, even had personal interaction with an Afghan person—their knowledge of the country is garnered through other people's accounts, interpretations, and opinions. In other words, knowledge is filtered and received secondhand, and as with most narratives that are told about the "East," it is predominantly Orientalist in nature. Edward Said (1978) describes Orientalism, among other things, as "a system of knowledge about the Orient, an accepted grid for filtering through the Orient into Western consciousness" (6) by "making statements about it, authorizing views of it, describing it, by teaching it, settling it, ruling over it" (3). The uninitiated Western reader receives and comes to understand the Orient through grids and codes provided by the Orientalist. In the case of Afghanistan, this "accepted grid" is constructed from the historical canon of novels, scholarly articles and books, news reports, images, and films that present the country to Western audiences. As the following examples demonstrate, Orientalist discourses on Afghanistan essentialize the country as static and undeveloped, with the same themes appearing across centuries.

In his account of a diplomatic mission to Afghanistan in 1808–1809 to conclude an agreement with the ruler, Shah Shuja Durrani, Mountstuart Elphinstone—an administrator with the East India Company—wrote,

> If a man could be transported from England to the Afghaun country [...] he would find it difficult to comprehend how a nation could subsist in such a disorder; and would pity those, who were compelled to pass their days in such a scene, and whose minds were trained by their unhappy situation to fraud and violence, to rapine, deceit, and revenge. (1815, 149)

Over two hundred years later, Western media has been indicted for shaping a "false world opinion" of Afghanistan by portraying Afghans as "savage, conservative and medieval people with no appetite and understanding for modernist, democracy and freedom" (Daud, 2020) and representing the country as "an abode of Taliban and extremism, a penitentiary for women, a narcotics den, a centre for Islamization, and a safe haven for Al-Qaida and Usama Bin Laden" (Shabir, Ali, and Iqbal, 2011, 83). A google search for "Afghanistan" produces a similar narrative of war, with countless images of foreign soldiers in camouflage wielding Kalashnikovs, military helicopters, and Taliban insurgents, and offers nothing of the country's culture, landscape, or citizens. Post-2001 popular fiction narratives have come under intense scrutiny for their Orientalist portrayal of Afghanistan and its people. Stories of the lives of Afghan "others" have become a mass-marketed commodity and are readily consumed by Western readers desperate to enjoy a story of human redemption from suffering. Katrine Ørnehaug Dale (2016) argues that a "new Orientalist" narrative found in American novels such as Khaled Hosseini's *The Kite Runner* (2003), Susan Froetschel's *Fear of Beauty* (2013), and Trent Reedy's *Words in the Dust* (2011) reinforces and emphasizes negative stereotypes and misconceptions of Afghanistan as primitive, less civilized, and lacking morality.

Particularly important to any discussion of the representation of Afghan women is Said's third characteristic of Orientalism, which describes the Western style of "dominating, restructuring, and having authority over the Orient" (1978, 3). Since the US-NATO invasion and subsequent fall of the Taliban in 2001, the lives of Afghan women and girls have been filtered through a particularly narrow Orientalist grid to construct the image of the archetypal Afghan women as silent, oppressed victims. This portrayal has been used by various international actors, including nation-states and transnational feminist networks, to justify, on a humanitarian level, the foreign military intervention in the country and the need to "save Afghan women" from their patriarchal prisons. In Hosseini's novel *A Thousand Splendid Suns* (2007), the author is accused of reproducing the media's dominant representation of Afghan women as passive victims of war and violence (Kazemiyan, 2012), while Sensoy and Marshall (2010) argue that colonialist discourses of Afghan girls as poor, uneducated, and constrained are evoked in Deborah Ellis's novel *The Breadwinner* (2000). As Gillian Whitlock (2005) notes, "The already deeply embedded interpretative frameworks of Orientalism, exoticism, and neo-primitivism through which the East is stereotypically and variously produced for Western consumption have hardened in ideological support of the war on terror" (56).

Representations of ANIM's female music students in the international media cement and perpetuate the Orientalist tropes of Afghanistan discussed above. Western media coverage of ANIM's female musicians and the Zohra Orchestra emphasize the violent family and community opposition experienced by the girls over any musical, aesthetic, or educational aspects of their activities. The students are portrayed as being subject to and overcoming violent family and community threats and condemnation in order to continue their musical education; "Afghan female orchestra faces DEATH THREATS for 'dishonouring families' over Davos concert" (Oliphant, 2017) and "even being disowned by their own families won't prevent some of these women from pursuing their dreams" (Channel 4 News, 2017). In particular, the media highlights the male protagonists of this violence, alluding to particular form of gendered Orientalism that views brown women as the victims of brown men (Spivak, 1998). In one arresting account of the conductor's lived experience, the media quotes her uncle who told her, "Wherever I see you, I'll kill you. You are a shame for us" (Oliphant, 2017) upon learning that she attended a music school.

The media's focus on this gendered violence serves to associate the students, despite their perceived bravery and defiance, with Chandra Mohanty's (1988) concept of "Third World [women]" who lack agency and are "objects-who-defend-themselves" (67). Mohanty argues that Western feminist writers discursively colonize the material and historical heterogeneities of the lives of women in the third world, thus reducing them into a homogenized "other" who are bound by family and tradition, domesticated, and victimized, and which ignores the diversity of experience within this group. Several scholars have identified and looked critically at analogous discourses that reproduce this image within the transnational feminist campaign to liberate Afghan women after the fall of the Taliban (Abu-Lughod, 2002; Bergner, 2011; Berry, 2003; Hunt, 2002; Mitra, 2020; Rich, 2014; Rostami-Povey, 2007). These feminist movements, it is argued, "collude with Orientalist tropes by constructing a singular, monolithic Afghan Woman, whose agency and heterogeneity is appropriated and controlled to advance a neo-imperialist agenda as part of the war against terror" (Chishti and Farhoumand-Sims, 2011, 123). In the current analysis, rhetoric such as "Afghan teenager braves threats, family pressure to lead women's orchestra" (Harooni, 2016) and "her uncles and brothers threatened to beat her for performing on television" (2016) reinforces the image of Afghan women as archetypal victims of gendered violence and firmly situates ANIM's female students within this Orientalist paradigm. While it is important not to critically dismiss these narratives and Zohra members' lived experiences, this aspect of their lives does not define their identities, either as women or as musicians.

Zohra members explicitly identify these orientalist representations—and the negative stereotypes they produce—as one of the reasons they want to present another view of Afghanistan and Afghan women to overseas audiences. In particular, the students wish to negate the Western misconception that all Afghan women are domesticated and prisoners in their homes. During a panel discussion at the World Economic Forum in 2017, one of the orchestra's conductors explained how "we [Zohra] want to tell to the other countries that Afghan women can do everything and they are not just sitting at home, like they are thinking" (World Economic Forum, 2017, 07:55), a sentiment that was echoed by another student in an interview with myself: "So we just want to show that [Afghan women] have power, we can do anything . . . like music, everything. We are not just at home or to work in home and wash and these things" (Orzala, interview, January 7, 2021). Similarly, on tour to the

United States in 2013, another female student (who later became a member of Zohra) wished to demonstrate Afghan women's abilities because "[Americans] think that the women are under the *burqa* and can't do anything" (Glasse, 2013), directly alluding to the image of the veiled Afghan women, which was used as justification by the United States to liberate Afghan women (Berry, 2003; Rich, 2014). Members of the orchestra take much pride in the knowledge that they have the agency to overwrite the dominant image of Afghan women as veiled, oppressed, and domesticated through musical performances which celebrate women's freedoms, strength, and abilities.

When an audience member sees a performance of the Zohra Orchestra, their view of Afghanistan and its people is significantly less filtered than when seen through the refracting Orientalist lens that shrouds a lot of international media and popular culture. Of course, Zohra's staged performances are tailored to meet the expectations and tastes of Western audiences and it is crucial to note that all the Afghan music presented is filtered through the (mostly white) Western faculty who select and arrange the repertory. However, public performances offer an interaction between groups of people in the same physical space rather than across the vast ideological space that is constructed by Orientalist discourses. These musical acts, therefore, stress "the importance of interactive aspects of diplomacy at people-to-people levels" (Lindsay, 1989, 429). Even when viewed on social media or television, the ensemble's performances are still less mediated by intervening opinions or interpretations and are only filtered by the camera through which they are filmed. In this way, Zohra's performances both expand the "accepted grid" through which Afghanistan is filtered to the West (beyond the examples discussed previously), remove much of the Orientalist filter through which the country is usually viewed, and thus let more of Afghanistan and its culture through to Western audiences. The orchestra shifts the frame of reference in which people around the world think about Afghanistan (and the Middle East region), expand the aperture through which the country is viewed, and overcome and manage relations of separateness between peoples that these Orientalist representations engender.

COMMUNICATING A POSITIVE IMAGE OF AFGHANISTAN THROUGH ARTS AND CULTURE

The desire shared by Zohra's members to challenge misconceptions and disprove Orientalist tropes about Afghanistan through their musical activities constitutes part of a growing movement among young Afghans (both in Afghanistan and the diaspora) that utilizes art and cultural production to confront hegemonic narratives of the country circulating in the West (Ghani and Fiske, 2020). Artists within this movement fundamentally see artwork as a way of communicating and expressing ideas, feelings, and identities that are difficult or impossible to be disseminated through more conventional means (120). Although their work is aimed primarily at domestic audiences, Kabul-based street artists, film makers, musicians, poets, and photographers use artistic mediums to represent themselves to the world *on their own terms* and to articulate an authentic Afghan identity that challenges Western stereotypes. This in turn can be understood as the manifestation of a wider obligation felt by Muslims to situate themselves on the "good" side of what critical theorist Mahmood Mamdani (2004) describes as a "Good Muslim/ Bad Muslim" dichotomy that has dominated US foreign policy since the Cold War. According to Mamdani's distinction, so-called Good Muslims are modern, secular, and Westernized while Bad Muslims are doctrinal, antimodern, and virulent. Until proven otherwise, all Muslims are presumed to be "bad" in the Western imagination. For Omaid Sharifi, cofounder of ArtLords, the responsibility to rewrite the narrative on Afghanistan and expand the knowledge grid lies with Afghans who have the opportunity to present themselves in new ways:

> I think we are the most misrepresented people in the whole world. The world really does not know about us. We are always misjudged, looked at very differently. I think there is so much room for writing about us, knowing us, and that also applies to us. The responsibility is on us to connect with the world and [show] the people who we really are.' (quoted in Ghani and Fiske, 2020, 118)

Street artist Shamsia Hassani makes a point of traveling overseas with her artwork "to show people a new Afghanistan, to show people something that until now they didn't know about" (quoted in Ghani and Fiske, 2020, 119). Similarly, the nonprofit organisation Free Women Writers, which has an online platform for disseminating Afghan women's writing in the English language (and thus directed at Western audiences), works to challenge the global media's misrepresentation and one-dimensional portrayal of Afghan women by elevating authentic Afghan voices.[18] Rather than being represented in the West by Western actors, these Afghan "cultural diplomats" *represent themselves* in the West through their own cultural products. However, the efficacy of culture as a vehicle to promote a positive image is not a new paradigm for Afghans and is not limited to influencing the Western imagination. During the Taliban rule, the musical activities of Afghan refugees in the Iranian city of Mashhad were recognized as a "way of presenting a more positive image of the Afghan refugee as someone with something to offer in the way of artistic activity" (Baily, 1999b, 11).

In the same way that Afghanistan-based artists communicate to both domestic and overseas audiences, the Zohra Orchestra wishes to impact both Afghans at home and the international community. The terms and scope of these two messages are slightly different: to domestic audiences, Zohra demonstrates the abilities of women beyond the domestic home and their equality within public space; and to international audiences, they want to communicate an image of strong, empowered women but also contribute to a wider reconfiguring of Afghanistan and its citizens within the West's popular imagination.

"'POSITIVE IMAGE OF AFGHANISTAN" THROUGH MUSICAL PERFORMANCE

> There is war, there is bad things, there is violence against women, but I'm so happy that today I got the opportunity, Zohra ensemble got the opportunity, to give a very positive image of Afghanistan to the world. [. . .] Afghanistan is beautiful, Afghanistan is not what you think. (As quoted by Zarifa Adiba, World Economic Forum 2017, 24:25)

Members of the Zohra Orchestra share a commitment and feel a responsibility to show a beautiful and positive image of Afghanistan to the rest of the globe. This image celebrates both Afghanistan's diverse and rich musical heritage and culture and the strong women of the country who have made significant progress in reclaiming their rights over the past twenty years. The primary mode through which this image is presented is public performance while touring overseas.[19]

Danielle Fosler-Lussier (2014) claims that musical performance enables "both the transmission of ideas through the content of the works (symbolic power) and a new understanding of self and other through the performative nature of the events (social power)" (271). Within a performance context, how does music function as a mediator and transmitter of ideas and values, and which actors are engaged in this exchange? To understand music's potential as a platform for cultural diplomacy and how broader discourses, meanings, and identities are articulated and produced by Zohra's overseas musical practices, we may turn to critical theories of multimodal discourse and more specifically, the assertion that "music can, and should, be analysed as discourse" (van Leeuwen, 2012, 319). In their theory of discourse semiotics, Gunther Kress and Theo van Leeuwen (1999) suggest that "images involve two kinds of participants, *represented participants* (the people, the places and things depicted in images), and *interactive participants* (the people who communicate with each other *through* images, the producers and viewers of images)" (377). Taking this "image participation" model and extending it to music, we are able to view the international musical performances of Zohra as "multimodal communicative acts" (McKerrell and Way, 2017, 8); that is, the music and the orchestra act as signifiers of a positive image of Afghanistan and its citizens (*represented participants*), which is communicated between the *interactive participants* (Afghan musicians and foreign audience members/institutions deploying these participants for cultural diplomacy) through the multimodality and multimediality of musical performance.

Beginning with the sonic experience of Zohra's performances, audience members are met with a unique sound that is achieved by blending traditional Afghan and Hindustani classical instruments—the rubāb, tanbur, dutar, tabla, and sitar—with Western classical orchestral instruments. According to an interlocutor from the World Economic Forum—the hosts of Zohra's first international tour in 2017—the orchestral nature of the ensemble (as opposed to a solely Afghan traditional group) played a crucial role in the cross-cultural dialogue between the Afghan musicians and their foreign audiences: "I think [the orchestra] had a huge impact because it was a way for the Zohra to come halfway to the understanding of the music that this audience is used to. It was an invitation to say, 'come and learn from our music.' [. . .] So I think that was very important in kind of creating a bridge for audience to be engaged in it" (interview, March 29, 2021). In other words, the minority culture of Afghanistan is neatly packaged within the majority culture of the European audience, increasing the music's legibility. To accommodate for Zohra's unique combination of instruments, Afghan folk and popular songs are specially arranged and orchestrated by the school's international faculty. By abstracting these traditional instruments and indigenous harmonic modes and rhythms from their normative discourse of Afghan music and adapting them within a Western classical orchestral framework, they act as cultural connotations.[20] The meaning potential, or "'symbolic power" to use Fosler-Lussier's term, of these connotations lies in their representation of the resilience and revival of Afghan music—and by association Afghan people—after nearly four decades of war. Equally, the physical and sonic union of Afghan and Western musical heritages articulates an East-West dialogue and acts as a symbol of the orchestra's endeavors to promote cooperation between Afghanistan and its global partners both on and off stage. The practice of collaborating with local young musicians—who become temporary members of the ensemble and sit side by side with their Afghan colleagues—provides another symbolism of international cooperation and reciprocity. In this way, the performance foregrounds peaceful musical and personal interaction over the antagonism and violent exchanges, which are most commonly associated with the ongoing conflict in the region. Finally, although Zohra's concerts predominantly showcase Afghan musical genres, the ensemble always extends a musical olive branch to their audiences by playing a specially arranged piece of music from their host country: in Sweden, a medley of ABBA songs; in the United Kingdom, "Greensleeves"; and in India, the Bollywood classic "Meera Joota Hai Japani." However, similar gestures by non-Western orchestras and ensembles have been critiqued in the past amid concerns about authenticity and the preservation of tradition. For example, following a performance by an ensemble from the Central Conservatory of Music in Peking at the 1979 Durham Oriental Music Festival that featured—alongside "modern" Chinese music—a rendition of the English song "Home, sweet home," debates erupted about the Westernization of Chinese "traditional" music (Kun et al., 1981).

Against a background of Western discourses that perpetuate the negative stereotype of Afghanistan as a patriarchal prison, an all-female orchestra conducted by a female conductor articulates and symbolizes the strength, autonomy, and determination of Afghan women. As one former student described, "Zohra was a message from Afghanistan to other countries that we [women] can do music. Our women have power" (female student, interview, January 9, 2021), directly challenging the Orientalist image of Afghan women without agency discussed earlier. Zohra's performances present a new narrative to the audience of Afghan women as independent and in positions that empower them. The legibility of this gendered image to foreign audiences is strong on account of the transnational discourses surrounding the (West's) ongoing efforts to improve women's rights and freedom in the country (see Bergner, 2011; Chishti and Farhoumand-Sims, 2011; Human Rights Watch, n.d.).

Returning to Kress and van Leeuwen's participation model, we have begun to conceptualize how certain images and values are articulated and communicated through musical performance. In turn, this may, or may not, engender more positive relations and foster mutual understanding between participants, in particular "the interactive participants" *attitudes toward* the represented participants' (emphasis added, Kress and van Leeuwen, 1999, 377). As David Clarke (2016) points out, uncritically treating cultural products as self-evident, portable, and contextless vehicles for communicating national values is an illusion. From the perspective of cultural theory, communication is understood as a social process of *coproduction* of meaning (Ang, Isar, and Mar, 2015, 377) and there is no straightforward causality between cultural products and the image that they represent and the desired outcomes of cultural diplomacy/relations.[21] The communication of a positive image of Afghanistan through musical performance is not a one-way process and the audience's role as active meaning-makers as they consume cultural products must be taken into account. Furthermore, even if in the moment these performances effect change in people's beliefs and opinions toward Afghanistan, it is difficult to know how these transformations fare over time.

LOCAL IMPACT

Reflecting on the substantial media response to Zohra's successful performance at the 2017 World Economic Forum (WEF) from within Afghanistan (see TOLOnews 2017a, 2017b), Nico Daswani (head of Arts and Culture at the WEF) believes that the "[WEF] platform was generative of a new national conversation [on women's issues] back home in Afghanistan" (Institut für Auslandsbeziehungen, 2018). Despite the promising image of women's empowerment that Zohra presents on the world's stage, female performers are still greatly stigmatized in Afghanistan and many women have difficulty participating safely in public life. At the time of writing (February 2021), the struggle of Afghan women to become legitimate actors in the public sphere took a particularly bloody turn with stories of female assassinations, targeted shootings, and knife attacks against women in public roles becoming a disturbing leitmotif in both national and international news bulletins.[22] As such, the Zohra Orchestra also speaks back to domestic audiences in an attempt to change perceptions on women's abilities and potential in Afghan society.

Discourses on cultural diplomacy tend to focus on exchanges that occur between different nations and overlook the important fact that the groundwork for international affairs begins with domestic policy (Istad, 2020). What is exported through cultural diplomacy activities is understood to reflect a country's values and the way in which it wishes to define itself and be seen on the global stage. While Gillian Howell (2020) argues that "Zohra's performances claim a more equal share of Afghanistan's cultural space, presenting women as contributors and leaders" (17), this observation is somewhat undermined by the increasing discrimination against public-facing women back at home. The disjunction between what is displayed and what is lived experience is exemplified by the story of Zahra Elham who, despite being the first woman to win Afghanistan's popular *Afghan Star* singing contest in March 2019, received insulting comments on her social media page throughout the contest's season. Thus, if Zohra's message of empowered and strong Afghan women is to be taken seriously by audiences, the country's domestic policy on women's rights needs to speak from the same page. From this perspective, the cultural diplomacy of Zohra constitutes a two-pronged attack that ultimately seeks to achieve equilibrium between what is practiced at home and what is exported overseas.

"TO SHOW THE TAXPAYERS": LEGITIMIZING THE "WAR ON TERROR" WITH MUSIC EDUCATION

The mobilization of musical works and practices in diplomatic activities is intimately linked to the issues of the pursuit and exercise of power (Velasco-Pufleau, 2019). Although cultural diplomacy is founded on the exchange of ideas, information, art, culture, and language between two (or more) nations to foster intercultural dialogue and mutual understanding, on occasion such interactions are co-opted for wider geopolitical agendas. US reporting on ANIM's 2013 tour to the east coast of the United States highlights the way in which the school's director and ANIM's international collaborators explicitly viewed and framed the event as an opportunity "to showcase what a decade of [US] investment has achieved" (Boyle, 2013) and ultimately strengthen US public support for the military intervention in the country:

> One of the major ideas behind the tour of the United States is to show the taxpayers who have been supporting the army in Afghanistan—people who supported the fight against terrorism in Afghanistan, people who have been eager to help the Afghan people stand on their own feet—to show the investment ... is not gone. (Ahmad Sarmast quoted in Druzin, 2013)

> We wanted Americans to understand the difference their tax dollars have made in building a better future for young people, which translates into reduced threats from extremists in the region. (Eileen O'Connor, US State Department, quoted in Boyle, 2013)

The timing of ANIM's tour to the United States could not have been more significant. At the end of following year (2014), the UN-mandated International Security Force Mission in Afghanistan—of which the United States was a major component—was to officially end, at which point the Afghan National Defence and Security Forces would take over full responsibility for the security of the country and the number of international troops stationed there would drastically drop. While the Afghan National Youth Orchestra impressed audiences at Carnegie Hall in New York City and the Kennedy Center in Washington, DC, ongoing negotiations over the Unites States' post-2014 role in Afghanistan were taking place. Thus, there was an urgent need to demonstrate both to the public and to policy makers what kind of nonmilitaristic benefit the United States' presence in the country was having on the people of Afghanistan and what was at risk of being lost should the intervention end prematurely. The unabashed politicization of Afghan music education inherent in the quotes above ultimately hijacks and operationalizes the educational success of young Afghan musicians as a symbol of international objectives, which is then used as evidence in what is increasingly seen as a failed intervention. At this point, an important question should be asked: To what extent is it the responsibility of young Afghan children to help justify the $882 billion[23] spent on the war in Afghanistan since 2001? This query becomes more pertinent when one considers that the US State Department (through the US embassy in Kabul) has been one of ANIM's primary donors since 2010. Echoing the centuries-old phrase "sing for your supper," Afghan students are, to some extent, put in a position where they have to "play for their education" (or at least the money through which it is funded).

The taxpayer narrative surrounding the 2013 tour brings to light the broader issue of outside states utilizing cultural diplomacy engagements to fulfil their own national agenda and achieve specific overseas politico-military outcomes. Staying with the United States as a case study, cultural diplomacy is viewed as the "linchpin of public diplomacy" (US Department of State, 2005) and has become a crucial tool in the country's bid to enhance national security, improve its international standing, and reverse the erosion of trust and credibility induced by the war on terror (US Department of State, 2005). In Afghanistan, US Army music is operationalized to assist with enhancing host nation relations and communicating national values and beliefs as part of what is known as "'defence support to public diplomacy" (Harmon, 2009). As David Hebert (2015) observes, the United States has seen a dramatic increase in the militarization of school music since 9/11 which, to some extent, appears to have been exported to the conflict zones in which the country is currently engaged. In November 2016, a group of ANIM students and staff collaborated with USFOR-A Band, 1st Cavalry (Bagram Air Base), to perform a joint concert hosted by the Public Affairs section of the US embassy in Kabul. Taking place deep within the Green Zone's[24] fortified blast walls and with an audience made up of mostly US embassy staff and Afghan government officials, this was as much a political performance as it was an intercultural exchange between musicians. Viewed as the latter, the event fulfilled the army's mission to foster friendship and cooperation through music in order to build trust, improve understanding and communication, and pave the way for increased cooperation between nations (Department of the Army, 2015). However, for the embassy staff and army musicians, the musical performance was also grounded in and shaped by American national interest. According to the US Army music doctrine, music performances and exchanges are seen as "'a low-threat opportunity to shape opinions and attitudes of local civilian populations" (Department of the Army, 2015, 1-1) and to "create, strengthen, or preserve conditions favorable for the advancement of U.S. interests, policies, and objectives" (1–2). At this point, music becomes a soft "power resource" (Nye, 1990) and is used to shape others' ideas and preferences to be aligned with one's (political) agenda. That three out of the four pieces played jointly by the U.S. Army musicians and the ANIM students were by American composers[25]—the other being an Afghan traditional song—suggests that while this event had a strong element of intercultural exchange, it also afforded an opportunity for the United States to communicate its "positive cultural values and ethics" through its own music. However, as Hebert (2015) cautions, "Music should be used wisely on behalf of all that is positive and admirable in [the United States], in ways that are globally appreciated" (82), raising questions about whether, in a society increasingly tired of active conflict and foreign occupation, army music is the best vehicle through which to promote American cultural values and ethics.

The examples given here do not necessarily suggest unilateral political imposition by US actors and it is important to stress the student benefits (professional development, cross-cultural dialogue, empowerment) afforded by these educational opportunities. However, when cultural diplomacy practices are analyzed and understood critically within their social, political, and ideological contexts, certain unequal power relations and neoimperialist agendas are brought into sharp relief. In the context of post-2001 reconstruction Afghanistan, the interplay between educational programs and broader political agendas underscores the importance of reflecting upon ethical pedagogical practices, especially when there are financial and military implications.

CONCLUSION

The intersection of ethnomusicology, cultural diplomacy, and music education offers a unique window into understanding music's place within contemporary Afghan society and culture, and in particular, the ways in which alternative images of places, nations, and peoples can be produced, articulated, negotiated, and articulated. Working within a framework of Said's Orientalist "accepted grid," this chapter has looked critically at the dominant narratives of Afghanistan circulating in the West and proposed that the Zohra Orchestra's overseas performances constitute a widening of the aperture and the grid through which Western audiences come to know the country. Zohra's musical performances operate like an automatic car wash for the mind; audience members enter the concert venue with a negative, harmful vision of Afghanistan and eventually leave an hour or two later with a fresh understanding of the country as a place of beauty, hope, and empowered women. At least that is the idea. The orchestra not only competes against a flood of other transnational flows of culture, ideologies, and discourses (e.g.,

Islamophobia, dominant war narratives), which threaten to drown out the ensemble's musical message, but also the increasing violence against public-facing Afghan women, which escalated in 2020 amid the ongoing foreign intervention negotiations and peace talks.

ANIM's engagement with cultural diplomacy and relations illustrates the growing conflation of interest-driven governmental agendas and ideals-driven non-state actor practices. At times, the school's musical diplomacy is situated at "the nexus of power politics and culture" (Gienow-Hecht, 2012, 19), as demonstrated by the examples given in relation to the public diplomacy agenda in the United States, which throws light on the uncomfortable reality that cultural diplomacy can be used to reinforce unequal power relations. However, it is important not to throw the proverbial baby out with the bath water and recognize the valuable space afforded by cultural diplomacy in which grassroots actors can engage in cross-cultural dialogue and build mutual understanding across borders. The importance of culture as a medium for communicating a positive image of Afghanistan to global audiences and as a vehicle for igniting intercultural dialogue will no doubt strengthen in the face the recent resurgence of extremist activity in the country.

NOTES

1. In the language of retaliation used by the Islamic State, the Crusader coalition refers to the group of countries who engage in military interventions on the Prophet's lands, such as Syria, Iraq, and Afghanistan (Bruun, 2019).

2. Following the 2015 refugee crisis, right-wing populism, Islamophobia, and xenophobia began to rise in Germany (Gedmin, 2019) and in 2017, the Far Right Alternative für Deutschland entered the federal parliament for the first time, becoming the country's biggest opposition party. Similar rises in Far Right nationalism have been witnessed in other countries in the European bloc.

3. See, for example, Paolo Petrocelli's initiative "Music Diplomacy" and the EMMA for Peace program. See https://www.musicdiplomacy.net, accessed 02/10/21.

4. On August 15, 2021, Kabul fell to the Taliban after a lightning offensive that lasted less than ten days. Shortly after taking over the country, the Taliban announced that music was banned once again and ANIM was forced to close indefinitely; the school's students went into hiding and a large-scale operation to evacuate the school began. This chapter is therefore situated in historical time, covering events from 2010 through early 2021. The research for this chapter was carried out between October 2019 and January 2021 and the chapter was written between February–March 2021.

5. Here I am borrowing Sakata's (2012) term used to describe the "Golden Age" of Afghan music during the same timeframe.

6. Leftist coup d'etat in April 1978 led by the People's Democratic Party of Afghanistan and named after the Afghan month in which it occurred.

7. An "unfretted flunked lute [. . .] with two strings" (Karimi, 2017, 730).

8. In her translation of the *Poems from the Divan of Hafiz* (1897), Gertrude Lowthian Bell notes that "Zohra is the planet venus, the musician of the heavens, and the protector of all musicians and singers upon the earth. Zohra played a part in very ancient mythology" (149).

9. There have been two notable films made exclusively about ANIM: *Dr Sarmast's Music School* (2012) directed by Polly Watkins and *Return of the Nightingales* (2013) directed by ethnomusicologist John Baily. Both offer a visual portrayal of the school's early music activities; the former focuses on giving a broad account of the story behind the school's establishment while the latter emphasizes the teaching, rehearsal, and performance of the music. There is also a written account of ANIM in the final chapter of Baily (2015). See also Forrest (2013) for an interview with Ahmad Sarmast.

10. In contrast, Baker (2014) provides a critical analysis of El Sistema and largely dismisses prevailing notions that the program is a force for positive social change.

11. See Doubleday (1988, 2011) for earlier accounts of women's music-making in Afghanistan.

12. The court patronage of North Indian musicians continued under the rule of King Zahir Shah (1933–1973) (Sakata, 2012).

13. Tensions between Afghanistan and Pakistan go back to the creation of the latter in 1947, which ignited conflicts along the border between the two countries (the Durand Line) (Ahmed and Bhatnagar, 2007, 159) and have increasingly worsened with the development of terrorist activity in the region (see Grare, 2006).

14. "Australia-Afghanistan Relations: Reflections on the 50 Year Anniversary of Afghanistan Australia Diplomatic Relations," available at https://afghanaustralia.com.au, accessed 02/03/21.

15. See https://www.sharedstudios.com/shared-spaces, accessed 02/22/21.

16. ArtLords is an art collective that paints murals on blast walls in Kabul and across Afghanistan to provide a positive visual experience and to raise awareness of important sociopolitical issues concerning the Afghan public. See https://www.artlords.co, accessed 03/03/20.

17. Pashto is one of Afghanistan's official languages, alongside Dari.

18. See https://www.freewomenwriters.org/about-free-women-writers/, accessed 02/22/21.

19. Since its establishment in 2014, Zohra has performed in eight different countries across three continents.

20. See van Leeuwen and Kress (1997, 120) for a discussion on the semiotic function of connotation.

21. A good example of musical diplomacy missing the mark is when the Tehran Symphony toured Europe in early 2010 with Majid Entezami's "Peace and Friendship Symphony." Despite the Iranian consulate handing out free tickets for the concerts, audience turnout was extremely low and in Geneva, protestors took to the stage in honor of recently-killed dissidents in Iran (Gienow-Hecht, 2012, 17).

22. Although many of the attacks are not claimed by any group, it is believed that both the Taliban and the Islamic State affiliate in Afghanistan, known as the Islamic State Khorasan, are behind the wave of attacks.

23. The total military expenditure (US Department of Defense) from October 2001 to September 2019 was $778 billion in addition to the $44 billion spent on reconstruction projects (US Department of State) (Reality Check team, 2020).

24. Walled-off enclave, also known as the "foreigner bubble," in the center of Kabul, which is home to a high concentration of foreign embassies and newsrooms.

25. Dizzy Gillespie's *Night in Tunisia* (1942), Steve Reich's *Clapping Music* (1972), and Victor Eijkhout's *Bubble Machine* (n.d.).

REFERENCES

Abu-Lughod, Lila. 2002. "Do Muslim Women Really Need Saving? Anthropological Reflections on Cultural Relativism and Its Others." *American Anthropologist* 104, no. 3: 783–90.

Ahmed, Zahid Shahab, and Stuti Bhatnagar. 2007. "Pakistan-Afghanistan Relations and the Indian Factor." *Pakistan Horizon* 60, no. 2: 159–74.

Ang, Ien, Yudhishthir Raj Isar, and Phillip Mar. 2015. "Cultural diplomacy: Beyond the National Interest?" *International Journal of Cultural Diplomacy* 21, no. 4: 365–81.

Arndt, Richard. 2006. *The First Resort of Kings: American Cultural Diplomacy in the Twentieth Century*. Washington, DC: Potomac Books.

Baily, John. 1979. "Professional and Amateur Musicians in Afghanistan." *The World of Music* 21, no. 2: 46–64.

———. 1988. *Music of Afghanistan: Professional Musicians in the City of Herat*. Cambridge: Cambridge University Press.

———. 1999a. "Music and the State." In *Garland Encylopedia of Music Volume 5 – South Asia: The Indian Subcontinent*, edited by Alison Arnold, 830–37. New York: Routledge.

———. 1999b. "Music and refugee lives: Afghans in eastern Iran and California." *Forced Migration Review* 6: 10–13.

———. 2005. "So Near, So Far: Kabul's Music in Exile." *Ethnomusicology Forum* 14, no. 2: 213–33.

———. 2015. *War, Exile and the Music of Afghanistan*. Farnham, UK: Ashgate.

Baker, Geoffrey. 2014. *El Sistema: Orchestrating Venezuela's Youth*. Oxford: Oxford University Press.

Bell, Gertrude. 1897. *Poems from the Divan of Hafiz*. London: Heinemann.

Bergh, Arild, and John Sloboda. 2010. "Music and Art in Conflict Transformation: A Review." *Music and Arts in Action* 2, no. 2: 2–17.

Bergner, Gwen. 2011. "Veiled Motives: Women's Liberation and the War in Afghanistan." In *Globalizing Afghanistan: Terrorism, War, and the Rhetoric of Nation Building*, edited by Zubeda Jalalzai and David Jefferess, 95–116. Durham, NC: Duke University Press.

Berry, Kim. 2003. "The Symbolic Use of Afghan Women in the War on Terror." *Humboldt Journal of Social Relations* 27, no. 2: 137–60.
Boyle, Katherine. 2013. "Orchestrating Change." *Washington Post*, February 3, 2013. LexisNexis.
Bruun, Laura. 2019. "ISIS, Air-Strikes and the Language of Retaliation." *Action on Armed Violence*. Last modified January 7, 2019. https://aoav.org.uk/2019/isis-air-strikes-and-the-language-of-retaliation/.
Campbell, Patricia Shehan. 1997. "Music, the Universal Language: Fact or Fallacy?" *International Journal of Music Education* 29: 32–39.
Channel 4 News. 2017. "This All-Female Orchestra in Afghanistan Isn't Going to Let Taliban Death Threats Silence Them." March 31, 2017. Video, 02:01. https://www.facebook.com/Channel4News/videos/10154703208196939/.
Chishti, Maliha, and Cheshmak Farhoumand-Sims. 2011. "Transnational Feminism and the Women's Rights Agenda in Afghanistan." In *Globalizing Afghanistan: Terrorism, War, and the Rhetoric of Nation Building*, edited by Zubeda Jalalzai and David Jefferess, 117–43. Durham, NC: Duke University Press.
Clarke, David. 2016. "Theorising the Role of Cultural Products in Cultural Diplomacy from a Cultural Studies Perspective." *International Journal of Cultural Policy* 22, no. 2: 147–63.
Cohen, Cynthia. 2008. "Music: A Universal Language." In *Music and Conflict Transformation*, edited by Olivier Urbain, 26–39. London: I.B. Tauris.
Cummings, Milton. 2003. *Cultural Diplomacy and the United States Government: A Survey*. Washington, DC: Center for Arts and Culture.
Dale, Katrine Ørnehaug. 2016. "What Happens in Afghanistan, Does Not Stay in Afghanistan: Understanding American Literary Representations of Afghanistan Through a New Orientalist Approach." Master's Thesis. University of Oslo.
Daud, Bilquees. 2020. "Perception of Afghanistan in the Western Media." *Afghanistan Center at Kabul University*. Last modified April 18, 2020. https://acku.edu.af/2020/04/18/perception-of-afghanistan-in-the-western-media/.
Department of the Army. 2015. *Army Music*. ATP 1-19. Washington, DC: Department of the Army, 2015. https://fas.org/irp/doddir/army/atp1-19.pdf.
Doubleday, Veronica. 1988. *Three Women of Herat*. London: Tauris Parke.
———. 2011. "Gendered Voices and Creative Expression in the Singing of 'Chaharbeiti' Poetry in Afghanistan." *Ethnomusicology Forum* 20, no. 1: 3–31.
Druzin, H. 2013. "In Afghanistan, Teaching Music to Overcome War's Percussion. *Stars & Stripes*. Retrieved from https://www.stripes.com/news/in-afghanistan-teaching-music-to-overcome-war-s-percussion-1.205380
Elliott, David J. 1990. "Music as Culture: Toward a Multicultural Concept of Arts Education." *The Journal of Aesthetic Education* 24, no. 1: 147–66.
Ellis, Deborah. 2000. *The Breadwinner*. Toronto: Douglas & McIntyre.
Elphinstone, Mountstuart. 1815. *An Account of the Kingdom of Caubul and its Dependencies in Persia, Tartary, and India*. London: Strahan.
Forrest, David. 2013. "The Afghanistan National Institute of Music." *Australian Journal of Music Education* 1: 76–82.

Fosler-Lussier, Danielle. 2014. "Afterword: Music's Powers." In *Music and Diplomacy from the Early Modern Era to the Present*, edited by Rebekah Ahrendt, Mark Ferraguto, and Damien Mahiet, 267–75. New York: Palgrave Macmillan.

Gedmin, Jeffrey. 2019. "Right-Wing Populism in Germany: Muslims and Minorities after the 2015 Refugee Crisis." Brookings Institute. Last modified July 24, 2019. https://www.brookings.edu/research/right-wing-populism-in-germany-muslims-and-minorities-after-the-2015-refugee-crisis/.

Ghani, Bilquis, and Lucy Fiske. 2020. "'Art Is My Language': Afghan Cultural Production Challenging Islamophobic Stereotypes." *Journal of Sociology* 56, 1: 115–29.

Gienow-Hecht, Jessica C. E. 2012. "The World is Ready to Listen: Symphony Orchestras and the Global Performance of America." *Diplomatic History* 36, 1: 17–28.

Glasse, Jennifer. 2013. "Afghan Orchestra Set to Hit the Right Notes." *Al Jazeera*, January 29, 2013. https://www.aljazeera.com/indepth/features/2013/01/20131298533390922.html.

Goff, Patricia M. 2013. "Cultural Diplomacy." In *The Oxford Handbook of Modern Diplomacy*, edited by Andrew F. Cooper et al., 419–33. Oxford: Oxford University Press.

Grare, Frédéric. 2006. "Pakistan-Afghanistan Relations in the Post-9/11 Era." Carnegie Papers 72. https://carnegieendowment.org/files/cp72_grare_final.pdf.

Gul, Ayaz. 2018. "Afghan Orchestra Flourishes Despite Violence, Social Pressure." Voice of America, September 22, 2018. https://www.voanews.com/arts-culture/afghan-orchestra-flourishes-despite-violence-social-pressure.

Hallam, Richard J. 2012. "Sistema: Where Academic, Educational, Musical, Personal and Social Development All Meet." In *Listen Out: International Perspectives on Music Education*, edited by Chris Harrison and Sarah Hennessy, 104–15. Solihull, West Midlands: National Association of Music Educators.

Harmon, Matthew. 2009. "Defense Support to Public Diplomacy: Options for the Operational Commander." Unpublished paper. Faculty of the U.S. Naval War College. https://apps.dtic.mil/dtic/tr/fulltext/u2/a502997.pdf.

Harooni, Mirwais. 2016. "Afghan Teenager Braves Threats, Family Pressure to Lead Women's Orchestra." Reuters, April 17, 2016. http://www.reuters.com/article/us-afghanistan-orchestra-idUSKCN0XF00X.

Hebert, David G. 2015. "Another Perspective: Militarism and Music Education." *Music Educators Journal* 10, no. 13: 77–84.

Higgins, Kathleen M. 2012. *The Music between Us: Is Music a Universal Language?* Chicago: University of Chicago Press.

Hosseini, Khalid. 2007. *A Thousand Splendid Suns*. New York: Penguin.

Howell, Gillian. 2018. "Community Music Interventions in Post-Conflict Contexts." In *The Oxford Handbook of Community Music*, edited by Brydie-Leigh Bartleet and Lee Higgins, 43–70. Oxford: Oxford University Press.

———. 2020. "Harmonious Relations: A Framework for Studying Varieties of Peace in Music-Based Peacebuilding." *Journal of Peacebuilding and Development* 6, no. 1: 85–101.

Human Rights Watch. n.d. "Afghanistan: Events of 2018." Accessed February 7, 2019. https://www.hrw.org/world-report/2019/country-chapters/afghanistan#49dda6.

Hunt, Krista. 2002. "The Strategic Co-optation of Women's Rights." *International Feminist Journal of Politics* 4, no. 1: 116–21.

Institut für Auslandsbeziehungen. 2018. August 15. "Nico Daswani: Touring with the Afghan Women's Orchestra." August 15, 2018. Video, 14:04. https://www.youtube.com/watch?v=6YG7q6dNk84.

Istad, Felicia. 2020. "Gender in Public Diplomacy." *CPD Blog* (USC Center on Public Diplomacy). Last modified February 20, 2020. https://uscpublicdiplomacy.org/blog/gender-public-diplomacy.

Jönsson, Christer, and Martin Hall. 2005. *Essence of Diplomacy*. Basingstoke: Palgrave Macmillan.

Karimi, Ali. 2017. "Medium of the Oppressed: Folk Music, Forced Migration, and Tactical Media." *Communication, Culture and Critique* 10: 729–45.

Kazemiyan, Azam. 2012. "A Thousand Splendid Suns: Rhetorical Vision of Afghan Women." Master's Thesis. Ottowa: University of Ottowa.

Kress, Gunther, and Theo van Leeuwen. 1999. "Representation and Interaction: Designing the Position of Viewer." In *The Discourse Reader*, edited by Adam Jaworski and Nikolas Coupland, 377–404. London: Routledge.

———. 1997. *The Multi-Modal Text*. London: Edward Arnold.

Kun, Fang, Keith Pratt, Robert C. Provine, and Alan Thrasher. 1981. "A Discussion in Chinese National Musical Traditions." *Asian Music* 12, no. 2: 1–16.

Letts, Richard. 1997. "Music: Universal Language between All Nations?" *International Journal of Music Education* 29: 22–31.

Lindsay, Beverly. 1989. "Integrating International Education and Public Diplomacy: Creative Partnerships or Ingenious Propaganda?" *Comparative Education Review* 33, no. 4: 423–36.

Lisack, Lucille. 2018. "A National School for Global Music: The Case of Uzbekistan in the Globalized Network of Western-Style 'Contemporary Music.'" In *Music Glocalization: Heritage and Innovation in a Digital Age*, edited by David Hebert and Mikolaj Rykowski, 190–217. Newcastle Upon Tyne: Cambridge Scholars Publishing.

Lui, Kevin, Nash Jenkins, and Tara John. 2017. "What to Know About the Berlin Christmas Market Attack." *TIME*, December 20, 2016. https://time.com/4607437/berlin-christmas-market-crash-what-to-know/.

Mamdani, Mahmood. 2004. *Good Muslim, Bad Muslim: America, the Cold War, and the Roots of Terror*. New York: Pantheon Books.

McKerrell, Simon, and Lyndon C. S. Way. 2017. "Understanding Music as Multimodal Discourse." In *Music as Multimodal Discourse: Semiotics, Power and Protest*, edited by Lyndon C. S. Way and Simon McKerrell, 1–20. London: Bloomsbury Academic.

Meharry, Joanie Eva. 2014. "Cultural Diplomacy with US Sends Crucial Message to Afghanistan's Young People." Asia Society. Last modified April 14, 2014. https://asiasociety.org/blog/asia/cultural-diplomacy-us-sends-crucial-message-afghanistans-young-people.

Mohanty, Chandra Talpade. 1988. "Under Western Eyes: Feminist Scholarship and Colonial Discourses." *Feminist Review* 30: 61–88.

Neuls-Bates, Carol. 1986. "Women's Orchestras in the United States, 1925–45." In *Women Making Music: The Western Art Tradition, 1150–1950*, edited by Jane Bowers and Judith Tick, 349–69. Urbana: University of Illinois Press.

Nye, Joseph S. 1990. *Born to Lead: The Changing Nature of American Power*. New York: Basic Books.

O'Grady, Siobhán. 2019. "For First Time, a Woman Won Afghanistan's Version of 'American Idol'." *The Washington Post*, March 23, 2019. https://www.washingtonpost.com/world/2019/03/23/first-time-woman-won-afghanistans-version-american-idol/.

Oliphant, Vickiie. 2017. "Afghan Female Orchestra Faces Death Threats for 'Dishonouring Families' over Davos Concert." *The Daily Express*, January 18, 2017. https://www.express.co.uk/news/world/755921/Afghanistan-first-female-orchestra-Zohra-DEATH-THREATS-Davos-concert.

Pascale, Louise. 2011. "Sharing Songs: A Powerful Tool for Teaching Tolerance and Honouring Culture." *General Education Today* 25, no. 1: 4–7.

———. 2013. "The Role of Music in Education: Forming Cultural Identity and Making Cross-Cultural Connections." *Harvard Educational Review* 83, no. 1: 127–34.

Reality Check team. 2020. "Afghanistan War: What Has the Conflict Cost the US?" BBC News. Last modified September 3, 2021. https://www.bbc.com/news/world-47391821.

Rice, Timothy. 2017. *Modeling Ethnomusicology*. Oxford: Oxford University Press.

Rich, Janine. 2014. "'Saving' Muslim Women: Feminism, U.S Policy and the War on Terror." *International Affairs Review*, Fall 2014. https://www.usfca.edu/sites/default/files/arts_and_sciences/international_studies/saving_muslim_women-_feminism_u.s_policy_and_the_war_on_terror_-_university_of_san_francisco_usf.pdf.

Rostamy-Povey, Elaheh. 2007. *Afghan Women*. London: Zed Books.

Said, Edward. 1978. *Orientalism*. New York: Pantheon Books.

Sakata, Hiromi Lorraine. 1976. "The Concept of Musician in Three Persian-Speaking Areas of Afghanistan." *Asian Music* 8, no. 1: 1–28.

———. 1983. *Music in the Mind: The Concepts of Music and Musician in Afghanistan*. Kent, Ohio: Kent State University Press.

———. 1985. "Musicians Who Do Not Perform; Performers Who Are Not Musicians: Indigenous Conceptions of Being an Afghan Musician." *Asian Music* 17, no. 1: 132–42.

———. 2012. "Music in Afghanistan." *Afghanistan: Multidisciplinary Perspectives* 17, no. 2: 1–5.

Santella, Anna-Lise P. 2012. "Modeling Music: Early Organizational Structures of American Women's Orchestras." In *American Orchestras in the Nineteenth Century*, edited by John Spitzer, 53–77. Chicago: University of Chicago Press.

Sarmast, Ahmad Naser. 2004. "A Survey of the History of Music in Afghanistan, from Ancient Times to 2000 A.D., with Special Reference to Art Music from c. 1000 A.D." PhD diss. Melbourne, Australia: Monash University.

Sensoy, Özlem, and Elizabeth Marshall. 2010. "Missionary Girl Power: Saving the 'Third World' One Girl at a Time." *Gender and Education* 22, no. 3: 295–311.

Shabir, Ghulam, Shahzad Ali, and Zafar Iqbal. 2011. "US Mass Media and Image of Afghanistan: Portrayal of Afghanistan by Newsweek and Time." *South Asian Studies* 26, no. 1: 83–101.

Sharp, Paul. 2009. *Diplomatic Theory of International Relations*. New York: Cambridge University Press.

Skyllstad, Kjell. 2008. "Managing Conflicts through Music: Educational Perspectives." In *Music and Conflict Transformation*, edited by Olivier Urbain, 172–86. London: I.B. Tauris.

Slobin, Mark. 1976. *Music in the Culture of Northern Afghanistan*. Tucson: University of Arizona Press.

Small, Christopher. 1998. *Musicking: The Meanings of Performing and Listening*. Middletown, CT: Wesleyan University Press.

Spivak, Gayatri Chakravorty. 1988. "Can the Subaltern Speak?" In *Marxism and the Interpretation of Culture*, edited by Cary Nelson and Lawrence Grossberg, 271–313. Chicago: University of Illinois Press.

Stobart, Henry. 2008. "Introduction." In *The New (Ethno)musicologies*, edited by Henry Stobart, 1–22. Lanham, MD: Scarecrow Press.

TOLOnews. 2017a. "Afghan Women's Orchestra Wins Freemuse Award." TOLOnews, January 23, 2017. https://tolonews.com/arts-culture/afghan-women's-orchestra-wins-freemuse-award.

———. 2017b. "Girls Welcomed Home After Swiss Tour." TOLOnews, February 2, 2017. Video, 02:14. https://www.youtube.com/watch?v=7zkNw897P-A&t=40s.

Tunstall, Tricia, and Eric Booth. 2016. *Playing for Their Lives: The Global El Sistema Movement for Social Change Through Music*. New York: W. W. Norton and Company.

U.S. Department of State. 2005. "Cultural Diplomacy: The Linchpin of Public Diplomacy." U.S. Department of State. Last modified September 15, 2005. https://2009-2017.state.gov/pdcommission/reports/54256.htm.

van Leeuwen, Theo. 2012. "The Critical Analysis of Musical Discourse." *Critical Discourse Studies* 9, no. 4: 319–28.

Velasco-Pufleau, Luis. 2019. "Music, Diplomacy and Emotions." *Music, Sound and Conflict*. Last modified December 19, 2020. https://msc.hypotheses.org/1800.

Watkins, Polly. 2012. *Dr Sarmast's Music School*. Film. Melbourne: Circe Films, 2012.

Whitlock, Gillian. 2005. "The Skin of the Burqa: Recent Life Narratives from Afghanistan." *Biography* 28, no. 1: 54–76.

World Economic Forum. 2017. "Davos 2017 – Press Conference with the Afghan Women's Orchestra 'Zohra.'" January 19, 2017. Video, 26:39. https://www.youtube.com/watch?v=OIg-Tgl8oZc.

Chapter Four

Music Festivals and Cultural Diplomacy in Uzbekistan

Elnora Mamadjanova and David G. Hebert

Among touring folk musicians and managers of international music festivals, the Central Asian nation of Uzbekistan is notable, as home to some of the world's most spectacular music events. In this chapter, we discuss cultural diplomacy in relation to two international music festivals in Uzbekistan, one of which, Sharq Taronalari (in Samarkand), has been operating for a few decades while the other, the International Maqom Festival (in Shahrisabz) is rather new. Sponsored by the government of Uzbekistan and endorsed by UNESCO (United Nations Educational, Scientific and Cultural Organization), Sharq Taronalari is certainly among the world's largest festivals for traditional music, attracting musicians and musicologists from each inhabited continent. This festival, which entails formal judging and competing for generous cash prizes, is held in Samarkand's magnificent Registan Square.[1] The festival includes a musicology symposium as well as stakes claim as the world's largest music competition in terms of the breadth of traditional genres included in the adjudication (Hebert, 2019). At each festival, a team of judges—including professional musicians, music industry managers, and ethnomusicologists—from multiple countries, accepts the formidable task of determining from an array of live performances, representing extremely diverse traditions, which musicians most deserve awards, and in which ranking. Begun in 1997 with participants from thirty-three countries, in 2019 Sharq Taronalari hosted participants from seventy-five countries. In 2017, another unique international event, the International Maqom Festival, was founded by the president of Uzbekistan Shavkat Mirziyoyev, according to his decree on "The Art of *Maqom*," to celebrate *maqom*-based music traditions. Held in September in one of the oldest cities in Uzbekistan, Shakhrisabz, the first maqom festival brought together more than 1,500 participants from seventy-three countries. In this chapter, we describe the impact of these major cultural events, how approaches to festival management have evolved across time, and how they define and promote Uzbekistan's national image at home and abroad in ways that "stimulate the expansion of cultural exchange with the international community" (Mamadjanova, 2016, 75).

BACKGROUND: MUSIC CULTURE OF UZBEKISTAN SINCE INDEPENDENCE

The year 1991 marked a new era in the history of Uzbekistan's people. The fall of the Soviet Union resulted in new sovereignty and recognition of the nation's distinctive cultural identity by the world community. In many spheres of social life, new priorities arose, including in the fields of arts and culture. The change in the status of the state entailed a series of reforms that touched, first, on such sectors as education, culture, and the arts. Importantly, this era provided new contexts for the recognition that the traditional culture of the Uzbek people should be paramount. Furthermore, since independence the national government has declared Uzbekistan's citizenry to be the inheritors of a great civilization, with a hopeful promise to share the nation's cultural values, achievements, and developments with the world. This objective has been facilitated in part by Uzbekistan's hosting of major international music festivals, symposia, and conferences, as well as the active participation of representatives from Uzbekistan at international events.

As part of efforts to define the main directions and priorities of the musical culture of Uzbekistan at the turn of the millennium, we note first and, perhaps most importantly, the revival of musical traditions that developed in ancient times. This cultural rejuvenation has resulted in increased interest from foreign countries, particularly from international music scholars. Consequently, the musical heritage of the people has risen to a new level. Indeed, the government of Uzbekistan actively supports sustaining traditional cultural heritage, even as part of its efforts to strengthen ties with foreign countries. This is accomplished by promoting international tours of Uzbek performers, supporting diasporic Uzbek cultural events in many countries across the world, as well as international competitions and festivals held within Uzbekistan.

Uzbekistan is increasingly recognized for its contributions to global musical heritage. The *shash maqam* (meaning "six maqams" in Arabic) is a notable body of repertoire considered the pinnacle of Central Asian classical music, mostly traceable to the city of Bukhara, near Samarkand in Uzbekistan. Maqam-based music is found across much of Asia due to the Silk Road, even from North Africa to Xinjiang, but Uzbekistan and Tajikistan are widely recognized as central sources for much of the historical repertoire. As Blum observed, "The *šašmaqom* became above all a repertory of pieces, each of which follows the norms and bears the name of a genre (such as *saraxbor, talqin, nasr*, and *ufar* in the main part of each *maqom*,[2] before the secondary groupings)" (2015, 169–70). Many recent musicians have helped to draw greater national and international attention to Uzbekistan's musical heritage, and despite what may be assumed in Western nations, women have a long history of participating in this music and continue to be among the most prominent performers (Merchant, 2015). Here we will briefly offer biographical profiles of a few notable Uzbek musicians to orient readers in the hope that they may explore them further.

Munojat Yulchieva (b. 1960), People's Artist of Uzbekistan and professor of traditional music at the Yunus Rajabi Institute, is a prominent singer of classical Uzbek traditional music, including shash maqam. She is "a frequent performer on Uzbek television as the most high-profile proponent of the tradition through several international tours and recordings" (Coppola, Hebert, and Campbell, 2020, 147). Yulchieva has collaborated for many years with Shavkat Mirzaev, who first "discovered" her and became her mentor while a student at Tashkent Conservatory. She focuses on older traditions, having received "the same Ustro-Shogrid training from her teacher, Professor Shavkat Mirzaev, as other Sufi singers in pre-Soviet times" (Sultanova, 2014, 85). Yulchieva has served as a contest judge for the Sharq Taronalari festival and is a previous contest winner of it as well. In addition, she frequently performs on Uzbek television, has toured internationally, and maintains multiple recordings. Yulchieva is revered as the most renowned proponent of the shash maqam tradition.

Nadira Pirmatova (b.1976), Honored Artist of Uzbekistan, is a well-known performer of maqoms from the traditional music heritage of Uzbekistan and other parts of Central Asia. She has a unique, mesmerizing voice, and her talent was first widely recognized at the Sharq Taronalari festival in 2005, where she won first place. Pirmatova's deep knowledge of Uzbek and Tajik poetry makes her one of the most outstanding performers of the poetic form *shiru shakars*, as well as the Fergana-Tashkent and Bukhara-Samarkand maqoms. She also accompanies herself on both tanbur and dutar, which is rare among performers in sedentary cultures.[3] Nodira Pirmatova was a pupil of such great Uzbek performers as Saodat Kobulova and Halima Nosirova. Today, she's an associate professor at the Yunus Rajabi Institute of Traditional Music in Uzbekistan.

Mahmud Tojibayev (1957–2020) was born in the Kuva District of the Fergana region. In 1984, he graduated from the Tashkent Conservatory. In addition to his formal education, he also learned directly from many traditional mentors such as Mamatov, Hajikulov, Mamadaliev, and Alimatov.[4]

Until he passed away in 2020, Tadjibayev was soloist of the Yunus Rajabi Maqom ensemble, a role he took on in 1984. In 1987, he won the Republican Competition of Performers named after Yunus Rajabi. In 2000, he became an associate professor at the State Conservatory of Uzbekistan. Widely regarded as the greatest musician and performer of maqom art, including shash maqom and Fergana-Tashkent maqoms, he became a People's Artist of Uzbekistan in 2000. As a poetic hafiz, Tadjibayev was known for his calm performance style, lyricism, sound, and musical balance. The late artist toured across Asia, the United States, Europe, and North Africa. His untimely death in 2020 was a great loss for Uzbek traditional music.

A major challenge to cultural policy since independence has been how best to ensure the preservation of Uzbek traditional musical heritage. Despite this concern, much has been achieved in this area across the thirty years of independence. However, there is still much to do to promote and sustain many forms of traditional music, an issue faced by most forms of ancient musical heritage from Central Asia (Levin, Daukeyeva, and Kochumkulova, 2016), and among the Uyghurs of Xinjiang (China), whose musical traditions especially share much in common with Uzbekistan (Harris, 2008). Opportunities for expansion in research and international exchange have dramatically changed with digitization and online communication, but the challenge of sustaining cherished genres of traditional music, both folklore and scholarly professional creativity, remains serious (Grant, 2014). Partly through support from UNESCO, ethnographic research on traditional music and culture is systematically conducted throughout Uzbekistan. Music competitions and festivals increasingly reveal the level of influence of modern innovations on these genres, styles, performance in general, as well as the degree of integration into the global sphere. Over the past three years, President Shavkat Mirziyoyev's administration adopted policies aimed at developing further the concept of national culture. Specifically, the first international music festivals were held on the art of maqom in Shakhrisabz, the art of Bakhshi in Termez, and the folklore festival in Margilan. International musicology conferences also continued to be held in tandem with the Sharq Taronalari International Music Festival.

UNESCO Recognition

Uzbekistan is rich in ancient architectural masterpieces and centuries-old traditions, and includes some of the world's most ancient cities, in some cases more than 2,700 years old. Unique ancient monuments are valuable not only for the Uzbek people, but also for humanity. Located at the crossroads of the Silk Road, which served as a conduit for the achievements of humanity in the scientific, technical, cultural, spiritual spheres, the region played an important role in the development of world civilization. In 1993, the country joined UNESCO, which advises cultural tourism development and highlights Uzbekistan's heritage. To unite all countries and organizations interested in the revival of the ancient Silk Road, in 1994, the United Nations World Tourism Organization, together with UNESCO, held its first international meeting in Uzbekistan, during which the Samarkand Declaration on Tourism along the Silk Road was adopted. UNESCO acknowledged that there are 8,138 objects of material and nonmaterial culture on the territory of the country, of which 4,732 are architectural monuments, 682 objects of monumental art, 580 places of pilgrimage, and others. UNESCO designates some cultural properties of the country as globally significant intangible cultural heritage, including the holidays of Navruz and Katta Ashula, traditional chants in the Fergana Valley and Askia, and the art of wit (satire). In 2019, the Khorezm dance "Lazgi" was included in the Representative List of the Intangible Cultural Heritage of Humanity. Thus, at present, this list includes seven traditions from Uzbekistan: Shashmakom art music genre (2008), Cultural Space of Boysun historical village (2008), Katta Ashula traditional song genre (2009), Askia comedic genre (2014), Culture and Traditions of Plov rice-based cuisine (2016), Navruz spring equinox festivities (2016), and the Khorezm dance "Lazgi" (2019).

Samarkand: Location of Sharq Taronalari

Sharq Taronalari ("Melodies of the East") is one of the most significant music events not only in Uzbekistan, but all Central Asia, and according to established tradition, is held in Registan, the central square of Samarkand. It has taken place in Samarkand since 1997 at the initiative of the founding president of Uzbekistan, Islam Karimov (1938–2016), who led the country for twenty-five years from 1991 until his death. The festival has been organized on a regular basis, once every two years. Some might wonder how such a grandiose event can be presented within what is arguably a sacred site in an ancient city. Indeed, since ancient times Samarkand was named by travelers along the Silk Road as the "Pearl of the East" for the beauty and magnificence of its architecture. Rome was known as the "great city" of the ancient West, while Samarkand was the "great city" of the ancient East.[5] As the capital of the vast medieval empire of Tamerlane (1370–1405), Samarkand gathered the best minds and talents of that era: scientists, artists, architects, poets, each of whom sang about this legendary eastern city in his own way.

The ancient city of Samarkand is rightfully included in the UNESCO register of tangible world heritage. Here, the paths of not only the caravans of the Silk Road crossed, but also meetings of great ancestors, and researchers of various types of arts, including literature and poetry, music, and painting took place. Great scholars laid the foundations of many sciences, formed philosophies and theories, including musicology (Turkestan being the birthplace of both Al Farabi and Avicenna during the Islamic Golden Age). Official state-sponsored cultural activities aim to sustain and transmit the invaluable cultural achievements of Uzbekistan's past to younger generations.

Registan Square is a magnificent architectural example of medieval times in the East. Today, centuries later, Samarkand has become a permanent venue for the music festival Sharq Taronalari. Once every two years, at the end of summer, hundreds of talented singers, dancers, and instrumentalists gather to celebrate the musical traditions of the world. Cultural bearers from across the globe come to Samarkand to present the cultural heritage of their countries at Sharq Taronalari. A huge open-air stage with fantastic illumination and acoustics is built on the historic Registan Square, surrounded by monuments of Eastern medieval architecture. The organizers do their utmost to make it a success: designing decorations, curating exhibitions, organizing conferences timed to coincide with the festival, and hosting many competitors, foreign guests, and representatives of the press.

Construction of Registan's Sher-Dor (or "Shil Dar") Madrassah was completed in 1636. Its name (meaning "adorned with tigers") comes from

Figure 4.1. Registan Square, Samarkand, Uzbekistan, during the 2019 Sharq Taronalari festival. Photo by David Hebert.

prominent images on its portal: two golden tigers carrying a sun—with a human face—on their backs and following deer. These images were engraved deep into the stone of the mosque at the time of its completion. Due to restrictions on Islamic art, these may be the only examples worldwide of a human face and animal figures represented on a mosque (figure 4.1).

Besides Registan, other notable sites in Samarkand include the Shah-i-Zinda necropolis, where according to legend, the spirit of the saint Kusam Ibn Abbas (cousin of Mohammed) still lives underground, as well as the ancient settlement of Afrasiyab, the mausoleum of the prophet Daniel (important in Judaism and Christianity, as well as Islam). Additionally, Samarkand is home to the madrasah of Ulugbek, the prominent medieval scientist and patron of science and art (as well as the grandson of Tamerlane), the Bibi-Khanum Mosque, and many other architectural monuments of the ancient city. During the festival, exhibitions of diverse Uzbek ethnic costumes, folk instruments, an art bazaar, and conferences are held. The festival itself lasts almost a week and ends with a grand gala concert, where the winners of the competition perform.

Organization of the Sharq Taronalari Festival

The stated goals and objectives of Sharq Taronalari are to widely popularize, preserve, and develop the best achievements of national musical art, educate the younger generation about national traditions, and further expand international creative ties. Supported by UNESCO, the festival is organized by the Ministry of Culture of the Republic of Uzbekistan, the National Television and Radio Company of Uzbekistan, the Union of Composers of Uzbekistan, Samarkand Regional Municipality Concert Association "UZBEKNAVO," and the governor of the Samarkand region. Local universities train their students to offer language support and insider knowledge of local heritage sites for hosting the festival.

Sharq Taronalari, in Samarkand, was not only the first international music festival to develop in Uzbekistan, but the first in Central Asia. Beginning in 2018, other international festivals in Uzbekistan (which will be discussed later), such as the International Maqom Festival, Bakhshi Art Festival (in Termez), and the Folk Arts and Crafts Festival (in Kokand) were also developed as part of what President Shavkat Mirziyoyev calls the Third Renaissance of Uzbek culture.[6] The number of countries participating in the Sharq Taronalari festival has increased nearly every year, with representatives from thirty-one countries at the first festival in 1997, to a total of seventy-three in 2019.

Competition winners of the festival have come from various parts of the world. At the first festival in 1997, the Grand Prix was awarded to the mugham performer Simara Imanova from Azerbaijan, while first place was taken by Munojat Yulchieva (Uzbekistan) and Shainu Hurama (India). At the second festival in 1999, the Grand Prix was won by Nasiba Satarova (Uzbekistan). In 2001, first place was taken by Alim Gasimov (Azerbaijan) and artists Sohibjon Niyazov and Abdunabi Ibrokhimov (Uzbekistan). In 2003, the Grand Prix was awarded to the Uranhai ensemble from the Republic of Tuva (Russia), while Dilnura Mirzakulova (Uzbekistan) and Fozil Jamshidiy (Iran) took first place. In 2005, Aygun Biylar (Azerbaijan) and Nodira Pirmatova (Uzbekistan) won first place awards. In 2007, the Grand Prix went to a group from the Kuwait Institute of Music, while first place went to a group from the Music Institute of South Korea. In 2009, the Honored Artist of Turkmenistan Lala Begnazarova was awarded the Grand Prix. An article in the *Diplomat* described the purpose of Sharq Taronalari as follows:

> The aims and objectives of the festival are to popularize widely the best achievements of national music art, to preserve and develop great traditions of peoples, to encourage talents in the musical- and vocal sphere, as well as to spread in further international creative ties, to strengthen cultural friendship and ideas of mutual sympath[y]. (Atjam, 2017)

Founded on the objectives of promoting the musical traditions of the peoples of the world, as well as the mutual enrichment of national cultures and the friendship of peoples, the festival also contributes to the development of tourism in Uzbekistan, the popularization of its historical heritage, and the formation of an attractive, tourist-friendly image for the country. The festival is of interest to many tourists who routinely announce their intention to attend the event more than six months in advance.

International Musicology Conference within Sharq Taronalari

The uniqueness of the Sharq Taronalari International Music Festival in Samarkand is that it brings together many participants, guests, and media representatives. Leaders of prominent international non-government organizations and entities such as UNESCO, the Shanghai Cooperation Organization, the International Folklore Organization, and the Asian Development Bank support attend the festival. The Sharq Taronalari festival is organized by UNESCO and recognized as a major international forum in the Resolution of the President of the Republic of Uzbekistan No. PP-4214, which states, "On measures to prepare for the Sharq Taronalari International Music Festival" dated February 26, 2019. In his welcoming speech at the opening ceremony of the International Music Festival "Sharq Taronalari" XII on August 26, 2019, President Shavkat Mirziyoyev stressed the importance of holding a scientific and practical conference within the framework of the festival.

During the 2019 Sharq Taronalari festival, the scientific conference "Prospects for the development of traditional music of the peoples of the East" was held in Samarkand. International scholars of music and cultural studies took part in the scientific-practical conference to discuss urgent problems related to the study of musical development, as well as issues of preserving the unique cultures of the peoples of Central Asia. The theme of the conference focused on the main problems of studying the state of traditional music of Central Asia in the third millennium. The international representation of the conference was extensive, with twenty-seven scientists from fourteen states taking part: Uzbekistan, India, the United States, Great Britain, China, Korea, Russia, Kazakhstan, Azerbaijan, Iran, Afghanistan, France, Moldova, and Norway.

The conference included a plenary session and two main sections: *"Tarikh va meros"* (History and heritage) and *"Nazariya va amaliyot"* (Theory and practice). The minister of culture of the Republic of Uzbekistan, Bakhtiyor Sayfullaev, opened the plenary session and emphasized the importance of holding the current festival and conference. Among the many notable reports were: "Transmission: a creative direction in the development of traditional music" by Rustambek Abdullaev (Uzbekistan); "Revealing the meanings through music: notes on the musical project *Bahariya* as an example of the dynamic recontextualization of mugham" by Jahongir Salimkhanov (Azerbaijan); "Shash*maqom* as a cultural and performing phenomenon in the education system of the West" by Razia Sultanova (Uzbek living in the United Kingdom); and "On the issue of local song genres of Dagestan folklore" by Patit Shakhnazarova (Russia). The work of the conference made it possible to exchange information on various Central Asian music genres, discussion of an array of issues in musicology, and the presentation of new publications. At the end of the conference, an exhibition of the latest ethnomusicology literature was held, and at its conclusion, a formal declaration on the main goals and objectives for the study of Central Asian music was adopted.[7]

The First International Maqom Festival

The historical formation of the mode and genre system of maqom across the vast region of Eurasia and Maghreb extended through a long process of change. It is difficult to establish with convincing accuracy exactly where and which subgenre of maqam-based traditions appeared before others. What can be said with confidence is that the international research base, which first established scientific principles for the study of maqom moe than one thousand years ago (in the seminal work of Al Kindi and Al Farabi), now includes many countries with studies in the form of scientific articles, monographs, and essays, as shown by the festival.

Due to the initiatives of President Shavkat Mirziyoyev, especially his decree on "The Art of *maqom*" in 2017, there is a new opportunity to take a fresh look at the musical heritage of the Uzbek people, expand the field of study, and introduce younger generations to this phenomenon. Since 2018, the new maqom center was established with several regional branches, which developed this field further along with departments at the State Conservatory of Uzbekistan. The International Maqom Festival, held in September 2018 in one of the oldest cities in Uzbekistan, Shakhrisabz, is one outcome of the multifaceted work in this field.

While there had previously been some minor scholarly symposia discussing maqom as an international phenomenon, the first International Maqom Festival was the first presented on a large scale. It brought together representatives from seventy-three countries; the total number of participants was about 1,500. The festival required organizers to physically modify the central part of Shakhrisabz city. They built a new amphitheater with several thousand seats, constructed a stage for broadcasting with high-tech screens, opened dozens of small hotels, and built a central square area. According to *Diplomat*, "One reason for launching the First International *Maqom* Festival is intended to *sensitize* and capture the attention of the youth and the general public. Making them aware of the potential of *Maqom*. Its artistic, vim and vigor as well as its esthetic musical heritage. Additionally, *Maqom* has the capability of fostering relations of friendship between nations" (Atjam, 2018).

This festival demonstrated to the world that the phenomenon of maqom art does not belong exclusively to any particular nationality. Representatives of many countries and diverse religions worldwide perform genres of maqom, study its features, and find points of commonality. For example, the competitive performances of musicians from Belgium (Lámekán Ensemble), Israel (Jaffa Maqam Quartet), Great Britain (Soufian Saihi), and even Japan captivated the audience of the festival. Indeed, maqom has even developed new popularity in the United Kingdom, with such student ensembles as Oxford Maqom (directed by ethnomusicologist Martin Stokes) and even Uyghur maqom ensembles. Representatives of Uzbekistan also performed well, including Bektosh Khudoyberganov and the Sakil ensemble.

Within the framework of the festival, a two-day scientific conference "The Art of *Maqom* and its Role in World Civilization" was held, and participants included representatives from Azerbaijan, Kazakhstan, Kyrgyzstan, Tajikistan, France, the United Stated, Korea, Tunisia, Turkey, Italy, India, and more than ten representative Uzbek scholars. In Uzbekistan, the most foundational works on maqom include "*Maqom*ot," "Bukhara macom," and "Khorezm macom" by Otanazar Matyakubov, "Fergano-Tashkent *maqom*s" by Okilkhon Ibragimov, and "Uzbek *maqom*s" by Ravshan Yunusov. Following these classic works, a new generation of maqom researchers study the subject with an approach that is also informed by globalization and scientific methods including the practical issue of sustaining maqom genres as invaluable cultural heritage.

Two days of the conference consisted of a busy schedule of roundtable discussions, presentations, and the exchange of new literature. At the end of the conference, a declaration was signed in which future tasks were identified and the main problems of the current state of maqom genres were highlighted. In the declaration, the participants emphasized the important role of forums of this kind and identified objectives for future meetings.

Immediately following the conference, preparations for the next one began, but this was inevitably disrupted by the global impact of the COVID-19 pandemic. For the next forum, the organizers aim to attract not only musicologists, but also vocal and instrumental maqom performers, and *ustozes* (master teachers). The festival also led to the creation of an international journal, *Eurasian Music Science Journal,* with representatives of different countries on its editorial board. An international mugam festival is also held every two years in Azerbaijan, and similar forums are held annually in different Arab countries of the Maghreb region. They share the goal of demonstrating maqom-based genres and unique performance features, while at the same time finding commonalities between different cultures.

These discussions demonstrate that changes brought about by modern lifestyles and communication systems profoundly impact maqom-related heritage, causing some genres to alter in performance style or simply disappear. For better or worse, many performers today feel a sense of creative freedom in interpreting maqom aesthetics. For example, while there may be positive aspects to this fact, many wish to preserve this treasury of musical heritage and do not feel it appropriate to incorporate maqom genres into popular music or offer performances under distracting conditions at weddings. Traditionally, the uniqueness of this art relies on one's absolute immersion, perception, and ownership during the performance; this is not meant as background music. According to some holders of this tradition, the centuries-*old* maqom art system risks collapse. There has also long been a need for revision of the system of music education (that had emphasized art music during Soviet times), which is now occurring in the field of traditional music. This problem not only concerns Uzbekistan but also other cultures that seek to sustain their traditional music (Coppola, Hebert, and Campbell, 2020). It is also an issue for composers who seek to develop music that meaningfully represents local identities while still communicating in forms recognizable to an international audience (Lisack, 2018).

Many questions arise: Who defines what counts as "traditional" music? In discerning and describing authenticity in traditional music, where does authority rest? How do changes in required learning processes, particularly time, impact the expected quality of performance style? For example, if it was expected that students spend fifteen to thirty years learning a particular style, how can one rationally say that with few years of music study, they become authentic tradition bearers? In Uzbekistan, to tackle these questions to successfully preserve these traditions, a new school of maqom art began and now teachers hope to achieve its mission, with expert pedagogy and the highest of academic and artistic standards.

Music scholars in almost all countries that sustain maqom traditions appear to be concerned about similar issues. Azerbaijan has a school of *mugham* art, and a similar structure might be applicable to all Central Asian countries, where there is an orally transmitted professional art. This may allow carriers of the genre to not only preserve and transmit their unique skills but also to promote them among the young generation of musicians and discover new talents. Otherwise, acquiring the skills of performing maqom only at the conservatory might lead to irreparable consequences of the loss of an entire generation of carriers of this art. In addition, if we call this art "traditional," then its teaching arguably should be within the framework of the traditional pedagogy of said tradition, of course taking into account the authentic conditions of era, place, and time. These statements are not intended to detract from the significance and role of the current generation of Uzbek maqom artists, whose names, such as Mahmud Tojiboyev, Munojat Yulchieva, honored artists Malika Rizayeva, Iles Arapov, and many others, are known outside of Uzbekistan.

Among the main shared concerns is that of ensuring appropriate contexts for performances. Vocal-instrumental cycles, such as maqom, *raga*, *mugham*, and *kui* are not originally intended for performance for a large audience of listeners, where sound is mediated through the use of electronic equipment for manipulating and amplifying sound. Few new concert halls are built with the needs of traditional music in mind, and it is common for acoustical and technical problems to hinder audience appreciation of this music. It is important to reflect upon general problems that arise in our rapidly developing time when so much is implemented through use of digital technologies. Indeed, the human factor, with centuries-old experience and traditions, must prevail to a greater extent to point young students in a sustainable direction. The establishment of scholarly forums, such as the first international festival of maqom art in Shahrisabz, promises to significantly expand the boundaries of both heritage appreciation and scientific knowledge.

Music Festival Management and Cultural Diplomacy

Music has been a notable part of the legacy of rich cultural exchange across Central Asia for millennia, and a vast array of traditions emerged from contact between traders and travelers across the Silk Road. The legendary trading route certainly passed through Samarkand, and has been described as "from Rome to Nara" (Winter, 2020, 904), with tributaries south to India (Ranade, 2006). Due to this long history of regular trade and migration, there is a strong rationale for analyzing "Eurasia as a single interconnected historico-cultural block" (Stride, 2011, 54). In earlier centuries, the Silk Road facilitated shared languages across a vast geographic space, which also had implications for *music* as the notion of nation-state emerged: "From Baghdad to Samarqand and Dushambe, this loss of multilingualism is one of several respects in which musical life suffered as state institutions promulgated doctrines (borrowed from Europe) of 'one nation, one language, one race'" (Blum, 2015, 168). Nation-states evolved, music genres matured, and the role of music in cultural diplomacy developed as well to meet the changing needs of society. Today, across the world, claims to history and identity are conveyed through digital media as a mechanism of official public relations, in which music continues to be of great symbolic value even while "we can access cultural experiences on our devices" (Goff, 2020, 33).

Presidential speeches at Uzbekistan's international music festivals, as we have shown, highlight the importance of these events for cultural diplomacy. During his speech at the opening ceremony of the ninth Sharq Taronalari International Music Festival in Samarkand (2013), the first president of Uzbekistan, Islam Karimov, said the following:

> It is difficult to overestimate the importance of such festivals as Sharq Taronalari, especially in our turbulent and extremely difficult time, which clearly demonstrate the boundless power and impact of musical art, which serves to comprehend the origins of values common to all mankind, in fulfilling the most important mission of bringing different peoples closer together, strengthening mutual understanding between them, peace and tranquility in the region and in the world as a whole.

This enthusiastic official endorsement of the festival, at the highest level of the state, seems to have only increased with the next administration. During the opening ceremony of the twelfth Sharq Taronalari (2019), President Shavkat Mirziyoyev stressed that the festival not only "gave wings for a creative launch" to many famous artists, but had also become a platform for dialogue between different cultures and civilizations, countries, and peoples. Moreover, he claimed that each artist on the stage of Registan Square represents the high ideals of humanism that unite all people regardless of their nationality, language, and religion. In our estimation, it is relatively unusual to encounter state presidents who explicitly make such statements regarding the diplomatic importance of an international music festival, but such events may attain greater prominence in nations that have not yet had an opportunity to host a World Expo or Olympic Games. Mirziyoyev especially noted that no technical means can replace the beauty of the human voice: "We accept you as true devotees of art and highly value you as ambassadors of peace and friendship." President Mirziyoyev also declared that "music as an art phenomenon has tremendous opportunities for the harmonious education of the younger generation. Young people, introduced to art, begin to relate to life differently, respect national and universal values. And I am sure that such young people who highly value the principles of humanism and tolerance are able to protect the world from a spiritual crisis."

It seems accurate to suggest that these international music festivals are the most notable vehicles of cultural diplomacy in Uzbekistan today, enjoying much public and private sector support. Preparation for each music festival and symposium requires the collaboration of a large team, and for several years the directorate of the Sharq Taronalari festival coordinated the annual event in Uzbekistan, but recently this has been expanded to multiple festivals. The directorate serves as a kind of headquarters, which manages various tasks: organizational and financial planning; meeting and "seeing off" of guests; logistics, food, and accommodations; providing invitations and visa arrangements; and coordinating music ensembles and academic conferences. As a rule, festivals are not held in the capital, Tashkent, but rather, mainly the regional centers and ancient cities of Uzbekistan: Samarkand (Sharq Taronalari festival), Termez (Festival of Bakhshi Art), Shakhrisabz (Festival of Maqam Art), and Kokand (Festival of Applied Genres and Crafts).

The main challenge to the management of the large international festivals lies with the logistics, including transporting participants to regional cities from the international airport at the capital. Modern communications, transport interchanges, and increasing developments to the infrastructure of Uzbekistan's cities now make it possible to do this quickly, which one could only dream of fifteen to twenty years ago. Still, there can be challenges to planning and communication.

It is enlightening to observe the reactions of international guests at the festivals. Some visitors only know a little about Uzbekistan before their trip. They may assume that Uzbekistan is a poor country that still suffers from the many problems of the post-Soviet period. But it is unusual for any country to receive several thousand guests, pay for both their flights and accommodations, and importantly, all this at the expense of the state reserve. Uzbekistan is clearly showing to festival guests that it is an important country interested in interacting more with the outside world. Guests discover not only the richest historical layers of a culture with many profound traditions, but also a modern state with a promising future. Most importantly, the government and the head of state directly support and participate in these international music events. Visitors to Uzbekistan, no matter as a guest or a participant in music festivals, as tourists, or for business, leave with impressions of this country where antiquity combines with modernity, where traditions coexist with innovative technologies, and much more. It is in this way that the music festivals serve as important vehicles for cultural diplomacy, since many who experience these events depart with positive attitudes toward Uzbekistan as well as an enthusiasm to explore what kinds of international collaboration might develop between other countries in the future.

NOTES

1. See www.sharqtaronalari.uz.
2. Note that maqom is transliterated in various ways by different authors: maqam, makom, maqom, etc.
3. In earlier eras, self-accompaniment was more common among solo male performers of epic songs who migrated across Central Asia, but due to modernization the lifestyles and identities connected to such traditions have changed.
4. Consistent with Central Asian tradition (and, coincidentally with APA style in the West), cited Uzbek scholars are indicated with only the first initial and surname in the text.
5. Context for these claims, commonly seen in tourism brochures, is offered later in the section on "Music Festival Management and Cultural Diplomacy."
6. The first high point being the Islamic Golden Age (eighth century to thirteenth century), followed by the early 1990s when Uzbekistan first gained independence from the USSR, and now the 2020s, under the post-Karimov presidency of Shavkat Mirziyoyev.
7. See Mamadjanova E. Грани научно-практической конференции «Перспективы развития традиционной музыки народов Востока» в спектре XII Международного музыкального фестиваля «Шарк тароналари».- Журнал «Мусика», 2019, № 3.- Facets of the scientific-practical conference "Prospects for the development of traditional music of the peoples of the Orient" in the spectrum of the 12th Sharq Taronalari International Music Festival. Journal "Musiqa," 2019, no. 3.

REFERENCES

Atjam, Roy Lie. 2018. "*Maqom*: The Soul of Uzbeki People." Diplomat (August 23). Retrieved from: https://diplomatmagazine.eu/2018/08/23/maqom-the-soul-of-uzbeki-people/.

Atjam, Roy Lie. 2017. "XI Sharq Taronalari Festival August 2017 Samarqand-Uzbekistan." *Diplomat* (October 5). Retrieved from: https://diplomatmagazine.eu/2017/10/05/xi-sharq-taronalari-festival-august-2017-samarqand-uzbekistan/.

Blum, Stephen. 2015. "The Persian Radif in Relation to the Tajik-Uzbek Šašmaqom." In *This Thing Called Music: Essays in Honor of Bruno Nettl*, edited by Victoria Lindsay Levine and Philip V. Bohlman, 167–79. Lanham, MD: Rowman & Littlefield.

Coppola, William J., David G. Hebert, and Patricia Shehan Campbell. 2020. *World Music Pedagogy, VII: Teaching World Music in Higher Education*. New York: Routledge.

Goff, Patricia M. 2020. Cultural Diplomacy. In *Routledge Handbook of Public Diplomacy*, edited by Nancy Snow and Nicholas J. Cull, 30–37. New York: Routledge.

Grant, Catherine. 2014. *Music Endangerment: How Language Maintenance Can Help*. New York: Oxford University Press.

Harris, Rachel. 2008. *The Making of a Musical Canon in Chinese Central Asia: The Uyghur Twelve Muqam*. London: Routledge.

Hebert, David G. 2019. "Competition in Music." *SAGE International Encyclopedia of Music and Culture*, volume 2, edited by Janet Sturman, 610–13. Thousand Oaks, CA: Sage Publications.

Levin, Theodore. 1997. *The Hundred Thousand Fools of God: Musical Travels in Central Asia (and Queens, New York)*. Indianapolis: Indiana University Press.

Levin, Theodore, Saida Daukeyeva, and Elmira Kochumkulova, eds. 2016. *The Music of Central Asia*. Indianapolis: Indiana University Press.

Lisack, Lucille. 2018. "A National School for Global Music: The Case of Uzbekistan in the Globalized Network of Western-Style "Contemporary Music." In *Music Glocalization: Heritage and Innovation in a Digital Age*, edited by David G. Hebert and Mikolaj Rykowski, 190–217. Newcastle: Cambridge Scholars.

Mamadjanova, Elnora. 2016. *Traditional Music of the Uzbeks*. Tashkent: Extremum Press.

Merchant, Tanya. 2015. *Women Musicians of Uzbekistan: From Courtyard to Conservatory*. Urbana: University of Illinois Press.

Ranade, Ashok. 2006. "Performing Exchanges: A Conceptual Inquiry with Reference to Indo-Iranian Experience." *Journal of the Indian Musicological Society* 36/37: 173–207.

Stride, Sebastian. 2011. "Samarkand: The Peripheral Core of World History." In *World and Global History: Research and Teaching*, edited by Seija Jalagin, Susanna Tavera, and Andrew Dilley, 47–57. Pisa: Pisa University Press.

Sultanova, Razia. 2014. *From Shamanism to Sufism: Women, Islam, and Culture in Central Asia*. London: Bloomsbury.

Winter, Tim. 2020. "Silk Road Diplomacy: Geopolitics and Histories of Connectivity." *International Journal of Cultural Policy*, 26(7), 898–912.

Chapter Five

Sufi Voices

Music as a Unifying Pathway toward the Divine

Chaden Yafi

IN SEARCH FOR CONTINUITY AND HARMONY

One way to reach a better understanding of the various cultures throughout the world is to reflect on how they differ from each other, what distinguishes each one and makes it unique. Another way, which constitutes my method and approach, is to analyze the common denominators found among diverse cultures and trace reciprocal influences and manifestations common across them. One would thereby view culture as a layered product of humanity rather than various juxtaposed ideas and *modes of being*: no oppositions, only continuity and harmony.

My viewpoint stems from the fact that I grew up in Syria and was subject to various cultural influences, yet I never felt any contradictions or conflict between them. My father's great-grandfather was the famous Sufi poet, Omar al Yafi, and my mother's great-grandfather was Sabri Mawlawi, a Sufi whirling *darwish*, follower of the Rumi order (figure 5.1).

My father, Dr. Abdul Karim Yafi, was an influential figure in the cultural and educational circles of the Arab world as a writer, philosopher, and teacher. He worked as a professor at Damascus University for sixty years and served as a diplomatic expert to the United Nations. My father was the first to create the Arabic version of the field of study known as "demography" and the first to teach it as a subject at Damascus University. For many years he was an active member of the International Union for the Scientific Study of Population. He was also the first professor to teach modern physics in relation to philosophy. My father wrote more than twenty-two books, some of which are still used as references in universities throughout the Arab countries.

My father studied at the Sorbonne in Paris, with brilliant twentieth-century French philosophers including Gaston Bachelard, Charles Lalo, and Louis

Figure 5.1. Family-owned painting of Sabri Mawlawi created by an Italian painter who visited Damascus in 1810.

Massignon, while obtaining several degrees in various fields of science and literature. His doctorate was in philosophy with a dissertation on the Sufi thinker Ibn al Fared. I once asked my father about his life in France and how he emotionally dealt with the fact that during that time (the 1940s), France was an occupying force in Syria, and the French air force was bombarding Damascus. He replied that Bachelard and Massignon (scholars) were not the ones bombing Syria. Years later, while I was a student at Boston University, that solitary statement floated back into my mind. I was just starting my doctorate, when the World Trade Center in New York City came under attack on September 11, 2001. As a result, US forces invaded Iraq. The media portrayal of the war was similar to a terrible reality show, and the images of destroyed places where I had spent my childhood years were heartbreaking. Still, I had learned from my father to separate culture from politics, and to keep focused on my studies. I realized that both culture and politics are powers: the first aims to connect, the second to control.

The house where I grew up in Damascus was a magnet for diplomats, ambassadors, and cultural attachés. They would come to visit my father and ask him questions about the Arab-Islamic culture of which he was an expert, and they also aspired to learn from his mastery of the Arabic language. My father's personal library held more than thirteen thousand books in different languages. These books shaped my own intellectual and spiritual life, for we are not merely the result of our biography, but also our *bibliography*.

My father was also frequently invited to lecture at conferences in Europe and the Middle East, mostly about the dialogue among cultures. He kept reminding the world of the glorious Arabic-Islamic civilization, a difficult task that he transmitted directly to me.

Since early childhood, I studied classical music with Russian teachers and was trained as a classical pianist. Almost all of my schooling was at the Ecole des Soeurs Franciscaines, which was established by the French during their occupation of Syria. I felt no contradictions in reciting Quranic verses one day and poems by Victor Hugo the next.

When I was young, I was chosen to perform Ludwig van Beethoven's *Piano Concerto No. 4 in G Major Op. 58* with the Syrian National Orchestra. The concert was in the summer, at the historical Al Azem Palace, which was very close to the Umayyad Mosque in the heart of downtown Damascus. Although scheduled to begin at 8:00 p.m., we were asked to delay for ten minutes, until after the call for prayer. I still remember hearing the striking sound of the Imams with their repetitive chant: *Allahu Akbar, la ilaha illa Allah* (God is the greatest! There is no God but God). Immediately after the prayer, I played the incredibly beautiful G Major chords that beckoned the rest of the orchestra to join in the glorious piano concerto! For me, Beethoven's music became a continuation of the call for prayer.

The goal of this chapter is to shed light on the philosophical knowledge introduced by the Muslim and Sufi thinkers with respect to Western art music. To some readers, this might at first seem to be a random juxtaposition, but I intend to demonstrate how recognition of this relationship is not only sensible, but holds the potential to play an important role in cultural diplomacy. Few musicians in Western countries today fully recognize that after the fall of the Roman Empire, and the music-related writings of Boethius (477–524), for centuries the most comprehensive and advanced theoretical writings on music were in Arabic, and later translated into Latin. Subsequently, when the first universities finally arose in Europe (long after higher education emerged in India, Egypt, and Morocco), *Grand Book on Music*, by Alpharabius (a Latin translation of Al- Farabi's work) was a prominent part of the music curriculum at Oxford and Paris. This was the outcome of a period of musicological development in the context of what later became known as either the Islamic Golden Age, or alternatively, the Dark Ages. It is useful to briefly explore what became of music during this period that might seem either "dark" or "golden," and to consider why this matters for the world of music today. This objective fits the notion of "decolonizing" (or "decanonizing") music history since in traditional narratives, European composers are treated much like saints in a thoroughly "Western" Eurocentric approach that minimizes long-term European musical interactions with Asia and Africa (see Kurkela and Vakeva, 2009).

To that end, this chapter is organized around three themes: 1) an overview of music in Islamic and Arabic culture, and Sufi literature, and how Middle Eastern contributions profoundly influenced what we know today as "Western music"; 2) how the work of medieval Arab and Muslim scholars relates to the present; and 3) how music education may be enriched from analyses that take these points into consideration. It is my hope that a better understanding of the intellectual influence of Arab-Islamic culture on Western art music may result in fostering mutually beneficial forms of cultural diplomacy between the West and the Middle East.

WHY MEDIEVAL MUSLIM PHILOSOPHERS?

Much of the work and theories of early Arab and Muslim philosophers, scientists, and theologians were available in Europe by the late medieval and Renaissance period through the translations of their books into Latin. European thinkers assimilated and embraced these books to the point where they often adopted them as their own, seldom giving reference to their origin, but among those who read in the original Arabic were philosophers Roger Bacon, Michael Scot, Robert Grosseteste, and Gilbert of Aurillac (also known as Pope Sylvester II).

In his book *Introduction to the History of Science*, the American historian George Sarton (1884–1956) brought attention to the significance and value of the content of Arab Islamic science. Sarton mastered Arabic, which enabled him to go to original sources. He also relied on Lucien Leclerc's *Histoire de la médicine arabe* (1876) that documented how the translation from Greek to Arabic, and later from Arabic to Latin, led to the thriving of the sciences in the West. Sarton also referred to the work of the French Orientalist Ernest

Renan (1823–1892) entitled *De philosophia peripatetica apud Syros* (see Mavroudi, 2015).

As for Sufism and the Sufi thinkers, their works were brought to Europe a few centuries later by St. John of the Cross, August Tholuck, Goethe, and even Ralph Waldo Emerson (Michon and Gaetani, 2006, xxi). Contrary to what is often assumed today, medieval Arab and Muslim philosophers had faith in reason, insisted on dialogue and openness to encounters, and honored the open debate of ideas as a way to gain and build knowledge (see Goody, 2012). Their works were never limited to a specific nation or group of people, and indeed mutual respect is evident between the writings of such notable contemporaries as Jewish philosopher Maimonides, Muslim philosopher Avicenna, and Christian philosopher Roger Bacon. When medieval Arab philosophers and scientists translated works by the ancient Greeks, they almost always gave credit to the original authors. They commented, added, and corrected many texts. In fields such as music, as for the works of Aristotle, most of the Greek texts were lost in Europe and it ultimately became necessary to rely on Arabic texts that were translated to Latin. A detailed account of this historical process in the field of music can be found in George Farmer's book *Historical Facts for the Arabian Musical Influence* (1930). For many, this book remains as the most valuable reference book in English, since George Farmer mastered music theory and was able to read the original sources in Arabic.

The courts of khalifa(s), during the Islamic era between the seventh and thirteenth centuries, were a cultural oasis where scientists, linguists, musicians, poets, and intellectuals of all kinds gathered to exchange ideas and debate. These encounters and debates aimed to resolve problems of life and achieve a common good for all, with the belief that philosophical deliberation leads to truth and knowledge. By listening to each other, scholars learned and realized that there were multiple ways of accessing reality and truth. These gatherings were often called *majales*, the plural term of majlis from the verb *jalas* in Arabic, meaning to sit down. The majlis, which often featured meals and musical performances, "brought together men and women of different legal status as audience, patrons, and performers" (Frishkopf and Spinetti, 2018, 228). Some of the concerts were performed outdoors in garden settings to enhance the aesthetic experience (27).

I find that the openness that characterized the approaches of the Arab and Muslim thinkers was manifested in two levels: 1) being open to ideas of people who came from other cultures and religions: Greeks, Byzantines, Persians, etc., 2) being open to an interdisciplinary approach to various fields of study. For example, a medical doctor could also be a logician, judge, linguist, musician, and so on. Some of the most influential scholars of medieval times, such as Al-Farabi and Avicenna, not only influenced philosophy, science, and medicine, but also produced important theoretical writings on music, which are well worth exploring.

Prominent Music Theorists

What we have today in terms of writing on music from Arab and Muslim scholars could be divided into two categories: 1) *The writings of the philosophers and scientists*, or what we refer to in Arabic as *Falasifa,* such as Al-Kindi, Al-Farabi, and Avicenna. They considered music, most of the time, a mathematical science and 2) *The writing of the Sufi thinkers*. They wrote aesthetical essays and poems about the role of music in life and considered music's ability to reach out for the divine. Considering this, I will give a brief overview of the work of the *Falasifa* before preceding to examine the Sufi narratives.

Al-Kindi (801–873)

Al-Kindi was known as "The Philosopher of the Arabs." This renowned philosopher also excelled in medicine, mathematics, physics, chemistry, and music. Born in Al-Basra, Iraq, he later moved to Baghdad where he was sponsored by the khalifa Abdullah Al-Ma'mun. Al-Ma'mun asked him to be in charge of the translations in the Bait-al hikma (the College of Science), which was the first Arabic library and university. He studied Syriac and Greek to be able to read original sources, translate them, and edit previous translations. He authored fifteen music books. Only five have survived. The most important treaties on composition were *Risala fi Khubr ta'lif al alhan*, which notably utilized Arabic letters for music notation. He was the first to use the term music "*Musiqa*" in Arabic. The term was later translated into Farsi and Turkish.

Al-Kindi used the terms *Luhun*, or *Taniniat* to refer to scales or what is known today in Arabic as *Maqamat*. The scale has twelve notes and was based on the Greek music scale of Pythagoras. He labeled notes with Arabic letters and emphasized the aesthetical and purposeful importance of the first note of each scale known today as the tonic (Shawqi, 1996, 96–99). For centuries, Al-Kindi influenced many writers who came after him, especially Ikhwan al Safa (The Brothers of Purity). Most of Al-Kindi's writings and theories on sound, from both physical and psychological viewpoints, were original (Farmer, 1929, 150).

While he dealt with sounds, modes, intervals, genres, rhythmic transitions, and many other aspects of musical composition, perhaps the most important thing is that he clarified how the Arabic music system is original and different from Persian or Byzantine music systems (as quoted in Farmer, 1929, 151).

Al-Farabi (870–950)

Al-Farabi studied the sciences in Baghdad and excelled in music. He was a virtuoso ud player. He was invited by Saif al Daula, the *Hamanid*, to come and live in Aleppo under his patronage. Along with his mastery of the ud, he wrote many important theoretical treaties on music. These music treatises were translated into Latin. He was known in Europe as Alpharabius. His work in music contributed to the cultural and musical renaissance in Europe. Roger Bacon (1219–1292) the medieval English philosopher, was influenced by Al-Farbi writings on music in his Opus majus and Opus tertium (Carpenter, 1953, 17). Al-Farabi was nicknamed the Second Master (*Magister Secundus*) to Aristotle.

His most famous book on music was the *Kitab al Musiqi al Kabir* (Grand Book on Music) (Carpenter, 1953, 175). Al-Farabi wrote this book out of frustration regarding documents he reviewed from Greek theorists translated into Arabic:

> Now, I found in all of them (the Greek Theorists) incompleteness in the various branches of the art, and Lacuna in many things in what they said. And the chief aim of most of them is speculative theory (al-'ilm al-nazari), but in the education of it, intelligible sayings have been employed in such a way that it is almost unthinkable that the ancient theorists (nazarun) should have been unable to deal with this art and did not attain to its perfection, considering their numbers and proficiency, and their eagerness for discovery in the sciences, and their preference for them over every other human thing, and the excellence of their understanding, and the transmission of it (their work) from generation to generation. Except (that we allow) that their writings in the perfection of this branch of knowledge have either perished, or what was handed down from them in Arabic were defective writings. (as quoted in Farmer, 1930, 287)

Even with the above criticism of the Greek philosophers, Al-Farabi studied in depth the works of Euclid, Ptolemy, and Themistus, and was, to some extent, influenced by them (Farmer, 1930, 330). He commented, explained, corrected, and added his own theories.

In the opening of his treaties, *Al Musiqi al Kabir*, Al-Farabi wrote:

> The aim of a writer in every theoretical art should be determined by three axioms. The first, a complete statement of fundamental principles. The second, the ability to elucidate what follows from these principles. The third, the ability to combat errors which meet him in that science, and strength to restrict the

opinions of others, to discriminate between the right and the wrong, and to rectify the imperfections of those whose opinions are obscure. (as quoted in Farmer, 1930, 67)

In the second book of Al-Farabi's treaties, he stressed again his mission in correcting what was obscure in the writings of the Greeks, noting that "we have explained the value of what each of these has attained . . . in this science, and we have rectified the errors of those who have fallen into errors" (Farmer, 1930, 68). Unlike Al-Kindi who was not himself a musician—or Ishaq al Mausili, who was a performer but lacked training in music theory, science, philosophy, or logic—it is clear that Al-Farabi mastered both the practical and theoretical art of music. Al-Farabi had a wide knowledge in various fields of study in addition to rigorous training in logic and philosophy that he was able to incorporate when he wrote about music. What is original about Al-Farabi's writings about music is that he combined theoretical knowledge with practice: "Whatever by its nature should be known and practiced, its perfection lies in it actually being practiced" (al-Talbi 1993, 353). Finally, Al-Farabi was not only concerned with the music of the Greeks but also described the practice of music in the Umayyad and Abbasid dynasties.

His treatise *Al Musiqi al Kabir* dealt with various aspects of music: the scientific aspect: exploring the acoustics and the physics of sound; the theoretical analytical aspect: compositional techniques, descriptions of intervals, melodies, rhythms, and modes, as well as instruments used in his time like the ud, *mizmar, rababa, tonbur*, etc.; performance practice issues: for both voice and instrumental music, describing the relation between the melody and words; and the social aspect: the function of music in the society, and its capacity to stimulate the imagination in humans, discipline their emotions, and lead them to wisdom.

A famous anecdote was recorded by Al-Farabi's contemporaries. Whether it is true or not, this story shows his perceived power, self-confidence, and ability to stand up to authorities. Al-Farabi was once invited to the court of Saif al-Dawla. Upon his arrival, the prince asked him to take a seat. Al-Farabi asked, "Should I seat myself where I am or where you are?" Then he started playing the ud in a certain way that made everyone laugh. He changed his tuning and played again and made everyone cry. In the end, he played again and made everyone sleep (al-Nasir, 2018, 31).

Despite his mastery of the ud and writings on instrumental music, Al-Farabi favored the human voice over all other instruments. He found that only the human voice can attain perfection in music. It is capable of unifying three important virtues of music: pleasing and calming effect, provoking certain feelings and images, and stimulating the imagination to inspire ideas for the audience (Michon and Gaetani, 2006, 172). His attitude brings to mind a well-known fact about Chopin, and how, despite his mastery of the piano, he would rarely go to hear piano concerts or any performances. Instead, he preferred the human voice and would go to operas to get inspired by the *bel canto*!

Ibn Sina (980–1037)

Ibn Sina was known to the West as Avicenna, but nicknamed in the Arab world as *Al Sheikh al rais* (The Chief Teacher). He was a scientist, doctor, and philosopher. Born in Bukhara, he was a prodigy and claimed to master all sciences by the age of eighteen (Farmer, 1930, 218). His book, *Qanun fil tibb* (Canon of Medicine) was translated to Latin in the twelfth century, and recognized as a reference textbook that was globally circulated during his lifetime and for centuries after his death (Gardet, 1979, 158). He wrote 450 books, of which only 240 survived and were all in Arabic except two in Farsi.

In his books *Shifa* and *Kitab al Najat*, Ibn Sina wrote about music and considered it among the mathematical sciences. He researched melodies, notes, in terms of harmony and dissonances, and explained various types of rhythms. Both books show Ibn Sina's knowledge of *Tarkib* (compound) and *Tad'if* (doubling), which the later European music theorists took under the name of organum. That was the earliest example of polyphonic writing in music. In *Kitab al Najat*, Ibn Sina wrote: "And as for the *Tarkib*, it is the blending in one beat, of the principal notes with a note agreeing harmoniously. And the most excellent of that blending is to be found in the large intervals, in the octave [and after that the fifth] and then the fourth" (as quoted in Farmer, 1930, 330).

In the twelfth century, Latin translations of the Arabic texts made their appearance in European cultures. Thus, the ideas of the great music theorists such as Al-Farabi and Ibn Sina were most likely taken by the author of Anonymous IV, Vincent de Beauvais, and Jerome of Moravia, among others (Farmer, 1930, 37). Music was taught in the Arabian colleges in Cordova, a city in Andalusia, in southern Spain, and that is how the art of organum was transmitted:

> That the European students were sitting at the feet of these music professors at Cordova, lends some colour to the suggestion that organum was being taught at this hub of Arabian culture and civilization. Otherwise, it is difficult to appreciate why European students were studying there at all, if it was merely homophony and not harmony that was being taught. (Farmer, 1930, 106)

In higher education in Europe and North America today, Western music history courses tend to begin with Gregorian chant in Europe, giving no mention of Arabic musicians and music theorists, or perhaps with a very brief discussion of ancient Greece before leaping across centuries to Gregorian chant. Indeed, in contemporary European and North American conservatory traditions, nearly all the history described here is erased, as if virtually nothing happened in centuries of "dark ages" between the ancient Roman Empire and the Renaissance.

SUFISM

Islamic philosophers not only influenced Western musical thought in medieval times, but also in later centuries as various European thinkers became impressed by Sufism. Sufism refers to the esoteric mystical dimension of Islam. The terms "Sufi" and "Sufism" have been used since the eighth century, at the start of the collection and codification of Islamic traditions. But the Sufi path and the esoteric way of conceiving the Islamic religion was known and practiced since the beginning of Islam in the early seventh century, without explicitly using the term "Sufism." Opinions vary about the origins of the word. It may be related to the word *Suf* in Arabic, meaning wool, referring to the garment made of coarse wool that Sufi wear to show their renunciation of comfort. The French scholar, Henry Corbin, adheres to another origin of the word, using for reference the Muslim scientist and scholar, Al Biruni, from the end of the tenth century who affirmed that the word, Sufi, comes from the Greek word, Sophia, meaning wisdom.

The Sufi themselves say that there are thousands of ways to define Sufism. William Chittick, one of the most prominent American scholars of Sufism, states that Sufism is "the way by which man transcends his own individual self and reaches God" (Michon and Gaetani, 2006, 21). His view is in accordance with the eleventh-century Sufi, Ansari, who similarly admonished, "Know that when you learn to lose yourself you will reach the beloved, there is no other secret to be learnt and more than that is not known to me" (Vaughn-Lee, 1995, ii).

Sufism started almost as a reactionary movement of asceticism after Muslims gained power in the world and started to immerse themselves in luxury, richness, and comfort. The early Sufis preached against being attached and attracted to the materialistic world and against being trapped in endless desires: "The Sufi al Bustami was asked: what do you want? He said I want not to want" (Yafi, 1999, 130). But soon Sufism surpassed that phase and became the path to reach for the love, wisdom, and knowledge of God.

The Sufis began to differentiate between the ascetic (*al Zahed*) and the knower (*al Aref*): the ascetic turns his back to the world and almost closes his eyes to its beauty, while the knower finds that everything in the world reveals the beauty of God. A universe of meanings appeared to the Sufi from the Quranic verse that says, "Wherever you turn, there is the face of God." Thus, the great Sufi al Bustami said, "The knower flies toward God while the ascetic only walks" (Yafi, 1999, 130). According to the Swiss scholar Jean-Louis Michon, many mystic scholars and contemporary thinkers who are "Seekers of Truth" "recognize Sufism as being not only the very heart of Islam but also a key that gives access to the deepest meaning of other sacred traditions" (Michon and Gaetani, 2006, xxi).

It is important to acknowledge that the Sufi were considered "heretics" by some fanatics who rejected their interpretations of Islam. In fact, some Sufis were condemned and killed, like Hallaj and Suhrawardi. Al-Hallaj was a brilliant theologian and Sufi, as well as a great poet, and when condemned to death, he was asked to choose how he would be executed, so he asked to be crucified. The ignorant fanatics could not understand his sublime words, metaphors, or poetry. After the tragic death of Al-Hallaj, the Sufi were cautious not to reveal all their visions, secrets, and mystical experiences to the public. While I write about the Sufi out of intimate personal familiarity with their literature, I also do so in a way that endorses the words of St. Martin, "All mystics speak the same language for they come from the same country" (Underhill, 1990, 80).

THE SPIRITUAL CONCERT *SAMA*: MUSIC AS PATHWAY TOWARD THE DIVINE

In Sufism, the word *"Sama"* was used to describe the aesthetic experience of listening to music. Sama usually translates to mean "audition," and it implies more than the act of listening. Sama describes a vast world of reflections and philosophical mediations on music, and how music reveals the glory of the Creator and reminds listeners of the primordial state of the souls:

> The heart of man had been so constituted by the almighty that, like a flint, it contains a hidden fire which is evoked by music and harmony, and renders man beside himself with ecstasy. These harmonies are echoes of that higher world of beauty which we call the world of spirits; they remind man of his relationship to that world, and produce in him an emotion so deep and strange that he himself is powerless to explain it. (al-Ghazzali, 2016, 64)

According to the Sufi Al Kashani, being capable of Sama is a special blessing that God offers to a selected few who are pure in heart: "He has purified the channels of audition in the hearts of His elect [asfiya'] so that the audition may be realized" (Frishkopf and Spinetti, 2018, 209).

Many Sufis analyzed their experiences listening to music and described the effect of music upon their souls, what it meant for them, and the images that music carries. For instance, the famous Sufi poet, Jalal al-Din al Rumi, mentioned Sama in many of his poems. "What is the *sama*? A message from those hidden within the heart. The heart-the stranger- finds peace in their missive. . . . It is a wind which causes the branches of the intellect to blossom, a sound which opens the pores of existence" (as quoted in Chittick, 1983, 326). Like many Sufis, Rumi felt that music was one of many ways to know God and glance at the glory of paradise: "The *sama* has become a window towards Thy rose garden; the ears and hearts of the lovers peer through the window" (327).

A relationship between music and heaven is found in a famous anecdote about Rumi. Rumi once said, "Music is the creaking sound of the door of paradise." One person objected saying, "I don't like the creaking sound of doors." Rumi answered, "I hear the sound of the doors that open, you hear the doors that close" (During, 1992, 153).

Rumi also expressed with metaphorical images the pleasing physical effects of music, having a sweet taste like candy: "A marvelous sweetness has appeared in the body, for the flute and the musician's lips give it all the sugar it wants" (as quoted in Chittick, 1993, 327). He went so far as to suggest that everything in nature hears music, and even the leaves on the trees are moved by it: "You do not see, but they can hear the leaves on the trees also clapping. You cannot perceive the clapping of the leaves—you need the ear of the heart, not the body's ear" (328).

Rumi is even credited with first creating the dance of the whirling dervishes. Despite the word "dance," this spiritual movement has little to do with the concept of dancing we know today. It is a specific ritual of the Rumi order of Sufism to worship God, even though today it is used as a performance. In this ritual, the Sufi turns himself around in circles, with his right hand open upward to the sky and his left hand down toward the earth, a symbolic gesture that he is collecting blessings from God and bringing them to Earth. The hat on the head of a dancing Sufi represents the tombstone, and the fast, whirling movement is reached when he feels one with the movement of the universe.

For the Sufis, music connects humans with spiritual beauty, while revealing the secrets of their inner world of feelings as well as the mysteries of the Divine world. By their nature, humans have hearts that are susceptible and responsive to music. Some Sufi even went so far as to find that music could be an epiphanic experience. As Dhu'l Nun said, "Listening (*Al sama*) is a divine influence which stirs the heart to see Allah, and those who listen to it spiritually attain to Allah, and those who listen to it sensually fall into heresy" (Farmer, 1929, 36). Sa'd al-Din Hamuyah expressed similar sentiments in this way:

> When the heart attends the spiritual concert (*sama*)
> It perceives the Beloved and lifts the soul to the abode
> of the Divine Mysteries. (Naser, 1987, 166)

Perhaps one of the most beautiful Sufi insights about music came from discussions of Al Ghazali's claim, "In the heart, there is a virtuous residue that the power of speech cannot utter with words, the soul expresses it with music" (Yafi, 1999, 134). This was many centuries before French author Victor Hugo observed that "music expresses what words cannot."

SUFI INSPIRATION IN THE WESTERN WORLD

One does not have to look hard to find examples of the influence of Sufi thinkers on their Western counterparts. In his book *La Escatologia Musulmana en la Divina Comedia* (1919), the Spanish scholar Asin Palasios asserted that Dante's famous work, the *Divine Comedy*, found its source of inspiration in the Islamic night journey (Levitation) [al-'Isra wal-Mi'rag] of the prophet Muhammad to the seven heavens. There are numerous similarities between both stories: the presence of a "Guide" (Gabriel in the Islamic text, Beatrice in the *Divine Comedy*), the description of hell, the exit from hell through purification, the presence of a woman at some point crossing the path in the journey (symbol of the worldly seduction), the guards of hell and heaven, and the structure of the spheres of heaven. All of this could not be a mere coincidence.

Another source that bears resemblance to Dante's masterwork is a text by the Persian Sufi thinker Farid al Din al Attar (1145–1221). Al Attar was a medieval Iranian poet, famous for his epic poem *Manteq al-Tayr* (*The Conference of the Birds*), in which he described a bird's journey (metaphor of human souls), and spiritual quest to reach the Divine. The birds were guided by the wise hoopoe who helped them travel through "Seven Valleys" to find the Simorgh, a mythical bird-deity commonly found in Persian literature. The first valley is called the Valley of Quest (which compares to Dante's purgatory or the purification of the soul.) It is the most difficult, tiring, and long journey where one must relinquish all earthly pleasures and become totally empty and vacant from desires. The second valley is the Valley of Love where one finds the illumination of mystical life (comparable to Dante's "Earthly Paradise"). Valley number three is the Valley of Knowledge (comparable to

Dante's "planetary heavens where each soul partakes of the Divine") (Underhill, 1990, 131–32), which is followed by the Valley of Detachment, Valley of Unity (comparable to Dante's condition in the last canto of *Paradise*), Valley of Amazement in which one suffers blindness in front of the Divine light and, finally, the few birds who could make it to the end, the Valley of Annihilation, the merging of the self with the Divine love.

The poems of Attar have this main story but many other subsidiary stories just like Dante's *Divine Comedy*. The seven valleys are comparable to the seven days in Dante's journey: two days in hell, four days in the purgatory, and one day in heaven. Dante's pilgrims were guided by the Eagle of Justice, as the pilgrims' birds in Attar, who were guided by the wise Hoopoe.

Another philosophical Sufi masterwork that made a huge impact in the Western world, influencing writers and philosophers for centuries, was a novel by Sufi Ibn Tufail (1105–1185), *Ḥayy ibn Yaqẓān,* known in Latin as *Philosophus Autodidactus,* and in English, *The Improvement of Human Reason: Exhibited in the Life of Hai Ebn Yokdhan.* This story became popular in Europe during the Enlightenment and it is not hard to see how, after six hundred years, the British writer Daniel Defoe borrowed its content to write his renowned novel *Robinson Crusoe*. The story of *Hayy ibn Yaqzan* is about

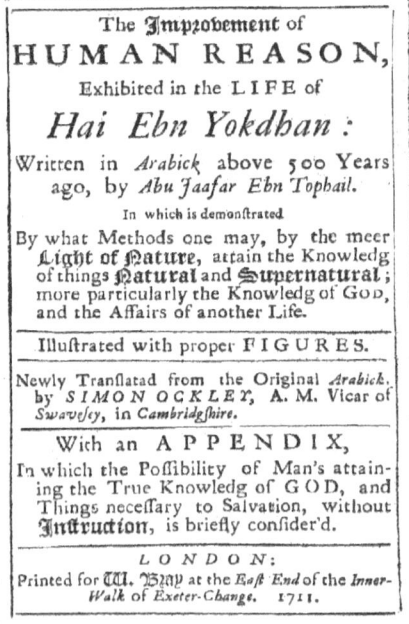

Figure 5.2. The cover of the novel in the English translation in 1711

a man who was born on a deserted isle. He grew up without a mother and father, and was adopted by a doe who had lost its fawn. The deer mothered him for seven years, then she died. Her death was his first spiritual awakening since he realized that her body was gone but his love for her remained. By observing nature and his surroundings, reflecting and thinking, feeling and contemplating, he discovered little by little the power of reasoning and judgment, and the highest ideas of science and spirituality. Gradually he thereby achieved faith in the creator (figure 5.2).

Moving ahead to the eighteenth century, the famous German poet Johann Wolfgang von Goethe (1749–1832), whose writings inspired the work of Franz Schubert and other composers, was among the many writers influenced by Sufi literature. Upon reading the poems of Hafez Shirazi (Persian Sufi poet from the fourteenth century), Goethe expressed immense interest, leading him to write his poetry collection entitled the *West-Eastern Divan*.

Among the metaphors that Goethe borrowed from Sufi tradition was the image of the butterfly to symbolize the human soul. This metaphor is often used by Sufi poets, as seen for instance in a poem by Al Attar that describes how true love consumes the soul with an annihilation of the self. Al Attar shows this by depicting the ways that three butterflies interact with a candle flame, the first of which claims to know love merely by flying close to it, while the second goes so far as to lightly touch it with its wings saying,

> I know how love's fire can burn.
> The third one threw himself into the heart of the flame
> and was consumed. He alone knows what true love is.
>
> Al Attar (from *The Conference of the Birds*)

In Goethe's poem "The Holy Longing," we find a similar image where he praises the butterfly that is attracted to a "silent candle burning" and "longs to be burned to death." Goethe thereby shows a lover in their "desire for higher love making":

> Now, arriving in magic, flying,
> and finally, insane for the light,
> you are the butterfly and you are gone . . .
>
> Goethe ("The Holy Longing")

Today, schools and colleges across the world teach Goethe's poems, the novel *Robinson Crusoe*, and *The Divine Comedy*, but are their Islamic origins ever mentioned? Perhaps this only occurs in departments of Islamic studies or the context of medieval Islamic cultures. The seemingly self-evident origin of "Arabic numerals" and of *algebra* itself in the teaching of mathematics seem to have met the same fate. What would change if people worldwide learned about other cultures through their intellectual heritage rather than by what they hear through news media? Probably the idea of a "different other" would diminish in the recognition that each culture had its share in building our common human heritage. As we begin the third decade of the twenty-first century, many would argue that we need to broaden our horizons by learning through meaningful dialogue, thereby becoming more open-minded. Perhaps then a less stigmatized appreciation of Islamic heritage could be attained. This task is possible by incorporating the theories of cultural diplomacy in our approach to various fields of study.

The modern theories and goals of cultural diplomacy do not imply a presumption of fixed and simple cultural models or clichés when examining the outcomes of various cultural heritages. Rather, they aim to open a space for discussions and dialogues based on respect, listening, and openness to shared cultural, spiritual, and educational experiences (Goff, 2013, 419). As mass media and social media bombard us with a flow of images from other cultures, we do not necessarily gain a deeper and more genuine understanding of each other: "Ironically, we have more information about each other, but we may not know more about each other" (423).

Many know the story of Malala Yousafzai, a female adolescent in Pakistan who was shot in the head in 2012 by fanatics who associated themselves with Islam, while on her way to school. As a result of this widely popular story, many now assume that Islam has long stood against women and not allowed them access to education. Few non-Muslims know the Hadith of the Prophet Mohammad that says: "To acquire knowledge is an obligation on every Muslim, male or female." The Arabic word "Hadith" and its plural "Ahadith" refer to the collected sayings of the Prophet Mohammad, and they constitute the second form of legislation in the Islamic religion after the Quran. Also, few are likely to know that the first degree-granting university in the world was established by a Muslim woman. Fatima al-Fihri founded the University of Al-Qarawiyyin in 859 AD in Fez, Morocco, considered the oldest university in history (UNESCO World Heritage Centre, 2021). The realm of cultural diplomacy aims to develop a compassionate consciousness and a feeling of responsibility to understand and share the world with others. Through this compassionate energy that combines softness and force, we can change the climate of humanity and propagate kindness, feelings of connectivity, and oneness not only between the East and the West but also between the past and the present.

BORROWING INSIGHTS: SPIRITUALITY AND MUSIC

I cannot count how many times, while I pursued professional music studies in Boston, Massachusetts, I was asked, "How come you play the piano? Isn't music forbidden in your religion?" I find it useless to debate the lawfulness of music in Islam since there is not even one verse in the Quran that prohibits it. However, I acknowledge the presence of many Muslim theologians and scholars who have defended music prohibition, relying on sayings (Hadith) attributed to the Prophet Mohammad. On the other hand, other sayings also attributed to the prophet *support* listening to music and singing, and essential features are shared between the deepest of musical and spiritual experiences.

SIMILARITIES BETWEEN MUSICAL EXPERIENCE AND THE MYSTICAL EXPERIENCE

Both music and religion arguably present spiritual views of the world, and both may be understood as gnostic experiences: a kind of mystical knowledge that transforms the state of the person. The musician spends a lifetime in seclusion, practicing an instrument, exploring, imagining, and speculating. With each note, they pours out all of the emotions of their heart and utter their most intimate words; and with each phrase, they live the ephemeral life of feelings. Shapes, colors, moods, events, created and re-created during hours of practice in solitude, musicians, drunk with the beauty of sounds, travel from the individual to the Divine, from the earthly to the sublime, from the physical to the metaphysical, creating a world of symbols to represent a world of symbols.

Like Sufism, music is not just cognitive knowledge, but an experience of the heart. Like Sufism, it is a lifelong spiritual journey of discovery and revelation; it is loving without expecting an outcome; trusting without needing proof; searching for fleeting moments of beauty that reflect the Eternal; and moving from the microcosm (lower-self) to the macrocosm (the Divine). The journey is long, and the discipline is hard. The task is even harder in a society that emphasizes commercial profitability. But the soul always seeks what is beyond material existence. How many famous lawyers, doctors, and businessmen turn, later in life, to music or other forms of spirituality after finding that all the money they accumulated cannot bring spiritual bliss of any kind? There is no escape from our eternal longing to the Divine, to the Home, to the lost paradise we knew in a primordial state of being, but music brings us close to the celestial world by attenuating our ontological thirst for the absolute and curing our wounds of separation.

Mystic scholar, Evelyn Underhill, points out how music, among all of the arts, is the closest to mystic writings.

> The Mystery of music is seldom realized by those who so easily accept its gifts. Yet of all the arts music alone shares with great mystical literature the power of waking in us a response to the life-movement of the universe: brings us—we know not how—news of its exultant passions and its incomparable peace. Beethoven heard the very voice of Reality, and little of it escaped when he translated it for our ears. (1990, 76)

There is another striking similarity between the mystical experience and the musical experience known to mystics as "the Dark Night." After going through an intense spiritual experience, or following a period of sustained mystical activity, sometimes, the mystics fall into a state of fatigue, stagnation, and depression. Nevertheless, with patience, they can overcome this period and consider it a phase of purification that will make them attain higher levels of consciousness. The medieval theologian, Sufi Al Ghazali, went through this period when he took time off from his four hundred students and traveled to Syria: "I went to Syria, where I remained more than two years; without any other object than that of living in seclusion and solitude, conquering my desires, struggling with my passions, striving to purify my soul, to perfect my character, and to prepare my heart to meditate upon God" (Underhill, 1990, 226).

Iconic French music pedagogue, Nadia Boulanger, explained in one interview about practicing a musical instrument and repeating passages many times, sometimes without a result. She mentioned how St. Teresa of Avila had days of "dry prayer when she would pray and pray without any results and then one day she would "hear." Boulanger associated this "hearing" with "inspiration" for musicians (Monsaingeon, 1985, 37).

Such spiritual fatigue is also common among musicians. Many composers go through periods where they cannot compose anything, like the case of Sergei Rachmaninoff. Even some great performers encounter this "Dark Night." Vladimir Horowitz, despite being a phenomenal pianist and having successful concerts, went through a period where he was doubting his abilities. He developed performance anxiety at the height of his career, and his insecurities prevented him from giving public concerts for years. Another world class pianist, Martha Argerich, took a two-year from solo performances in 1980. After the withdrawal, she returned to performing, stronger than before.

INTERPRETATION AND HERMENEUTICS

Shared insights from music and Sufism are also notable in the sphere of interpretation and hermeneutics. When deciphering a musical score, the performer has the mission of reading and comprehending not only what is written on the page but the meanings and ideas behind the written notes while detecting the feelings and emotions the music could carry to the listeners. The performer gives life to the score to create the musical work anew. There are infinite ways to approach a musical text, but for most performers, the goal is to be as close as possible to what the composers indicated in the music score. Most composers specify the tempo (speed) of the piece, and sometimes, they give a hint of the overall character of the music (joyful, sad, sarcastic, etc.) Within these remarks, the execution varies much from one performer to another. It is interesting to notice also that some performers might obey literally what is in the text and play all the correct notes in the correct rhythms and speed, yet their playing can be dull and fail to captivate the hearts of their audience. What speaks to the hearts and minds of an audience and what stirs their feelings is something commonly perceived as spiritual and not physical. It relates to the degree of inspiration the performer may have while on stage. Can we analyze this inspiration? Is there a way to define it? Why do some performers possess this magic and are able to mesmerize their listeners while others do not? The issue here seems to be related to one thing: interpretation.

Interpreting a text of music is the process of taking what is written (in the case of notated traditions) and foreseeing what lies beyond the notes and what worlds of meanings and feelings those notes create when they come to life and are played on musical instruments. It is going from the *physical* (written notes on a page and the actual capacity of the given musical instrument) to the *imagined*. As Theodor W. Adorno wrote: "Only what is imagined convincingly can become meaningful and convincing. Any uncertainty of imagination is projected onto the result. This is a basic rule" (2006, 153).

In an interview, American concert pianist Abbey Simon explained the difficulty of understanding what is on the printed page. "It is not easy to understand what a composer has written because it is just a clue in a series of clues" (Noyle, 1991, 122). The performer has to read between the lines and make sense of all the written and hidden clues. Boston based Japanese conductor Seiji Ozawa spoke in an interview about his teacher Maestro Herbert von Karajan, and how he used to tell his students this advice: "Read what's behind the score" (Murakami, 2016, 91).

The performer must also follow the tradition of interpreting certain works and never destroy their main ideas. The freedom of interpretation is related to what is left unsaid and unmarked in the musical text. Adorno finds that musical interpretation has many different layers: "The analytical recognition of the sense, i.e., the truth of the work. . . . The adequate imagination. . . . The realization" (2006, 130).

In an interview, Czech American classical pianist Rudolf Firkunsy said the following:

> When we start to study a piece, we have to be extremely humble and follow every possible marking which the composer gave us . . . because this is the only contact we have with the composer's version. After we know the notes, then we have to read between the notes, something which is not printed, something which is not there. That is when your process starts as an interpreter, when you can show what you understand in the piece, what you feel, what makes a good interpretation or bad interpretation. (Noyle, 1991, 84–85)

The exciting challenge of a piece of music brings to the performer the multiple ways of interpretation it can inspire. Of course, it is better to try to be as close as possible to the composer's intentions, but sometimes, as musicologist Richard Taruskin explains, to limit the meaning of a piece of music only to the intentions of the composer would impoverish it (1997, 474).

A rich musical text always inspires various interpretations and ways of execution. This is the case with J. S. Bach's keyboard music. Bach left most of the scores without articulations, dynamics (loud or soft), or phrasing slurs, trusting that the keyboardists of his period would know how to interpret them, and perhaps, more importantly, giving them the freedom to do so depending on the "effect" they wanted to produce in their audience.

I find that the process of interpretation in music resonates with the process of interpreting religious sacred texts. There have been some studies relating hermeneutics with musical interpretation, but a comparison with the interpretation of Islamic texts does not seem to have been approached. The word, "hermeneutic" means the interpretation of sacred texts, typically from the Bible or Talmud, and when it comes to the Quran, the Arabic word used is *Ta'wil*. In all cases, the challenge is not to be trapped in the literal meanings of words, but to use the imagination and travel beyond, seeking a deeper understanding of all the symbols and metaphors that the text contains.

Henry Corbin, the famous French scholar of Sufism, defined Ta'wil in this way: "*Ta'wil* is the name that one gives in general to all symbolic exegesis . . . it is a science which has as its pivot a spiritual direction and a divine assistance" (as quoted in Cheetham, 2003, 187). Before Corbin, the eighteenth-century philosopher Johann Georg Hamann researched the world of hermeneutics by speaking about a three-way relationship between the author, the reader, and the text. For Hamann, the depth and meaning of a text go beyond the author's own contribution and are the responsibility of the interpreter: "Few authors understand themselves, and a proper reader must not only *understand* his author but also be able to *see beyond him*" (Griffith-Dickson, 2017). The interpreter, therefore, must say what the author left unsaid, transcending the limitation of the presented text.

Corbin also explained Ta'wil in terms of its opposite: "In Ta'wil one must carry sensible forms back to imaginative forms and then rise to still higher meanings; to proceed in the opposite direction (to carry imaginative forms to the sensible forms in which they originate) is to destroy the virtualities of the imaginations" (1998, 240). A simpler definition of Ta'wil is presented by Tom Cheetham, an American Corbin scholar:

> Hermeneutics is an unveiling. It is not an operation on a text in anything like the modern sense of criticism, whether historical or literally. It is not a linguistic exercise at all in the usual sense or a conceptual manipulation based upon reasoning. It is an uncovering, a process by which we participate in the blossoming not of ideas or words, but of images. It occurs in the imaginal space between the soul and the text. (2003, 115).

INSPIRATION AND REVELATION FOR THE MUSICIAN AND THE MYSTIC

In any artistic creation or spiritual realization there are two sides: the sender and the receiver, a manifestation and an arrival, a force that gives and another that understands, an energy that reveals, and another that hears. In the end, a concept will be formed: a musical idea, or a spiritual vision, or a verse of poetry, and so forth.

Sufi thinkers correlated inspiration to a flash of brief lightning that brightens the heart: "something which descends upon the hearts of the mystics regardless of their intentions, their attempts to attract it or their desire to earn it ... [the states are] like flashes of lighting ... they alight upon the heart only to leave it instantaneously. (Al-Qushayri, 2007, 78). However, the person capable of receiving a revelation must possess the prerequisite knowledge and aspiration. For the Sufi, inspiration is a process of uncovering (*Kashf*) or unveiling, penetrating the fabric that envelops the mind and conceals the truth. It is not an intellectual inquisition, but rather a mystical perception of the soul of what already exists. Thus, the great Sufi master, Ibn Arabi, explained in his book *al-Futūḥāt al-Makkiyya* how a Sufi gets inspired to write:

> The heart clings devotedly to the door of the Divine Presence, watchful for what unfolds when the door is opened, in poverty and need, empty of all knowledge.

Whatever comes to it from behind that curtain, the heart hastens to obey and sets it down according to the measure appointed in the divine command. (Hirtenstein, 1999, 232)

Some artists and poets expressed how they don't feel that they are creating the work but are transmitting it. Their task is to reveal a work that already existed somewhere in the universe before they conceived it, or in other words, it was inspired to them first, and then they had to put an effort to realize and complete it.

It is important to note that the French Sufism scholar Eric Geoffroy differentiated between three different terms that the Sufi used in their rhetoric: the Inspiration (*ilham*), the Revelation (*wahi*), and the Unveiling (*Kashf*). He said that only the prophets receive the revelation. As for the unveiling, "It constitutes for the Sufis the principal mode of access to the supra-sensible world . . . it permits the raising of the veils that the world of the senses (*mulk*) throws over man, which then allows him to reach the world of the spirit (*malakut*) or even the world of the Divine (*jabarut*)" (Michon and Gaetani, 2006, 51).

Successful performances for musicians or actors depend not only on their training but also on the degree of inspiration they feel on the day of the show. It is the ability to disconnect from all the surrounding environment and surrender to the role of the play or the character of the musical piece played. Often people comment on a show saying, "He was inspired" or "That was inspiring" when the performer stirs in their hearts various feelings, sometimes even ones they did not know they were capable of experiencing. The performance becomes an experience or a revelation, and it lasts in the memory for years. We can all recall a certain concert that touched us more than others, or a certain actor who has the capacity of changing the way we feel. The question is not about talent and the ability to show great control of the mind and body, it is something more, something we cannot easily describe. It is the "je ne sais quoi" and the "*presque-rien*" that the French philosopher Vladimir Jankelevitch talks about in his books, a mysterious component that only some have and can share with the world.

CONCLUSION

Today, in our digital age bathed in materialism, where success is measured by the financial profit one gains, is there anything one can learn from medieval Muslim philosophers? There are various dimensions of arguments presented in this chapter that I believe remain pertinent to our world today:

1. *The openness and embrace of other cultures by viewing how they are all related to one unified culture: that of all humanity.* Arabs and Muslim philosophers studied and translated ancient texts they obtained from the Greeks (whom they called *al Kudama'a*, meaning the ancients.) They elaborated and commented on these texts and handed them to Europe in the early Renaissance. During this "Golden Age," there was an openness to other cultures and various influences from Persia and the Byzantine Empire, which enhanced and advanced knowledge. Thus, although the situation in many Arab countries seems deplorable now, we should not forget that they had their share of profound contributions in the chain of global culture.

   Today, in the twenty-first century, many in the West like to think that they, too, are open and understanding toward others in various parts of the world. We are led to believe that social media has made people more open and aware of others, but in many ways it has imprisoned people in isolated bubbles, content to live in a state of solipsism. Moreover, it has canceled essential debates by making people only "hang out" with those who share the same opinions. In his book *The Shallows* (2011), Nicholas Carr brilliantly describes in detail the influence and consequences of such digital advancements on our behaviors and ways of thinking (See also Hebert & Rykowski, 2018; Hebert and Williams, 2020).

2. *An interdisciplinary approach to various fields of study.* Many renowned Arab Muslim philosophers were also medical doctors, logicians, musicians, theologians, and scientists. Fields of knowledge enhance each other and are interrelated. With the development of universities, learning has moved toward more specialization. Knowledge today is separated into various disciplines and seekers of knowledge often cannot see beyond the limitations of their own subject. It would be beneficial to incorporate some of the ideas of a well-rounded education, not only in primary schooling but at all levels of study. Science, philosophy, literature, and the arts are all important to give different forms of access to truth.

3. *The need for the spiritual in a rapidly changing world.* The origin of the word religion is from the Latin verb *religare*, which means to link, or to connect. We live in a time where people have a prejudice against this word. When you say this person is "cultured," it is often perceived as a compliment. However, when you say a person is "religious," it brings to most people's minds limits and rigidity. In my opinion, the flaws of certain cultures are often wrongly attributed to religion.

We also live in a time when "science" is revered and deemed as the highest and most "real" form of knowledge. We are trained to think that science has all the answers to all questions and phenomena that we encounter in our existence. Yet, even philosopher Friedrich Nietzsche, who was not religious, warned that having only a scientific interpretation of the world "is the most stupid of all possible interpretations" and "one of the poorest in meanings reducing the world to a mechanical and meaningless one." The example that he uses is music: "Assuming that one estimated the value of a piece of music according to how much of it could be counted, calculated, and expressed in formulas: how absurd would such a "scientific" estimation of music be! What would one have comprehended, and understood, grasped of it? Nothing, really nothing of what is 'music' in it!" (Nietzsche, 1974, 336).

The essence of music is both physical and metaphysical. There are many questions in music that remain unanswered and even unapproached and ineffable. Metaphysical studies of music are rare. There is, for example, the question of inspiration, genius precocity, and the enigmatic issues of creativity and talent that made composers like Mozart and Handel able to produce mature works at a very young age. The effect of music in itself has been examined and studied in various books from a scientific point of view without really coming to satisfying results.

Science is far from being able to explain the existence of music. From Darwin, who declared that music was biologically meant to attract mates, "I conclude that musical notes and rhythms were first acquired by the male or female progenitors of mankind for the sake of charming the opposite sex. Thus, musical tones became firmly associated with some of the strongest passions an animal is capable of feeling, and are consequently used instinctively" (Levitin, 2016, 251) to the modern French scientist, Dan Sperber, who declared that music is "an evolutionary parasite" (294).

This is not to say that the study of metaphysics will bring definite answers. Yet, it is the investigation of the realms of suprareason, and the transhistorical wisdom of previous generations, that might illuminate and guide some aspects of musical research that have been neglected.

In the end, I must admit that all I wrote in this chapter could be summarized with the following poem by Rumi:

> I am neither Christian nor Jew, neither Magian nor Muslim,
> I am not from east or west, not from land or sea,
> not from the shafts of nature nor from the spheres of the firmament,
> not of the earth, not of water, not of air, not of fire.
> I am not from the highest heaven, not from this world,
> not from existence, not from being.
> I am not from India, not from China, not from Bulgar, not from Saqsin,
> not from the realm of the two Iraqs, not from the land of Khurasan.
> I am not from the world, not from beyond,

not from heaven and not from hell.
I am not from Adam, not from Eve, not from paradise and not from Ridwan.
My place is placeless, my trace is traceless,
no body, no soul, I am from the soul of souls.
I have chased out duality, lived the two worlds as one.
One I seek, one I know, one I see, one I call.

(Nicholson, 1898; reprinted without alteration in McNeil and Waldman, 1973, 242)

REFERENCES

Adorno, Theodor W. 2006. *Towards a Theory of Musical Reproduction*. Cambridge: Polity.
al-Ghazzali. 2016. *The Alchemy of Happiness*. Translated by John Murray. Glastonbury: The Lost Library.
al-Nasir, Muhammad Abi Ras. 2018. *Al-Maskari: Healing the Deaf and Healing the Sick in Proverbs and Wisdom*. Dar Al-Kutub Al-Ilmiyya.
al-Qushayri, Abu 'l-Qasim. 2007. *Al-Qusharyri's Epistle on Sufism: Al-Risala Al-qushayriyya Fi 'ilm Al-tasawwuf* (*Great Books of Islamic Civilization*). Translated by Alexander Knysh. Reading, UK: Garnet Publishing.
al-Talbi, Ammar. 1993. *"Al Farabi." Prospects: The Quarterly Review of Comparative Education*. Paris, UNESCO, vol. XXIII, nos.1/2: 353–72.
Carpenter, Nan Cooke. 1953. "The Study of Music at the University of Oxford in the Middle Ages (to 1450)." *Journal of Research in Music Education* 1: 11–20.
Carr, Nicholas. 2011. *The Shallows: What the Internet is Doing to Our Brains*. New York: Norton.
Cheetham, Tom. 2003. *The World Turned Inside Out, Henry Corbin and Islamic Mysticism*. Woodstock: Spring Journal Books.
Chittick, William. 1983. *The Sufi Path of Knowledge: Ibn Al-Arabi's Metaphysics of Imagination*. Albany: State University of New York Press.
Corbin, Henry. 1998. *Alone with the Alone Creative Imagination in the Sufism of Ibn 'Arabi*. Princeton, NJ: Princeton University Press.
During, Jean. 1992. l'Oreille Islamique Dix Années Capitales de la Vie Musicale en Iran: 1980-1990." *Asian Music* 23, no. 2: 135–164.
Farmer, George. 1929. *A History of Arabian Music to the XIIIth Century*. London: Luzac and Co.
———. 1930. *Historical Facts for the Arabian Musical Influence*. London: Reeves.
Frishkopf, Michael and Federico Spinetti, eds. 2018. *Music, Sound, and Architecture in Islam*. Austin: University of Texas Press.
Gardet, Louis. 1979. "L'attitude Philosophique et Religieuse d'Ibn Sina: En Son Contexte Historique." *Roczniki Filozoficzne / Annales De Philosophie / Annals of Philosophy* 27: 157–67.

Goff, Patricia M. 2013. "Cultural Diplomacy." In *The Oxford Handbook of Modern Diplomacy*, edited by Andrew F. Cooper, Jorge Heine, and Ramesh Thakur, 419–35. Oxford: Oxford University Press.

Griffith-Dickson, Gwen. 2017. "Johann Georg Hamann." Stanford Encyclopedia of Philosophy. Stanford University, July 6. https://plato.stanford.edu/entries/hamann/.

Goody, Jack. 2012. *The Theft of History*. Cambridge: Cambridge University Press.

Hebert, David G. and Mikolaj Rykowski, eds. 2018. *Music Glocalization: Heritage and Innovation in a Digital Age*. Newcastle: Cambridge Scholars Publishing.

Hebert, David G. and Sean Williams. 2020. "Ethnomusicology, Music Education, and the Power and Limitations of Social Media." In *Oxford Handbook of Social Media and Music Learning*, edited by Janice Waldron, Stephanie Horsley, and Kari Veblen. New York: Oxford University Press.

Hirtenstein, Stephen. 1999. The Unlimited Mercifier: The Spiritual Life and Thought of Ibn 'Arabi. Oxford: Anqa Publishing.

Kurkela, Vesa and Lauri Vakeva, eds. 2009. *De-Canonizing Music History*. Newcastle: Cambridge Scholars Publishing.

Levitin, Daniel J. 2016. *This is Your Brain on Music, the Science of a Human Obsession*. New York: Dutton.

Mavroudi, Maria. 2015. "Translations from Greek into Latin and Arabic during the Middle Ages: Searching for the Classical Tradition." *Speculum* 90, no. 1: 28–59.

McNeil, William H. and Marilyn Robinson Waldman, eds. 1973. *The Islamic World*. New York: Oxford University Press.

Michon, Jean-Louis and Roger Gaetani, eds. 2006. *Sufism: Love and Wisdom*. Bloomington, IN: World Wisdom.

Monsaingeon, Bruno. 1985. *Mademoiselle: Conversations with Nadia Boulanger*. Manchester: Carcanet Press.

Murakami, Haruki. 2016. *Absolutely on Music: Conversations with Seiji Ozawa*. New York: Alfred. A Knopf.

Nasr, Seyyed Hossein. 1987. *Islamic Art and Spirituality*. Albany: State University of New York Press.

Nietzsche, Friedrich. 1974. *The Gay Science*. Trans. Walter Kaufmann. New York: Vintage Books.

Noyle, Linda J. 1991. *Pianists on Playing: Interviews with 12 Concert Pianists*. Lanham, MD: Scarecrow Press.

Shawqi, Yousef ed. 1996. *Risala fi Khubr ta'lif al alhan*, ed.. Cairo: Dar al Kutub.

Taruskin, Richard. 1997. *Defining Russia Musically: Historical and Hermeneutical Essays*. Princeton, NJ: Princeton University Press.

Underhill, Evelyn. 1990. *Mysticism*. New York: Doubleday.

UNESCO World Heritage Centre. 2021. "Medina of Fez." UNESCO World Heritage Centre. Accessed November 10. https://whc.unesco.org/en/list/170/.

Vaughan-Lee, Llewellyn. 1995. *Sufism, the Transformation of the Heart*. Point Reyes Station, CA: Golden Sufi Center.

Yafi, Abdul Karim. 1999. *Bada'at Al-Hikma*. Damascus: Dar Tlass.

Chapter Six

Soft War and Multilateral Musical Pathways in Iran

Nasim Niknafs

While music education scholarship has embraced concepts such as culturally responsive teaching, diversity, and antioppressive practices in music classrooms, and the impact of policies on music learning, few have hitherto considered transformative approaches to music education through the discourses of cultural diplomacy, soft power, and their local and global affective outcomes. Questions central to this chapter include how such discourses can make music education either a powerful means of expressive communication or an obsolete practice in the bedrock of governmental tendencies toward outwardly displaying attractiveness through public diplomacy while inwardly conveying strength. Considering Iran, a country where music has been a contested sphere since the 1905 constitutional revolution, I examine how top-down cultural policies through means of soft power and cultural diplomacy have inadvertently provided opportunities for the flourishing of bottom-up musical and educational movements. According to an ethnomusicological orientation, rather than only considering cultural policies in terms of political control, it is helpful to notice the implicit influence of *everyday cultural practices* on policies (see Nettl, 2005). Perhaps music policies can be conceived as a silver lining for a collectively self-sufficient and creative music education that may benefit from a more open space of cultural expression and circulation, reaffirming Raymond Williams's notion of the evolution of literacy: "There is no way to teach a man to read the Bible which did not also enable him to read the radical press. A controlled intention became an uncontrollable effect" (as quoted in Sreberny and Khiabany, 2010, 10). In this chapter, I consider the literature on music education in Iran after the 1979 revolution, intertwined with scholarship on cultural diplomacy and "soft war" to demonstrate a more nuanced and complex cultural sphere than a pure dichotomy between the perceived democratic and authoritarian regimes and their cultural artifacts. This approach fits with the poignant concept of cultural intimacy, by which Michael Herzfeld suggests that instead of looking at cultural practices through the binary prism of top-down versus bottom-up, one can "treat 'top' and 'bottom' as but two of a host of refractions of a broadly shared *cultural engagement* (a more processual term than the static culture" (Herzfeld, 2016, 6). It follows that the aim of this chapter is not so much to dwell on authoritarian cultural policies through soft power and soft war, but rather their actual effects on the ground, and to consider whether such policies conceived as propaganda can inadvertently create uncontrollable spaces in which musicians can thrive.

A SURVEY OF MUSIC AND ITS EDUCATION AFTER THE 1979 REVOLUTION

There is no linear trajectory and straightforward way to portray the impact of cultural policies on music education in Iran after the 1979 revolution (see Lucas, 2019). Therefore, I depict a more reflective picture of its intricate existence and circulation in the country and abroad. For the first two decades after the revolution, cultural policies in the country seemed to depend upon the elected president's social and cultural policies drawn from Mehdi Semati's characterization of the four post-revolutionary periods: "the war years, the reconstruction era, the reform era, and the post-reform era" (2008, 4). Yet, it gradually became clear that there was a discrepancy between the presidential orientation and, as Narges Bajoghli remarked, the *regime*'s (*Nezam*) intentions, which is the Islamic Republic's cultural ethos:

> Although some of my interlocutors were a part of the Revolutionary Guard, some were Basijis, and some referred to themselves as hezbollahis, their common denominator was their belief in the regime (*nezām*). Defending the nezam was their ultimate red line. . . . I heard over and over again in their debates with independent film makers, as well as in debates among themselves, "Criticism of the government [*dowlat*] is ok, but not criticism of the nezam." (2019, 13)

These divergent ambitions have created years of ambivalence in music education.

Mohammad Reza Pahlavi's reign was complex in that while music was encouraged in many ways, it was also censored in others. Having been wedged between a westernized modernization agenda of the Pahlavi era and the historically dominant social and religious practices, music went through an "identity crisis" leading to stark polarization between Western and Persian modes of musical delivery and transmission that, according to

Hossein Alizadeh, a well-revered contemporary tar player, still persists today (Bastaninezhad, 2014, 9). The prevailing modernizing cultural policies based on Western ideologies alienated many traditional musicians and substituted the oral/aural musical transmission of traditional Persian music with notated version and education. Ali Naqi Vaziri was the pioneer of this movement who established the "Madrese-ye Aliy-e Mosiqi" in 1924, based on his music education in France and Germany (9). Some well-respected musicians followed this path and earned their musical degrees outside of Iran. Music educators such as Sharif Lotfi and Siavash Baizai both pursued Western classical music education in Germany. Hormoz Farhat, ethnomusicologist, and Azin Movahed, flutist and pedagogue, studied in the United Sates, and Alireza Mashayekhi, composer, in Austria (12). At the other end, a movement began to take shape toward the end of the Pahlavi era in terms of "cultural self-awareness" to revive Persian music against the advances of Western ideologies. The most well-known radio program within this movement, Golhā, had a profound influence on attracting the Iranian populace to Persian musical tradition that to this day is still cherished (14).

Around the 1979 revolution, the unpredictable, volatile, and gendered circumstances of cultural practices in Iran made many classes of cultural workers, specifically musicians, leave the country to pursue their musical educational and professional opportunities. Farzaneh Hemmasi has evocatively tracked the evolution of *pop-e-Losāngelesi*, focusing on a generation of musicians popular in the music scene before the revolution and their re-establishment in Los Angeles (see Hemmasi, 2020). Hemmasi critically assesses the circulation of their music and its impact on the consumption of such music in Iran, colloquially known as *dambūli,* which is considered illegal and therefore disseminated on the black market.

Notwithstanding, it was not only prerevolutionary musicians with Western popular music inclinations who left the country, but also their Western classical counterparts after the revolution. For the first two decades of the Islamic era, which were marked with eight years of war followed by the presidency of Hassan Rafsanjani (the "reconstruction era"), public performances of Western classical music were considered extraordinary events. Students interested in learning this style of music did so in secret at private studios. If one intended to enter the university to study music, one could do so only by properly playing a Persian traditional instrument such as the *tar*, *setar*, or *santur*. It was during the presidency of Mohammad Khatami (1997–2005), at the time of the "reform era," that students wishing to pursue Western classical music could finally study at the university level. However, the thriving cultural scenes, or as Laudan Nooshin describes it, "cultural thaw" that occurred during Khatami's presidency, did not stop graduating students from moving abroad for further musical studies (Nooshin, 2005a, 231–72). Anecdotally, a cursory look at the substantial percentage of the first cohort of Western classical music graduates who left the country upon graduation demonstrates the unsteady ground on which music and its public education in Iran were formed. At least 50 percent of students of a cohort of about twenty-five who entered the University of Art-Tehran in the 1999–2000 academic year left the country to pursue further studies in music. I am among those students. Nevertheless, the situation was not limited to musicians who were socialized into Western aesthetics through classical or popular styles and genres. Persian classical and folk musicians were also subject to the unpredictable regulations imposed on musical production and education. It took painstaking energy, dedication, and devotion of determined and highly regarded musicians such as Mohammad Reza Shajarian, Mohammad Reza Lotfi, Hossein Alizadeh, and Parviz Meshkatian to make Persian classical music more accessible.

Beginning at the constitutional revolution of 1905, Arya Bastaninezhad presents a clear historical understanding of music pedagogy in Iran through what he classifies as "five major chronological events referred to as Nationalism, Modernism, Conservatism, Neo-traditionalism (Shirin-navazi), and Revivalism of Traditions" (Bastaninezhad, 2014, 5). Still, current public school education is not yet permitted to offer music as part of its curriculum, leaving music education to private studios, institutions, and cultural centers. Focusing on twenty years after the revolution, Ameneh Youssefzadeh provides a comprehensive picture of the official space of music detailing the ways in which a musician, regardless of the practicing genre, had to navigate their way into publishing an album or performing in public. Official recognition of a musician or ensemble can only be attained by gaining permission (*mojavez*, مجوز) from the Ministry of Arts and Islamic Guidance (وزارت فرهنگ و ارشاد اسلامی, vezārat-e farhang-o ershād-e eslāmi). This remains an arduous process with layers of administrative intricacies. According to Laudan Nooshin, because of the overly complicated procedure, a great many musicians forgo the process at the expense of not being formally legitimized (Nooshin, 2018, 353). To compound this problem, the system does not easily allow most Iranian women musicians to be officially recognized. Active musicians realize that those with the greatest number of views of their YouTube videos, the greater are their chances of being invited to international music festivals (362). Therefore, being a successful musician or music educator in Iran requires strategy and tact, as one has to constantly predict and gauge their moves either officially or unofficially, publicly or privately, nationally or internationally, online or offline, democratically or authoritatively. Here, I am not attempting to cast a binary outlook over the practice of music in Iran but would like to highlight the complex intersections of cultural policies in the day-to-day lives of Iranian musicians.

Even to this day, women cannot publicly perform solo in front of a mixed-gendered audience if they are vocalists. Rather, a combination with other voices is always necessary for public singing by women to be permissible. However, the billowing situation of music has not been limited to only women musicians. Men from a lower socioeconomic status also face discrimination. Nooshin, along with other scholars such as Bronwell Robertson and Nahid Siamdoust (2012), details these unpredictable conditions through analysis of prominent musical movements that occurred after the 1979 revolution, when President Khatami, under the auspices of the "Dialogue of Civilizations," opened spaces where music and specific genres such as rock, metal, and progressive jazz could flourish. Following the revolution, these genres were tightly gripped by hard-hitting regulations and banned from being practiced or publicly acknowledged. The major reason for the illegality of such genres after 1979 was their Western roots, perceived imperialism and colonialism, and ties to the shah's unequivocal bend toward U.S. foreign policies in the region. Music festivals, such as the 2006 Iranian Intergalactic Music Festival in Zaandam, The Netherlands, and music competitions, such as The Underground Music Competition in 2002, that was hosted by tehranavenue.com, increased the exposure of these genres and the musicians that performed them (see Nooshin, 2005b and 2008). This, ironically, helped to legitimatize them, albeit unofficially. However, it should be noted that these musical practices have been mainly the enterprise of male middle-class musicians, excluding for the most part, female musicians, and male musicians from the lower socioeconomic strata.

The internet has not only accelerated the growth of such genres but has also provided a much needed alternate space for musicians to find like-minded artists in Iran and abroad. It has allowed them to present their works with fewer constraints, and portray themselves as they wish, negotiating the complex musical identities that both national and international media assign to them (Nooshin, 2018, 345). Commenting on this phenomenon, Nooshin states, "The Internet thus provided a serendipitous lifeline through which musicians could reach both local and more geographically dispersed audiences, including those who might not have had access to the music event with a sanctioned public presence within Iran" (353). More specifically, Niknafs (2020) details the presence of the internet in the music of bands such as B-Band, where it became a crucial part of their collective identity. The internet was crucial for this band's survival due to their geographical isolation and distance.

Other musical genres that gained momentum were more inclusive of a diverse array of socioeconomic statuses. *Pop-e Farsi* was completely sanctioned by the state and freely broadcasted on state radio and TV, and with the inclusion of hip-hop, it became a contested, yet cherished, site for people of all walks of life, especially women from historically disenfranchised neighborhoods and cities. Writing on *rap-e Farsi* in Tehran, Nooshin features a female emcees' emergence to prominence stating that, "[Koli's story] conveys the social opprobrium attached to music performance for women, particularly in the domain of popular music . . .female rappers such as Koli face both social pressures—resistance to hip-hop per se and reputational risks to themselves and their families—and considerable legal risks" (2011, 21). Because poetry has been traditionally held in such high esteem in Iranian culture, rap-e Farsi enjoys a vibrant popularity for its accessibility and textual prominence.

The election of President Mahmoud Ahmadinejad in 2005, "the post-reform era," has yet again dramatically altered the face and content of cultural production in Iran. Many bands and musical genres that previously enjoyed relatively easy access to educational opportunities, practice, and performance, retreated to their proverbial basements and rooftops. Rooftops in Iran occupy a significant role in the political, social, and cultural life of the public. As they can be considered semiprivate spaces of the home, they have been used in many shapes and forms by the public throughout the years to circumvent the strict political and cultural regulations pre- and post-revolution. Examples such as prerevolutionary nighttime chanting during the shah era, or "hiding" the satellite dishes as contraband, or practicing or producing music videos on the rooftops are only a few examples demonstrating their significant role in assisting the circulation of sociocultural practices and political movements (see Alikhah, 2008; Leone, 2012; and Kheshti, 2015.

These new restrictions resulted in another wave of musicians leaving the country. Ahmadinejad's disputed, and much debated, 2009 second term presidential victory made the situation even more complicated. Political repression after the green movement cast a dark shadow over the content and aesthetics of what was musically permissible. Anecdotally, I have also heard from Iranian colleagues that the quality of music education and delivery in universities deteriorated greatly during Ahmadinejad's presidency. However, with the presidency of Hassan Rouhani in 2013, new hope was injected into the country. Rouhani promised a more lenient outlook toward social life and hoped to negotiate with the West concerning the country's nuclear program. As a result, the number of public popular music performances increased, more women musicians performed publicly, and a plethora of private schools launched music education programs that emphasized the value of a more comprehensive education. Rouhani's two terms as president coincided with that of Donald Trump's presidency in the United States. Trump's withdrawal from the hard-won 2015 Joint Comprehensive Plan of Action once again complicated cultural policy in the country and cultural diplomacy outside its borders and, in the end, resulted in dissatisfaction with Rouhani's performance as a president.[1] Today, much remains unclear concerning the political and cultural affairs of Iran, both domestically and internationally. One must wait to see the shift in cultural tides in the country, which may again depend on the new president's cultural policies in accord with the regime's guidelines.

Thus far, I have only briefly portrayed the state of official and unofficial music in Iran after the 1979 revolution, with the hope of demonstrating the complex and malleable relationships between cultural policy, music performance, and music education. I illustrated the impact that top-down cultural policies and bottom-up cultural materialization have on each other. A more thorough description of individual genres is beyond the scope of this chapter. All musical practices in Iran are mediated and directly influenced by cultural policies dictated by the state. Changes in presidencies and their contingent reliance on the regime's goals and ethos, combined with the variety of music afforded to the public by the World Wide Web make it a difficult labyrinth to navigate for musicians and music educators. Even a slight change in the lyrics, instrumentation, musicians, or audiences can shift the official discourse and its consequences. For example, the number of public performances of Persian pop has skyrocketed to the extent that it is making *pop-e Losāngelesi* (literally, pop music from Los Angeles) obsolete. At least three out of five musicians with whom I corresponded preferred the more open space of music-making, even if one of them lamented that such space also allowed what they deemed as the proliferation of lower quality or *bad* music (interview with participant, November 22, 2017).[2] Yet, the same musicians acknowledged that the progression and development of quality music directly depends on the quantity of music being produced, performed, and taught. Despite the audience being encouraged not to stand up from their seats or dance to the music, rock and metal bands have found a way to publicly perform their music by couching it as fusion music (*moosighi-e Talfiqi*). All these nuances shape a broader agenda of the Islamic Republic, which they term *soft power*. Considering this situation, I propose that cultural production, education, and consumption are very much integrated, highly contextualized, and influenced by both the public (bottom-up) and the state (top-down); neither of which are constructed by homogenous and uniform ideologies but of human actors with diverse worldviews, opinions, and corresponding actions. The ever-changing realities, goals, and agendas of state and public actors remind us that "the sign whereby we convey 'self-evident truths' have histories of their own," especially in the case of Iran (Herzfeld, 2016, 78).

SOFT WAR CULTURAL POLICIES

Throughout my research working with Iranian rock musicians in Tehran and the diaspora from 2014 until 2019, I witnessed a significant expansion in the kinds, genres, and education of musical practices in the country.[3] This period saw growth in the number of home studios, an increase in public performances, more live music in cafes, and even a surge in street musicians in the crowded streets of Tehran. A bustling city like this gives one a feeling of hope, especially after years of restrictions placed on music production, circulation, and education. Nonetheless, it was clear from both personal experience and research that this might only be a façade or a phase very much dependent on the elected president and his cultural policies, as was also clearly highlighted by one musician, King Raam, with whom I conducted interviews: "I'm working so hard nonstop because you never know. Some shit might go down and it all may come apart, as good as it is right now [referring to early Rouhani years]" (Niknafs, 2016, 360). Unfortunately, his speculations excruciatingly turned out to be true, as he lost his father in the Iranian political prison system. In the bedrock of the regime's decisive cultural policies against what they perceive as cultural invasion of the West, they adopted a "vaccination" strategy against *soft war* (Bajoghli, 2019, 39).[4]

The term *soft war* in Iran is an adaptation of Joseph Nye's concept of soft power, described as "the ability to get what you want through attraction rather than coercion or payments" (2004, 256). This resignification of a Western political term, or as Annabelle Sreberny remarks as a "clever play" and "linguistic reconstruction," is not unprecedented in the Iranian political discourse (2013, 802). Terms such as "axis of resistance" directly modified from George W. Bush's "axis of evil," or "dialogue of civilizations," coopted by President Mohammad Khatami from Samuel Huntington's "clash of civilizations" are but only two examples that illustrate the Islamic Republic's "considerable attention to Western foreign policy discourses" (2013, 802). According to Emily L. Blout (2017), the term *soft war* emerged around the turn of the century in Iran but its use and circulation in the media doubled between 2008 and 2009, tripled after the disputed 2009 elections, and became ubiquitous in the rhetoric of the regime since then (212).

Domestic and international debates around the definitions of the term *soft war* and its cultural implications in Iran abound. Generally, inside the borders the term implies that Iranian affairs remain under constant covert threat from the outside. More specifically, in Farzan Sabet and Roozbeh Safshekan's terms, "Soft war is the exercise of soft power by the United States on Iran such that it creates security challenges for the Islamic Republic and forces it to respond" (2013, 4). This rhetoric creates a mythical and unassailable enemy that could benefit and justify the restricted and heavily regulated cultural policies. Blout argues that this mythical narrative is deeply communication-centric and hits the media arena the hardest (2017, 221). However, what is unequivocal is Iran's sustained historical wounds from Western nations' implicit and explicit invasions, or their proxies' offensives toward it, throughout the years. This, many argue, fortuitously gave rise to the Islamic Republic's conspiratorial rhetoric (221). For example, the MI6-planned and CIA-operated coup d'état against the elected prime minister Mohammad Mosaddeq in 1953 following his nationalization of the Anglo-Iranian Oil Company in 1951, resulted in the impression that Iran was leaning toward the Soviet Union's communist agenda (see Abrahamian, 2013). Another example is the Iran-Iraq war of 1980–1988, which was "characterized by trench warfare and chemical weapons . . . [where] most Arab Countries supported Iraq, and regional and international powers played the two countries against one another" (Bajoghli, 2019, 4). There is also abundant ongoing evidence that the "story of the conflict the Islamic Republic calls soft war is in many ways the story of the exercise of U.S. soft power on Iran" since the mid-nineteenth century (Sabet and Safshekan, 2013, 6). A recent example is the Iran Democracy Fund that was initiated by George W. Bush's administration in 2006 "as part of an approach to regime change in Iran" (Price, 2012, 2402). The current controversial quagmire of Iran's nuclear program with the P5+1 group is another example of Western nations' interest in the country's affairs, demonstrating that "the interventions were not only a physical commandeering of the state, but also of the Iranian mind through manipulation of news and public opinion" (Blout, 2017, 215).

In such contexts, it is unsurprising that official state rhetoric would take advantage of these historical moments, exploit national sentiment, and consolidate the somewhat opposing views of the national vis-à-vis Islamic identity in the country. Thus, from the Iranian state perspective, there would be an organic inclination to accept and adapt the discourse of soft power with its affordances in "attracting" and alluring the domestic and international audience over "hard responses" (Sabet and Safshekan, 2013, 17). These hard responses can manifest in many forms, such as confiscation of cassettes, satellite dishes, and alcohol; rejection of album permissions, public performances and displays of love and affection; or prevention of dancing, busking in the streets, and wearing outfits considered Western. Seeking to keep the prevailing narrative intact in the face of clear anxieties regarding how to sustain the ethos of the Islamic Revolution, the regime's media producers are thinking creatively about ways to keep the younger generations interested in such discourse given that the younger generation of Iranians have no collective memory and lived experiences of the shah era, the 1979 revolution, and the Iran-Iraq War (see Bajoghli, 2019). Consequently, "the old slogans of the revolution [do] not represent many of their needs" (Sabet and Safshekan, 2013, 15). The rhetoric of soft war thus becomes handy to keep public opinion attracted and loyal to the Islamic Republic.

Blout argues that the conspiratorial rhetoric of the Islamic Republic through soft war and propaganda campaign, even if well-founded, is merely a myth that works as an offensive strategy to have a grip on the social and political life of the residents. By blocking certain websites and applications, reducing internet access, and later the launch of "Permanent Bureau for Soft War" to resist against foreign powers' intrusions, Iran can use a perceived Western threat to maintain control over access to information (Blout, 2017, 219). Blout further explicates, "As a variation of the myth of foreign conspiracy, soft war helps explain the enmity between the governments of the United States and Iran, as well as the distribution of power within Iran.... As interpreted by the proponents of this narrative, the specter of soft war necessitates a security state and corresponding censorship and restriction of expression and press" (221). However, Sabet and Safshekan (2013) paint a different picture on the soft war rhetoric in Iran highlighting that as much as the Islamic Republic was successful in its coercive responses to "US primary currencies (hard response), it has been much less successful in creating attractive indigenous primary currencies (soft response) ... because [they] are not monopolized by the state but are mainly produced by civil society" (17). Not dismissing or downplaying the harsh realities and frustrating materialities of cultural censorship through soft war's rhetoric, I further expand Sabet and Safshekan's proposition that not all this soft war discourse is effective, nor is it persuasive concerning cultural practices. Rather, I suggest that it is the cultural workers and, in our case, musicians who dictate the cultural intricacies on the ground despite the outright and restrictive regulations from above. Soft war rhetoric has the capacity to be molded. The public, too, can also coopt the soft war rhetoric to its own benefit and shift the discourse.

MUSICAL IMPLEMENTATIONS OF THE SOFT WAR RHETORIC

According to Narges Bajoghli, there exists an acute cultural and media campaign for (re)educating Iranian youth to pull them back into the early war rhetoric, a backbone narrative of the Islamic Republic (see Bajoghli, 2019). Although taking the lives of millions, the Iran-Iraq War solidified the Islamic Republic's hold of power. Now in control of the narrative, it is unsurprising that authorities continue to make a "conscious decision" to "transform the war from a military confrontation with Iraq to a cultural and social confrontation in Iranian cities and towns" (60). Yet, for this narrative to take hold again, I argue that the artistic and cultural language of the youth need to first be coopted by the state. Critiquing the regime's tactics, one of Bajoghli's interlocutors from the ruling regime remarked,

> We need to stop framing our story as one that's just about the Islamic Republic ... it needs to be about Iran. Our young people may not defend the regime because they don't feel a part of it, but they will rise up to defend Iran as the thing that we're all defending, not just a regime or ideology ... that's why we need to make films that people don't think we made. We need to hide the fact that we're the ones making the films they see. (5)

I would argue that this is not a unilateral relationship, and the reverse can concomitantly happen. The statespersons in the Islamic Republic as living actors can also be very much influenced by the everyday cultural and musical practices and embody a shared cultural intimacy (see Herzfeld, 2016). This is appositely highlighted by Herzfeld, "The state so fully adopts the cultural signs of that intimacy in order to permeate the oppressed citizens' every sentient moment that it reciprocally exposes itself to greater day-to-day manipulations by the same citizens" (31). Cultural wars remain as a continuation of class wars of the revolution. According to Bajoghli, although ruling class and their families have gained economic capital throughout the years, they still struggle to have access to the social and cultural capital that (*gheyr-e khody*) outsiders enjoy (2019, 80). Therefore, it is critical to examine cultural artifacts and creative processes to unravel the relationships and interconnectivity between these various sides.

One of the music videos of the all-boy band Safir-e Eshgh's (Harbinger of Love), reflects the notion that musicians and music educators maintain a more significant role in the cultural shifts than one would assume. On their homepage, front and center, sits a clean shot of the current adolescent members in slick grey suits but with a peculiarly updated and westernized version of modest attire. Their hands rest one over the other, with heads slightly lowered to show humility and modesty. Below the photo is a quote by the supreme leader: "Deeply understanding cultural concepts, both for the people and for the authorities, while increasing their awareness can prevent from cultural cracks and this is one of the most important characteristics of a right cultural activity" (Rahimpour, 2021).[5] The essence of this quotation is further elaborated in the "About Us" section where the significance of cultural activities, along with economic ones, are meant to generate meaningful pathways in any society and government. Under the umbrella of "right cultural activity," this ensemble's musical activities solidify the soft war rhetoric that "culture" is the place to put the most attention.

Yet, it is in their music video, *Qalb-e Ārām* (Calm Heart), where we see the clearest statement for this notion (Safir Eshgh International Symphony Ensemble YouTube video, 2021). The video begins with an out of focus shot of these young men in their sharp suits and sweater vests, coming from the far end of an alley and entering a mosque that seems to be the Haram-e Motahhar (Mausoleum of Ruhollah Khomeini). Following the ritual of removing shoes before entering the hall, they showcase their respect toward this spiritual and holy place. At the bedrock of a lamenting piano and electric guitar, the group begins singing in unison and in English: "Khomeini is the second name of Iran." In the following shot coinciding with the line, "A man of deep thinking and of his words," the audience sees these singers without their shoes and jackets, but creating a semi-circle, symbolizing the preparation for *namāz-e jamā'at* (congregational prayers). While continuing the praise of Khomeini, the lead singer at 0:39 seconds, with his acute theatricality of a solo singer, begins the first verse.

Overlooking the cinematography and imagery of this music video, the song itself in B minor can be considered a catchy pop/rock song with a memorable chorus emphasized by its drumbeat, which sounds to be either highly edited samples or programmed on a drum machine. While the chord progression switches often, except in the 2nd and 4th choruses and 1st and 2nd interludes, the solo guitar with its raw sound shines through, ironically reminiscent of the lyrical style of Joe Satriani or Steve Vai of the 1990s. The lyrics reflect a sense of nationalism:

> So, Iran will forever last and of course,
> Khomeini is the second name of Iran

Yet, the neumatic ornamentations of the solo vocalist betray a contextualized song in the style of *maddāhi*, a Shi'a-oriented eulogy recitation in praise of persons of high piety and sanctity in Shi'a Islam. Combining it with a touch of deep dynamic rock vocal style in the second verse, the solo vocalist attracts a young audience who does not necessarily engage with typical cultural productions of the regime (Bajoghli, 2019, 100).

With the full production value, musical genre, and practice that for years has been banned from public live performances, radio, and TV, this *Namāhang* music video (a combination of *namā* (view) and *āhang* (song, tune) highlights the regime cultural producers' PR campaign that "have begun to pour money and resources into producing music videos that they hope young people will not only consume but also make viral on Instagram and Telegram" (Bajoghli 2019, 105). The producers employ an acute tactic to intermingle Khomeini with nationalism through showing his *jamārān* home and direct references to "Iran" rather than the "Islamic Republic." The lyrics of the song are entirely in English, showcasing the ensemble's hopeful reach to the international market. The caption below the video, along with introducing the production team and musicians, notes this was commissioned by the Setād-e Bozorgdāsht-e Hazrat-e Emām Khomeini (Committee for Celebration of Imam Khomeini) to be broadcast by all national and international channels. By getting "soft" on the permissible musical genres and dress codes, this music video highlights a "projected counter-strategy (beyond the much-recognized processes of censorship and control of the press and broadcasting)" (Price, 2012, 2407).

There are more such examples, now prevalent in the official domestic and international TV channels and media outlets employing similar strategies "to resonate with their desired audience; [the regime media producers] needed a unifying story. This new story presented itself in the form of populist nationalism in general population" (Bajoghli, 2019, 100). For instance, Amir Tataloo's controversial collaboration with the regime media producers through the music video, *Nuclear Energy* (2015, YouTube video), was an outright violation of their own musical regulations on the ground. Bajoghli extensively discusses this music video highlighting

> The video, with clear support from the regime and its military apparatus, shocked many Iranians, given that officials have snubbed rappers as Westernized thugs at best and fomenters of evil at worst. The military's participation in a music video with an underground artist who flaunts his tattoos, long hair, and piercings, perplexed many Iranians. However, I had seen the Revolutionary Guard's media producers use this strategy since the rise of the Green Movement. (2019, 104)

As much as these examples depict shrewd soft war tactics in attracting the younger generation and selling them Islamic Republic rhetoric, they also reveal the regime's limited grip on the pulse of cultural practices in the country, and even on their own side of the regime. Tataloo's participation and collaboration in this music video not only dramatically reduced his street cred as a sellout, but it brought about controversy within the regime, specifically with the Islamic Revolutionary Guard Corps that "Iran's armed forces 'are more dignified than to become propaganda for such an infamous singer'" (Kashani, 2015, para. 5). The matter of complex soft war tactics is not only about *sounding* or *looking* like what the public already consumes or engages in, but whether the state actors are already and intimately enjoying such cultural artifacts as their guilty pleasures. The soft war rhetoric, in this vein, is opening avenues for both levels of the state and the public—with vastly diverse ideologies, modes of thinking, and doing even within each group—to intelligently, but perhaps covertly to enjoy a certain level of "grassroots social, political, and cultural freedom" (Sabet and Safshekan, 2013, 20).

CONCLUSION

In Iran, the state of music constantly and rapidly changes to the point that even in the timespan of a research project, delineations alter, and sociological concepts of music education and production shift in new directions. This can indeed be traced back as much to the cultural policies imposed or implied on musicians as to the semantic and sociopolitical discrepancies between the internal and external debates around the ruling authority in the country, and what is considered to be the *regime* (the Islamic Republic) versus the government (*Dowlat*).[6] Yet while the change of presidencies has unquestionably given music different lights, the constant denominator was its challenging stance as an individual and collective mode of expression.

Thinking through Goff's perceptions of cultural diplomacy as endeavours that "can offset negative, stereotypical, or overly simplistic impressions arising from policy choices or from hostile portrayals," the Iranian regime has the opportunity to open conversation both within and outside the borders to cast a better picture of indigenous cultural practices (Goff, 2013, 442). Yet, according to Sabet and Safshekan, there are two general reasons that attempt to create "attractive indigenous sources of soft power" that have been relatively unsuccessful: "the lack of a vibrant economy," and more importantly, "the Islamic Republic's restrictions on both elite and grass-roots social, political and cultural freedoms, as well as poor state-civil society relations" (Sabet and Safshekan, 2013, 20).

The above-mentioned music videos exemplify the regime's soft war rhetoric, par excellence. Employing popular means through cultural production or nationalistic and spiritual sentiments, the two examples showcase the regime's *selective* leniency toward media and cultural practices on the ground. Yet I cannot help but also think that this outwardly acceptance of youth culture in Iran is not merely a soft war strategy, but an implicit inclination toward expanding cultural practices that sees a shift in "power distribution" among the cultural workers of the regime and public (Herzfeld, 2016, 69). I maintain that it is not as much about soft war cultural policies where musical practices have yielded to more open renditions and, perhaps, global aesthetics. Rather, this is an intricate, emergent cultural action from the bottom-up, attempting to find its newly developed voice through the rise of global national populism. Irrespective of the ruling regime, nuclear quagmire with Western nations, the media's unequivocal influence on the circulation of factual and fake information, and public relations' contested domination over the actual cultural narratives on the ground, the everyday influences of the soft war within the country should be examined from a more empirical outlook rather than an abstract binary of official cultural policies and diplomacy vis-à-vis grassroots endeavors of the public (2016). Neither of these bodies could be essentialized into opposing homogenized entities. The regime and the public comprise of living actors who share "embarrassing but comforting intimacies" through cultural intimacy that offer "the counter-vision of a 'common humanity' (*anthropia*) that incorporates the idea of accepting moral responsibility for what one does to others" (158–59).

Soft war strategies or not, these open spaces of cultural practice afford citizens the means to decipher and establish *relationships* among one another in voicing the said apprehensions and anxieties. Not limiting themselves to the top-down cultural policies, the public has a covert influence on how these policies shift in discourse, which disrupts a linear and simple justification of prolonged years of restrictive musical and cultural regulations in the country. One should not look at the cultural, musical, and educational practices in Iran through a binary prism. Rather, I argue that a circular and shifting discourse and dissemination of power is at play between those in power at the top and those who make music in the streets, *and* everyone in between.

NOTES

1. According to Patricia M. Goff, "Cultural diplomacy rests on the assumption that art, language and education are among the most significant entry points into a culture," which can soften strenuous relations between opposing parties (2013, 419). Trump's withdrawal from the 2015 JCPOA not only hardened the already strained relations between the two nations, but also made it extraordinarily difficult for the cultural workers in the country to create welcoming and thriving cultural spaces. At the writing of this chapter, Iran had agreed to permit UN personnel to monitor its nuclear program with the hope of lifting US sanctions, https://www.theguardian.com/world/2021/sep/12/iran-agrees-deal-with-un-on-monitoring-of-nuclear-programme.

2. These five well-known musicians are King Raam, Behzad Khiavchi, Behzad Omrani, Dara Daraie, and Kaveh Salehi all of whom have also experienced the Khatami era's cultural thaw.

3. This period coincided with the presidency of Hassan Rouhani, a reformist whose pledge to reopen cultural spaces after the harsh years of Mahmoud Ahmadinejad tremendously helped his campaign. However, the tides have changed since then, and a major part of the population is dissatisfied with his economic outcomes.

4. The rhetoric of cultural invasion of the West in Iran has historical roots in the pre-revolutionary years. The shah's outright adoption of Western modernity's

ideologies and implementation of their corresponding policies in a country with a highly contextualized history with religious rituals and traditions made a great many people dissatisfied. Moreover, these "modernizing" policies created great economic, cultural, and political chasms in the country. Accordingly, one of the largest messages of the post-revolutionary ethos was to go against any political, cultural, and social movements that represented even a sliver of the West, which could only bring devastation, colonialism, and political dependence. One can trace these thoughts in the writings of the supreme leaders Khomeini (1981) and Khamenei (1994).

5. After the revolution, dress codes both for women and men have been a demarcation of allegiance to the Islamic Republic. While compulsory hijab for women has been a regulating force of their bodies, men were also encouraged, and at times forced, to comply with the Islamic codes of conduct. According to Bajoghli, "In an attempt to do away with 'frivolous' Western fashions, which has been advocated in the Shah's regime, the Islamic Republic outlawed neckties." (2019, 78). What makes this image and attire in the music video peculiar are the collared shirts with open buttons rather than the "yaqeh akhundi" (cleric's collar) shirts that should remain untucked, which for years has been the signature look of men allied to the ruling class; the word for word translations are by the author.

6. Narges Bajoghli has profoundly contextualized this dichotomy and offered a persuasive account of the difference between these two entities.

REFERENCES

Abrahamian, Ervand. 2013. *The Coup: 1953, The CIA, And the Roots of Modern U.S.-Iranian Relations.* New York: The New Press.

Alikhah, Fardin. 2008. "The Politics of Satellite Television in Iran." In *Media, Culture and Society in Iran: Living with Globalization and the Islamic Republic*, edited by Mehdi Semati, 94–110. Abingdon: Routledge.

Bajoghli, Narges. 2019. *Iran Reframed: Anxieties of Power in the Islamic Republic.* Stanford, CA: Stanford University Press.

Bastaninezhad, Arya. 2014. "A Historical Overview of Iranian Music Pedagogy (1905–2014)." *Australian Journal of Music Education 4*, no. 2: 5–22.

Blout, E. L. 2017. "Soft War: Myth, Nationalism, and Media in Iran." *The Communication Review 20*, no. 3: 212–24.

Calmheart Safir Eshgh International Symphony Ensemble. 2021. YouTube video. https://www.aparat.com/v/ZlvDC.

Goff, Patricia M. 2013. "Cultural Diplomacy," In *The Oxford Handbook of Modern Diplomacy*, edited by Andrew F. Cooper, Jorge Heine, and Ramesh Thakur, 419–34. Oxford University Press.

Herzfeld, Michael. 2016. *Cultural Intimacy: Social Poetics and the Real Life of States, Societies, and Institutions.* Abingdon, UK: Routledge.

Hemmasi, Farzaneh. 2020. *Tehrangeles Dreaming: Intimacy and Imagination in Southern California's Iranian Pop Music.* Durham, NC: Duke University Press.

Kashani, Hanif. 2015. "Iranian Rapper Drops Bomb with Pro-Nuke Video." *Al-Monitor*, July 14. https://www.al-monitor.com/originals/2015/07/FOR%20WED%20iran-rapper-tataloo-video.html.

Khamenei, Seyyed Ali. 1994. *Farhang va Tahajom-e Farhangi*. Tehran, Iran: Sazman-e Farhangi-e Enqelab-e Eslami.

Khomeini, Ruhollah. 1981. *Velayat-e Faqih: Hokumat-e Eslami*. Tehran, Iran: Amir Kabir.

Kheshti, Roshanak. 2015. "On the Threshold of the Political: The Sonic Performativity of Rooftop Chanting in Iran." *Radical History Review* 2015, no. 121: 51–70.

Leone, Massimo. 2012. "My Schoolmate: Protest Music in Present-Day Iran." *Critical Discourse Studies* 9, no. 4: 347–62.

Lucas, Ann E. 2019. *Music of a Thousand Years: A New History of Persian Musical Traditions*. Berkeley: University of California Press.

Nettl, Bruno. 2005. *The Study of Ethnomusicology: Thirty-one Issues and Concepts*. Urbana: University of Illinois Press.

Niknafs, Nasim. 2016. "In a Box: A Narrative of a/n (Under) Grounded Iranian Musician." *Music Education Research* 18, no. 4: 351–63.

———. 2020. "Music Education as the Herald of a Cosmopolitan Collective Imperative: On Being Human." *International Journal of Music Education* 38, no. 1: 3–17.

Nooshin, Laudan. 2005a. "Subversion and Countersubversion: Power, Control, and Meaning in the New Iranian Pop Music," In *Music, Power and Politics*, edited by A. J. Randall, 231–72. New York: Routledge.

———. 2005b. "Underground, Overground: Rock Music and Youth Discourses in Iran." *Iranian Studies* 38, no. 3: 463–94.

———. 2008. "The Language of Rock: Iranian Youth, Popular Music and Iranian Identity." In *Media, Culture and Society in Iran: Living with Globalization and the Islamic Republic*, edited by Mehdi Semati, 69–93. Abingdon: Routledge.

———. 2011. "Hip-Hop Tehran: Migrating Styles, Musical Meanings, Marginalised Voices." In *Migrating Music*, edited by Jason Toynbee, and Byron Dueck, 92–111. Abingdon: Routledge.

———. 2018. "'Our Angel of Salvation': Toward an Understanding of Iranian Cyberspace as an alternative Sphere of Musical Sociality." *Ethnomusicology* 62, no. 3 (Fall): 341–74.

Nye, Joseph. 2004. "Soft Power and American Foreign Policy." *Political Science Quarterly* 119, no. 2: 255–70.

Price, Monroe. 2012. "Iran and the Soft War." *International Journal of Communication* 6: 2397–415.

Rahimpour. 2021. گروه هم آوایی بین المللی صفیر عشق [Safir Eshgh International Symphony Ensemble]. Accessed November 11. http://www.safire-eshgh.ir/.

Robertson, Bronwen. 2012. *Reverberations of Dissent: Identity and Expression in Iran's Music Scene*. London, UK: Continuum.

Sabet, Farzan, and Roozbeh Safshekan. 2013. "Soft War: A New Episode in the Old Conflicts Between Iran and the United States." *Iran Media Program*. https://repository.upenn.edu/iranmediaprogram/9.

Semati, Mehdi. 2008. *Media, Culture and Society in Iran: Living with Globalization and the Islamic State.* Abingdon: Routledge.
Siamdoust, Nahid. 2017. *Soundtrack of the Revolution: The Politics of Music in Iran.* Stanford. CA: Stanford University Press.
Sreberny, Annabelle. 2013. "Too Soft on 'Soft War:' Commentary on Monroe Price's 'Iran and the Soft War.'" *International Journal of Communication* 7: 801–04.
Sreberny, Annabelle and Gholam Khiabany. 2010. *Blogistan: The Internet and Politics in Iran.* London, UK: I. B. Tauris.
Tataloo, Amir. 2015. Energy Hasteei YouTube video, 3:19. July 12. Amir Tataloo. Energy Hasteei.
Youssefzadeh, Ameneh. 2000. "The Situation of Music in Iran since the Revolution: The Role of Official Organizations." *British Journal of Ethnomusicology* 9, no. 2: 35–61.

3

EAST ASIAN VIEWS

Chapter Seven

Cultural Diplomacy in Collaborative Music Projects between China and Europe

Marianne Løkke Jakobsen and David G. Hebert

This chapter presents insights from innovative musical collaborations between China and Europe developed through one author's long-term role as director of the Music Confucius Institute (MCI) in Copenhagen and the other author's residency as a Hanban Visiting Scholar at the Central Conservatory of Music, Beijing. The chapter offers a multifaceted exploration of several related themes: (1) Chinese music activities and approaches to leadership at the MCI, (2) reflections of Chinese traditional instrument pedagogues on their experience of teaching for both the MCI in Copenhagen and Central Conservatory of Music in Beijing, and (3) observations and recommendations concerning the Confucius Institute system as a form of "soft power" and Chinese cultural diplomacy, and the prospective role of music in such international initiatives.

BACKGROUND

Today, China is known worldwide as a major power in such fields as research, technology, and manufacturing, and the nation has become increasingly active in international affairs. Since the mid-twenieth century, Chinese musical heritage has been sustained by such elite institutions as the Central Conservatory (in Beijing), China Conservatory (also in Beijing), and Shanghai Conservatory. Chinese traditional music entails invaluable heritage that is fully recognized by an array of cultural policies within China, but it is also increasingly relevant beyond national borders. In addition to China boasting the world's largest national population, across recent centuries there has also been a large population of Chinese living outside the country, especially in Southeast Asia, but also the United States, and the total overseas Chinese population is now estimated to be approximately fifty million (much larger than the total population of many countries). Among such overseas Chinese, traditional Chinese music has long been taught and learned in community schools as a way of sustaining cultural connections with the homeland, but in recent times elite music schools in Europe have also begun offering professional level studies in Chinese traditional music, often to non-Chinese students. The purpose of such education is entirely different from that of diasporic Chinese learning heritage of their homeland, and is better understood as part of cultural diplomacy initiatives that support internationalization by broadening global appreciation for Chinese cultural heritage (Goff, 2013). Such teaching of Chinese music in diverse contexts deserves more attention, as indicated in multiple studies (Ho, 2018, 2021; Yao 2012).

MCI was a successful and high-profile institution in Scandinavia for nearly ten years, funded by Hanban as part of its global network of Confucius Institutes (CIs) and related educational and cultural initiatives. While most CIs have emphasized Chinese language learning, a small percentage have a special focus, which can be, for instance, on martial arts, Chinese traditional medicine, or music, among other possibilities. According to Hanban's website (hanban.org), "Benefiting from the UK, France, Germany and Spain's experience in promoting their national languages, China began its own exploration through establishing *non-profit public institutions which aim to promote Chinese language and culture* in foreign countries in 2004: these were given the name the Confucius Institute." Until 2020, Hanban's website also explained the purpose of CIs as "a platform for cultural exchanges between China and the world as well as a *bridge reinforcing friendship and cooperation between China and the rest of the world and are much welcomed across the globe.*" However, rather than universally being warmly welcomed, these institutions ultimately faced a complicated reception in many countries, leading to major redevelopment of the entire system. In 2020, Hanban was replaced by the Centre for Language Education and Cooperation, as the CI system was restructured, then sixteen years after its initial launch with explosive global expansion.

This chapter reflects the authors' personal experiences, juxtaposed against relevant theories and research findings. As such, it is useful to begin by sharing something about our experience in the field. Marianne Løkke Jakobsen worked for nine years as founding director of MCI in addition to her main role as director for international affairs at the Royal Danish Academy of Music in Copenhagen, Denmark. As MCI director, her responsibilities included a variety of tasks typically related to operations and management. In the beginning, much of her work focused on the establishment and implementation of the institute. This included developing its reputation, based on a form of reciprocal exchange with Scandinavia rather than purely a promotion of traditional Chinese culture. As director, it was essential to determine the organizational role (political, artistic, educational, or managerial) of each appointed board member from two partner institutions in Copenhagen and Beijing together to create a shared visionary strategy. Later, her work transitioned to stakeholder management on both institutional and national levels, which included mapping Sino-Danish relations in Denmark, possible regional community collaborations, and ongoing diplomatic and foreign relations engagement. In terms of daily operations, her duties as director included planning activities, fiscal management, implementation of quality assurance and evaluation procedures, and Sino-Danish staff training and collaborations.

David G. Hebert has lectured for twelve universities in China and in 2018 served as Hanban Visiting Scholar at the Central Conservatory of Music, Beijing, where he researched expert Chinese instrument teachers who had teaching experience in both Europe and China. Aware of both the opportunities and alleged threats attributed to CIs, he later spent three years carefully negotiating the development of a Hanban-sponsored Chinese Music Classroom in Bergen, but before it could be launched, the institution in Norway—under both political and financial pressure—withdrew its contract. Instead, it will now have a Vietnamese musician in residence for three years as a Swedish Research Council-funded postdoctoral researcher. Still, he remains active in China and has been awarded funding for online collaborations at the doctoral level in Hong Kong and Hainan.

The cases that serve as the basis for this chapter are unique in certain ways, and our close familiarity with directors at other CIs enables us to also report more broadly on the Hanban system as a whole. Moreover, the prominence of this case in terms of professional-level Chinese *music* activities abroad merits attention irrespective of the extent to which its features might be generalized to other CIs (Xing, 2009). Although musical activities and learning of various kinds were ultimately included at other CIs worldwide, the MCI in Copenhagen was the very first CI to specifically focus on music, and most likely the first conservatoire in Europe to specialize in professional level training within a specific East Asian music tradition. This has made it interesting for other schools in the field of cultural diplomacy.

PROFILE OF COPENHAGEN'S MUSIC CONFUCIUS INSTITUTE

The Central Conservatory of Music (CCOM) in Beijing and The Royal Danish Academy of Music (RDAM) established the Music Confucius

Institute in Copenhagen in 2012. Physically located within the RDAM, the MCI operated for eight years and closed in December 2020. The institute organized activities that included lectures, workshops, and concerts in collaboration with local partners, businesses, Danish/Chinese organizations, and RDAM students in the Copenhagen area. Every year MCI hosted a group of six to eight dispatched musicians with world-class expertise in playing and teaching traditional Chinese instruments. CCOM, a leading music conservatory in Beijing, selected the Chinese musicians. The institute was comanaged in collaboration with Chinese vice directors during those eight years. The first vice director was a Chinese percussion player; the second was a musicologist with expertise in the field of world music. Every year, the MCI had several recurring activities as well as other pioneering stand-alone ("one-off") projects, all of which depended on high levels of musicianship in order to brand MCI as an institute that promoted intercultural artistic collaboration.

One important initiative was the national high school collaboration that brought young high school music students together with Chinese musicians (graduate students from CCOM, categorized as voluntary teachers). The MCI's annually growing number of concerts, which were well attended by a diverse audience, as well as its teaching activities expanded the public outreach for RDAM. In addition to traditional classical music attendees, these opportunities attracted younger people with personal interests in China and others who intentionally sought out different cultural experiences. However, the MCI faced limited internal engagement due to RDAM's profile as an institution mainly charged with educating professional performers in the field of Western classical music.

Growing political tensions between the United States and China also created negative media attention around the very notion of CIs as a concept based on the assumed ambition of Chinese global control. Our focus on the vision of relationship building and artistic cocreation was a challenge in a period of polarization between East and West. The COVID-19 pandemic's severe travel restrictions prevented the MCI from continuing its range of activities and the decision from Hanban to change the overall structure of CIs with a more articulated focus on language learning from August 2020 challenged the MCI in new ways. The increasing obstacles and the vision of the MCI ultimately did not match. Maintaining the brand and image of MCI as an institute bringing cultures together became extremely difficult to maintain. Eventually, a proposal was initiated by RDAM to close the MCI, which finally ceased operations at the end of 2020.

CASE STUDIES: CHINESE INSTRUMENT TEACHERS IN EUROPE AND CHINA

In 2018, Hebert conducted research on the experiences of elite Chinese instrumental musicians who had taught at both the MCI, the European Union's first MCI, and the CCOM in Beijing. The purpose was to explore the intercultural music teacher exchange experience as well as consider the perceived differences between Chinese and Scandinavian music students and the milieu of higher education institutions. Hebert visited the MCI multiple times, and as part of the case study research, he spoke several times with the Chinese and Danish directors and interviewed musical instrument teachers who had returned to Beijing where he also observed their teaching and collected relevant documents, including curriculum, teaching materials, and concert programs.

Intercultural exchange was identified as an important goal shared by the music teachers in these case studies. As one of the Chinese music teachers explained, "Nowadays, many foreigners only know that Confucius Institute teach Chinese [language], but as people all over the world grow to love Chinese music, they will know more and more about the height and depth of Chinese culture." Another explained that "the main advantage of studying Chinese music in a Confucius Institute is not only to learn musical instruments but also to have a comprehensive understanding of Chinese culture."

The Chinese instrument teachers used various pedagogical techniques, some of which are different from their counterparts in Europe. For example, when observing *pipa* and *guqin* lessons in Beijing, David Hebert noticed how the one-on-one lessons were very intense yet still maintained a positive and friendly atmosphere. The pipa teacher used narrative approaches to explain the meaning of the songs but also had the student practice specific techniques, such as a tremolo from a very soft pianissimo, with a steady crescendo to fortissimo, and back again to pianissimo, while maintaining even tremolo with perfect control. In terms of narrative, she explained to the student how in the case of "Ambush from all Sides" (a famous traditional piece), the most passionate part of it indicates the fear and desperate cries as soldiers attack from all directions. As a contrast, "Dancing in the Mountain" (a contemporary piece) illustrates the pure and heartfelt sentiments of young love, specifically between teenagers.

At the guqin lesson, a nineteen-year-old student was learning the famous piece "Recalling an Old Friend" (Li and Zhao, 2017, 141). During the lesson, the student played the instrument but never asked questions, only nodding, and making brief affirmations, the equivalent of "yeah" or "okay." The teacher frequently interrupted to demonstrate better ways of phrasing and use of finger techniques, often emphasizing the importance of expressive phrasing. The teacher very often sang in solfege as she demonstrated how to play phrases more expressively, repeating something the student had played but with added nuance. The teacher emphasized subtle issues, especially the quiet grace notes at the ends of phrases, as well as finger techniques, when to pluck, and when to rely on the energy from a previous pluck to advance to the next notes without plucking. The teacher also focused almost entirely on the student's hands, with a clear focus on technique.

The teachers gave interesting responses when asked about the differences between teaching Chinese instruments to Chinese and European students. One explained that "in terms of learning methods, most Chinese students are more willing to spend a lot of time in contact, and are more likely to achieve a good level of technique. But Western students' learning methods are more diversified and creative." They also noticed differences in student motivation. For instance, one observed that "the learning motivation of Chinese and foreign students varies from person to person, some for interest, some for academic research, and some for practical work." Overall, the experience of teaching abroad seemed quite worthwhile to them. As one explained, "If I only teach here [in China], I only have one perspective on education in pipa. When teaching abroad we stay more at the introductory level, but we get another way, another angle to seeing and understanding the pipa." In terms of challenges associated with living abroad, they reported only minor issues: "When I was in Europe, I only missed the convenience of living in China, especially in Beijing. China progresses so fast and has express delivery for anything. When I came back to China I just missed the way of thinking of European friends."

Some general findings were reached through these case studies:

- European students and Chinese students tend to study Chinese musical instruments for different reasons. In general, European students of Chinese instruments are more interested in using music to approach a more general study of culture and aesthetics, while Chinese students are more interested in developing competence in performance and knowledge of repertoire.
- All teachers reported deep personal growth—with reflective insights into both teaching and music—upon returning to China after their experience teaching abroad. All teachers missed China while abroad but also found positive aspects of life in Europe.
- Many Europeans still only associate CIs with Chinese language instruction, so more can be done to promote their broader role for Chinese culture studies (including CIs that specialize in martial arts, Chinese traditional medicine, arts, and music, etc.).

- The power of music might be even more widely utilized in cultural diplomacy, with a larger number of CMIs CIs that offer some music studies, since music is an especially attractive form of culture and "soft power" that strongly connects to emotions and naturally evokes empathy and goodwill.

A STRATEGIC VIEW: DIPLOMATIC IMPACT OF MCI ACTIVITIES

It is useful to consider how MCI activities look from the perspective of its management. The selection of MCI activities developed as its directors attained a sense of what worked well for the stakeholders and the communities it served. It is important to note that RDAM is a small art school with approximately four hundred students. The MCI functioned as a platform for learning activities that created new opportunities for RDAM students: tai chi for musicians, Chinese language learning (based on musical encounters), Chinese instrument lessons, Chinese culture studies, and seminars on music-related topics. Additionally, the MCI brought music cultures together through new ensemble formats, including both traditional Chinese and Western instruments, and created many projects with composers for contemporary music creation. To meet the cost/benefit goals in terms of outreach and quantitative measures, a number of collaborative projects with high schools, community outreach, and concerts covered a considerable proportion of the institute's portfolio of activities.

The MCI established diverse institutional collaborations to ensure its scope of successful outreach activities. The institute aimed to serve rather different kinds of partners, roughly divided into five categories: (1) educational collaboration activities from primary school to higher education level, (2) governmental Sino-Danish relations, (3) community outreach—elder care, cultural events on the municipal level, (4) Sino-Danish organizations (e.g., Danish Chinese business forum), and (5) cultural institutions, with various concert activities toward new audiences. This diverse range of collaboration partners demonstrates an institute that served as a hub for cultural diplomacy in both implicit and explicit ways. The annual activity plan for the MCI was developed through discussions with and support of various stakeholders from different fields. Planning of the projects needed to consider a mixture of political expectations, institutional expectations, artistic creativity, and artistic expertise, as well as public interest. One significant challenge for creating success within the CI structure was to embrace and identify the two sides of cultural brand and image. Cultural diplomacy through the MCI was based on choosing activities that could attract collaboration partners from both sides, but most importantly, to engage the artists involved from both countries and their respective institutions.

IMPLICATIONS OF THE "SOFT POWER" CONCEPT

Lo and Pan (2016), Song (2017), and Zhou and Luk (2016) have raised various debates in relation to CIs and the "soft power" concept. Considering Jakobsen's years of experience managing the MCI in Copenhagen, she notes how practical experience leads one to either agree or disagree with such theoretical debates. Writings in this field sometimes make valid points, but they can also appear unbalanced, lacking in nuance, and even fail to offer data to support the authors' interpretations. CI-related articles are numerous, but the vast majority are naturally limited since their authors lacked direct access to the inner workings of a CI.

CI research during 2005–2012 emphasized the rapid development of CIs during this period. CIs were widely seen as an effort by China to craft a positive image of itself in a world fraught with danger (Paradise, 2009, 662). This notion of image merits careful consideration, particularly when assessing the outcome of soft power initiatives in this context, since it illustrates the important distinction between hard power and soft power. CIs in this way are conceptualized as "a tool of China's public/cultural diplomacy, which China uses to shape its global image" (Hartig, 2015, 54).

Research that appears a full decade after the initial establishment of CIs, from around 2014, instead tends to describe the institutions as ineffective initiatives expanding out of control (Lien and Miao, 2018; Sweet, 2017), and some even report that CIs are viewed as political institutions only representing Chinese government power connected to information control, particularly in Tibet, Taiwan, Xinjiang, and Myanmar (Zhou and Luk, 2016). For example, Paradise (2009) and Sweet (2017) focus on the rapid growth of CIs, the danger and fear of Chinese control, and soft power as something unpleasantly situated within East-West conflict. Even the standard contract issued by Hanban for the establishment of CIs, which we will discuss later in detail, is cited as proof of excessive Chinese control. Some later research offers a more nuanced and interdisciplinary perspective that does not portray the institutes in an excessively negative light (Li, 2017; Song, 2017).

A third perspective on CIs comes from research funded by the Chinese government to document return of culture sector investment (Lien, Yao, and Zhang, 2017; Lien and Miao, 2018). Such studies have demonstrated the many positive effects of CIs on tourism, finding that the "CI improves international friendship, cooperation and recognition" (Lien, Yao, and Zhang,

2017, 3682), while also identifying legitimate concerns, such as problems with the "evaluation system and supervision mechanisms," with the conclusion that "Hanban is lacking in the overall management" of CI-affiliated Chinese partner universities (Lien and Miao, 2018, 142–43). Considering some of the critiques of CIs, it is helpful to reflect on why this discourse tends to offer existential pros and cons instead of more nuanced discussions of the problems raised and recommendations for how to improve relations with CIs for the betterment of each international partner. CIs have a history now of more than fifteen years and the experiences connected with them are rather diverse worldwide.

Based on our experience and critical review of literature, it is clear that CIs with fewer problems tend to be those established with two directors of different nationalities, one Chinese and one local host. On paper, one will always be Chinese and another always "foreign," but in reality what happens, often in the United States for instance, is that many CIs are jointly managed by two Chinese directors—one sent by a Chinese university and dispatched to the foreign country, while the "foreign director" is actually a Chinese American often placed in charge of the university's China Studies program. This structure potentially leads to disagreements regarding how best to integrate into the host university on an American campus in a way that fits with US university norms. Many CIs are isolated and detached from the main campus in large university settings, and this, too, creates certain difficulties that arguably could be avoided if the original idea of having a local director recognized by the foreign host university was more universally engaged and not underestimated as a basic organizational principle.

ADMINISTRATIVE CHALLENGES

Running a CI from the "foreign side" is a comprehensive and multifaceted responsibility. The most common conditions for CI establishment are that the local director already has many duties (as dean of the university, head of its Asian Studies program, its international relations manager, or director of a cultural institute, etc.) and on top of these preexisting responsibilities comes the leadership of a CI. The local directors tend to be characterized by a deep interest in Chinese culture, as well as languages and intercultural communication. A passion for China typically inspires the local director to accept what turns out to be challenging working conditions, which require constant problem-solving due to both cultural and intercultural factors, including ensuring the well-being of dispatched staff, and solving financial issues related to the funding system of Hanban. Many host universities do not have the human resources and specialized knowledge necessary to deal with staff dispatched from China, many of whom often encounter language and cultural misunderstandings. In the beginning, the CI is driven by passion and enthusiasm, but in time, the local director is often affected by a continuous overload of work and struggles with the integration and insufficient understanding of China from the host university. Moreover, local criticism of China (often appearing in local news media) creates additional challenges and reduced motivation for high-profile projects.

Another issue is quality differences and diverging managerial responses to the quantitative operational objectives of CIs. Hanban's reward system evaluation mechanism is primarily based on the number of students learning Chinese (Gil, 2008). This cost benefit concept is exacerbated in situations where the host university chooses to only offer teaching facilities and "in-kind" contributions without direct financial investment. Little is at stake locally in such scenarios, so the host university allows the CI to run itself into a corner without a shared vision connected to the host university's strategy. These situations ultimately produce misunderstandings regarding the basic structure of CIs, which are meant to be a joint venture fifty-fifty model that is locally supported.

Note that soft power in Nye's definition implies "the ability to get what you want through attraction rather than coercion or payments," and several scholars have interpreted CIs as major instruments of soft power (Cho and Jeong, 2008, 455). Indeed, here there is no *coercion*, but the activities are in the framework of *attraction*, so what allegedly makes the soft power of CIs false? When the investment is unbalanced—China is paying—with little appreciation or willingness for reciprocal investment from the host university, then the soft power is arguably no longer soft power. Then it is inevitably perceived as an insistent form of one-sided public diplomacy, which does not fit the original intention of CIs where attraction can work if the codirectorship between Chinese and foreign sides is genuine, and investment and resources equal with mutual appreciation.

An often-discussed issue is the question of true collaboration versus concerns that CIs might be independent institutions fully under Chinese control (or even as some have alleged direct Chinese Communist Party control). While politics plays a role in any large institution, it is important to recognize that Hanban has recently been restructured and renamed, most likely to distance itself from the appearance of direct party control in response to international criticism of CIs. Still, structurally the legal framework for CIs is built upon a jointly signed international agreement, envisioned as jointly managed, for the benefit of both parties. As a director of international affairs, one investigates many international contracts and memorandums of understanding, which contain similar approaches to joint collaboration. There appear to be sound reasons why these agreements are built upon the same structure, thereby making it clear how to jointly manage, as well as the financial conditions, solve disputes, and terminate the agreement.

The Hanban/CLEC agreement is composed as a document to be used on a global level, applicable to hundreds of CIs worldwide that use it as a framework document. Critiques of the Hanban/CLEC legal framework often relate to a lack of negotiation because the foreign side apparently sometimes does not know that negotiation is possible, while the carrot—the payments (as Nye would describe it)—is too tempting to leave space for a thorough reading that would identify any possible "dangers." This is exacerbated by a tendency for the language of the contracts to be in a form of "Chinglish," so the original Chinese text of the contract may differ somewhat from the English version. This issue has been improved throughout the years of CI history but there is a common assumption that China seeks unusually extensive control because the translated text often uses words and expressions that are not commonly seen in other kinds of contracts. For instance, the often-cited contract includes a phrase that tends to scare some in the Western world: "Abide by the rules of the Peoples Republic of China," which is a commonly-used formulation in official government documents in China and is similar to what one would expect of a European university seeking to establish a project in Asia. Still, such phrases tend to stimulate disproportionate concern. This could easily be accommodated by Western readers with the following meaning: "The activities should be in accordance with the regulations set by the Chinese Government." Maybe such a minor revision to the translation would reduce attacks on the very framework of CI agreements, or maybe not?

Since CIs were initiated by Hanban, it is natural to let China choose the wordings and focus on friendship and good faith between countries as a prerequisite for entering into any formal agreement. Such an approach should reduce conflicts by underscoring that mutual trust is the first step, while contractual words are merely necessary for formal purposes. However, such an approach is not in accordance with common ways of thinking among attorneys, especially those unfamiliar with foreign legal systems.

If one compares Hanban's contracts with those used in the European framework agreement of educational collaboration—the Erasmus program, based on the European Charter for Higher Education—one mostly notices many similar components to the Hanban contract. The basic idea of fifty-fifty investment, the basic conditions that members should abide by the EU's conditions, and that the funding structure is based on priorities and strategies decided by the EU is in many ways the same. Cost benefit review is an important part of the project application system, like Hanban. Of course, the EU is a framework that belongs to the member states and cannot be criticized in the same way as Hanban, which is exclusively associated with the single nation of China and solely decides on the basic terms and conditions.

RECOMMENDATIONS

Careful reflection on both personal experience and observations of managers at various CIs leads us to propose some suggestions for institutions contemplating establishment of such an internationally comanaged institute. Both Hanban/CLEC and the foreign host universities arguably should jointly consider offering more local staff resources to ensure the smooth running of the CIs. There are likely similar staffing challenges in other educational or diplomatic systems of this kind. The quantitative emphasis on increasing global numbers of CIs may have been sensible for a time, but now it makes sense that the number of CIs would be reduced for a focus on *quality*, to meet the demand of better qualified dispatched staff and better quality and evaluation procedures of CI teaching activities. Hanban's original focus on training and hosting joint conferences (including open feedback and evaluation processes) was notable, but recently with a new foreign policy approach, international programs have been replaced or reduced, and the "carrot" is becoming smaller while in some ways the cultural gap is growing larger.

To conclude, our general reflections on these challenges suggest that the negative images attributed to the entire CI project as a whole are related to the Western world having a rather fixed focus on general power relations between East and West rather than the actual scope or quality of CI activities. Thus, discussions tend to draw the picture of a colonizer (China) and oppressed ("foreign country"). It is also clear that CIs in developing countries are criticized less than in developed countries. This may be worth careful consideration in future engagements of joint venture soft power collaborations. The fact is that China is known for having a top-down and centralized system for its vision, strategy, and goals, but at the same time a system based on negotiation and increasingly, global interaction.

China will surely continue to act as a powerful country wishing to interact with the entire world while seeking to be a central power of the East that is respected by the West (Hunter, 2009). This predictable trajectory should cause the Western world (Europe and the United States) to recognize that any expectations for China to adopt Western thinking and principles are unrealistic. The future requires shared activities based on stimulating curiosity and developing mutual understanding. This is where soft power can play an important role as long as the reasons to engage are sincere and based on realistic assessments. The potential is great, and the history of CIs have—irrespective of critical views, and both good and bad stories—certainly expanded global knowledge of China, Chinese culture, and the number of Chinese language learners. This achievement is worth wide recognition and something future collaborations with cross-continental stakeholders may learn from.

TOWARD MUTUALLY BENEFICIAL SOLUTIONS: FINDING A MIDDLE GROUND

Realistic expectations, and a sense of how to find a middle ground through delicate compromises, are essential components of diplomatic projects, including in the field of culture. The strategic goals of an organization like Hanban (or similar institutions in other countries) are often not completely in line with what may be desired by local institutions in other countries with which they collaborate, so local directors frequently experience the challenge of negotiating between competing interests, in the hope of sufficiently satisfying multiple parties with different values. This requires empathy, diplomatic skills, and effective strategies for communicating with different approaches to reach acceptable compromises. Among Hanban's main interests is the international promotion of a positive image of Chinese cultural heritage, in the assumption that this may counteract some of the negative press and stereotypes often connected to China. Locally, however, institutions tend to have very practical concerns, such as how to schedule facilities and ensure sufficient student numbers, as well as educational quality. In the local press, on the other hand, there may be overconfident claims about what supposedly is "really going on" in educational activities promoted by a foreign power. Such complex forces tend to create substantial leadership challenges and sometimes it is not possible to satisfactorily resolve them. Unfortunately, academia has not always been helpful, when it ideally *should* serve as a helpful sphere for bolstering mutual understanding. This can even be a problem in the Nordic countries, in which scholarship is often assumed to take a very balanced approach but does not always meet such an ideal.

In 2019, we participated in an international conference in the field of China Studies and gave a panel presentation related to the topic of this chapter. Several of the conference participants, viewed locally as "China experts," were professors who clearly had negative views of China, yet upon discussion, we kept discovering many had not been to China for several years. We recall meeting a professor from a leading university from a Nordic country who claimed to know much more about Confucianism than any scholar in China, and insisted that the Chinese are incapable of correctly interpreting their own heritage, and that open discussion of philosophy is completely forbidden at

Chinese universities. When we expressed surprise at this perspective and explained how much his perceptions contradicted our own recent experiences in China (at the nation's leading law schools, for instance), he reluctantly admitted he had not been to China for many years and was only familiar with departments at a few universities. We also met an American who held an esteemed position as an endowed chair at a European university, who insisted that China would invade Taiwan in the coming months (explicitly predicted in the title of his speech!). Obviously, that did not happen, nor was there even any widespread concern of such a risk, yet somehow his speech was accepted. He seemed obsessed with the treatment of the Uyghur people in Xinjiang (which is a legitimate concern), but also insisted that China is militarizing Africa and outer space, that the very purpose of CIs is espionage and propaganda, and other rather extreme statements. Then there was a keynote speaker, a retired professor who also had not been to China for many years, and who displayed an offensive cartoon, intentionally disrespectful to the president of China, on an enormous screen for more than twenty minutes, while he complained about human rights in China, all based on anecdotes without reference to any scientific data or relevant social theories. Such arguments failed to acknowledge that most of the very same complaints they made about China would also apply to most of China's neighbors—North Korea, Russia, Vietnam (even South Korea and Singapore)—as well as much of entire regions, such as the continent of Africa, the Middle East, and Latin America. China was singled out as the one country that deviates from "international norms," and somehow Scandinavia had become the main "norm" for comparison. As we spoke with these "China experts" we increasingly doubted the legitimacy of their views while regretting the influence they doubtlessly wield in some European countries. Based on such views, it would seem inevitable that Chinese teachers insert propaganda into the middle of their music lessons, but we had never seen any evidence of this happening. Instead, what actually occurred at CIs were many unsurprising challenges due to cultural differences, and yet we find there is still so much to be gained from struggling to make such intercultural encounters successful.

It is important for those involved in intercultural work, especially when across a major divide, to recognize that propaganda is incessant (including sometimes even from academia), and it occurs in many directions, while cultural diplomacy seeks to offer a safe space in which people from very different worldviews (too often with negative assumptions about each other) can meet with mutual respect through a positive recognition of what may be eternally good in human artistic achievement (Goff, 2020).

What we have sought to demonstrate through this chapter is how music offers a special field in which international relations can be steered toward a direction that is potentially positive for all. It is worth noting that we have considerable recent experience in many different situations in different parts of China, and recognize that it has a long and complex history, with norms and attitudes that are rather different from Western countries; but we also know that most of the world today is quite different from Western Europe and North America, and that the rise of BRICS (Brazil, Russia, India, China, and South Africa) economies is rapidly changing the world's political and economic landscape. Rather than dismissing other countries as impossibly different, there is much to gain by engaging with mutual respect and empathy, with a sincere interest in understanding different beliefs and aims. An important first step is to attain mutual respect, toward which the arts are invaluable. As scholars based in Europe, we should take our share of responsibility to actively support the European (and increasingly, global) agenda of equity and equality, and as those involved in management or teaching in art schools, we should be active in contributing to the agenda of decolonization. Cultural diplomacy is a powerful tool for reaching these noble objectives that benefit us all.

CONCLUSION

How are we to make sense of the broader phenomenon of Chinese traditional instrument teachers offering lessons to Europeans as part of a major diplomatic initiative? Clearly, this fits the changing logic of the contemporary world, for Chinese students have been studying piano and violin for years, and now the pendulum is swinging in the other direction, requiring "glocalization" and "easternization" to be considered along with such familiar concepts as globalization and westernization (Hebert and Rykowski, 2018; Lam, 2008). Elsewhere it has been suggested that "by applying concepts from East Asian social theory in our 'cultural translation' work, we may not only develop more robust scholarly understandings but also directly engage in those forms of 'intellectual entrepreneurship' that ultimately lead to desirable social transformations" (Hebert, 2018, 343). The kind of cultural exchange that we see when Chinese approaches to music are shared in Europe can indeed be deeply meaningful, yet its meaning may be elusive if only approached from one direction. In other words, Chinese social theory requires attention in our interpretations, since as Qi has claimed, common Western theory "holds that the world comprises two sectors; one of these is Europe, where invention, innovation, and change naturally occurs, and the other—non-Europe—is stagnant" (Qi, 2014, 68). Much to the contrary, China is clearly changing and increasingly influencing the world across the spheres of business, technology, diplomacy, arts, and scholarship.

Indeed, China continues to challenge "well-established institutions of capitalist modernity while integrating itself into the capitalist world system more passionately than any other" (Kang, 2013, 573). In forthcoming work, it seems appropriate to consider how Chinese theories may best explain the rapid growth of CIs and related initiatives as strategic components of Chinese-style international relations (Qin, 2018). We can be confident that music, as one of the most meaningful human practices, will continue to serve as an important bridge across cultural divides, enabling all to better recognize what is good in the other, while generating mutual respect and empathy toward all of humanity. It is through listening to the other (Östersjö, 2020) that we apprehend the beauty in human life.

REFERENCES

Cho, Yong Nam, and Jong Ho Jeong. 2008. "China's Soft Power. Discussions, Resources, and Prospects." *Asian Survey* 48, no. 3: 453–72.
Gil, Jeffrey. 2008. "The Promotion of Chinese Language: Learning and China's Soft Power." *Asian Social Science*, 4, no. 10:116–22.
Goff, Patricia M. 2020. Cultural Diplomacy. In *Routledge Handbook of Public Diplomacy*, edited by Nancy Snow and Nicholas J. Cull, 30–37. New York: Routledge.
———. 2013. "Cultural Diplomacy." In *The Oxford Handbook of Modern Diplomacy*, edited by Andrew F. Cooper, Jorge Heine, and Ramesh Thakur, 419–39. New York: Oxford University Press.
Hartig, Falk. 2015. "Communicating China to the World: Confucius Institutes and China's Strategic Narratives." *Politics* 35 nos. 3–4: 245–58.
Hebert, David G., ed. 2018. *International Perspectives on Translation, Education and Innovation in Japanese and Korean Societies*. New York: Springer.
Hebert, David G. and Mikolaj Rykowski, ed. 2018. *Music Glocalization: Heritage and Innovation in a Digital Age*. Newcastle: Cambridge Scholars Publishing.
Hunter, Alan. 2009. "China on a Global Stage." *Chinese Journal of International Politics* 2, no. 3: 373–98.
Ho, Wai-Chung. 2018. *Culture, Music Education, and the Chinese Dream in Mainland China*. Cham: Springer.
———. 2021. *Globalization, Nationalism and Music Education in the Twenty-first Century in Greater China*. Amsterdam: Amsterdam University Press.
Kang, Liu. 2013. "The Frankfurt School and Chinese Marxist Philosophical Reflections Since the 1980s." *Journal of Chinese Philosophy* 40, no. 3–4: 563–82.
Lam, Joseph. 2008. "Chinese Music and its Globalized Past and Present." *Macalester International* 21. Retrieved from: https://digitalcommons.macalester.edu/macintl/vol21/iss1/9/.
Li, Siyuan. 2017. *China's Confucius Institute in the Discourse of Power in International Relations: A Case Study of the Confucius Institute in Africa*. Doctoral dissertation, University of Leeds.

Li, Xiangting and Xiaoxia Zhao. 2017. *Easy Steps to Chinese Music: Guqin*. Beijing: Central Conservatory of Music Press.

Lien, Donald and Liqing Miao. 2018. "Effects of Confucius Institutes on China's Higher Education Exports: Evidence from Chinese Partner Universities." *International Review of Economics and Finance* 57:134–43.

Lien, Donald, Feng Yao, and Fan Zhang. 2017. "Confucius Institute's Effects on International Travel to China: Do Cultural Differences or Institutional Quality Matter?" *Applied Economics* 49, no. 36: 3669–683.

Lo, Joe Tin-Yau and Suyan Pan. 2016. "Confucius Institutes and China's Soft Power: Practices and Paradoxes." *Compare: A Journal of Comparative and International Education* 46, no. 4: 512–32.

Östersjö, Stefan. 2020. *Listening to the Other*. Ghent: Orpheus Institute.

Paradise, James F. 2009. "China and International Harmony: The Role of Confucius Institutes in Bolstering Beijing's Soft Power." *Asian Survey* 49, no. 4: 647–65.

Qi, Xiaoying. 2014. *Globalized Knowledge Flows and Chinese Social Theory*. New York: Routledge.

Qin, Yaqing. 2018. *A Relational Theory of World Politics*. Cambridge: Cambridge University Press.

Song, Jiaying. 2017. *The Manifestation of China's Soft Power Agenda in American Higher Education: The Case of the Confucius Institute Project in America*. Doctoral dissertation, University of California, Los Angeles.

Sweet, Diana L. 2017. "The Art of Winning Hearts and Minds: Explaining Divergent Outcomes of Confucius Institutes in the U.S." PhD dissertation, Fairfax, VA: George Mason University.

Xing, Rong. 2009. "Research on the Development of China's National Music Against the Background of Cultural Soft Power." *Advances in Social Science, Education and Humanities Research* 283: 668–72.

Yao, Yijun. 2012. "The Pedagogy of Chinese Traditional Music at the China Conservatory of Music." *Journal of Music History Pedagogy* 2, no. 2: 179–83. Retrieved from: http://www.ams-net.org/ojs/index.php/jmhp/article/view/63.

Zhou, Ying and Sabrina Luk. 2016. "Establishing Confucius Institutes: A Tool for Promoting China's Soft Power?" *Journal of Contemporary China* 25, no. 100: 628–42.

Chapter Eight

A Gap in Cultural Policy

Non-Japanese Experiences of Learning Japanese Music

Koji Matsunobu

Japanese music has become widely practiced outside Japan in recent decades. An in-depth analysis of non-Japanese studying Japanese music, however, does not support the conclusion that they are necessarily interested in—or learning—Japanese culture more generally. Those who are passionate about the spiritual (e.g., Zen) aspects of this music may see its cultural dimensions as universal rather than culture-specific, and even as a series of hindrances to outsiders who seek access to music's underlying spirituality. Their views provide a unique perspective that prompts questions about what it means to fully understand foreign cultures. This chapter highlights a gap between the Japanese government's cultural policies and the views of non-Japanese shakuhachi practitioners through in-depth analysis of policy documents, as well as expressed attitudes and beliefs.

Across recent decades, many genres of traditional Japanese music have become widely practiced outside Japan. The tradition of *taiko* (drumming), for instance, is now widespread across the world. Many taiko groups in North America compose pieces as musical hybrids, performing their own musical identities by incorporating theatrical movements and other instrumental sounds (Ahlgren, 2018; Bender, 2012; Izumi, 2001; Terada, 2001; Powell, 2003; Wong, 2019). Serious shakuhachi learners travel from distant countries to participate in *hogaku* (traditional Japanese music) competitions in Japan. A highly competitive competition at the Nagatani Kengyo Memorial Hogaku Music contest has awarded several non-Japanese shakuhachi players.[1] Serious learners not only take music lessons in Japan but also participate in weeks-long study tours (Day, 2015; Matsunobu, 2011). In addition, one-day workshops for beginners are available for non-Japanese speaking tourists who desire a taste of Japanese music.[2] Since 2010, the Japanese government has promoted Japanese culture as soft power under the popular slogan "Cool

Japan," trying to explore the international market and supporting content creators and producers of both traditional and popular culture.[3] State-run NHK World-Japan broadcasts English programs catered for non-Japanese audiences, such as *Cool Japan*, *Japanology*, *J-Melo*, and *Blends*, and introduces Japanese performers of traditional and modern music.[4]

Despite increased exposure to Japanese culture, an in-depth analysis of the experiences of non-Japanese participants in Japanese music reveals that they do not necessarily develop broader interests in Japanese culture that require deeper understanding. Those who are passionate about the spiritual (e.g., Zen) aspects of this music may see its cultural dimensions as universal rather than culture-specific, and even as a series of hindrances to outsiders who seek access to music's underlying spirituality. Their views provide a unique perspective that prompts questions about what it means to fully understand foreign cultures. The case to be described in this chapter focuses on a group of North American practitioners of shakuhachi music who are drawn to deconstructed approaches to cultural practice. It thereby resembles Park's (2005) description of spiritual seekers in the United States who find the unique religious and spiritual realms of Japanese manga important—different from what their culture can offer—and thereby create their own cultural and spiritual practices.

In what follows, I first discuss traditional music in Japan's cultural policy and highlight a gap between the government's emphasis on cultural policies and foreign practitioners' interest in culture. I then introduce an in-depth analysis of foreign practitioners' views through interview data, which is followed by a discussion and summary of findings.

PRIORITY OF TRADITIONAL MUSIC IN JAPAN'S CULTURAL POLICY

To help preserve the traditional arts, the Agency for Cultural Affairs (Bunkacho)[5] has instituted a policy of intangible cultural properties (*mukei bunkazai*). To this end, the rank of important intangible cultural properties (*jūyo mukei bunkazai*) and living national treasures (*ningen kokuhō*) is bestowed upon those groups and individuals who are considered to have achieved the highest level of artistry within the traditional arts, such as music, dance, theater, painting, ceramics, and dying. As of 2015, fifty-eight individual artists and thirteen groups have been awarded this recognition in the field of the performing arts; in that of the fine arts, it is the same number of individual artists and fourteen groups. In return for receiving this highest of artistic honors, the grantee is obligated to give concerts, hold exhibitions, and train high-quality students, all of which are concerned with the objective of *maintaining the tradition* rather than *entertaining the public*. The emphasis is placed on the transmission of traditional artistry, rather than on exercising innovative creativity.[6]

The selection process of living national treasures is also somewhat political, and its criteria appear to have never been explicitly explained by Bunkacho.[7] In the field of Japanese traditional music, simply being a highly successful player does not automatically guarantee becoming an awardee of the *national living treasure* rank unless the player is also a member of Sankyoku Kyokai (the Japan Sankyoku Association[8]) and has become the *iemoto* ("head of household") of an established *ryū*. As a result, some of the top shakuhachi players, such as Katsuya Yokoyama, have failed to be officially designated as living national treasures. The iemoto is the physical embodiment of the tradition, the personification of the musical style practiced by the school, and the symbolized authority that alone can set the artistic standard. In addition to granting licenses to teach and perform the art (Keister, 2001),[9] the hierarchy of the iemoto system is also characterized by such ranking as *shihan* (master's license) and *junshihan* (teaching license). Some shakuhachi schools confer even higher ranks on their members with ever more nuanced names, such as *dai-shihan* (grandmaster license) and *chikusui* (bamboo master). The iemoto system is the dominant form of artistic transmission in Japan. The fact that the government does not grant the national living treasure rank to those who are outside the iemoto system suggests that they are less traditional, and thus lacking in embodiment and inheritance.

Five shakuhachi players have been awarded the rank of national living treasure since the establishment of the system. These players emanated from two representative schools (or ryū) of the shakuhachi tradition, namely the *tozan* and *kinko ryū*. The kinko ryū was formed by Kurosawa Kinko (1710–1771), the foremost shakuhachi player of the eighteenth century, who collected *honkyoku* solo pieces of the time. Later, much of the significant repertoire of this school also included *sankyoku* ensemble pieces. The largest shakuhachi school, however, is the *tozan ryū*, which was founded and established by Nakao Tozan (1876–1956) based on a new repertoire of music, including his own modern compositions. A systematic notation system (figure 8.1), which he also invented, allowed for easy access and wider dissemination of the repertoire, thereby ensuring his success. In addition, he created a hierarchical ryū system based on a centralized licensing mechanism, which resulted in great financial rewards and allowing his school to expand significantly.

The fact that all the national living treasures have emanated from these schools means that these two groups are officially under the protection of the Cultural Affairs Agency.[10] In contrast, the temple-based lineages of

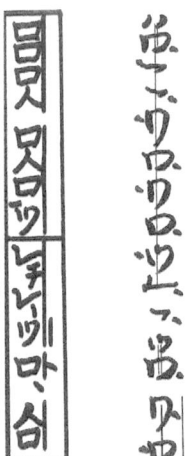

Figure 8.1. Comparison of the Tozan and Kinko notations. *Note.* Tozan notation (left) and Kinko notation (right) of the same piece rokudan no shirabe, handwritten by the author.

shakuhachi players, often known generically as *myoan ryū*, have effectively been left behind. Although these players are also concerned with transmitting their artistic lineages to successive generations, they are afforded a less legitimate status within the national system of intangible heritage. There may be several reasons for this: for instance, they are often amateur players concerned primarily with performing honkyoku solo music; since they do not play sankyoku ensemble music, they are not members of the Japan Sankyoku Association. Furthermore, their practice is focused more on the spiritual dimension of musical experience, rather than performance quality, a gap that is evident in the honkyoku tradition.[11]

Observing the gap between the spiritual and secular orientations to shakuhachi practice, Shimura (2002) argues that the former—what he calls the first world—is characterized by the pure focus on the honkyoku repertoire, whereas practitioners in the secular orientation, or the second world, play a variety of music, ranging from sankyoku ensemble music to pop music. In the first world, the meaning of practice is determined and acquired by experiencing the spirit of the Fuke Zen shakuhachi tradition through performing honkyoku music. While the emphasis of practice in the second world is often placed on enhancing musicality, the practice of the first world is characterized by its spiritual orientation, often explained through the notion of *ichion-jobutsu* ("one tone, enlightenment"). This notion suggests that depth of experience can be attained through perfecting a single tone rather than performing a tune musically. It is often emphasized when alluding to the role of the shakuhachi as a tool of self-cultivation. Shimura argues that there is no distinction between professional and amateur players in this first world, nor is there an audience who pays for admission to a professional performance. The chief goal of their music practice is to achieve personal and spiritual maturity through the realization of the "ultimate tone."

The kinko and tozan schools are more inclined toward the second world. The Cultural Affairs Agency promotes and protects their artistic lineages over the spiritual tradition. This means that the second world is the shakuhachi tradition officially promoted by the government. Indeed, shakuhachi players nominated and supported by the Cultural Affairs Agency for its cultural exchange program, in which selected artists spend weeks and months abroad introducing and promoting Japanese culture, are all from these schools. However, a gap is confirmed between what the government promotes as the shakuhachi tradition and what non-Japanese learners hope to study, as will be explored through a specific case in this chapter.

SHAKUHACHI PLAYERS AS CULTURAL AMBASSADORS

Today, many Japanese shakuhachi players have opportunities to perform and teach in foreign countries. Some live abroad as shakuhachi players and teachers. They serve as cultural ambassadors and facilitate intercultural understanding between Japan and their respective countries through music. An earlier attempt at direct teaching by Japanese players was already evident in the 1960s. Yamaguchi Goro (1933–1999) was one of the first as an artist in residence at Wesleyan University in Connecticut between 1967 and 1968. As a kinko-school master and later a living national treasure (since 1992), he taught many non-Japanese students. Another notable player and teacher was Yokoyama Katsuya, the founder of the Kokusai Shakuhachi Kenshukan (the International Shakuhachi Training Center), who hosted the first International Shakuhachi Festival in Okayama in 1993.[12] He taught many Japanese and non-Japanese students. They played an important role in organizing the International Shakuhachi Festival in Boulder, Colorado (1998), New York (2004), Sydney (2008), Kyoto (2012), and London (2018). They also held regional organizations, such as the European Shakuhachi Society, the Shakuhachi Summer Camp of the Rockies, and the Australian Shakuhachi Society. Today, many universities offer shakuhachi courses (e.g., Wesleyan University), and some offer a master's degree in music performance with a major in shakuhachi performance (e.g., Sydney Conservatorium of Music) taught by non-Japanese teachers.

Shakuhachi is widely practiced and appreciated outside Japan.[13] Several shakuhachi players outside of Japan are highly acknowledged inside and outside Japan, such as John Nepture Kaizan, David Wheeler, Riley Lee, and others. This is a significant point of difference from other Japanese instruments: while most professional koto (a Japanese zither) or shamisen (a Japanese three-stringed banjo) players are Japanese, a significant number of shakuhachi players are non-Japanese from North America and Europe (Tsukitani, 2008).[14] The rapid development of shakuhachi communities in the West has seen a third generation of shakuhachi players who are trained predominantly outside Japan and granted the shihan qualification by non-Japanese players. The shakuhachi is also gaining popularity in Chinese-speaking countries. Underlying the emerging popularity of the shakuhachi in China is a shared narrative among Chinese practitioners: originating in the Tang dynasty, the shakuhachi has finally returned to its birthplace and is regaining its "authenticity" as a Chinese instrument. With an expansion of international adherents and the rise of multilingual spaces, the shakuhachi has seen changing boundaries of membership and shifting notions of musical identity and musical ownership.

SPIRITUALITY OF THE SHAKUHACHI

American shakuhachi expert David Wheeler identifies three factors in the rising popularity of shakuhachi in North America: (1) it is easy to carry; (2) it is a wind instrument and requires no understanding of Japanese lyrics; and (3) it is linked to Zen Buddhism. He observed:

> Many people are surely attracted to the meditative, spiritual aspect of training, even though the number of those people may be decreasing as people realize that any instrument could be used for the same purpose.... In many cases, people start learning honkyoku after being fascinated by the tone of the shakuhachi rather than a melody of honkyoku. (Mitsuhashi et al., 2002, 49)

Part of the international popularity of the shakuhachi is because, like other indigenous flute music, shakuhachi music now is often categorized in the subgenre of new age, spiritual, and healing music within the broader market of world music. Just as other forms of world wisdom traditions have been commodified, world music, including sacred music traditions, is also widely consumed in the global market, and Shakuhachi music is no exception.[15]

One of the chief reasons that world flute music has become globally popular and widely practiced outside its original cultural contexts is that the simple construction of the flutes allows people to make their own flutes without becoming professional instrument makers. The shakuhachi, in particular,

Figure 8.2. A variety of ji-nashi shakuhachi (left) and an image of its inside (right). Note. This is the author's own collection. Four from the left and two of the lying shakuhachi are myoan shakuhachi made in the towari method. Some are "modern" ji-nashi and well-tuned. Some have both features of edo and modern ji-nashi. Photos by author

serves as a unique case because of its practitioners' degree of involvement in the instrument-making process.[16] They mostly make the classical type, *ji-nashi* shakuhachi (figure 8.2).

Whereas the modern type of the shakuhachi (called *ji-ari*) is made with filling material, placed inside the bamboo to control the diameter of the inner bore of the bamboo and thus to produce tuned pitches, the ji-nashi traditionally is made out of a single piece of bamboo with minimal artificial modification to maximize the character that the individual bamboo segment naturally bears (figure 8.3). Because of this feature, each ji-nashi has different musical qualities (timbre, pitch, playability) that depend on

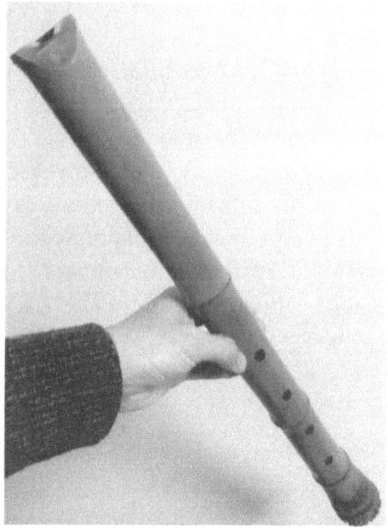

Figure 8.3. A nineteenth-century shakuhachi. *Note.* This particular piece was owned and played by the author's great, great grandfather. Photo by author

the nature of the bamboo and the artist–maker who has fashioned it into a shakuhachi (Shimura 2002).[17] The result is an instrument that demonstrates less standardization and allows for a greater degree of variation.

On one hand, this feature of the ji-nashi renders the instrument unsuitable for playing in an ensemble and limits the instrument to solo performance of the honkyoku repertoire. On the other hand, it displays a wide degree of differences in terms of playability, sound, and intonation. Thus, it allows the practitioner to develop his or her relationship (attachment and association) with the instrument. The rhythm of honkyoku playing, which is determined largely by one's breathing patterns, also allows for a great degree of personalization. This individual aspect of honkyoku playing is emphasized greatly by some independent-minded foreign students in the West (Keister, 2004, 2005).

The interest in the ji-nashi shakuhachi has been continually increasing outside Japan, which may be due to its tendency to be perceived as having an especially organic or "earthy" sound (Keister, 2004). Because the instrument is minimally processed and closely resembles the bamboo's natural state, practitioners can incorporate an organic feeling into their experience of its music. It is this aspect of music experience that has attracted many practitioners, including my participants in this study.

CULTURE AS A HINDRANCE TO SPIRITUALITY

Honkyoku as Universal: Many Western shakuhachi practitioners, like my participants, are drawn to honkyoku playing. They find playing honkyoku more satisfying and liberating than playing sankyoku pieces, *minyo* folk songs, or other kinds of Japanese music. They also find that the primitive nature of ji-nashi leads more toward the fulfillment of their spirituality. This perspective was expressed, for instance, by Liam (all names are pseudonyms). The following conversation occurred when speaking with a Japanese teacher about the differences between the modern (ji-ari) and the classical (ji-nashi) shakuhachi. Liam said,

> Most Westerners haven't heard it [the ji-nashi shakuhachi]. But immediately when they hear ji-nashi, wow! This is how I feel. [In contrast] when I hear ji-ari, I relate it more to Japanese folk music and modern music, which, I am not Japanese, so it's not that meaningful to me. Sankyoku, minyo too. I am not Japanese. It doesn't touch me because I don't have any of the background to understand it. . . . Russian folk music, I don't really understand it. I'll have to study Russian history and culture. With Japanese folk music, I have to study a lot more Japanese history to understand it. Chinese folk music, I'll have to study

a lot of stuff including language. But the most basic—sometimes it's a religious form of music—is easier for everyone to understand.

Liam was a serious student, having taken six years of shakuhachi lessons in his home country. In addition, he traveled to Japan every few years to take lessons with Japanese masters. Thus, it is not appropriate to interpret his remark above as a lack of commitment or a sign of unwillingness to engage in a more serious study of shakuhachi music that requires more than a sound-only approach. What he indicated was that, while playing folk music required an understanding of the culture (language and history) of the place in which the music originated, the experience of honkyoku playing was more immediate: It directly reached his heart. It allowed him to experience the depth of its spirituality without taking a detour. Liam continued to speak slowly word by word, sentence by sentence, so that his Japanese teacher would understand his point well in English:

> When I hear honkyoku on ji-nashi, I think it's universal. Some Westerners maybe think it's a little weird. But it's natural. It sounds like nature. It sounds like something that isn't cultural. It's not a cultural entertainment. It's like someone speaking more from the heart. So even though I am not Japanese, honkyoku on ji-nashi makes a lot of sense to me. It's obvious that there is something very primitive, very fundamental there. But ji-ari and minyo or ji-ari and sankyoku, it's constructed. It's a complicated construction of men. I have to be Japanese to understand it better. But I think I can eventually understand honkyoku [without becoming Japanese]. Ji-nashi is natural. Honkyoku is natural. It takes us back down to the universal experience. The rawer you go, the more people in the world I think would understand it.

Liam thought that the attraction and the pleasure of playing the ji-nashi lay in its "primitive" nature, meaning its elegant simplicity as essentially a natural piece of bamboo with holes cut into it. While the ji-ari for him represented the culture, the ji-nashi signified the organic and the primitive. Thus, it was fundamental. In the above narrative, he also revealed his view was "a complicated human construction" accumulated on the universal commons that already existed before cultures arose. According to him, these universal commons were not complicated constructions but rather simple: They were the roots of today's distinctive cultures in the world and thus shared by people of different places and times. He saw the culture as restricting and hindering the access of cultural outsiders. Understanding the culture involves years of commitment to the mastery of not only the music itself but also the social and moral values, which are often transmitted through the feudal *iemoto* ("head of household") system (Malm, 2000; Trimillos, 2004) and are not easy for foreign practitioners to understand and acquire.

For Liam, the difference between the ji-ari (modern) and the ji-nashi (classical) shakuhachi and between studying folk music and honkyoku was likened to understanding a foreign religion: One way is through perusing scriptures and joining rituals; the other way is to approach directly by experiencing its spirituality. The latter deals more with inspiration, energy, wholeness, mystery, and an organic engagement with life experience. In contrast, the former for him was parochial and formulaic. Although he acknowledged the importance of following the traditional path to the mastery of music from other cultures, he also believed that following the conventional way did not necessarily guarantee its result as spiritually satisfying.

Expression of Simplicity as Universal: Liam stated above that "the rawer you go, the more people in the world would understand it." By this he meant that simple forms of cultural expression of the world have much in common. In other words, the more complex a cultural expression is the more difficult it is for outsiders to understand its essence. He indicated that spirituality is a universal trait of human experience and often is acquired through simpler expressions, such as a single tone of a simple flute. Such a perspective was provided by Andrew, another North American shakuhachi student with an extensive range of knowledge and experience of performing jazz and hip-hop music. He was more involved in the act of blowing into a piece of bamboo, which gave him a corporeal feeling of "vibration," than into playing honkyoku as "music."

Andrew suggested that the awareness of the properties of music, such as rhythm and pitch, could be hindrances to gaining the most intimate, organic experience of music. Simplicity was the key for him to the experience of shakuhachi playing, through which he transformed his view of music. He remarked,

> Everything about the shakuhachi is conducive to just ... very in tune with, every feeling, every change of mind. You don't have to add meter. You even don't have to have that pitch really. You can do anything. You can just make noise. You find a tune to yourself as a human being because it [the shakuhachi] is a vessel for that; music just follows, which is much different than any other instruments. So simple and raw and natural. That's how you hear the sound. . . . As soon as you give up the idea that everything has to be twelve-tone Western scale and you open yourself up to the possibility of just sound, and if you think about sound and nature like rock falling down a hillside or the sound of water, or any of those kinds of things, you realize really how beautiful and how powerful your breath is as a tool of creation. It doesn't have all those restrictions. It can blossom into something that is much more powerful than what the normal music is.

In a way, Andrew was much more into what has been believed to be the essence of shakuhachi playing: *ichion-jobutsu*, or "the attainment of enlightenment through perfecting a single tone" (Gutzwiller, 1995; Matsunobu, 2007). The idea of pursuing spirituality by focusing on a tone traditionally has been sought after by practitioners in the Fuke sect of Japanese Zen who play the shakuhachi for a meditative practice. The chief goal of ichion-jobutsu is not to experience aesthetic pleasure but to achieve personal and spiritual maturity through the realization of the "ultimate tone" (called *tettei-on*). The emphasis of its expression is placed more on the shade and color of each tone than the structure of music.

Andrew explained this aspect of shakuhachi experience using his knowledge of jazz. To him, the sound that the shakuhachi makes expresses "no structure, no restrictions, but merely tension and energy," which is similar to his experience of jazz. He explained,

> Jazz is very much like that. It's more about feeling than it is about rules. And the best people of the time, Coltrane and Miles Davis, from a technical standpoint, they are sloppy because they surpassed technical things and went on more to spiritual excellence, more about feeling. That's what I am more interested in. Definitely, that's harder to cultivate. Shakuhachi is a much purer form of jazz, pretty much contains every element that jazz strives to be because the whole idea of jazz is freedom, free form of music.

Andrew, believed that indigenous instruments such as the ji-nashi carry the sensitivities of native people, those who are more in tune with nature, sensitive to the spiritual dimension of life, and deeply connected. When playing such instruments, according to Andrew, we are reminded of the organic dimension of life and experience it vicariously in the way native people used to feel it. Therefore he explained, "the real beauty of shakuhachi is that it's a way to directly remind the self of a more organic self. Just by holding it, looking at it, you realize it." He continued,

> It [the shakuhachi] has elements that are like yoga. It's almost like a kind of combination of all different things in life you do. It makes you interested in the past, history, and all those kinds of things. If you play electronic guitar, you might be interested in Jimmy Hendrix. But that is much more immediate. Shakuhachi has this thing. It's like reaching back to the ancient world into a time where there isn't any history. If you go back to the most basic thing, you go back to the roots of everything we have now, so in a way bamboo is the root of [the] computer. If you want to get down to the source of life, start back to the basics. It answers the biggest question.

Here, Andrew points out that one significant aspect of learning indigenous forms of music is to develop a sense of connection to the past. Indigenous musical practices that developed long ago inevitably carry a sensitivity of the time and remind us of what it would be like to engage in music and life organically. In the case of the ji-nashi shakuhachi, this feeling of connectedness is gained not only from playing old vintage flutes that were made hundreds of years ago but also from engaging in the process of making flutes out of self-harvested bamboo. Andrew emphasized that playing what he understood to be a primitive instrument was "like reaching back to the ancient world into a time where there isn't any history." He observed that, by engaging in the ji-nashi practice, players feel that they are connected to a more profound sensitivity and spirituality. Like Liam, Andrew observed that the shakuhachi can bring players the feeling of something organic (primitive), natural, fundamental, and thus universal.[18]

IMPRESSION OF THE EARTH ENERGY

As represented by Andrew, the shakuhachi was often experienced and characterized by my participants as a vibration of energy rather than a construction of sounds, or music. This was also the case with Pamela. Speaking more pointedly than Liam and Andrew, she stated that the shakuhachi is a pipe through which the energy flows in and out of her body in a similar way to how she experienced energy through qigong practice, a method of cultivating energy through slow breathing and body movements. According to Pamela,

> When I play shakuhachi I feel a very strong connection to the earth's energy [qi or ki]. . . . The longer ji-nashi allows me to rest the root-end on the earth as I play. I feel then that, as I produce a sound, the energy comes up from deep in the earth, travels through the instrument, and then vibrates out through the sound into the surroundings. This feeling is so much stronger when I play outdoors that I feel certain this must be what is happening.

Pamela's long root-end flute literally reached the ground. She felt that she was an extension of the flute as if she was the pipe, through which the air naturally went in and out of her body. She thought that she felt this connection for several reasons:

> Firstly, the wider bore [of the ji-nashi] means that I can breathe/sigh into the instrument to produce a sound, without feeling that my breath is restricted, or squeezed along its length as with narrow bore flutes. Secondly, I feel that the softer sound emanating from the ji-nashi integrates with nature's sounds, rather than cutting across them. Thirdly, the longer ji-nashi allows me to rest the

root-end on the earth as I play.... I feel that the natural sound of the ji-nashi shakuhachi emulates the sounds of nature far better than any other musical instrument.

Like Andrew, Pamela strongly sensed that playing the ji-nashi was an act of feeling, embodying, and circulating the energy. For Pamela, playing the ji-nashi served her as a medium through which to connect herself to nature.

This suggests that playing the ji-nashi for Pamela (and Andrew) was experienced as a realization of qi (ki). Qi refers to a cosmology that explains the self-directed natural movement of life force (Yuasa, 1987,1993). By sensing the flow of qi, the practitioner can feel as if he or she is connected to the universe governed by the circulation of qi. Music, like other aesthetic forms and martial arts, can be a powerful medium to realize and embody the flow of qi (Matsunobu, 2007). Tuning into qi is thus a state or a process of being and becoming spiritual. The practitioners who participated in this study clearly expressed that their flutes allowed them to embody the qi energy, become part of the universe, and cultivate their spirituality.

BIOLOGICAL, PHYSICAL, UNIVERSAL PERSPECTIVES ON MUSIC

Shakuhachi students in this study perceived that the cultural aspect of music often manifests itself differently in a variety of sounds and scales that characterize each culture's expression of music. For Liam, honkyoku was less cultural but more spiritual because it sounds much simpler, so simple that it does not seem to form any scale, theory, or complicated construction of music perceived as a cultural expression. Andrew observed that playing shakuhachi involves no restrictions or set of rules defined and imposed by each culture. Similarly, the shakuhachi sounded like nature for Pamela rather than music. They all found the primitive nature of the ji-nashi as leading more to the fulfillment of spirituality than to musical excitement. It was through such forms of decontextualized musical practice that they became aware of what I interpreted as their innate primitive, organic sensitivities that allowed them to feel the energy of the universe. I observed that this realization, in turn, brought them a sense of oneness—an experience of aliveness of mind and body, self and world as a unity. It seemed as if they saw this type of music experience as a universal, biological human reaction to sound.

Whether this view is objectively justifiable or not, they reported feeling more in tune with their spirits through such decontextualized approaches. How can we interpret these practitioners' rendering of Japanese music as a source of spirituality? How can we locate this mode of intensified musical engagement within the curriculum? One way is to explore it from a biological perspective. Acknowledging that the emphasis of conventional music education has been placed on the musical, DeNora suggested that music studies need to examine more of the bodily reaction to music than its cultural properties:

> Thinking about the ways that we attend to and make connections between cultural and bodily music may open new avenues for thinking about music's role as a social medium in senses that also include its roles as a medium of physiological ordering in daily life. As such, music studies encompass the musical not only cross-culturally, but also biologically, albeit a biology that is understood to interact with culture, custom, and conviction. (2007, 802)

DeNora indicates that humans, of any culture and time, would share, to a great extent, similar biological reactions to music. Similarly, Dissanayake (2000) proposes a view that all humans share the biological makeup for aesthetic expressions. Observing human interactions through early rhythmic-modal experiences between mother and infant, she raises a vision of homo-aesthetics that underscores proto-musical operations of human interactions based on such processes as formalization, repetition, exaggeration, dynamic variation, and manipulation of expression (Dissanayake, 2008). She posits that humans inherit and develop these operational behaviors through ritualization and that this process was both cultural and biological. Like DeNora, Dissanayake suggests looking at biological aspects of human musical traits.

Whether spirituality is a biological trait or not is no more relevant than asking if music is a universal longing. What is important is that my participants' experiences of shakuhachi playing are better captured by the view of music as a biological rather than cross-cultural experience. Again, what made them interested in honkyoku music was not so much the cultural aspects of Japanese music, but rather biological aspects of human experience identified in Japanese music, such as the embodiment of the earth's energy, the corporeal feeling of being connected to ancient times, and the revitalization of humans' primitive, organic sensitivities. These aspects of music for my informants were universally experienced regardless of cultural differences. This is to suggest that for these serious practitioners of Japanese music, spirituality was experienced as a universal language.

DISCUSSION

The aforementioned discussion on the universal dimensions of shakuhachi playing exhibits a variety of views on what counts as authentic shakuhachi playing (Matsunobu, 2018). While the classical view of authenticity posits that an appropriate answer resides in the music, authenticity also acknowledges the dimension of "personal authenticity." Schippers (2010) argues that most music practices today are recontextualized.[19] What counts as an authentic performance may vary from generation to generation, from lineage to lineage, in each place of practice. He posits that recontextualization is achieved by moving strategically from static to dynamic views of tradition, from a single to multiple senses of authenticity.

The nontraditional context of shakuhachi practice outside of Japan—free from the social and cultural constraints originating in Japanese society—has facilitated a space for non-Japanese practitioners to adopt deconstructed shakuhachi practices. Non-Japanese practitioners, especially those in the West, tend to be drawn to such practices, which often differ from traditions that the government promotes as "pure" forms of Japanese culture. In this sense, the shakuhachi is like anime, as an art that is embraced abroad largely irrespective of official cultural policy: "It is the 'Otherness' of anime rather than its specific 'Japanese-ness' that is one of its fundamental appeals to the fans" (Napier, 2001, 255). Indeed, compared to taiko, the shakuhachi is arguably *too* "Japanese" (Izumi, 2001). While taiko—a rhythm instrument ensemble—rather easily allows for the production of cultural hybrids with other instruments (not limited to Japanese instruments), the shakuhachi is fundamentally a solo instrument with five finger holes, which, on the one hand, makes a performance of traditional pieces (especially those in the minyo pentatonic scale) easier; on the other, an execution of heptatonic and chromatic scales challenging. This nature remains the same even with a shakuhachi with seven finger holes as it is catered for Japanese *in* scales. This means that for many, the shakuhachi, especially for beginners, bears limited transcultural expressions. As such, shakuhachi lovers outside Japan tend to play either solo honkyoku pieces or the new age kind of music. Compared to the taiko, the shakuhachi in North America is actively practiced by those who have no cultural roots in Japan (e.g., Caucasians and non-Japanese Asian Americans) and whose orientation to the shakuhachi tends to be musical and spiritual rather than social and political.[20]

What implications can we draw for cultural diplomacy from the case analysis? First, there should be a better acknowledgment of a possible gap between what the government tries to export as Japanese culture and how it is perceived and practiced outside Japan (Akagawa, 2015). As the case analysis indicated, the kind of cultural experience that non-Japanese practitioners would expect is not necessarily what the government promotes as an authentic experience. Just as taiko is practiced for fitness exercise, traditional music in Japan can be approached (and appropriated) in a myriad of ways.

By acknowledging that cultural diplomacy is not merely to export a set of knowledge, art forms, and patterns of actions, the government should support diverse ways of approaching and appreciating the culture and target a wider audience, inviting foreign practitioners. Clarifying the notion of musical diplomacy, Einbinder argues that "in building cross-cultural musical programs we should not use predefined musical concepts but look at how different cultures and people create, perform and characterize music" (2013, 38).

Cultural diplomacy aims to achieve mutual recognition and mutual understanding. It takes bilateral (rather than unilateral) approaches to form common grounds (Goff, 2013). This means that cultural diplomacy is facilitated by mutual interactions. In the case of shakuhachi, there have been myriad responses and innovations brought by non-Japanese practitioners. An interest in the ji-nashi shakuhachi in North America led to a production of a new style ji-nashi made by bamboo dust compound. Metal and 3-D printed shakuhachi seem more popular in China than in Japan. These new forms of development will, in return, enrich the Japanese scene of shakuhachi music, just as American shakuhachi player and maker John Neptune Kaizan, widely known for his fusion music, did in Japan. There has been a conservative attitude against the changes brought by foreign practitioners; a concern similar to what the color change of Judo uniform from sacred white to blue created decades ago.[21] Although the change was originally unthinkable for many Japanese practitioners, it also facilitated internationalization and bridged people of diverse cultures. Music can play the same role.

The inclusion of popular culture in cultural diplomacy is another issue. Traditional cultural diplomacy depended on high culture (Goff, 2013). This was the case in power-war Japan cultural diplomacy in which the uniqueness of Japanese culture was promoted through traditional arts and language teaching abroad (Katzenstein as cited in Goff, 2013). The current Cool Japan policy led to the export of popular culture, such as manga, anime, and J-pop. The shakuhachi is also present in Japanese popular culture. Anime fans have been exposed to the sound of the shakuhachi and other traditional Japanese instruments through the soundtracks of internationally popular anime series Naruto (2002). *Ghost of Tsushima*, a video game released on PlayStation 4 in 2020, featured the shakuhachi sound and attracted many anime fans. So did *Sekiro: Shadows Die Twice*, an action-adventure video game released in 2019. A flute branded as "shakuhachi—Japanese bamboo flute as heard in Ghost of Tsushima and Sekiro" is available on Amazon's website.[22] The emergence of Wagakki Band changed the public image of traditional Japanese instruments from submissive and nostalgic to innovative and transcultural instruments that can play hybrid rock music with Western instruments. The combination of popular and high culture of Japanese music contributed to the allure of

Japanese culture as soft power, the messages strongly communicated in the NHK World programs (e.g., Blends). On the one hand, popular culture has opened a window for many people to experience Japanese culture that might otherwise be inaccessible. Many foreign learners of the Japanese language today are drawn to Japanese popular culture rather than high culture. On the other hand, as indicated in the aforementioned case analysis, popular culture is not necessarily the interest of serious music learners, and some may not be interested in learning the culture behind the sounds. This may suggest that effective cultural diplomacy needs to target a variety of audiences through a variety of cultural heritages and innovative creations. While the potential of popular culture as a tool in intercultural communication is yet to be explored as the "greatest untapped resource in the cultural diplomacy" (Schneider, 2003, 14), it can help to overcome the "limitation" of Japanese popular culture as soft power in certain Asian countries.

Musicians are also engaged in the creation and performance of cultural hybrids in a cross-cultural context of musical sharing and making. This was the case with Japanese musicians who were sent abroad as cultural ambassadors on Bunkacho's Japan Cultural Envoy program. They were drawn to the cocreation of cultural hybrid with local musicians catered for a local audience. Yamaji Miho, a koto/shamisen player and a member of the 2014 cultural envoy, engaged in improvisation with local musicians in Finland, a violinist, and pianist in Slovakia, ensembles with *kokle* players in Latvia, while teaching local students and providing workshops in these countries. Noh actor and player Tatsumi Manjiro, a member of the the 2013 cultural envoy, upon his envoy activities in Korea, stressed the need for mutual interactions through expressing the culture of their own as well as embracing the culture of their counterparts in Japan. A member of the 2019 cultural envoy, Honjo Hidejiro, a shamisen player, performed twenty-one newly commissioned works by local composers with local musicians in nine countries (Turkey, the United States, Italy, France, the United Kingdom, Germany, Czech Republic, and Russia).[23] Although these musicians took the role of promoting Japanese musical heritage, their activities led to the development of a common ground through musical creation and cocreation. These musicians' experiences corroborate Channick's observation:

> Artists engage in cross-cultural exchange not to proselytize about their own values but rather to understand different cultural traditions, to find new sources of imaginative inspiration, to discover other methods and ways of working, and to exchange ideas with people whose worldviews differ from their own. (2005, 4)[24]

These musicians also reported an increased interest in the Japanese culture: through the interactions with unfamiliar musical and cultural expressions, they gained fresh insights into their own practices and traditions. In his dissertation, Momii (2021) sheds light on the intercultural environment and activities in which Japanese musicians, such as Honjo Hidejiro and Miyata Mayumi (a gagaku player), engage in the production and communication of intercultural meanings through Japanese music. Their performances, dialogues, and collaborations challenge conventional views of cultural purity, homogeneity, and authenticity, in line with the argument discussed in this chapter.

Miscommunication and misunderstanding can easily occur in a cross-cultural context (Einbinder, 2013). Teachers of traditional Japanese music often experience a gap between the Japanese teaching methods (Halliwell, 1994) and a more "understanding-oriented" pedagogy requested by non-Japanese students (McCollum, 2018; Matsunobu, 2009). Gutzwiller (1995) suggests that shakuhachi instructors teaching outside Japan need to modify their methods to suit the needs and expectations of foreign practitioners. Sometimes, the gap is so wide that it leads to a high level of frustration among both parties. An Australian student was once told by a Japanese teacher: "You don't deserve any music lesson in any country with any teacher." Musicians and music teachers as cultural ambassadors should have abilities to accommodate themselves to the needs of foreign cultures so that the results are intercultural understanding and respect. As experts in traditional music, they may not be proficient in the musical practices of other cultures but must be open to other cultures' values, beliefs, and aesthetics. Cultural diplomacy should support their intercultural training and involve them in cultural exchange programs.

CONCLUSION

The shakuhachi is widely practiced and appreciated by a variety of people in many countries. The number of such people is ever increasing not only in Europe, North America, and South America but also in Asia. These people will potentially serve as ambassadors for intercultural understanding and communications. The shakuhachi also provides a gateway to understanding how people in a specific place approach their music in a decontextualized way. Such diverse and global forms of music practice will be of interest to those who are involved and interested in cultural diplomacy, trying to develop a sustainable international relationship. This chapter is a reminder that musicians and teachers can play an important role in facilitating intercultural communication and understanding as music diplomacy (Einbinder, 2013).

NOTES

1. A list of winners is available at: http://www.kumahou.com/result/.
2. Examples can be found at https://www.veltra.com/en/asia/japan/tokyo/ctg/197141:taiko_workshop/.
3. The Cool Japan policy document by the Ministry of Economy, Trade and Industry (in Japanese) is available at https://www.meti.go.jp/policy/mono_info_service/mono/creative/180205CooljapanseisakuFeb.pdf. The Cool Japan strategy by the Cabinet Office is available at https://www.cao.go.jp/cool_japan/index.html. (see Akbas 2018)
4. NHK *Blends* is on Youtube at https://youtu.be/Ufdmc-K8GO0.

Japanology Plus featured "traditional music in modern life in Japan" (originally aired on July 10, 2017) and introduced a new wave of traditional music together with its sister program Blends with a narration: "Blends is dedicated to broadcasting these innovative performances. Today's guest Akihisa Kominato himself performs on Blends, and he serves as the show's music producer. He is striving to pioneer a new style of traditional Japanese music" (https://www.dailymotion.com/video/x7lv1gn).

5. Officially established in 1968, the main role of Bunkacho, or the Cultural Affairs Agency, has been to promote culture and the arts, support artists and artistic communities, and to engage in social education and cultural exchange. In the 2017 revision of the 2001 Basic Act on the Promotion of Culture and the Arts (Bunka geijutsu suishin kihon hō), the definition of culture and the arts and the range of promotion activities are expanded to emphasize tourism, town development, international exchange, social welfare, education, and industry. More information is available at https://www.bunka.go.jp/seisaku/bunka_gyosei/shokan_horei/kihon/geijutsu_shinko/index.html.
6. This view is not necessarily shared by artists themselves. Interviewing two living national treasures, Arisawa (2011) revealed the innovative side of performing arts practices in the traditional realm.
7. The statement regarding the selection of living national treasures is "those who embody and represent the designated performing arts and craftsmanship at the highest level" (https://www.bunka.go.jp/seisaku/bunkazai/shokai/mukei/). The government's agendas to promote and protect traditional arts through designating living national treasures have been consistent since the establishment of the Cultural Properties Protection Law in 1950 and the first grantees of ningen kokuho in 1955. What seems to be changing, however, is the definition of performing arts and folk performing arts, as pointed out in Arisawa (2012), and a broader cultural policy of the country, as argued in this chapter.
8. The website of Japan Sankyoku Association is www.sankyoku.jp.
9. Hebert (2005) observes that the *iemoto* model appears to have had an immense influence on the institutionalization of Western music in Japanese conservatories where "pedagogical lineage" and "authority" are associated with the *iemoto* system of Japanese schools of Western music.
10. The website of the Cultural Affairs Agency is https://www.bunka.go.jp/.

11. Implicit criteria have been discussed by Arisawa (2012) and Alazewska (2012) as determining points for eligible grantees of ningen kokuho: professional over amateur artists, nationwide over place-bound groups, artistic over entertainment orientations, and secular over religious activities. Shakuhachi players of temple-based lineages and so-called *myoan* schools are not eligible because they are typically amateur practitioners, inclined more into the spiritual than aesthetic values. It is, however, important to note that there are shakuhachi players outside the major schools who are recognized and granted to be intangible cultural *waza* holders at the prefectural level. For instance, five shakuhachi players of Nezasaha Onezasaharyu Kinpuryu Shakuhachi in Hirosaki, Aomori Prefecture are granted to be *kengigei* (県技芸) artistry holders (https://www.pref.aomori.lg.jp/soshiki/kyoiku/e-bunka/kengigei_01.html). This may suggest, as Arisawa (2012) argues, that these performers and groups are considered as practitioners of "folk" rather than "classical" art.

12. Other renowned teachers who taught and teach foreign students include, but are not limited to, Aoki Reibo, Fukuda Teruhisa, Furuya Teruo, Ishikawa Toshimitsu, Kakizakai Kaoru, Kanzaki Ken, Kawase Junsuke, Kurahashi Yodo, Mitsuhashi Kifu, and Okuda Tatsuya.

13. Definitions of Japanese terms regarding shakuhachi music may help the reader understand this chapter. Honkyoku refers to the classical repertoire of shakuhachi music, often dubbed as Zen music. Sankyoku is a Japanese chamber ensemble, consisting of voice, koto (zither), shamisen (lute), and shakuhachi. Minyo are Japanese folk songs, which often are accompanied with the shakuhachi. The shakuhachi traditionally has been used in these genres of music.

14. This phenomenon typically was observed, for example, at the seminar on Japanese music held at the School of Oriental and African Studies at the University of London in 2006. Whereas most of the invited koto and shamisen players were Japanese, more than half of the invited shakuhachi players were non-Japanese from North America and Europe. Indeed, there are a number of shakuhachi players who are not Japanese but highly acknowledged inside and outside Japan (see, for instance, a list of registered shakuhachi teachers on the website of the International Shakuhachi Society: www.komuso.com/teachers.html). These players are engaged actively in disseminating shakuhachi music and organizing shakuhachi events including the Shakuhachi Summer Camp of the Rockies (annual) and International Shakuhachi Festival (semi-annual).

15. The discussion here is based on my personal communication with Bruno Nettl, one of my doctoral supervisors. There is no market-based data for the shakuhachi. However, mere internet search for shakuhachi music leads to a number of websites promoting Zen, healing, healing, yoga, meditation, and a number of recordings promoted through these images.

16. In fact, ji-nashi making workshops organized in Europe and North America attract many participants. The number of questions and discussions about shakuhachi-making posted on the online discussion forum exceeds that of postings in other areas such as technique and notation.

17. Shimura (2002) reports the results of his acoustic, physical, and historical analysis of ji-nashi shakuhachi from the edo-period onward. Ji-nashi shakuhachi

from these periods were made through a proportional method, such as the *towari* method, which means the distance between the finger holes is one-tenth of the entire length. This often results in some notes (such as "chi") sharper and some notes (such as "tsu") flatter, depending on the thickness of the internal bore. He concluded that the ji-nashi as an instrument is highly capable of executing a variety of tone colors, while the modern shakuhachi, he characterized, is inclined into accuracy of pitch and homogeneity of quality. While Shimura's analysis focused on vintage classic ji-nashi, Day (2011) analyzed modern ji-nashi, including those made by contemporary makers whose shakuhachi training is in the ji-ari shakuhachi. Many ji-nashi shakuhachi produced today are functional in terms of pitch and volume and thereby can respond to today's musical demands. Another characteristic of modern ji-nashi is its size: compared to the myoan shakuhachi (typically, around the size of 1 shaku 8 sun or 54.5 cm), modern ji-nashi are much longer (see figures 2 and 3).

18. The word "primitive" is often used in this chapter. The modern shakuhachi is a sophisticated instrument, requiring years of training and craftmanship to build. However, it should be noted that there are also practitioners in Japan, as reported in Matsunobu (2007), who barely process the bamboo but make the shakuhachi right away so that they can enjoy the smell and the feel, even if the bamboo shrinks and cracks in time. The participants in this study were also exposed to these Japanese practitioners in their "bamboo roots pilgrimage" journey led by the author. For outsiders, treating indigenous forms of music as primitive can be offensive, leading to the promotion of noble savage romanticization and cultural misappropriation. It is not my intention to promote a naïve portraiture of the shakuhachi tradition.

19. In the same vein, "strategic inauthenticity" is the term coined by Timothy Taylor (1997) to describe musicians who intentionally stay away from the authentic or fixed sense of tradition and instead explore new influences and expressions. Trimillos (2004) identifies staged authenticity in a real performance context in which the performer, as a culture bearer (of traditional music), expresses his or her authentic self (Taylor, 1991) while corresponding to a specific need of the situation.

20. While the taiko in North America has widely been practiced by Japanese immigrants, the shakuhachi has been more popular among non-Japanese practitioners. Among the Japanese immigrants, the taiko was an effective tool to overcome negative stereotypes toward Asian Americans and the resulting self-depreciation and self-denial (*Izumi*). For later generations, the reason for playing the taiko was more "physical fitness, spiritual growth, and communalism" (Terada, 2001, 51–52).

21. In his blog (http://houscidou.blog.fc2.com/blog-entry-438.html), influential shakuhachi maker-seller-player Ohashi Taizan introduced his encounters with conservative shakuhachi practitioners who observed, "the son of Araki Kodo V looks almost foreigner [the son is half Japanese]. That's unacceptable on the stage for classic music." Ohashi heard this kind of remarks many times. In the same blog, however, he also introduced a non-Japanese master who mentioned, "Nobody gets surprised to see humans balance on a ball, but if it is done by a bear, it is an applause," indicating that foreign shakuhachi players are praised for their "unprecedentedness." The author has also heard several remarks on judges of hogaku music competitions that they were

biased toward non-Japanese. "If competitors are senior Japanese players, there is no way to win. Novelty is gold."

22. "Shakuhachi—Japanese Bamboo Flute," Amazon, accessed February 2, 2021, https://www.amazon.co.uk/Shakuhachi-Japanese-Tsushima-Playing-Instructions/dp/B08D3P455W.

23. The reports of Japan Cultural Envoy forum are available at https://www.bunka.go.jp/seisaku/kokusaibunka/bunkakoryushi/index.html.

24. In the same article, Channick writes more specifically for US policy makers: "Listen to artists, who have been working internationally for all these years—collaborating artist-to-artist and artist-to-audience—finding shared values, mutual respect and understanding in the midst of difference. They are the true cultural diplomats—emphasis on the cultural" (2005, 4).

REFERENCES

Akagawa, Natsuko. 2015. *Heritage Conservation and Japan's Cultural Diplomacy: Heritage, National Identity and National Interest.* New York: Routledge.

Akbas, Ibrahim. 2018. "A 'Cool' Approach to Japanese Foreign Policy: Linking Anime to International Relations." *Perceptions* 23, no. 1 (Spring): 95–125.

Ahlgren, Angela. 2018. *Drumming Asian America: Taiko, Performance, and Cultural Politics.* New York: Oxford University Press.

Arisawa, Shino. 2011. Cultural Properties Protection Law: Aspects of Preservation and Innovation in the Protection of Intangible Cultural Properties of Japan. *Quadrante*, no. 12/13: 103–15.

———. 2012. "Dichotomies between 'Classical' and 'Folk' in the Intangible Cultural Properties of Japan," in *Music as Intangible Cultural Heritage: Policy, Ideology, and Practice in the Preservation of East Asian Traditions*, edited by Keith Howard, 181–95. London: Routledge.

Bender, Shawn, 2012. *Taiko Boom: Japanese Drumming in Place and Motion.* Berkeley: University of California Press.

Channick, Jan. 2005. "From the Deputy Director: The Artist as Cultural Diplomat." *American Theater* 22, no. 5 (May): 4.

Day, Kiku. 2011. "Changes in the Construction of the Jinashi Shakuhachi in the Late 20th and Early 21st Centuries." *European Shakuhachi Society Journal* 1: 62–85.

———. 2015. "Zen Buddhism and music: Spiritual shakuhachi tours to Japan." In *The Changing World Religion Map*, edited by Stanly D. Brunn, 2815–831. Dordrecht: Springer.

DeNora, Tia. 2007. "Interlude: Two or More Forms of Music." In *The International Handbook of Research in Arts Education,* edited by Liora Bresler, 799–802. New York: Springer.

Dissanayake, Ellen. 2000. *Art and Intimacy: How the Arts Began.* Seattle: University of Washington Press.

———. 2008. "If Music is the Food of Love, What about Survival and Reproductive Success?" *Musicae Scientiae* 12, no. 1 (March. Special Issue: Narrative in Music and Interaction): 169–95.
Einbinder, Mary. 2013. "Cultural Diplomacy: Harmonizing International Relations through Music." Unpublished master thesis. New York University.
Goff, Patricia. M. 2013. "Cultural Diplomacy." In *The Oxford Handbook of Modern Diplomacy* edited by Andrew F. Cooper, Jorge Heine, and Ramesh Thakur, 419–35.
Gutzwiller, Andreas. 1995. "Adapting Traditional Japanese Teaching Methods to the Western Teaching Situation." In *Teaching Music of the World: The Second International Symposium, Basel*, edited by Margot Lieth-Philipp and Andreas Gutzwiller, 180–82. Affalterbach, Germany: Philipp Verlag.
Halliwell, Patrick. 1994. "Learning the Koto." *Canadian University Music Review* 14: 18–48.
Hebert, David G. 2005. "Music Competition, Cooperation and Community: An Ethnography of a Japanese School Band." Doctoral dissertation, University of Washington. Ann Arbor, MI: Proquest-UMI.
Izumi, Masumi. 2001. "Reconsidering Ethnic Culture and Community: A Case Study on Japanese Canadian Taiko Drumming." *Journal of Asian American Studies* 4, no. 1 (February): 35–56.
Keister, Jay Davis. 2001. "Shaped by Japanese Music: Kikoku Hiroaki and Nagauta Shamisen in Tokyo." Unpublished doctoral dissertation. University of California, Los Angeles.
———. 2004. "The Shakuhachi as Spiritual Tool: A Japanese Buddhist Instrument in the West." *Asian Music* 35, no. 2 (Spring–Summer): 99–131.
———. 2005. "Seeking Authentic Experience: Spirituality in the Western Appropriation of Asian Music." *World of Music* 47, no. 3: 35–53.
Matsunobu, Koji. 2018. "Making Instruments to Create an Authentic Experience: Overcoming the Constraints of Tradition." *International Journal of Creativity in Music Education* 6: 37–46.
———. 2011. "Spirituality as a Universal Experience of Music: A Case Study of North Americans' Approaches to Japanese Music." *Journal of Research in Music Education*, 59, no. 3: 273–89.
———. 2007. "Japanese Spirituality and Music Practice: Art as Self-Cultivation." In *International Handbook of Research in Arts Education*, 1425–42. Dordrecht: Springer.
McCollum, Jonathan. 2018. "Embodying History and Pedagogy: A Personal Journey into the Dokyoku Style of Japanese Shakuhachi." In *International Perspectives on Translation, Education and Innovation in Japanese and Korean Societies*, edited by David G. Hebert, 255–78. New York: Springer.
Malm, William. P. 2000. *Traditional Japanese Music and Musical Instruments*. Tokyo: Kodansha International.
Mitsuhashi, Kifu, et al. 2002. "The Future of Shakuhachi: Symposium at the Tokyo International Shakuhachi Summit." *Hogaku Journal* 189: 42–53.

Momii, Toru. 2021. *Music Analysis and the Politics of Knowledge Production: Interculturality in the Music of Honjoh Hidejirō, Miyata Mayumi, and Mitski*. PhD dissertation, Columbia University.

Napier, Susan J. 2001. *Anime from Akira to Princess Mononoke: Experiencing Contemporary Japanese Animation*. New York: Palgrave.

Park, Jiu Kyu. 2005. "Creating My Own Cultural and Spiritual Bubble: Case of Cultural Consumption by Spiritual Seeker Anime Fans." *Culture and Religion* 6, no. 3 (August): 393–413.

Powell, Kimberly A. 2003. "Learning Together: Practice, Pleasure and Identity in a Taiko Drumming World." Unpublished doctoral dissertation. Stanford University.

Schippers, Huib. 2010. *Facing the Music: Shaping Music Education from a Global Perspective*. New York: Oxford University Press.

Schneider, Cynthia P. 2003. "Diplomacy that Works: 'Best Practices' in Cultural Diplomacy." In *Cultural Diplomacy Research Series*. Center for Arts and Culture. Retrieved from http://www.interarts.net/descargas/interarts645.pdf.

Shimura, Satoshi. 2002. *Kokan Shakuhachi no Gakkigaku* [*The Study of Old Style Shakuhachi Instruments*]. Tokyo: Shuppan Geijutsusha.

Taylor, Timothy D. 1997. *Global Pop: World Music, World Markets*. New York: Routledge.

Terada, Yoshitaka. 2001. "Shifting Identities of Taiko Music in North America." In *Transcending Boundaries: Asian Musics in North America*, edited by Yoshitaka Terada, 37–59. Osaka: National Museum of Ethnology.

Trimillos, Ricordo D. 2004. "Subject, Object, and the Ethnomusicology Ensemble: The Ethnomusicological 'We' and 'Them.'" In *Performing Ethnomusicology: Teaching and Representation in World Music Ensembles*, edited by Ted Solis, 23–52. Berkeley: University of California Press.

Tsukitani, Tsuneko. 2008. *The Shakuhachi and its Music* (translated by Charles Rowe). In *The Ashgate Research Companion to Japanese Music*, edited by Alison McQueen Tokita, and David W. Hughes, 145–67. Aldershot, Hampshire, UK: Ashgate.

Wong, Deborah Anne. 2019. *Louder and Faster: Pain, Joy, and the Body Politic in Asian American Taiko*. Berkely: University of California Press.

Yuasa, Yasuo. 1987. *The Body: Toward an Eastern Mind-body Theory*. Albany: State University of New York Press.

———. 1993. *The Body, Self-cultivation, and Ki-energy*, translated by Shigenori Nagamoto and Monte S. Hull. Albany: State University of New York Press.

Chapter Nine

Cultural Diplomacy and Transculturation through the History of the *Vọng Cổ* in Vietnam

Nguyễn Thanh Thủy and Stefan Östersjö

This chapter discusses how low-level processes of cultural diplomacy may be studied through intercultural collaboration. Or rather, it seeks to understand the more long-term processes of intercultural collaboration that ultimately comprise transculturation and how these may inform our understanding of cultural diplomacy. The empirical material was collected in the south of Vietnam between 2018 and 2019, as part of Musical Transformations, a research project that combines methods of ethnomusicology and artistic research in music.[1] The project studied the emergence of a piece called *Vọng Cổ* in southern Vietnam, seeking to understand the impact of the hybrid context in which the piece was created and altered through time. An additional aim was to address the classic emic/etic problem[2] (Nettl, 2005; Östersjö, 2020) through analysis of artistic intercultural collaborations using "stimulated recall" approaches[3] developed by the Vietnamese/Swedish group The Six Tones,[4] of which the two authors are founding members. Accordingly, the main arguments in this chapter are built either on historical sources or findings developed jointly by the research team and the master performers of *Vọng Cổ*, drawn from the stimulated recall sessions carried out in 2018–2019. The design of this analysis seeks to give voice to all participating musicians and to build the analysis on shared understandings articulated in the stimulated recall sessions that were carried out in recording studios as part of the artistic working processes.[5]

INTERCULTURAL COLLABORATION, TRANSCULTURATION, AND CULTURAL DIPLOMACY

Notions of cultural diplomacy often reference short-term symbolic events such as a tour of a symphony orchestra to a foreign country.[6] In their seminal book, Ahrendt, Ferraguto, and Mahiet note how "music's power has been constructed and experienced, as both a metaphor for and a practice of international relations" (2014, 2). Indeed, we see the impact of music's ability to speak across national and cultural boundaries as early as 1528, when Italian diplomat and musician Baldassare Castiglione discussed the potential of music to enhance diplomacy, claiming that "music is not only no hindrance in the pursuits of peace and war, but is very helpful therein" (1901, 63). Ahrendt, Ferraguto, and Mahiet point to the impact of historical practices of musicians and diplomats, such as Castiglione in the sixteenth century, in conceptualizing musical performance as a "space to imagine political change and conceive social alternatives" (2014, 6). Mark Ferraguto (2018) illustrates how many diplomats in the eighteenth century played important roles as facilitators and collaborators with musicians and composers, reflecting on the mutual benefit between music and diplomacy. In this same historical vein, this chapter considers cultural diplomacy as a component of intercultural, and sometimes transnational relations, between Vietnam and the colonial power of France across the twentieth century.

In a paper discussing Alain Destandau's *Antigone Việt Nam*—a play presented at the Huế Festival in Vietnam in 2008—Matthew Spangler underscores the lasting impact of colonial hegemonic power, and therefore, how intercultural theater performance "may unwittingly, though nonetheless perfectly, reinscribe an imperialist discourse of otherness and rough-handed plunder even as they outwardly seek to claim a progressively avant-garde, anti-imperialist stance: the worst kind of cultural appropriation and hypocrisy" (2010, 82). For The Six Tones, as a platform for intercultural artistic collaboration, it has been essential to continually return to such (self) critical perspectives. Just as other forms of short-term interactions, typical of much cultural diplomacy, can create division and amplify structural injustice (see for instance Pundziūtė-Gallois, 2018), intercultural collaboration may also do the same. Hence, it is only through interrogating its fundamental principles that intercultural collaboration may achieve its goals. Spangler continues his reflection by noting how the challenge of intercultural collaboration should be taken seriously since successfully designed intercultural artistic collaboration holds the potential to

> [R]adically throw open the boundaries of presentational form and reinvent the very possibilities of performance itself. They mark and simultaneously transcend political and cultural borders by bringing together diverse artists in an equitable collaboration that otherwise would not take place. They create transformational experiences for performers and audiences alike through embodied practices of making meaning that emerge in, through, and beyond the performance itself, the effects of which have the capacity to interrogate oppressive structures in the

social world in ways that reimagine that world through avenues of agency for the disempowered. (2010, 82)

We are particularly interested in how intercultural collaboration in music may instigate more long-term change, processes that take embodied form in individual musicians as well as collectives, or material form in the re-formation of musical instruments and other artifacts. Similar long-term changes, across embodied, material, and institutional domains, have also been observed as an outcome of colonization. As argued by Denning, colonial musical practice has tended to institute

[N]ew disciplines of the body—new ways of singing, of dancing, of marching, of playing instruments. To speak of the colonization of the "ear" is thus a metonymy: for the reshaping of the musical subject is not only a reshaping of the individual's musical muscles—the articulated flesh and bones that make up the singing voice, the instrument-playing hands and lips, the dancing feet and hips. It is also the reshaping of the order of the group—the creation of marching bands and church choirs: a colonization not only of the body, but also of articulated bodies. (2016, 36)

Following Margaret Kartomi (1981), we see the long-term processes of such encounters as examples of *musical transculturation*, which, she argues, occurs "only when a group of people select for adoption whole new organizing and conceptual or ideological principles—musical and extramusical—as opposed to small, discrete alien traits" (244).[7] She continues to observe how the impetus for such processes often has been extramusical, related to the prestige of colonial culture, the social or economic advantage of conforming with a majority culture, or the potential of creating a unified form of expression across several groups without a shared culture. She finally notes how:

The final stages of a complete process of transculturation are reached after the tensions between two or more musical cultures have interacted and been resolved into a new unity, through successive generations. Such musical interactions creatively unite and transcend the partly antithetical parent musics to create a new, independent style or genre that is accepted in its own right by the relevant group of people as being representative of their own musical identity, whereupon the processes of musical transculturation may begin all over again. (245)

We further acknowledge how processes of transculturation in music have proven to be sometimes violently destructive and, at other times, a source for creative transformation. In the latter case, as observed by Kartomi and Blum, transculturation "may result in a greater level of individual and corporate creativity than before" (1994, ix). Indeed, the history of *Vọng Cổ* holds several important examples of the proximity between transculturation and hybridity,[8] and we now turn to a historical perspective of the emergence of this music.

CẢI LƯƠNG AND *VỌNG CỔ*: TRANSCULTURATION BETWEEN TRADITION AND MODERNITY

Ever since the end of the seventeenth century, the Mekong plain has been populated by Chinese, Khmer, and Vietnamese, and by the middle of the eighteenth century it has been home to six of Vietnam's provinces (Keith Weller Taylor, 1998). As noted by Keith Weller Taylor, already at this time it was "a place of cultural and ethnolinguistic encounter" (966), sometimes described as a cultural melting pot full of potential for creative innovation, but Philip Taylor observes that, at the same time, "it is precisely such places marked by intense communications, where collisions between people, ideas and memories are quotidian, that offer fertile ground for the development of distinct ethnic consciousness" (2007, 4). With French colonization, beginning in the south in 1862, further transnational influence and the modernization that followed further enhanced the coexistence of different cultures and languages. This laid the ground for the development of hybrid cultural forms that have proven to be remarkably sustainable into the day.

However, the first step in the developments that we will outline in the following two sections is the emergence of *Đờn Ca Tài Tử*,[9] a movement for the revival[10] of traditional Vietnamese chamber music traditions, as musicians migrated south, leaving the royal court in Huế (Cannon, 2012). At the end of the nineteenth century, an anti-French movement gained prominence across Vietnam, wherein Confucianism became a symbol of the fight against colonialism. Many intellectuals left the cities, seeking to lead a life according to traditional values in the countryside (Lê, 2003). Some of these migration streams brought *Huế* music to the south, but also a value system that promoted the learned but nonprofessional performer (*Tài Tử* is Sino-Vietnamese for "talented gentleman" or "talented person"). Hence, Đờn Ca Tài Tử can be understood as sustaining traditional heritage, but also as a movement that embraced traditional Southeast Asian culture as a form of resistance against colonization.

Đờn Ca Tài Tử spread quickly in the south of Vietnam, across different social groups in the nineteenth century. The 1900 Paris exposition became a radical turning point, introducing a novel element of cultural diplomacy, instigated by the French colonial rule. For the exposition, a group of Tài Tử musicians was invited to take part in a performance, which also involved Cambodian traditional dance, (paradoxically) performed by the French choreographer and dancer Cléo de Mérode, selected more for her potential to attract a large audience during the five months of the expo than for her artistic skills in Asian dance, assisted by a group of Italian dancers. It should be noted that de Mérode merely studied the Cambodian dance she was asked to perform for photos, and then created her choreography (Nguyễn and Nguyễn, 2014). Hence, its authenticity may be put in doubt, and it should be further noted that the production contained very little intercultural exchange. Then again, and as pointed out by Nguyễn and Nguyễn (2014), the event at the expo, which was performed for the entire five months of the fair, appears to have been successful as cultural diplomacy, by giving renewed energy to the Tài Tử musicians involved, and also attracted a large international audience.

In 1906, at the Colonial Expo in Marseille, a group of Tài Tử musicians led by Nguyễn Tống Triều again visited France and met with audiences and artists from around the world. While the motivation for these intercultural exchanges has remained relatively unclear, they gained prominence through their impact in the increasingly hybridized culture that was developing in the south of Vietnam. Inspired by the settings in Western theaters, Đờn Ca Tài Tử began to perform in theaters and drew out of the expressive content of traditional songs, a gestural performance style in vocal performance, which became known as Ca Ra Bộ.[11] These developments, as well as a wish to adapt traditional Hát Bội theater[12] to audiences in the shifting context, were related to colonial urbanization, which also entailed an alienation from the Chinese language of Hát Bội (Nguyễn, 2007; Trần 1970). However, Cải Lương was not only built on forms drawn from traditional music and theater, but gained prominence through its development of hybrid forms, which (paradoxically) combined influences drawn from this anticolonial movement of revival with elements from Western theater and music. In the 1920s, Sài Gòn had become the greatest harbor city in all French Indochina (Logan, 2005). Also, jazz was becoming fashionable and was the music most often heard in hotels and restaurants. But these were also the venues for Đờn Ca Tài Tử performance.[13] Tradition and modernity became increasingly entangled. As observed by Erich DeWald (2012), since 1930, when Radio Sài Gòn started its international broadcasts, radio became an exposition of modernity in the south of Vietnam. Indeed, "jazz was a particularly popular programming option," but traditional theater was equally popular, and DeWald claims that its "modernity was just as conspicuous as that of jazz from France" (155). At around the same time, Western motion pictures were also introduced in Vietnam and soon became a central source of inspiration for the theatre troupes performing Cải Lương.

Drawing on all these sources, Cải Lương was already at the outset, built around the juxtaposition of Western songs and traditional music. During the 1920s, it was common to incorporate a group playing military band instruments, and an ensemble of traditional instruments, with musicians from Đờn Ca Tài Tử (Gibbs, 2003). Luu (2014) underlines how many agents, ranging from media, theater directors, playwrights and song composers, actors, and musicians carried out this "cultural transfer" (104) to the growing audience. The diplomacy carried out by these agents was concerned not only with the weaving together of Western and Vietnamese musical forms and theatrical forms of expression, since Cải Lương also encompassed influences from China, Japan, and some minority cultures found in the south of Vietnam.

The growing performing arts industry, including theaters, cinemas, record labels, and radio stations in Vietnam at this time, all thrived from the attraction of the modern, of the novelty inherent to the diplomacy between culturally distinct modes of expression. The incorporation of Western songs, as well as aspects of Western theater, evidently pleased audiences. On the other hand, Gibbs (2003) points to historical evidence of how "many Vietnamese listeners during the 1920s and 1930s found it difficult to reconcile Western music with this familiar affect system. Even encountering these songs during intermissions or scene changes was a shock to some" (64). The experience of cultural collision, as well as of excitement for novelty, is amply captured in Sài Gòn newspapers from the period (Nguyễn and Nguyễn, 2013). In this setting, wherein the wish to sustain Vietnamese and ancient Asian traditions was contrasted by novel forms of expression, embracing the modernity launched by colonial urbanization, *Vọng Cổ* emerged. This piece of music had its roots in Đờn Ca Tài Tử but became the central music, which always was played in a *Cải Lương* performance. Its popularity has lasted into the present day, and it remains emblematic of the nostalgic expressiveness of *Cải Lương*.

Vọng Cổ developed gradually from another composition, *Dạ Cổ Hoài Lang*, which was composed in 1920 by Cao Văn Lầu[14] from Bạc Liêu in the Mekong Delta. Even though the earliest developments are not possible to trace in any detail since much of this history took place either under colonial rule or during a civil war, it is important to note that *Vọng Cổ* has been subject to extraordinary processes of transformation, much due to its great popularity, but also, as we will argue, due to processes of transculturation, launched initially by the hybrid context in which it was first created.[15] Still, there are many layers to unpack in the history of musical change, and the development of *Vọng Cổ* can also be related to the wish of musicians to obtain more space for improvisation within the original framework of the song.

The historical development of the Vietnamese guitar is a substantial example of material transculturation. Starting in the late 1920s, musicians experimented with ways of adapting, first the mandolin and then also the guitar, to the performance of *Cải Lương* and *Vọng Cổ*, seeking ways to enable the performance of the ornamentation that characterizes this music. Their method was to modify the fretboard by creating deeply scalloped frets. In addition, the development of the Vietnamese guitar entailed extensive experimentation with different tuning systems (see Östersjö, forthcoming). The latter process was also characterized by negotiations between performance practices either related to the Western mandolin (adapted to the guitar) or to the đàn kìm,[16] an instrument central to the music of Đờn Ca Tài Tử. Hence, material transculturation was closely dependent on different forms of embodied transculturation in the process of creating the Vietnamese guitar.

MUSICAL TRANSFORMATIONS

The first part of the Musical Transformations project started in autumn 2018. Funded by Sweden's Wallenberg Foundation, this international project sought to better understand the development of *Vọng Cổ* by exploring both past and present transformations through fieldwork in the south of Vietnam. The four members of The Six Tones carried out this work in collaboration with American ethnomusicologist David G. Hebert. Musical Transformations seeks to document *Vọng Cổ* heritage while gaining additional insights from collaborating in recordings of both traditional music and experimental forms that combine Vietnamese and Western art music traditions. Such projects may be understood as a form of cultural diplomacy among artists via intercultural negotiation of musical sound and instrumental practices.

When traveling in the Mekong Delta region in August 2018 we interviewed several local musicians in the city of Long Xuyên. One of them was Linh, an amateur performer of Đờn Ca Tài Tử who plays both the *đàn kìm* and violin. We were particularly interested in his relation to the latter instrument, and he told us a story that started in the time of the "American war." Although he lived in the south, he joined the northern side and was soon engaged as the manager of a group of artists supported by the Việt Cộng, performing at the front. In 1970, as part of the supplies they received from Hà Nội, they were given a violin. Since no one in the group knew how to play it, Linh held on to this violin. He describes how it was difficult to play the instrument at the outset, and he had to practice far out in the rice fields so that others wouldn't be annoyed with his playing. During all the wartime travels, he would bring the violin along and always practice far from camp. He had learned to play Đờn Ca Tài Tử from his father, and already knew how to play the *đàn kìm* and the guitar, but found that the violin was also suited for this music since it immediately would afford both the intonation and ornamentation typical of this music. At this time, there were several Vietnamese violinists famous for their performance of *Vọng Cổ*, and he studied the recordings of Hai Thơm, Văn Còn, and others. After the war, he worked as the director of a *Cải Lương* group, wherein he also played the violin. But he remained an amateur performer, the characteristic carrier of the traditions of Đờn Ca Tài Tử and *Cải Lương*. We asked him whether he thought of the violin as a Western instrument, which was brought into hybrid use in *Cải Lương*, and, referring to the instrument he was holding during the interview, he said he did not think of it as such.

> I have a Vietnamese soul, thinking and emotions, therefore all of my playing is absolutely Vietnamese, not Western. The person who holds the instrument is Vietnamese, therefore the instrument is just a means to project a Vietnamese soul. Therefore I think of this instrument as Vietnamese. (Đặng Hoàng Linh, Stimulated recall interview,[17] August 4, 2018)

Returning to the observations of Philip Taylor, perhaps Linh's relation to the violin can be seen as an expression of how South Vietnam has been characterized as "a place of intense flows of people, goods and ideas, the delta has been described as a melting pot" (2007, 4). Taylor continues to note how its "cultural identity has been defined as one of constant change, a passion for the new, a product of voracious combination and constant reinvention" (4). In the Transformations project, we sought to understand the potential for further musical development in the present, through the openness to change, and the reinvention of cultural practices and artifacts, which we found to be characteristic of the history of *Vọng Cổ*. But we were equally interested in how the identity of this music had at the same time been characterized by preserving core elements of ancient traditions, all in the spirit of Đờn Ca Tài Tử.

Although we met a great number of musicians in the reconnaissance trips in the Mekong Delta in the initial stage of the project, for the recording project we decided to work with three musicians, who also were the core members of a group and often perform as a trio (typically also with one or more singers). There is an interesting dynamic in their group, which can be related to its generational spread. Phạm Công Tỵ, who plays two versions of the two-stringed fiddle, the đàn gáo, and đàn cò,[18] is the oldest. Phạm Văn Môn is a leading performer of the Vietnamese guitar, and he recorded with Phạm Công Tỵ for the first time on an album released in 1998. The first sessions, in which The Six Tones first worked with these three musicians, took place in October 2018, in the recording studio of the youngest member of their group, Huỳnh Tuấn, who plays the đàn kìm.

DIPLOMACY AND TRANSCULTURATION THROUGH INTERCULTURAL COLLABORATION

When initiating a project, The Six Tones always make time for sessions where all participating artists are able to present their previous work. The first day in Tuấn's studio was spent sharing audio recording and video of the work of the two ensembles, as well as some live playing by each group. Here, The Six Tones presented many examples of experimental music, which combined elements of traditional music from the south of Vietnam with texturally driven work with instruments and live electronics. We have found it important to remain in this stage for a while, without aiming to produce anything, thinking of this stage more as a way of setting the grounds for the negotiations. Having said this, it is vital to also to bear in mind that the listening that takes place here can at best function as a way of evoking curiosity and that these initial presentations are bound to often create misunderstandings. We understand cultural diplomacy in music as a matter of musicians tuning their ears to the Other, seeking intersubjective understanding, also across culturally defined ways of listening. In this section, we will look at examples of how such processes took shape across this collaboration, building on video documentation and audio recordings collected between October 2018 and October 2019, when The Six Tones made the final recording sessions in the Việt Tân studio in Sài Gòn.

In the initial sessions, we also presented the Musical Transformations project along with its dual aims of first documenting the living tradition of *Vọng Cổ*, with a particular interest in its history of musical change, and second, to experiment with this music to invite new approaches to these traditions. As part of the overall method of building trust[19] between all participating musicians, we then entered the second stage, in which we would document trio and solo versions of *Vọng Cổ*. We were interested to find that, even though Ty, Môn, and Tuấn are leading masters of this tradition, they were not entirely comfortable with recording their solos. Although solo recordings became influential already with the introduction of *Vọng Cổ nhịp* 32—for instance as heard in a recording on the Lam Sơn label in the late 1950s with the *đàn kìm* master Năm Cơ (Gibbs et al., 2013, 89), and perhaps even more striking through the solo recordings of the guitarist Văn Vĩ in the 1960s—they were much more confident with their trio playing. Recording their solo performances of *Vọng Cổ* was a challenge for them, and they clearly took the challenge seriously. They described how they had been preparing extensively for these first recording sessions, and both Môn and Tuấn asked to redo their first recordings in later sessions. As the project developed, Stefan took on the role of a record producer, for instance, by challenging Môn to shape his solo playing on the Vietnamese guitar across all registers, in the process of preparing for the final recordings of their solos for the double album. The way in which the project immediately challenged the traditional practice of the three performers became a purposeful means for building trust, and also increasing understanding, among the participants. Further, when the final recordings were made a year later, substantial development was evidenced, for instance in the striking mastery in Tuấn's solo recording of *Vọng Cổ nhịp* 32. The recordings were made using high-quality microphones, and a rough mix was made in the evening of each day so that we could listen back to their performances the next morning. This, too, enabled us to continue building trust. When Ty heard his solo recordings, he claimed they were the best quality recordings he had ever made![20]

At the end of the second day, we made the first recordings of all musicians playing together. It was an explicit wish that Ty, Môn, and Tuấn should retain a structure from *Vọng Cổ*, and The Six Tones would seek ways to interact with their playing. We made several takes that afternoon, some with just one of them, and sometimes all at once. These recordings were mixed in the evening and on the morning of October 31, 2018, and we listened back to these takes, with the agreement that any one of us could stop the playback to comment on a certain moment. Ty was the first to comment, saying that the music sounded "wonky, muffled as if from a creased cassette tape" [laughing]. "I wanted to listen to *Vọng Cổ* but I don't know what people were playing in here . . . sounds funny" (Phạm Công Ty, Stimulated recall interview, October 31, 2018).

The atmosphere was friendly, but Ty, Môn, and Tuấn appeared to be similarly unsure of what to make of the music they listened to, and all of them laughed. One shared concern was that of structure. Ty suggested that it might be helpful for the listener if some parts were *Vọng Cổ*, played properly, and other parts were not and that the division between the two would be more articulated. Tuấn similarly expressed that also for himself, "there should be a sound or something to keep the time, in order to know where we are" (Huỳnh Tuấn, Stimulated recall interview, October 31, 2018).[21] Such discussions of structure would be a recurring topic in the negotiations across the coming year. Môn pointed to how a Vietnamese listener would hear this music differently than a Westerner, and their expectations on what to listen for in a performance of *Vọng Cổ* may be a concern, since they may feel lost in this music. These concerns are very similar to those expressed in the early negotiations between Western and Vietnamese music in *Cải Lương*, as discussed above. But Môn continues to say that, after the working sessions the day before, he was

[T]hinking of how to create something new in *Vọng Cổ*, which people would like to listen to, in some parts we could combine different versions of *Vọng Cổ*, sometimes we play original, pure *Vọng Cổ*, sometimes we decompose the piece, but just a little: similarly to how it is sometimes done in pop songs. But the main point is that we need to have harmony, if we do not want normal *Vọng Cổ*, we need to work with harmony. (Phạm Văn Môn, Stimulated recall interview, October 31, 2018)[22]

Hence, all three engaged in negotiating how we might approach the aim of creating novel versions of *Vọng Cổ*, proposing to work with the large-scale form or introduce harmony as a different structuring element. Still, the general impression is that they all felt that what we played the first day is hard for them, but also for their audience, to relate to.

We continued the work on this day by testing smaller constellations, working mostly in trios with two instruments and electronics. When combining Ty's đàn gáo with Trà My's đàn bầu, the first take that seemed to attract everyone in the group was recorded. These are two melodic instruments, and in this recording, they wove similar lines, going in and out of the traditional frameworks of *Vọng Cổ*, although Ty had the role of keeping a basic structure going throughout the piece.

The next morning, we again started by listening back to the recordings made the day before. Perhaps most experimental piece recorded that day was a trio with two Vietnamese guitars (played by Môn and Stefan) and electronics. When listening back to the recording, Môn asked Stefan how he found it "working with *Vọng Cổ* this way," asking him to compare it to earlier projects with traditional music that were presented on the first day. He asked more specifically, "Do you have different methods, or do you have a different experience?" Stefan replied, outlining some general artistic methods in the two pieces:

I was looking most of all for a sound, with the two guitars, that works. And that the two guitars would be, all the time, in different musical spaces. But to have a sound that works. To me, there was never an intention for this to really work, it was really a way of experimenting, but also, I wanted to challenge him [smiles and looks at Môn]. (Stefan Östersjö, Stimulated recall interview, November 1, 2018)[23]

Seeking experimentation rather than immediate success may be understood as a method in itself. Certainly, creating challenges for the Other can also be a form of cultural diplomacy, and in this conversation, Môn agreed that he could see that this was part of it. He continued to note how he could himself see that at this point, he was not yet able to "find many ways to interact with Stefan's playing, I try, sometimes I stop, but then I do not find anything to go along with what Stefan was doing, and then I return to playing *Vọng Cổ*" (Phạm Văn Môn, Stimulated recall interview, November 1, 2018).[24] In a study of early interactions between the members of The Six Tones, Thủy noted (when looking back at video documentation ranging back to 2007), "I see now how my biggest challenge in the work we did in the spring of 2009 was to develop a different individual voice,[25] which could be shared in this context" (Östersjö, 2020, 100). What Môn mentioned here appears to be a similar observation of how the development of a shared voice in musical performance may sometimes first demand the creation of a new individual voice. We propose that such microprocesses of transformation of voice are typically a continual and reciprocal process in intercultural collaboration. Hence here, diplomacy instigates change both in self and the other, and thereby becomes a matter of internal growth and development through which new modes of interaction become possible. The most integrated interactions we found were in the trio performances with Tỵ, My, and Henrik, which everyone had liked the day before. Môn enthusiastically compared the two voices of the *đàn gáo* and the *đàn bầu* to two snakes, like weaving patterns. Tỵ says he "likes this one. It follows the framework, but not the *Vọng Cổ* figurations."[26] This constellation was also the first to be considered a "keeper" for the CD release, and when returning to workshops at the end of the year, this trio would again be rehearsing, seeking to further refine this music.

A new phase in the negotiations started in the afternoon of the same day when we agreed to start discussing the form of a concert we were to play at the Hanoi New Music Festival in December. To address the requests from several performers for a structural framework, The Six Tones proposed to decide on a large-scale form for the entire concert. In the afternoon session, we gradually developed formal ideas and made one run-through of the version we had at the end of the day. A fundamental idea with this concert was that we would design it as a double trio event, with the trio of Tỵ, Môn, and Tuấn and The Six Tones playing on their own in substantial parts of the performance. Hereby, we would secure moments in the concert in which the audience could experience *Vọng Cổ* in its traditional form, and build moments of friction between our respective practices through which its framework was challenged. From this point, the interactions shifted from the experimenting mode of a workshop to the production mode of rehearsal. In December 2018, we knew that we would only have one day for rehearsals before the concert, so it was necessary to establish a robust performance before closing these first sessions. At the end of the day, after the run-through, everyone seemed to agree that we were in good shape for the concert.

Meeting up in Hà Nội was a shift of scenery that had positive effects on the interaction between all performers. Now, The Six Tones were the host ensemble and would bring the other players around to rehearsal and concert venues, cafes, and restaurants. We also rehearsed the music we had created with the improviser and composer Lương Huệ Trinh, who was replacing Henrik Frisk, playing live electronics in the concert in Hà Nội. The concert, at L'Espace, a concert venue that forms part of the French embassy in the city center, was a success and was played to a full hall. Members of the project were interviewed by several TV stations, and the entire event certainly brought the group together even more. First and foremost, to be successfully rehearsing and giving concerts constitutes the most fundamental level of building trust among musicians. But the social interactions outside the professional work was proving to be more and more important too, as we all flew back to Sài Gòn for further workshops, now held in a lecture/performance space at Vietnam National Institute of Culture and Arts Studies (VICAS), a national center for musicology in Sài Gòn.

On the first day, we spent time listening back to versions of the piece we had played in Hà Nội. One comment made by Môn is particularly important since it had a central function in our further development of artistic approaches to the modal framework of *Vọng Cổ*. He again related to the idea of working with harmony, as discussed in the initial sessions. His question was posed at the end of the session, and certainly adopted a diplomatic tone:

> I am not so acquainted with contemporary music, but I wonder, when we play for instance in *Hò* 1, should the other trio play in the same key? I hear that in some parts we do not play in the same key, it sounds a bit jarring (*nghịch tai*)[27] to the ear. I only wonder if this is intentional or not? (Phạm Văn Môn, Stimulated recall interview, December 29, 2018)[28]

In the section that Môn refers to, we had agreed that The Six Tones would introduce a different tonality, and it is this use of polytonality that Môn refers to. We agreed to continue working on that section in the afternoon to find a way of playing it so that everyone was happy with. However, the concept of polytonality in the performance of *Vọng Cổ* would surface again, gaining increasing prominence in the final recording sessions.

Ty, Trà My, and Henrik also rehearsed this day. After they recorded the first take, Trà My asked Ty how he found it, and he replied he thought it was "so-so." He continued to observe how, in the parts where he played, *Vọng Cổ* and Trà My was "disturbing," and it "sounded better, because when you play *Vọng Cổ*, I sometimes was not sure where you are, and then I did not know what to do" (Phạm Công Ty, Conversation in rehearsal, December 29, 2018).[29] Trà My responded by first stating that she thought his "interruptions" sounded good to her. She then tried to convince him that it wouldn't matter if his layer of music would not be aligned with a specific structural downbeat in the *Vọng Cổ* she is playing: "Just play what you want, do something you like and find something new!" They agreed to create a more flexible form and expand the space for more free interaction in the piece, an approach that was retained also in the final recordings for the CD. At the end of our sessions at VICAS, we made stimulated recall interviews with the trio, looking back at recordings of solo and trio recordings of *Vọng Cổ*, made in August and December 2018. While many important topics were covered across those interviews, we will only touch on one aspect here, which is how Tuấn expresses that so far, he was not pleased with his solo playing. He found that he was still not quite able to structure the phrases (*Lái*) so that he could avoid exact repetition of figurations.[30] This, as well as Môn's comment from the initial "stimulated recall" session, looking back at the performance in Hà Nội, are two pointers toward the work we were to do in the Viết Tân Studio in October 2019.

While Henrik Frisk and Stefan Östersjö had carried out all audio recordings thus far, Torbjörn Samuelsson, a sound engineer who made a name for himself as a leading name in acoustic recordings in Scandinavia, made the recordings for the double CD.[31] Hence, when we all got together in Sài Gòn to carry out the recording sessions, it was clear that our ambitions were higher, and that our focus was on getting the most out of the artistic potential of the group. The general plan was to start with trio recordings of *Vọng Cổ* and then finish all solo recordings of the piece (knowing that they were still most concerned about getting these right) and then move to the more experimental work, in different constellations.

Tuấn's solo recordings were the first truly magical moment. As mentioned above, he had thus far been discontented with his playing in the previous recordings. But his playing in *Vọng Cổ nhịp* 32 was now virtuosic, at the same time as it had a new depth. Most of all, his structural grasp and large-scale phrasing now enabled him to shape the piece in much larger chunks, with crystal clear shaping of each *Lái*.

On the second to last day of the recording sessions, we had individual interviews with all three players. Here, we invited them to reflect on their experience of the entire working process. In the interview with Tuấn, the development in his solo playing was the first obvious topic. He first confirmed that he felt that the project had forced him to develop new aspects of his playing, and he referred to the listening practice, the high-quality recordings that were made each time, and the repeated joint listening back to them, as a central factor. He described it as follows: "When I listen back to recordings of my playing, several months or a year ago, I often think that 'I did it like that then, but I would do it differently now.'" He also explains that, in his solo playing, he is not interested in preparing a fixed version. Instead, he wants to "only focus on the context, in the moment, I listen to my sound. When I play solo, I can hear it well, and I can be very focused," and he finds this approach to be one reason for the recordings coming together as they did. On the other hand, he describes how the project has made him practice solo playing at home, and voice together with the critical and attentive listening practice in the studio work, he has developed an increased awareness of "the way I bring the Lái to closure, bringing the Lái to the Hò, how I make several Lái more interconnected, sometimes I want to create rhythmical tension," but also how he seeks "to play less figurations, and focus more on the ornamentation (. . .) when I play solo, I think more of the softer qualities, and then I build toward a culmination" (Huỳnh Tuấn, interview, October 16, 2019).

Tuấn continued by reflecting on how his experience of playing the more experimental pieces, with The Six Tones, has changed over time. He described how he "feels more integrated in the group now." The concerns he expressed in the first stimulated recall session, and his wish for clearer structures, something to help keep the time "in order to know where we are" is here turned into a rather different description of working in this group:

> I feel deep inside that it makes my playing very free. Since your playing is so free, I can also play anything. There is no constraining composition or timeframe, it is free. Therefore I feel very free and comfortable. (Huỳnh Tuấn, interview, October 16, 2019)[32]

As can be seen above, the task of creating clear structures and frameworks for the more experimental approaches to *Vọng Cổ* was central to the negotiations within the group beginning in October 2018. Before we managed to achieve this, the freedom that Tuấn expressed above, by the time of the final recordings, would not have been possible. In the same interview, he reflects on this shift, and notes how when playing in the larger ensemble "I do not have to play a lot or play little. It could be anything, following your concept. Before I understood this, I worried whether, if I do this or that, is it good or not? When I listened back, I felt there was something inorganic" (Tuấn, personal communication, October 16, 2019). In an interview on the same day, Ty expressed how he felt that a mutual understanding has emerged in the group:

> Comparing between the last time we met and now, last time I was not familiar with this kind of work, and we didn't know each other as well as now. In my opinion, I didn't know how to do free improvisation, or what it was. . . . In Vietnamese traditional music we have a melodic framework, but we do not have free improvisation like this. This year, we really understand each other. It was really good, much better than last year. Last year we tried, but we did not understand. This year we have a mutual understanding, really intertwined. It was really

good. Even in the free improvisations we understand each other very well. (Tỵ, personal communication, October 16, 2019)[33]

Returning to the question of tonalities, on the second to last day, Tỵ came up with a new idea for how to approach this problem, proposing that the trio should try to play *Vọng Cổ* in three different keys simultaneously. Perhaps in reference to our previous discussions of polytonality at VICAS, this proposal became a very important final turning point in the project. We first recorded the trio on its own, playing without common tonal connecting points at the beginning of each Lái. The result was a piece of extraordinary music that retained the rhythmic vitality of *Vọng Cổ*, but provided a sense of polytonal harmony that brought out novel timbral qualities in the constellation of instruments in the trio.

We agreed to continue by making this polytonal playing of *Vọng Cổ* a building block in performances with the whole group. The further structuring idea was to play as a "double-trio" again, as in the concert in Hà Nội, but now with quick shifts between us. Hereby, we created some of the most integrated interactions in the CD track, with music that moves seamlessly in and out of *Vọng Cổ*. On the final working day in the studio, when all recordings were finished, we set up a longer conversation with all musicians to summarize our shared experiences. Here, Môn compared playing *Vọng Cổ* in three different keys to how his listening also had changed when playing with the musicians of The Six Tones, using a Vietnamese phrase that could be translated as listening with an "inversed ear":

> Because when playing that version, my listening to their two instruments was inversed, just like I have been experimenting and playing with other kinds of instruments. It is not about playing the best version of *Vọng Cổ*. It is about experimenting with the piece. That was a good idea to try out.
>
> Thủy: Can you talk more about :inversed listening?"
>
> Môn: Inversed . . . unfamiliar but interesting. Traditionally, *Vọng Cổ* needs to be played together, in one key. Sometimes you can go to another key, but you need to return very soon. You cannot go very far from the central key. But in this version in three modes, my listening was really inversed. If you are not a master of *Vọng Cổ*, you wouldn't be able to play in this way. (Phạm Văn Môn, Stimulated recall interview, October 16, 2019)[34]

Môn's account of the change in his listening, and the notion of the "inversed ear" strikes a note similar to how we have previously discussed intercultural collaboration through the pair of musical and musicianly listening, taken from Pierre Schaeffer's typology.[35] Michel Chion observes how musical listening or invention refers back to traditional heritage, to established and accepted structures and values, which it attempts to rediscover or recreate; whilst musicianly hearing or invention seeks rather to locate interesting new phenomena or to innovate in the facture of sound objects. The musical attitude rests on old values; the musicianly attitude actively seeks new ones. (2009, 39)

Intercultural collaboration may demand musicians to modify their listening habits.[36] What Môn describes could be analyzed as a process of transculturation, instigated through musicianly listening. With such an observation we are deep below the surface layers of cultural diplomacy and considering the fundamental workings of the processes it may initiate. At the same time, it is also important to note how Schaeffer regards the pair of musical and musicianly listening as complementary. For a musician navigating conflicting aesthetic and social systems related to musical performance, such an oscillation between attitudes related to tradition and the searching modes of musicianly listening appears to be a key to the artistic possibilities inherent to intercultural exchange. Certainly, in the negotiations between Môn, Ty, Tuấn and The Six Tones, such oscillation can be seen in all musicians, in ways that resemble the historical processes that led to the creation of *Cải Lương*. Hereby, one could argue that, paradoxically, by challenging the traditions of *Vọng Cổ* performance, foundational principles of this music are at the same time reenacted.

DISCUSSION

The histories of colonization and hybridity, such as those found in the origins of *Vọng Cổ* in *Cải Lương*, have many parallels across the world. One instance is the introduction of jazz to the people of Haiti starting with the American occupation in 1915. Mervin L. Butler (2014) discusses how Haitian musicians created the idiom of "djaz," a creolized term referring to their response to this colonial influence, incorporating local forms of dance music with Afro-American jazz. Butler proposes that the term may be seen as "emblematic of social and political actions that transcended both the domain of musical practice and the borders of the Haitian nation-state" (212). Similarly, Nguyễn (2007) observes how *Cải Lương* "created a means of imagining a vision of a dynamic and syncretic Vietnamese identity out of contemplations about the performance of gender and identity" (20). As we suggest above, this development was sparked through processes of transculturation, which are active still today. Hence, we find Butler's explorations of the role of intercultural musical collaboration to be a pertinent source of comparison with the findings in our study.

If we return to the performance of Tài Tử music at the Paris expo of 1900, might it make sense to question whether an event like this, bringing music from a colony to the colonizing country, is at all a matter of cultural diplomacy? Is it perhaps better understood as an attempt at creating unity within an empire, not to negotiate relations, but as a means to build the cultural expressions of the colonies into the identity of the French mainland?

To avoid becoming a means for extended nation branding, musical diplomacy through intercultural collaboration must be built on an ethics of listening, emerging, following Cobussen and Nielsen (2012) "in the space between listener and music, in the resonance of the listening and the sounding body, in the dynamic encounter of the listener and the sensory material. Instead of relying on predetermined principles, ethical values need to be worked out in an effort of engagement" (165). We argue that when Môn describes the experience of listening with an "inversed ear" in the latter and more experimental performances of *Vọng Cổ*, constitutes an expression of such an engagement, which, returning to Denning (2016), initiates "new disciplines of the body" (36) but now as a post-colonial experience of transculturation. In the intercultural practice of The Six Tones, stimulated recall has been a method for negotiating shared understanding through listening. In Musical Transformations, we have aimed to share this practice with Môn, Ty, and Tuấn, seeking an intersubjective listening that cuts across cultural boundaries. This we understand as the very foundations of musical diplomacy, and in particular, for diplomacy that wishes to create change, both in individuals, institutions, and eventually, in nations.

NOTES

1. Artistic research was implemented in most European countries in the early 2000s. The term is less common in the United Kingdom where practice-as-research is a rather synonymous approach (Nelson, 2013). However, the term has gained currency also in the United Kingdom, as can be seen in recent publications such as Blain and Minors (2020). It should be noted that in most countries there is a prehistory of gradual development of formats for artistic research in conservatories dating back to the 1970s. In Finland, doctoral degrees were awarded in academies of fine and performing arts already in the late 1980s. For further reading see Biggs and Karlsson (2011) and Östersjö (2019).

2. Bruno Nettl (2005) summarizes the negotiation of insider and outsider perspectives that entails as the challenge of unpacking "what it is about the way a culture works, in its core, that causes its practitioners to make certain kinds of conceptual, behavioral, and acoustic distinctions in their music" (229). The Musical Transformations project has aimed to achieve such intersubjective negotiations through the use

of stimulated recall methods, and hereby, to give voice to all participating musicians. The two Vietnamese members of The Six Tones, both teachers in the traditional music department in the Hanoi National Academy of Music since the early 2000s, today have different relations to the musical cultures of traditional music in Vietnam. This is indeed complex already in the relation between the aural traditions upheld by master performers outside the academy, and the priority given to scored music, as is the teaching model in the academy. Since 2006, when the group was created, the two Vietnamese performers have been increasingly engaged in international projects, and one has carried out a PhD in Sweden. However, in the work carried out in Transformations, their grounding also is in studies with masters from the south, and previous recordings of these repertoires constituted the initial building block in the creation of the project, providing both emic understanding and a foundation of trust between the performers.

3. Stimulated recall is a qualitative research method that has been used in music research to an increasing extent across the past decades. The term was coined by Benjamin Bloom in 1953 in a study that used audio recordings of classroom teaching as stimuli to allow students to relive the original experience and give accounts of their original thought processes. While Bloom selected clips from the teaching situation, Kagan and colleagues developed the method further by asking each subject to view the entire documentation and to stop it to identify moments that required comment (Kagan and Krathwohl, 1967). For a further discussion of the use of stimulated recall in the work of The Six Tones see Östersjö (2020).

4. The Six Tones are Nguyễn Thanh Thủy (who plays đàn tranh-Vietnamese zither) and Ngô Trà My (who plays đàn bầu-*monochord*), Swedish guitarist Stefan Östersjö (also playing many other stringed instruments), and Swedish composer and laptop improviser Henrik Frisk. The group was formed when the two Vietnamese performers were visiting Sweden as guest teachers in the Malmö Academy of Music in 2006. Since then, The Six Tones have been developing an artistic practice that challenges hierarchical constructions of musical experience and instead puts the focus on how music is essentially a shared phenomenon. The group invites composers, performers, and artists in other fields to collaborative projects that cross the boundaries between arts disciplines and cultures. Initially, The Six Tones had the aim of creating an amalgamation of art music from Vietnam and Europe. An important figure of thought has been how the transmission of a tradition always involves an element of transformation. Over the first few years, the group developed artistic strategies for playing traditional Vietnamese music in hybrid settings for Western stringed instruments and traditional Vietnamese instruments, improvising in traditional and experimental Western idioms, and commissioning new music by composers in Asia as well as Western countries.

5. The Transformations project produces a repository with data collected in Vietnam. As part of this work, a subpage holds video clips that contain the data referenced in this chapter. The repository is created as an exposition in the Research Catalogue and the subpage related to the present chapter is found following this link: https://www.researchcatalogue.net/view/1301475/1302055.

6. Cultural diplomacy through music is indeed a multifaceted phenomenon that has gained increasing attention ever since the days of the Cold War between the United States and the Soviet Union (Gevinson, 2017). The first notable Cold War musical diplomacy event was a tour of the USSR by the New York Philharmonic and its conductor Leonard Bernstein. It was intelligently designed by combining music by Russian composers who had previously been banned by the Soviet regime with music by American composers. It has been claimed that one outcome of this tour was the beginning of a reconsideration of Stravinsky's role in Russian music (see Gevinson, 2017; Schwarz, 1983). But, while this tour became a source for a renegotiation of relations between American and Russian musics, many other examples of cultural diplomacy by touring symphony orchestras instead have become expressions of a colonial understanding of Western art music as a universal language.

7. For a more detailed discussion of the individual processes of transmission, either within a musical culture or across cultures, see Schippers (2010), who discusses such systems of transmission from a series of overarching perspectives, while underlining that "transmission" relates not only to learning musical material but also to the enculturation of approaches to a musical style or genre at large" (62). These perspectives entail technical (instrumental and vocal) skills; repertoire and performance practice; theory (explicit or implicit); creativity and expression; and lastly, culture and values. The relation between these domains, and the nature of transmission within it, varies between different musics. In our understanding, transculturation takes place when systems of transmission are altered by inclusion of processes and practices (embodied transculturation) or through the adaption of instruments and other tools (material transculturation).

8. Welsch (1999) sees transculturality and hybridization as consequences of the "inner differentiation and complexity of modern cultures" (p. 197), affecting all levels of contemporary society, from institutional structures to individual experience.

9. *Nhạc Tài Tử* (Tài Tử music) is a genre of chamber music that has origins in the court music of Huế (Central Vietnam) and developed further in southern Vietnam. Đờn Ca Tài Tử refers to Tài Tử music performed also with singers.

10. As discussed by Hill and Bithell (2014), the notion of revival of musical traditions is a complex one, characterized by a span between continuity and reinvention. They note how "each instance of supposed revival results in some sort of transformation or innovation, whether it be a new musical style, new methods of transmission and performance, new functions and meanings, or even a new music (sub)culture" (5). Such processes were indeed characteristic also of the revival of Hát Bội through the development of *Cải Lương*.

11. Literally meaning "singing with gestures."

12. Hát Bội is a form of traditional theater (also often referred to as *Tuồng* theater), which developed in Vietnam in the thirteenth century, and which carries traits from Beijing opera. See Nguyễn (2007, 25–26) for further detail on the role of *Cải Lương* in the process of renewal.

13. The *Đờn Ca Tài Tử* group led by Tống Triều, which performed in France on several occasions, became the leading exponent of this music. Starting in 1910 they first gave regular performances at the Minh Tân hotel near Mỹ Tho station and soon the band became popular and instead made the Cửu Long Giang hotel in Sài Gòn

their regular venue. This place was also a central venue for artists, journalists, and intellectuals, and hereby *Đờn Ca Tài Tử* was established as a part of modern city life (Tuấn,1997; Vương, 1991).

14. He is often, as is customary in Vietnam, referred to as Sáu Lầu, "sáu" (six) since he was the sixth child in the family.

15. In 1937, a piece titled *Vọng Cổ* was recorded for the first time on the Asia label, the first Vietnamese label to emerge on the scene, with the singer Năm Nghĩa (Gibbs et al., 2013). Here, the pitch structure of *Dạ Cổ Hoài Lang* had expanded to eight bars per phrase (this version is therefore from here on referred to as *Vọng Cổ nhịp* 8). This can also be understood from how the smallest unit in the phrase structure, the Lái, is gradually stretched through these transformations. Hence, the Lái is two per bar in *Vọng Cổ* nhịp 4, one per bar in *Vọng Cổ nhịp* 8, stretches across two bars in *Vọng Cổ nhịp* 16, and across four bars in *Vọng Cổ nhịp* 32 (Bùi, 2017). Hereby, just as in the performance of a traditional piece in Tài Tử, the performers were given a greater window for improvisation on this melodic framework. *Vọng Cổ nhịp* 16, was first recorded in 1938, also on the Asia label (Kiều, 1997). The song was called *Tình mẫu tử*, the singer was Tư Sạng, and the guitarist was Bảy Hàm. Another recording of *Vọng Cổ nhịp* 16 on the Asia label, which became very popular, was *Tôn Tẩn Giả Điên*, made some years later with the singer Út Trà Ôn (Kiều, 1997).

16. A two-stringed lute, often referred to as moon lute, due to the shape of the body of the instrument.

17. In "stimulated recall" interviews, we play selected parts of either video or sound recordings for participants as stimulation to prompt deep and detailed discussions about specific aspects of the musical sound, an approach we have found to be invaluable in this research. The citation is found in video 1 following this link: https://www.researchcatalogue.net/view/1301475/1302055.

18. Both are bowed string instruments and part of the larger family of two-stringed Asian fiddles.

19. For a further discussion of the potential role of trust and empathy in intercultural music collaboration see Nguyễn and Östersjö (2019).

20. It should also be noted that we all found his performances breathtakingly beautiful. One of those solo recordings have since then been used in an experimental version of *Vọng Cổ* created through remote interaction with The Six Tones, produced for a series of concerts and lectures of telematic performance.

21. These two citations are found in video 2 following this link: https://www.researchcatalogue.net/view/1301475/1302055.

22. The citation is found in video 3 following this link: https://www.researchcatalogue.net/view/1301475/1302055.

23. The citation is found in video 4 following this link: https://www.researchcatalogue.net/view/1301475/1302055.

24. The citation is found in video 5 following this link: https://www.researchcatalogue.net/view/1301475/1302055.

25. For a discussion of the concept of voice, as well as the further notions of shared or discursive voice, see Nguyễn and Östersjö (2019).

26. The citation is found in video 6 following this link: https://www.researchcatalogue.net/view/1301475/1302055.

27. Interestingly, this is the same term as is used by Môn in the later interview, where we instead suggest the translation of *nghịch tai* as "inversed ear." The difference in meaning and expression we find striking, but so is also the personal development which the two occasions suggest.

28. The citation is found in video 7 following this link: https://www.researchcatalogue.net/view/1301475/1302055.

29. The citation is found in video 8 following this link: https://www.researchcatalogue.net/view/1301475/1302055.

30. The citation is found in video 9 following this link: https://www.researchcatalogue.net/view/1301475/1302055.

31. Samuelsson had previously worked extensively in Vietnam, documenting the music of minority peoples in collaboration with the ethnomusicologist Håkan Lundström. But he may be more well-known for recording a central album with the Vietnamese moon lute player and guitarist Kim Sinh.

32. This and the above citations from the same interview are found in video 10 following this link: https://www.researchcatalogue.net/view/1301475/1302055.

33. The citation is found in video 11 following this link: https://www.researchcatalogue.net/view/1301475/1302055.

34. The citation is found in video 12 following this link: https://www.researchcatalogue.net/view/1301475/1302055.

35. It should be noted that our reference to Schaeffer turns his research, a central building block in the Eurocentric project of musical modernism, into a vehicle for understanding musical processes of transmission, also in intercultural practices.

36. The notion of a listening habitus is discussed, with reference to Bourdieu's sociological concept, by Judith Becker (2010), but also forms part of the theory of voice put forth by Gorton and Östersjö (2019).

REFERENCES

Arendt, Rebekah, Mark Ferraguto, and Damien Mahiet, eds. 2014. *Music and Diplomacy from the Early Modern Era to the Present*. New York: Palgrave Macmillan.

Becker, Judith. 2010. "Exploring the Habitus of Listening: Anthropological Perspectives." In *Handbook of Music and Emotion: Theory, Research, Applications*, edited by Patrick N. Juslin and John A. Sloboda, 127–57. New York: Oxford University Press.

Biggs, Martin and Henrik Karlsson, eds. 2011. *Routledge Companion to Research in the Arts*. London/New York: Routledge.

Blain, Martin and Helen Julia Minors. 2020. *Artistic Research in Performance through Collaboration*. New York: Palgrave Macmillan.

Butler, Melvin L. 2014. "Haitian *Djaz* Diplomacy and the Cultural Politics of Musical Collaboration." In *Music and Diplomacy from the Early Modern Era to the Present*, edited by Rebekah Arendt, Mark Ferraguto, and Damien Mahiet, 209–29. New York: Palgrave Macmillan.

Bùi, Thiên Hoàng Quân. 2017. "Cấu trúc Bảy bản Lễ nhạc Tài tử Nam Bộ." *Tạp chí khoa học đại học Sài Gòn* 50, no. 25: 18–25. https://123doc.net/document/6004463-cau-truc-bay-ban-le-nhac-tai-tu-nam-bo.htm.

Cannon, Alexander M. 2012. "Virtually Audible in Diaspora: The Transnational Negotiation of Vietnamese Traditional Music." *Journal of Vietnamese Studies* 7, no. 3: 122–56. doi:10.1525/vs.2012.7.3.122.

Castiglione, Baldesar. 1901. *The Book of the Courtier by Count Baldesar Castiglione.* Leonard Epstein Opdycke (Trans.). New York: Charles Scribner's Sons.

Cobussen, Marcel and Nanette Nielsen. 2012. *Music and Ethics*. Farnham: Ashgate.

Chion, Michel. 2009. "Guide to Sound objects." Translated by John Dack and Christine North. Accessed February 24, 2021. http://ears.huma-num.fr/onlinePublications.html.

Denning, Michael. 2016. "Decolonizing the Ear: The Transcolonial Reverberations of Vernacular Phonograph Recordings." In *Audible Empire: Music, Global Politics, Critique*, edited by Ronald Radano and Tejumola Olaniyan, 25–44. Durham, NC: Duke University Press.

DeWald, Erich. 2012. "Taking to the Waves: Vietnamese Society around the Radio in the 1930s." *Modern Asian Studies* 46, no. 1: 143–65.

Ferraguto, Mark. 2018. "Eighteenth-Century Diplomats as Musical Agents." In *International Relations, Music and Diplomacy: Sounds and Voices on the International Stage*, edited by Frédéric Ramel and Cécile Prévost-Thomas, 43–64. Palgrave Macmillan.

Gevinson, Alan. 2017. "Khrushchev Doesn't Know Beans about B-Flat": Music and Cold War Cultural Diplomacy. *Music Educators Journal* 103, no.3: 16–18.

Gibbs, Jason. 2003. "The West's Songs, Our Songs: The Introduction and Adaptation of Western Popular Song in Vietnam before 1940." *Asian Music* 35, no. 1: 57–83.

Gibbs, Jason, David D Harnish, Terry E. Miller, David Murray, Sooi Beng Tan, and Kit Young. 2013. *Longing for the Past: The 78 RPM Era in Southeast Asia*. Atlanta: Dust to Digital.

Gorton, David and Stefan Östersjö. 2019. "Austerity Measures I: Performing the Discursive Voice." In *Voices, Bodies, Practices: Performing Musical Subjectivities*, by Catherine Laws, William Brooks, David Gorton, Nguyễn Thanh Thủy, Stefan Östersjö, and Jeremy Wells, 29–79. Leuven: Leuven University Press.

Hill, Juniper and Caroline Bithell. 2014. "An Introduction to Music Revival as Concept, Cultural Process, and Medium of Change." *The Oxford Handbook of Music Revival*, edited by Caroline Bithell and Juniper Hill, 3–42. New York: Oxford University Press.

Kagan, Norman and David R. Krathwohl. *Studies in Human Interaction*. Lansing: Educational Publication Services, 1967.

Kartomi, Margaret J. 1981. "The Processes and Results of Musical Culture Contact: A Discussion of Terminology and Concepts." *Ethnomusicology* 25, no. 2: 227–49.

Kartomi, Margaret and Stephen Blum, eds. 1994. *Music Cultures in Contact: Convergences and Collisions*. Basel: Gordon and Breach.

Kiều, Tấn. 1997. "Cây Đàn Ghita Phím Lõm." *Shriften und Dokumente zur Politik, Wirtschaft und Kultur Vietnams*, no. 9, edited by Schwaen, K., Jähnichen, G. and Wischermann, J. Berlin: Deutsch-Vietnamesische Gesellschaft.

Lê, Tuấn Hùng. 2003. "Huế and Tài Tử Music of Viet Nam: The Concept of Music and Social Organisation of Musicians." Accessed February 24, 2021. https://sonic-journal.files.wordpress.com/2014/01/hueandtaitumusic.pdf.

Logan, William Stewart. 2005. "The Cultural Role of Capital Cities: Hanoi and Hue, Vietnam." *Pacific Affairs* 78, no. 4: 559–75.

Luu, Trong Tuan. 2014. "Cai Luong (Renovated Theatre): a cultural transfer journey." *Creative Industries Journal* 7, no. 2: 92–107.

Nelson, Robin. 2013. *Practice as Research in the Arts: Principles, Protocols, Pedagogies, Resistances*. New York: Palgrave Macmillan.

Nettl, Bruno. 2005. *The Study of Ethnomusicology: Thirty-One Issues and Concepts*. 2nd ed. Champaign: University of Illinois Press.

Nguyễn, Đức Hiệp and Nguyễn Lê Tuyên. 2013. "Hát bội, đờn ca tài tử và sự hình thành Cải Lương từ cuối thế kỷ 19 đến đầu thế kỷ 20." *Tạp chí Nghiên cứu và Phát triển* 100, no. 2: 34–50.

Nguyễn, Lê Tuyên and Nguyễn, Đức Hiệp. 2014. "Quan hệ văn hoá Pháp-Việt đầu thế kỷ 20 qua sự kiện Triển lãm Toàn cầu 1900." *Văn hóa học* 6, no. 16: 31–36.

Nguyễn, Thanh Thủy and Stefan Östersjö. 2019. "Arrival cities: Hanoi." In *Voices, Bodies, Practices*, edited by Catherine Laws, William Brooks, David Gorton, Nguyễn Thanh Thủy, Stefan Östersjö, and Jez Wells, 235–95. Leuven: Leuven University Press.

Östersjö, Stefan. 2020. *Listening to the Other*. Orpheus Institute Series. Leuven: Leuven University Press.

———. Forthcoming. "The Vietnamese Guitar: Tradition and Experiment." In *Rethinking the Musical Instrument* edited by Mine Dogantan-Dack. Newcastle: Cambridge Scholars Publishing.

———. 2019. "Art Worlds, Voice, and Knowledge: Thoughts on Quality Assessment of Artistic Research Outcomes." *ÍMPAR Online Journal for Artistic Research* 3, no. 2: 60–69.

Schippers, Huib. 2010. *Facing the Music: Shaping Music Education from a Global Perspective*. New York: Oxford University Press.

Schwarz, Boris. 1983. *Music and Musical Life in Soviet Russia: Enlarged Edition, 1917-1981*. Bloomington: Indiana University Press.

Spangler, Matthew. 2010. "Performing Intercultural Hybridity: Alain Destandau's Antigone Việt Nam at the Hue Festival." *Text and Performance Quarterly* 30, no. 1: 81–99.

Taylor, Keith Weller. 1998. "Surface Orientations in Vietnam: Beyond Histories of Nation and Region." *The Journal of Asian Studies* 57, no. 4: 949–78.

Taylor, Philip. 2007. *Cham Muslims of the Mekong Delta: Place and Mobility in the Cosmopolitan Periphery*. Honolulu: University of Hawaii Press.

Trần, Văn Khải. 1970. *Nghệ thuật sân khấu Việt Nam: Hát bội, cải lương, thoại kịch, thú xem diễn kịch*. Saigon: Nhà sách Khai Trí.

———. 1992. "The Concept of *Dieu* in Vietnamese Musical Tradition." In *Von Der Vielfalt Musikalischer Kultur: Festschrift für Josef Kuckertz*, edited by R. Schumacher, 551–60. Anif/Salzburg: Verlag Ursula Müller-Speiser.

Tuấn, Giang. 1997. *Ca nhạc và sân khấu Cải Lương*. Nxb Văn hóa dân tộc.

Vương, Hồng Sển. 1991. *Sài Gòn năm xưa*. Tp Hồ Chí Minh: Nhà xuất bản Trẻ.

Welsch, Wolfgang. 1999. "Transculturality: The Puzzling Form of Cultures Today." In *Spaces of Culture: City, Nation, World*, edited by Mike Featherstone and Scott Lash, 194–213. London: Sage.

4
AFRICAN INSIGHTS

Chapter Ten

Cultural Policies and Music Production across Ethiopian Regimes

A Historical Study

Abraha Weldu and Jan Magne Steinhovden

This chapter aims to critically explore the development of cultural policy in Ethiopia during the last three consecutive regimes. Particular emphasis is given to the period of Haile Selassie's imperial government (1930–1935 and 1941–1974), the Derg socialist government (1974–1991), and the incumbent federal government (1991 to present) in order to illustrate how cultural policies were designed and administered by successive rulers and in what way music and popular culture were affected. Much of our data concerning Ethiopian regional and ethnic music, theater, drama, and paintings is based on field research by Ethiopian and foreign writers. However, historical research on Ethiopian popular culture and cultural policy offers an opportunity to appreciate the nation's cultural heritage and to shed new light on the trajectories of Ethiopian cultural dynamics. Conflicts seen in parts of Ethiopia today may be interpreted as merely one unfortunate outcome of a deeper historical struggle to forge a cohesive nation-state. Cultural policies have often failed to effectively utilize music and other arts for ethnic integration and social cohesion. Instead, the cultural sector has been used for propaganda in some eras and neglected in others. In other words, the potential role of music in cultural diplomacy has yet to be fully realized internally, in terms of inclusivity, and externally in Ethiopia's foreign relations.

Ethiopia is often depicted as a multicultural country. Italian scholar, Conti Rossini even went so far as to refer to the country as a "museum of peoples" because of its cultural diversity (as cited in Tibebu, 1995, 66). Still, Ethiopian studies have primarily featured cultures of northern Ethiopia, the Semitic language groups,[1] and primarily the Amhara (Pankhurst, 2001, 21–22). However, as with many African nations, pre-1950s popular culture and policy in Ethiopia are underrepresented in scholarly research, particularly in the south. Musicological scholarship has tended to focus on traditions in the northern highland areas, especially the Amhara-speaking people. For example, Aleqa Taye Gebremariam (1860–1924) collected Ethiopian folk songs and children's songs, which were later, in 1907 and 1910, published by Eugen Mittwoch, and is therefore acknowledged by some as the first Ethiopian ethnomusicologist (Simeneh Betreyohannes, 2010, 21). These songs were all Amharic, which illustrate an early bias in favor of the Amhara.

General introductions to Ethiopian music, such as Mondon-Vidailhet's *La Musique éthiopienne* (1922; reprinted in Mondon-Vidailhet, 2003) and later studies, such as those by Powne (1968), Ashenafi Kebede (1971a), and Zenebe Bekele (1987)[2] also focus on the music of the Amhara-speaking people and some other Semitic-speaking highland peoples, leaving out many ethnic groups of modern Ethiopia and Eritrea. In particular, Powne's *Ethiopian Music: An Introduction*, which is frequently referenced and even described by Simeneh Betreyohannes as "one of the most authoritative books about Ethiopian music" (2010, 22), explicitly describes some ethnic groups as "properly" Ethiopians while excluding others (Powne, 1968, 11).[3] It is also interesting to see that an official publication by the Ministry of Information (1968), published the same year as Powne, focuses on the musical traditions of the highland peoples.

Other general introductions to the music of Ethiopia attempt to present music that represents a broader range of the population, although they still emphasize the music of the highland people. Sárosi's study, "The Music of Ethiopian Peoples" (1967) includes songs from the Oromo, the Tigray, the Somali, and what he describes as the *Kaffichos*.[4] However, Sárosi's writing reflects both his Eurocentric, and Amhara-centric[5] views, calling the Oromo people the derogative term *Galla*[6] and using such descriptions as "rather civilized" when describing pentatonic melodies as less developed than melodies based on diatonic scales.[7] Kimberlin's textbook chapter "The Music of Ethiopia" (1980) has for many years served as the primary introduction to Ethiopian music for many Western music students. The main part of this chapter is concerned with the music of the highland people, but some descriptions of instruments are found among several groups in Ethiopia. Kimberlin also includes some musical examples from lowland peoples, such as "Muslim Drum Styles" (240–42) and a vocal style from Harar[8] (244–47).

A major figure that contributed to the development of wider interest for and study of traditional Ethiopian music, including places other than the Ethiopian and Eritrean highlands, is the Egyptian-born, and later American citizen, composer Halim El-Dabh.[9] According to Sutton, "Halim traveled north by Land Rover as far as Keren and Agordat in Eritrea, and south to Arba Minch in distant Gemu-Gofa, recording all the local musicians he could find along the way" (2007, 2). During his stay in Ethiopia (1961–1964), El-Dabh also established the Orchestra Ethiopia,[10] a folk music ensemble, which "made an important contribution to the task of collection, especially in the southern provinces, so rich yet so little explored musically up to that point—because looked down upon in general" (Falceto, 2007b, 26).

Through the support of the German embassy, Orchestra Ethiopia was able to make their first recordings at a major radio station in Addis Ababa,[11] and through the efforts of Charles Sutton, an American Peace Corps volunteer, they toured the United States. However, Tsegaye Debalke, music director for Radio Ethiopia, harshly criticized the Blue Nile Group[12] in the *Ethiopian Herald*,[13] calling its musicians "incompetent to perform in the U.S., and the dupes of a foreign exploiter" (Sutton, 2007, 8). After their success in the United States, the ensemble also became popular in Ethiopia. They became regular performers in the major hotels in Addis Ababa, recording their first LP album,[14] and even performed for the emperor Haile Selassie (Sutton, 2007, 9).

Another early collector and contributor to Ethiopian and Eritrean music recordings is Jean Jenkins. Jenkins's recordings from the 1960s were published by Tangent Records as three separate LPs in 1970, which are also available in CD format (Jenkins, 1994).[15] Ashenafi Kebede (1938–1998) gives Jenkins credit for presenting music from various ethnic groups and geographical places within Ethiopia (Ashenafi Kebede, 1971b, 196).

More specific studies on traditional Ethiopian and Eritrean music cultures have also largely focused on highland traditions, dividing the genres into either sacred or secular music (Shelemay, 1982, 52). Kimberlin's PhD dissertation "Masinqo and the Nature of Qenet" (1976) focuses on the secular music of the Ethiopian wandering troubadours. Ashenafi Kebede examines highland secular and sacred music in his respective articles "The Bowl-Lyre of Northeast Africa. Krar: the Devil's Instrument" (1977) and "The Sacred Chant of Ethiopian Monotheistic Churches: Music in Black Jewish and Christian Communities" (1980). Kay Kaufmann Shelemay (1977) studied the liturgical music of the Falasha[16] in her PhD dissertation and continued to focus on this group as well as the Orthodox Christian highlanders in her subsequent publications (Shelemay, 1982, 1986, 1992; Shelemay and Jeffery 1993, 1994, 1997; Shelemay, Jeffery, and Monson, 1993). The performance traditions of the country's plethora of ethnic groups, mainly those from non-Christian highlanders, have also suffered from lack of research (Ashagrie, 1996).

Although Ethiopia has an unusually rich cultural heritage, which deserves international attention and could potentially support tourism, its cultural policy has a relatively short history. Historically, musicians were among the lowest castes in Ethiopian society. Despite this situation, they played important roles for rulers. For example, they performed marches before officials on wind instruments such as the *meleket* (trumpet) and *embilta* (flute),[17] or as *azmaris* (wandering minstrels), who played the *mesenqo* (a single-stringed instrument played with a bow).[18] Still, as musicians belonged to the lowest castes, they were often treated as slaves (Falceto, 2005, 19).

Ethiopian music also tends to intersect with other performing arts, so it is important to consider the context of theatrical traditions. Before Emperor Haile Selassie's coronation on November 2, 1930, modern theater was only staged in select schools across the country. The schools were highly confined to the capital city, which ironically attracted neither large audiences nor talented performers.[19] In 1921, the first modern performance, *fabula: ye'awrewoch komedy* (Fabula: The Comedy of Animals) by Tekle Hawaryat Tekle Mariam, was prepared for staging at the Imperial Court. The work was adopted from the fables of *La Fontaine and Krylov* and is said to have been made for Lej Iyasu (c. 1908–1916). In this play, Tekle Hawaryat Tekle Mariam excoriated Ethiopian autocrats and was therefore it not performed due to resistance from conservatives. This had the unfortunate effect of the total closure of drama performances until the ban was lifted again by Haile Selassie (Zabolotskikh, 2010, 830). The emperor sought to use plays to both highlight his modern credentials and uplift his imperial status.

CULTURAL PRODUCTION AND POLICY UNDER EMPEROR HAILE SELASSIE (1930–1974)

Cultural production under Haile Selassie can be described as Amhara-driven, but also one that pushed for a Western educational style. Music traditions during this period were strategically used as tools for representing the people, part of early efforts to unify the polyethnic state. At Selassie's coronation, *Ethiopia Hoy*, the first national anthem of Ethiopia (composed by Armenian music professor Kevork Nalbandian with Amharic lyrics) a brass band performed for the very first time.[20] Nalbandian later composed several other marches honoring the emperor and also authored some of the earliest Ethiopian plays.[21] Only a year before the coronation, in 1929, the Imperial Bodyguard Orchestra was established to present Western music at state events and welcome visiting dignitaries (Shelemay, 2007). By the time fascist Italy occupied Ethiopia in 1935, "at least two hundred fifty musicians had been trained in the Empire's various military garrisons" (Falceto, 2005, 39).

From 1930 to 1935, Haile Selassie employed popular culture such as theater and drama as political tools for propaganda.[22] The imperial regime not only subjected popular culture to censorship but also sponsored writers to develop scripts for theater productions. For example, the emperor commissioned playwrights such as Yoftahe Nigussie and Melaku Begashaw to produce five plays for special court production (Plastow, 2010, 940). The works of this period were all in Amharic, and more "emphasis was put on fine, flowery language" (940). Acting and actors were viewed as less important, with roles often played by untrained schoolchildren.[23]

Yehager Fikir Mahber (the Ethiopian Patriotic Association) was established in July 1935 on the eve of the Italian invasion of Ethiopia. The principal initiative came from Mekonnen Habtewold, then director-general of commerce and communication. It was founded mainly to "do agitation work among the population, drawing on the resources of such influential writers as *blattengeta* Welde Giorgis Welde Yohannes and *qengn geta* Yoftahe Néguíe, who wrote exhortative tracts" (Ashagrie,1996). Moreover, speakers exhorted the people at various rallies, where artilleries were also put on display to promote the war effort. Following the Italian occupation, this organization was dissolved. But some members continued the fight as "inner patriots" (*yewst arbegnoch*). Yoftahe and Mekonnen, who preferred exile, established similar organizations in Sudan and France, respectively (Plastow, 1996).

The Aftermath of the Italian Occupation

Under the fascist occupation of 1936–1941, cultural production was completely suppressed. Several musicians were killed, especially the *azmari*, the traditional minstrels who were accused of bringing messages in favor of resistance (Falceto, 2005, 44). The return to liberation in 1941 led to the establishment of Ethiopia's first professional theater company: yehager feqer mahber (Ethiopian Patriotic Association), later changed to *hager feqer tiyater* in 1957/1958. This venue staged various shows that continue to be popular (Plastow, 2010, 940; see also Ashagrie,1996).

By and large, during the immediate aftermath of the five-year Italian occupation, cultural productions, particularly in music and visual arts, featured patriotic themes (Getahun and Kassu, 2014, 89). Popular songs from the Italian occupation of 1935/1936–1941 were composed in praise of Emperor Haile Selassie and the patriots and originally sung by crowds and professional azmari in the rebel-held areas.[24] Other ethnic groups that were non-Amhara have had relatively limited prospects to develop their culture during this time. Subsequently, they were mostly obliged to orally transmit their cultural heritage, including songs and historical narratives.

The theater company was used for political ends by the imperial regime and became an important organization for supporting unity and freedom. Influential in this revolution were Tekle Maryam and Iyoýel Yohannés. In 1953, Télahun Gessese, described by Falceto as "The Voice for Ethiopian listeners" (2005, 97), started his career at the early age of twelve years old at this theater and worked with them for three years. The Hager Fiqer also appeared as a pioneer of Western music and drama, traveling, not only to provinces but also staging concerts abroad, as they represented the country at the International Negro Art Festival in Dakar, Senegal, in 1966. In addition, Hager Fiqer also performed in nightclubs and were involved in the publication of two Amharic periodicals, successively *Menen* and *Hager Feqer* (Zewde, 2005, 966–67).

A few modern institutions and infrastructures were also established beginning in 1946. One of the most interesting achievements was the opening of the St. Yared Music School, named after a highly respected saint of the Ethiopian Orthodox Tewaḥedo Church. Alexander Kontrowicz, a Polish violinist, served as the initial director of the music school with forty part-time students and three instructors in a house in Addis Ababa. In 1948, this center would ultimately become the National School of Music, which aimed to host both national and global repertoires, although its emphasis has tended to be on European art music. In 1967, it became an institute that was later renamed the St. Yared School of Music (Segert and Boorogligeti, 1983, 1085).

The later years of imperial rule brought about a new era in the history of Ethiopian music. From the 1950s onward, many Ethiopian musicians began to produce their own popular songs through a process that has been described as "creative incorporation" (Levine, 1965, 13). This period led to the development of many new styles of musical performance in the country, partly thanks to the impact of radio and commercial recordings. Although Addis Ababa became the permanent headquarters of the Organization of African Union, one would be hard-pressed to recognize any pan-African influence. Rather, the dominant impulses came from Europe and, especially the United States (Falceto, 2005, 83–85). Early jazz bands such as the Haile Selassie I Theatre Orchestra (with saxophonist Getachew Mekurya) combined global and local (Ethiopian) sounds that led to what has been called the "golden age" of Ethiopian popular music, producing renowned Ethiopian musicians such as Tlahoun Gèssèssè, Mahmoud Ahmed, Bzunesh Beqele, and Alemayehu Eshete. Similarly, in the early 1970s, the most well-known Ethiopian composer Mulatu Astatke, educated abroad, returned to Ethiopia to introduce Ethio-Jazz (Shelemay, 2007, 1085).

The 1950s and 1960s were also periods in which modern Eritrean music developed, music that is closely linked to the secession movements of the Eritrean Liberation Front and the Eritrean People's Liberation Front. Some of the more prominent musicians were recruited into cultural groups as children. The objective of these troupes, such as Keyhati Embaba (Red Flowers), was to mobilize for war and maintain the people's morale (Kimberlin,

2013). Several prominent Eritrean musicians, including Tewelde Redda, Atewerbehand Segid, Tebereh Tesfa Hunegn, Bereket Mengisteab, Tsehaytu Beraki, Abrar Osman, Alamin Abdel-Latif, Yemane Baria, and Abraham Afewerki performed in protest of Ethiopian authorities and consequently experienced harassment. Ultimately, many of these musicians ended up in exile.

Despite certain developments, the imperial government generally remained unsupportive of independent cultural works and promoted an ambiguous policy that did not fully incorporate diversity. To put it bluntly, the state did not generate a comprehensive cultural policy framework. Culture principally served as a political tool. When theater became relatively popular, for example, Emperor Haile Selassie directly participated in the censorship of plays. The emperor, "who obsessively and personally read and censored all plays put forward for production," also partly obstructed the production of independent cultural production in the country (*Ethiopian Herald*, 1981). The same was true for music transmitted through Ethiopian radio. An example is Afran Qallo,[25] an Oromo cultural group from Dire Dawa in eastern Ethiopia, which received legal recognition from the Ethiopian emperor Haile Selassie, and was permitted to transmit one weekly Oromo song on Mondays at 4:00 p.m. over the radio in the early 1960s. This permission was obtained after the emperor had received a sample song by Ali Shabboo, one of the members of the group, which featured lyrics that praised the emperor for chasing out the invading Italian forces. The radio station had to pay 30 birr[26] for every song it broadcasted. Shortly after, when the Bale insurgency started (1963), the songs of Afran Qallo were banned.

In addition, the state did not devise an independent institution to manage and develop the sector (*Ethiopian Herald*, 1981). Throughout the imperial period, cultural issues were regulated either by the Ministry of Education and Fine Arts or the Ministry of Information. The absence of a government body directly responsible for cultural issues coupled with the country's serious literacy problem partially hampered the development of cultural equality and production. The imperial government not only failed to ensure the right of the people to use, preserve, and promote their own cultures, but also failed to employ culture for sustainable development (*Ethiopian Herald*, 1981).

CULTURAL PRODUCTION AND POLICY UNDER THE DERG SOCIALIST GOVERNMENT (1974–1991)

It was after the overthrow of the imperial regime in 1974 that the socialist government took power. Little changed in the cultural sphere under the new government. As an antifeudal government that hijacked the national question of self-determination of the peoples and nationalities of Ethiopia, it necessarily wanted to give at least lip service to the cultural production and cultural distinctiveness of different ethnic groups. But caught up in socialism, cultural production became only a medium for further state propaganda making. In reality, the socialist government proclaimed new programs to bring about a cultural revolution in what has arguably persisted as quasi-feudal conditions in Ethiopia.[27] On July 8, 1974, a new policy called *Etyopiya Tiqdem* (Ethiopia First) was announced with thirteen important points. The central aspects of this policy were, among other things, the proclamation of a new constitution, amendment of the labor law, elimination of antiprogressive traditions and cultural elements, and assistance for famine-afflicted regions in the country.

Despite the intention to promulgate cultural policies from a socialist perspective, the earliest policy of Etyopiya Tiqdem had no solid ideological economic or political foundation.[28] The first two points of the declaration reflected the Derg's aspiration for establishing a sort of constitutional monarchy with a nominal emperor at the center. Cultural productions such as literature, theater, and songs hitherto were critical of the wealth and power of the royal family and the feudal aristocracy. Marxist revolutionary literature began to appear; however, these publications were not significant in number.[29]

In the following years, the Derg endeavored to ensure cultural equality. According to the September 29, 1975, proclamation, equality was declared for the cultural expressions of all "nationalities" of Ethiopia.[30] Although Amharic continued to serve as the official language, other languages were increasingly accepted in schools. Some languages of the Ethiopian people and nations, for instance, were also half-heartedly encouraged as the basis for new literature. Compared to the imperial government, the Derg, at least initially, accomplished some temporary but momentous decisions to expand popular culture. Indeed, with the issuance of the New Democratic Revolution Programme (NDR) on April 20, 1976, the Derg attempted to strengthen the cultural and linguistic equality of all ethnic groups (*Addis Zemen*, 1976).

Politically, the NDR took an anti-imperialist and antifeudal stance. It advocated for the uniting of all ethnic groups under a working-class party. Regardless of the main political purposes, the NDR called on all Ethiopian peoples to organize (*Addis Zemen*, 1976). It advocated for some awareness among the masses to congregate for cultural and linguistic autonomy. In addition, the NDR supported regional autonomy for all nations of Ethiopia (Eshete, 1982, 21–22). In fact, some informants claimed that the NDR defended the cultural and linguistic equality of a multiethnic Ethiopia. The Derg primarily launched the NDR as a tool for political purposes (especially communist propaganda) communicated via music, art, literature, and film.[31]

The 1974 political revolution had an impact on cultural production and policy. Serious attempts were carried out to forge a cultural revolution. Various cultural fields, particularly literature, art, theater, and music were designed to suit the program and ideology of the socialist government. Various youth associations were created at the *kebelle* level (neighborhoods or subdivisions of a town) and produced plays explaining the new state revolutionary ideologies. There is also evidence that, for some years, this propaganda machine became a widespread means for disseminating information to the semiliterate rural population. The content and form of the works were consistent with the framework of the NDR program. The Derg not only sabotaged creative or independent cultural productions that did not fit within their ideology but also discouraged all works from the past, which were viewed with suspicion as antirevolutionary in orientation (*Addis Zemen*, 1976).

Informants who belonged to this generation recount that cultural production was instrumental in disseminating socialist and antifeudal propaganda among the masses.[32] Alem Eshete (1982) carried out a thorough study of the cultural situation in socialist Ethiopia. Eshete's findings indicate that the form and content of cultural production during the Derg regime were largely consistent with the NDR programs.

Because of the continued pressure from the government, creative culture was suppressed, leaving many playwrights and musicians with no choice but to leave the country. By the 1980s, for example, musicians compelled to leave the country went to such places as Washington, DC, where a large Ethiopian diaspora community took shape. Performers such as Aster Aweke and Ejigayehu Shibabaw established careers there. These musicians performed and released recordings abroad that remained widely popular in Ethiopian music history (Shelemay, 2007, 1085).

Still, the popular music scene in Addis Ababa did not abruptly vanish. Some musicians who remained in the capital city continued to perform, make recordings, and establish famous bands such as the Ethio Stars and the Roha Band, both of which that gave concerts in many Ethiopian hotels during the 1980s (Shelemay, 2007, 1085). In addition, some playwrights also continued in earnest. In February 1974, the playwright Tseggaye Gebre Medhin threw his support behind the Derg. As a result, once Emperor Haile Selassie was deposed in September 1974, theatrical arts faced relatively less censorship compared to other forms of art. Playwrights like Abbe Gubegna, Tesfaye Gessesse, and Mengistu Lemma all put on works disparaging the ousted imperial government and recommended strategies for political change (Plastow, 2010, 941; see also Aboneh, 1996).

However, during the late 1970s, the Derg tightened its grip on theater and continued to use it for propaganda. For example, in 1977 at the *hager fiqir tiyatir* (formerly, the Ethiopian Patriotic Association), the national theater in Addis Ababa, several Oromo cultural groups were invited to give an Oromo concert, but due to fear of the consequences of a pan-Oromo unity, the Derg regime regretted the invitation. In the end, the event was boycotted by the Ethiopian News Agency and not reported in media. Eventually, all new Oromo cultural groups were banned and performers and leaders of the existing groups were arrested (Mollenhauer, 2011, 64). According to Asafa Jalata, who attended this event, "The junta imprisoned, tortured or murdered most of the participants, both organizers, and performers" (Asafa Jalata, 2005, 188).

Despite the construction of two new theaters in Addis Ababa during this time, by the late 1970s theatrical productions were completely under government control. As a result, playwrights changed their focus from politics toward more historically-oriented plays, comedies, and noncontroversial translations of foreign classics.

The Derg not only compelled many prominent artists and performers to leave Ethiopia, but also failed to redress the ongoing concerns of cultural autonomy and equality in the country. For the Derg, the declaration of cultural rights was thought to address the age-old discrimination and inequality. As a result, the Derg regulated cultural production to spread its ideology. It accused the deposed imperial government at large of perpetuating the stagnation of the country. Both cultural works and their producers were obliged to contribute toward the Derg's political and moral values. To compound this, the socialist government was reluctant to promote and support the plethora of Ethiopian ethnic groups, let alone to support artists.[33] But the Derg's coming to power contributed to the formation of various youth associations. It organized partisan artists and playwrights at the *kebelle* level to perform at public stages.

In addition, the Derg established the Ministry of Culture and Sports by its proclamation in August 1977. This was arguably the first time in Ethiopia's modern history when culture was instituted and managed by an independent office. In contrast, the imperial government paid little attention to culture and left its administration to the Ministry of Education or the Ministry of Information. It was also during this period that the ministry generated five departments to dispense the abovementioned responsibilities. These were the Department of Arts and Theatre, Department for the Study and Preservation of the Cultural Heritage, National Library and Historical Archives Department, Ethiopian Language Academy, and Department of International Cultural Relations (Ethiopian Ministry of Culture and Sports 1998, 2–4; 2010, 1–3). However, the departments were largely confined to implementing the

Derg's ambitious political program and ideology. Regardless of the Derg's achievement in creating a ministry of culture, it provided only lukewarm support for multiculturalism and independent creativity. As with preceding regimes, it sought to impart its ideological interest in the production of popular culture (Aleme, 1982, 38).

CULTURAL POLICIES AND THE CREATIVE INDUSTRIES UNDER THE FEDERAL PARLIAMENTARY GOVERNMENT (1991–2022)

In marked contrast to preceding governments, the current federal parliamentary government brought multiculturalism to a new level of importance by including legislation that protects the cultural rights and concerns of all peoples of Ethiopia directly into the constitution. In 1991, the EPRDF (the Ethiopian People Revolutionary Democratic Front) toppled the Derg and instituted a federal state structure. One of the pressing issues for the seventeen-year armed struggle of the EPRDF, under the auspices of the Tigray People's Liberation Front, was to uphold the cultural, religious, and linguistic equality among all "nationalities" of Ethiopia. From the very beginning, the primary purpose of the EPRDF was to redress these long-lasting "inequalities."[34]

To overcome these historical inequalities, the EPRDF promulgated a federal constitution in 1995. Article 39/2 of the constitution states that "every nation, nationality, and people shall have the right to . . . promote its culture, helps to grow and flourish, and preserve its historical heritage" (Constitution of the Federal Democratic Republic of Ethiopian, 1995). In theory, it appears that the issue associated with cultural inequality is now fully addressed (1995). The constitution also promises equality to all of the more than eighty ethnic groups, and cultural diversity appears to be publicly celebrated. Nevertheless, it seems that cultural rights and equality remain undefined. In some cases, censorship continues unabated and genuine development of creative industries remains well below expectations.

A little-known cultural policy of Ethiopia was approved by the Council of Ministers in October 1997, which ensured equal access and protections for all peoples. However, critics say that this "equality" is really only for government-sponsored groups, such as Biftu Oromia (Mollenhauer, 2011, 206). This was an effort by the former Ministry of Youth, Sport, and Culture to put an end to discriminatory practices made by previous regimes (Ethiopian Ministry of Culture, 2004, 7). This policy was broad and promised development of important programs, even extending to Ethiopia's infrastructure and the restructuring of the ministry (Proclamation No. 4/1995). In other words, the proclamation aimed to create an Office of Cultural Affairs that worked properly. However, it was not until October 2010 that the proclamation came into effect and at long last, the Ministry of Culture and Tourism was established (Ethiopian Ministry of Culture, 2004, 7).

Although the new ministry was developed to govern culture and cultural products, long-term problems persisted. Although the new legislation on cultural policy theoretically ensured cultural rights and equality, it had limitations in terms of practical implementation: (1) there were still ethnic groups that did not receive equal attention; (2) despite its references to sustainable development, operational activities were discouraging and the state failed to generate income from culture and cultural industries; (3) the policy implications have rarely been examined and only limited monitoring mechanisms exist within civil society or in public organizations; (4) it was primarily connected to collective cultural rights regarding the use of mother tongue in education and public life.[35]

With the change of government in 1991 many anticipated that bearers of cultural expression would gain more freedom, but the expectation has not been completely realized. During the 1990s, several important musicians fled the country, such as Ilfinesh Qannoo, Hirphaa Gaanfure, and Abebe Abeshu, and all Oromo musicians. They left Ethiopia and settled in Bergen, Norway, and received UN quota for refugees due to harassment and several imprisonments by the EPRDF (Steinhovden, interview with Ilfinesh Qannoo and her daughter Hawwi, January 13, 2017). Dawite Mekonen, another Oromo musician, went into exile after refusing to perform for soldiers on the war front during the Eritrean-Eritrean war in 1998. Teddy Afro, possibly the most successful musician in Ethiopia during this time, was also imprisoned in 2008, three years after the release of songs interpreted as critical toward Ethiopian authorities, and in 2014 he experienced two last-minute cancellations of his concerts.

Importantly, a small youth theater movement arose, but as a result of inexpensive video technology, as in other African countries, many prominent theater performers shifted to free video production where financial gains are often much greater than in live theater (Plastow, 2010, 942). Equally, Ethiopian musicians appeared to be influenced by global developments. The import of popular music from outside, an active local recording industry, and a large Ethiopian diaspora have deepened the influence of foreign music and, at the same time, increased their global audience.

Since the 1990s, anthropologists and ethnomusicologists have begun analyzing the music of previously unstudied Ethiopian communities, giving long-overdue attention to the peoples of the south and southwest (Ohinata, 2009).[36] Many musicians have also increasingly included the songs of various marginalized ethnic groups from Ethiopia in their repertoire (Shelemay, 2007, 1082). After the 2015 UN conference on culture, Ethiopia issued a new national cultural policy that appears to have strengthened cultural diversity and support for meaningful development of creative industries, harmonious coexistence, and unity of the people. This was arguably demonstrated when Betty G. performed during the ceremony of the Nobel Peace Prize for Ethiopian prime minister Abiy Ahmed in 2019 (Nobel Prize, 2019, 4:16). A similar spirit was shown when Eritrean musician Dawit Shilan performed during Abij Ahmed's first visit to Eritrea in July 2018, and at a celebration in Mekelle, Ethiopia, in 2019, both as part of the peace agreement between Eritrea and Ethiopia. Such performances suggest that in some ways the notion of music in cultural diplomacy is alive today in Ethiopia (Gebrenigus, 2018, 11:37; Zion Tube, 2018, 12:03).[37]

CONCLUSION

This chapter chronicles Ethiopian state policy vis-à-vis cultural policies and cultural production throughout the history of modern Ethiopia. Efforts have been made to discuss the similarities and differences between each successive government toward ensuring and expanding cultural rights, cultural autonomy, and cultural production.

Until recent times, there was no separate institution to regulate culture, and governments have largely neglected the development of cultural policy. Both Haile Selassie and the Derg used cultural expressions as tools for political gain. In addition, cultural production under Haile Selassie was defined by a Western educational style, Western-influenced music and theater, and Amhara-driven cultural norms at the neglect of cultural rights of other ethnic groups. In 1974, the Derg government led dramatic control over creative expression and suspicion of past cultural works as antirevolutionary in orientation.

The federal parliamentary government placed multiculturalism as an important priority by incorporating the rights of all ethnic groups in its constitution. However, although cultural rights, equality, and sustainable development have become widespread within cultural policy documents in recent times, the actual conceptual and operational implications often remain vague. Today, Ethiopia remains turbulent partly because some of the issues discussed in this chapter were never fully resolved.

We began by noting that Ethiopia is known as a multicultural country. However, as this discussion has shown, successive regime's cultural policies have failed to effectively harness the power of music and performing arts as forms of cultural diplomacy to foster mutual respect and coexistence across the diverse ethnicities of this nation-state. Instead, either little attention and support were offered to the cultural heritage sector, or it was misused for propaganda. In this way, the case of Ethiopia currently illustrates not only successes but also failures of cultural diplomacy despite the nation's undeniably rich musical traditions. We can only hope that future governments will recognize the underappreciated value of Ethiopia's music traditions and other forms of cultural heritage and develop policies that promote music as cultural diplomacy both internally, for improved social cohesion, and externally for global appreciation of the nation's unique artistic contributions.

NOTES

1. Linguistically, the people are divided into four groups: 1) the Semitic includes Tigray, Amhara, Gurage, and Adere, 2) the Cushitic comprises the Oromo, Afar, Agaw, and Beja, 3) the Omotic language group also speaks by the people around the Omo River. This language group includes the Gemira, Welayta, and Kaffa, 4) the Nilo-Sahara includes Gumuz, Anuak, and Kunama.

2. A leaflet, which when reviewed by Baumann in *Yearbook for Tradition Music*, was described as "definitely not a scholarly work" (1989, 119), but is still frequently referenced in scholarship (a likely reason being the modicum of scholarly work on this topic).

3. Additionally, Powne uses pejorative terms to describe other ethnic groups in Ethiopia, for example, *Gallas, negro, negroid, Shankallas, Falashas.*

4. These are probably the people living in the former region of Kaffa.

5. This word was coined to indicate the biased way that some Amhara people have viewed other ethnic groups in Ethiopia, for example, via the use of derogatory names such as *Galla* (Oromo) or *Geleb* (Dassanetch), and putting their own names on already existing cities, such as Addis Ababa (Finfinne), Debre Zeit (Bishoftu), and Nazareth (Adama).

6. Galla was the commonly used name of the Oromo people at this time in history, but later developed derogatory connotations when it came to be used by the ruling Amhara people to refer to the Oromo.

7. A prevalent view among ethnomusicologists during that period, inherited from Victorian anthropologists, was that cultures developed from simple to more advanced, or from primitive to civilized. Such interpretations have now been rejected for more than a half-century.

8. Harar is also a Semitic-speaking group, but they live in a very different area than the other large Semitic-speaking groups Amhara and Tigrinya, and the music of Harar is not included in several other presentations of Ethiopian music.

9. Before coming to Ethiopia, Halim studied with Aaron Copland and Irving Fine, and established a considerable reputation in New York City (Sutton, 2007, 1).

10. Halim led Orchestra Ethiopia from 1962–1964, followed by Peace Corps volunteer John Coe from 1964–1966, and the Ethiopian Tesfaye Lemma from 1966–191974. Peace Corps volunteer Charles Sutton managed to receive support and organize a tour for Orchestra Ethiopia to the United States in 1969. This trip became a success and finally made the music group finally popular in Ethiopia (Sutton, 2007, 3–9).

11. Their first recordings were made with the Radio of the Gospel, a major radio station located in the heart of Addis Ababa. This was made possible after Halim had approached the German embassy and received support of five hundred dollars. Later, Halim successfully persuaded the director of the radio station to pay royalties to the musicians (Seachrist, 2013, 85–86).

12. In the United States, Orchestra Ethiopia was billed as "the Blue Nile Group."

13. Ethiopian newspaper.

14. Some of their recordings are available on *Ethiopique,* volume 23 (Falceto, 2007a).

15. The quality of these recordings is considered good, although their liner notes are criticized for being inaccurate and superficial (Suttner, 1970; Ashenafi Kebede, 1971b).

16. Often referred to as "the Ethiopian Jews."

17. See photograph (Falceto, 2005, 11).

18. See perhaps the first authenticated photograph of musicians in Ethiopia (Falceto, 2005, 10).

19. Muluworq Kidanemariam and Hailu Habtu, interviews by Abraha Weldu Hailemariam September 17, 2018, Mekelle, Ethiopia.

20. In 1897, the tsar of Russia sent about forty brass instruments to Ethiopia in tribute to Menelik's victory at Adwa. In 1924, Ras Tafari, later to become Haile Selassie, visited Jerusalem and was so impressed by the brass band welcoming him that he hired Armenian orphans to become the official band of Ethiopia (Falceto, 2005).

21. *Gebre-Maryamm the Gondare, Ato Men-Alle* (Mr. What'sthe-Matter), *The Shepherd Tefera, The War of Adal, The Freedom Fighters* (Falceto, 2005, 33).

22. The overall description is based on the interviews that took place on September 24, 2018, in Mekelle with Dinar Amare and Hailu Habtu, PhD.

23. Hailu Habtu and Dinar Amare, interviews by Abraha Weldu Hailemariam, Mekelle, Ethiopia, September 17, 2018.

24. *Arbegna* Endawek Assires and *Arbegna* Belay Kassaie, interviews by Abraha Weldu Hailemariam, Addis Ababa, Ethiopia, November 23, 2017.

25. See Asafa Jalata (2005, 186) Gadaa Melbaa (1999), Mollenhauer (2011, 62–63,) and Tesfaye Tolessa Bessa (2012, 89–91). Thomas Osmond and Francis Falceto describe Afran Qallo as "one of the main actors of Oromo nationalism in eastern Ethiopia" (2014, 12). Note there are multiple spellings for this group: *Arffan Qallo* (Asafa Jalata, 2005), *Afraan Qalloo* (Falceto and Osmond, 2014), *Afran Qallo* (Mollenhauer, 2011) and *Afran Qalloo* (Tesfaye Tolessa Bessa, 2012). This group is also known by the name *Urjii Bakkalchaa* (Gow, 1999, 131).

26. Birr is the local currency. At the time of this writing, the exchange rate from birth to U.S. dollar was approximately 2.5. See https://knoema.com/atlas/Ethiopia/topics/Economy/Financial-Sector-Exchange-rates/Exchange-rate (accessed July 2, 2021).

27. Hailu Habtu and Dinar Amare, interviews by Abraha Weldu Hailemariam, Mekelle, Ethiopia, September 17, 2018.

28. Habtu and Amara, interviews, September 2018.

29. Marxist literature was undeveloped during this period.

30. *Memehir* Muluworq Kidanemariam and Hailu Habtu, interviews by Abraha Weldu Hailemariam, Mekelle, Ethiopia, September 17, 2018.

31. Habtu and Amare, interviewsSeptember 2018.

32. Alem Kahsay, Berihu Habte, and Andargachew Mekurya, interviews by Abraha Weldu Hailemariam, Addis Ababa, Ethiopia, September 21, 2017.

33. Dinar Amare, interview by Abraha Weldu Hailemariam, Mekelle, Ethiopia, September 17, 2018.

34. *Memehir* Muluworq Kidanemariam, interview by Abraha Weldu Hailemariam, Mekelle, Ethiopia, September 17, 2018.

35. Kidanemariam, interview, September 2018.

36. The UNESCO/Norway Funds in Trust cooperation project (2005–2008) supported studies of Maale, Ari, Oromo, and Dareshe.

37. These musical peace performances are however controversial, like the peace agreement between Ethiopia and Eritrea itself. The peace agreement was not between the former enemies, the Eritrean ruler Isaias Afwerki and the TPLF-led coalition controlling Ethiopia. It was negotiated between the Eritrean ruler Isaias and the new Ethiopian leader, Abiy Ahmed, who in November 2020 became part of an armed conflict with TPLF.

REFERENCES

Ashagrie, Aboneh. 1996. "Popular Theater in Ethiopia." *Ufahamu. Journal for the African Activist Association* 24, nos. 2 and 3: 32–41.

———. 1976. "April 29." Addis Ababa, Ethiopia: Māstāwaqiyā Ministar.

Aleme, Eshete. 1982. "The Cultural Situation in Socialist Ethiopia." *Studies and Documents on Cultural Policies*-UNESCO.

Asafa Jalata. 2005. *Oromia & Ethiopia: State Formation and Ethnonational Conflict, 1868-2004*. Trenton, NJ, and Asmara, Eritrea: The Red Sea Press.

Ashenafi Kebede. 1971a. *The Music of Ethiopia: its Development and Cultural Setting*. PhD diss. Wesleyan University.

———. 1971b. "Review of Jenkins Recordings: Review of Ethiopia: Vol. 1, Music of the Central Highlands; Ethiopia: Vol. 2, Music of the Desert Nomads; Ethiopia: vol. 3, Music of Eritrea, Jean Jenkins." *Yearbook of the International Folk Music Council* 3:196–98.

———. 1977. "The Bowl-Lyre of Northeast Africa. Krar: the Devil's Instrument." *Ethnomusicology* 21, no. 3: 379–95.

———. 1980. "The Sacred Chant of Ethiopian Monotheistic Churches: Music in Black Jewish and Christian Communities." *The Black Perspective in Music* 8, no. 1: 21–34.

Baumann, Max Peter. 1989. "Review: Music in the Horn: a Preliminary Analytical Approah to the Study of Ethiopian Music, by Zenebe Bekele." *Yearbook of the International Folk Music Council* 21: 118–19.

"Constitution of the Federal Democratic Republic of Ethiopia." 1995. Addis Ababa, Ethiopia.

Dawit Mesfin. 2006. "Eritrea: Songs of the Patriots." *The Rough Guide to World Music: Africa & Middle East*, edited by Mark Ellingham, Jon Lusk, Duncan Clark and Simon Broughton, 103–107. London: Rough Guides.

Ethiopian Herald. 1981. "October 24." Addis Ababa, Ethiopia: Ethiopia Press.

Ethiopian Ministry of Culture. 2004. "Reports of the Ministry of Culture." Addis Ababa, Ethiopia.

Ethiopian Ministry of Culture and Sports. 1998. "Reports of the Ministry of Culture and Sports: Cultural Policy of FDRE." Addis Ababa, Ethiopia.

Ethiopian Ministry of Culture and Tourism. 2010. "Reports of the Ministry of Culture and Tourism; Cultural Policy of FDRE." Addis Ababa, Ethiopia.

Falceto, Fancis. 2005. *Abyssinie Swing -a Pictorial History of Modern Ethiopian Music*. 2nd edition. Addis Ababa, Ethiopia: Shama Books.

———. 2007a. *Orchestra Ethiopia*. France: Buda Music.

———. 2007b. *Orchestra Ethiopia* France: Buda Music.

Falceto, Francis, and Thomas Osmond. 2014. "Liner Notes." Ali Mohammed Birra. *Éthiopiques 28: Great Oromo Music*. Buda Musique 860233. CD.

Gadaa Melbaa. 1999. *Oromia: An Introduction to the History of the Oromo People*. Minneapolis, MN: Kirk House Publishers.

Gebrenigus, Nahom. 2018. "Dawit Shilan—Tezaweri New Eritrean Music 2018." Accessed June 15, 2021. YourTube video, 11:37. https://www.youtube.com/watch?v=M07EWqFwPE4.

Getahun, Solomon Addis and Wudu Tafete Kassu. 2014. *Culture and Custom of Ethiopia*. Oxford: Greenwood.

Gow, Greg. 1999. "The Language of Culture and the Culture of Language: Oromo Identity in Melbourne, Australia." PhD dissertation. Victoria University of Technology.

Jenkins, Jean. 1994. *Music from Ethiopia*. Topic Records TSCD910. CD.

Kimberlin, Cynthia Tse. 1976. "Masinqo and the Nature of Qenet." PhD diss. Los Angeles: University of California.

———. 1980. "The Music of Ethiopia." In *Musics of Many Cultures: an Introduction*, edited by Elizabeth May, 216–31. Berkeley: University of California Press.

———. 2013. "Eritrea." *Grove Music Online. Oxford Music Online.* New York: Oxford University Press.

Levine, Donald Nathan. 1965. *Wax and Gold: Tradition and Innovation in Ethiopian Culture*. Chicago-London: University of Chicago Press.

Ministry of Information. 1968. "Music, Dance, Drama; In Ethiopia." In *Patterns of Progress*. Vol. IX. Addis Ababa, Ethiopia: Publications & Foreign Languages Press Department.

Mollenhauer, Shawn. 2011. "Millions on the Margins: Music, Ethnicity, and Censorship among the Oromo of Ethiopia." PhD diss. Riverside: University of California.

Mondon-Vidailhet, Casimir. 1922. "La musique éthiopienne." *Encyclopédie de la musique et dictionnaire du Conservatoire* 3179-96. Paris: Librairie Delagrave.

———. 2003. "La musique éthiopienne (réédition du texte publié en 1922)." *Annales d'Ethiopie* 19: 149–87.

Nobel Prize. 2019. "Betty G performs Yamlu Mola's 'Sin Jaaladhaa' at the 2019 Nobel Peace Prize Ceremony." YouTube video, 4:16. Accessed June 14, 2021. https://www.youtube.com/watch?v=GyGjS3Re3gw.

Ohinata, Fumiko. 2009. "Progress of the UNESCO/Norway Funds in Trust cooperation project (2005-2008): 'Ethiopia—Traditional Music, Dance and Instruments.'" *Proceedings of the 16th International Conference of Ethiopian Studies* 1249–57, eds. Svein Ege, Harald Aspen, Birhanu Teferra and Shiferaw Bekele. Trondheim: International Conference of Ethiopian Studies (16th).

Pankhurst, Richard. 2001. *The Ethiopians: A History*. Oxford: Blackwell Publishing.

Plastow, Jane 1996. *African Theatre and Politics: The Evolution of Theatre in Ethiopia, Tanzania and Zimbabwe*. Rodopi, 47–54, 91–103, 144–58, and 203–28.

———. 2010. "Theatre in Ethiopia." In *Encyclopaedia Aethiopic*. Vol. 4. Wiesbaden: Harrassowitz Verlag.

Powne, Michael. 1968. *Ethiopian Music: An Introduction*. New York: Oxford University Press.

Sárosi, Bálint. 1967. "The Music of Ethiopian Peoples." *Studia Musicologica Academiae Scientiarum Hungaricae* 9 vols. 1/2: 9–20. Budapest: Akadémiai Kiadó.

Seachrist, Denise. 2013. *The Musical World of Halim El-Dabh*. Kent, OH: Kent State University Press.

Segert, Stanislay and Andras J. E. Boorogligeti, eds. 1983. *Ethiopian Studies: Dedicated to Wolf Leslau on the Occasion of his Seventy-Fifth Birthday*, November 14, 1981, by Friends and Colleagues. Wiesbaden.

Shelemay, Kay Kaufman. 1977. "The Liturgical Music of the Falasha of Ethiopia." PhD diss. Ann Arbor: University of Michigan.

———. 1982. "Zema; A Concept of Sacred Music in Ethiopia." *The World of Music* 24, no. 3: 52–67. VWB - Verlag für Wissenschaft und Bildung.

———. 1986. *Music, Ritual, and Falasha History*. Ethiopian Series 17. Edited by Harold G. Marcus. Michigan State University, East Lansing: African Studies Center.

———. 1992. "The Musician and Transmission of Religious Tradition: The Multiple Roles of the Ethiopian Däbtära." *Journal of Religion in Africa* 22, no. 3: 242–60.

———. 2007. "Music in Ethiopia." In *Encyclopaedia Aethiopic*. Vol. 3. Edited by Siegbert Uhlig, 1082–86. Wiesbaden: Harrassowitz Verlag.

Shelemay, Kay, Peter Jeffery, and Ingrid Monson. 1993. "Oral and Written Transmission in Ethiopian Christian Chant." *Early Music History* 12: 55–117.

Shelemay, K, and Peter Jeffery, eds. 1993. *Ethiopian Christian Liturgical Chant, an Anthology (Vol.1), Recent Researches in the Oral Traditions of Music*. Madison, WI: Published with the assistance of Subventions from the National Endowment for the Humanities and the American Musicological Society.

———, eds. 1994. *Ethiopian Christian Liturgical Chant, an Anthology (Vol.2), Recent Researches in the Oral Traditions of Music*. Madison, WI: Published with the assistance of Subventions from the National Endowment for the Humanities and the American Musicological Society.

———, eds. 1997. *Ethiopian Christian Liturgical Chant, an Anthology (Vol.3), Recent Researches in the Oral Traditions of Music*. Madison, WI: Published with the assistance of Subventions from the National Endowment for the Humanities and the American Musicological Society.

———Simeneh Betreyohannes. 2010. "Scholarship on Ethiopian Music: Past, Present and Future Prospects." *African Study Monographs. Supplementary Issue* 41:19–34.

Suttner, Kurt. 1970. "Review. Jean Jenkins: An Anthology of African Music. The Music of Ethiopia: Volume 1: Music of the Ethiopian Coptic Church. Volume 2: Music of the Cushitic Peoples of South-West Ethiopia (Record Reviews)." *Ethnomusicology* 14, no. 3: 530–32.

Sutton, Charles. 2007. "Tezeta (PDF-file included on CD 'Orchestra Ethiopia.'" *Ethiopiques* 23. France: Buda Music.

Tesfaye Tolessa Bessa. 2012. "A History of Oromo Cultural Troupes in the Making of Oromo Political Struggle (1962-1991)." *Star Journal* 1, no. 3: 88–96.

Tibebu, Teshale. 1995. *The Making of Modern Ethiopia: 1889-1974*. Trenton, NJ: The Red Sea Press.

Zabolotskikh, Maxim. 2010. "Täklä Hawaryat Täklä Maryam." In *Encycopaedia Aethiopica*. Vol. 4. Wiesbaden: Harrassowitz Verlag.

Zenebe Bekele. 1987. *Music in the Horn: A Preliminary Analytical Approach to the Study of Ethiopian Music*. Stockholm: Författares bokmaskin.

Zewde, Bahru. 2005. "Hagär Féqér Tiyatér." *Encyclopaedia Aethiopic*. Vol. 2. Harrassowitz Verlag, Wiesbaden.

Zion Tube. 2018. "Dawit shilan - ሰሚዐኪ '዁ | Live Performance (Official Video) 2018 መቃል ሽኮር ኮንሰርት 1 ዳዊት ሽላን." YouTube video, 12:03. Accesssed June 15, 2021. https://www.youtube.com/watch?v=602xarprl3k.

Chapter Eleven

Musical Activism from South Africa
The "Soft Power" of Cultural Diplomacy
Ambigay Yudkoff

In an African folktale, a lion's aggression toward the people of a village during a famine is quelled by the sound of a young boy singing. The lion is so captivated by the music that he miraculously starts to dance. The boy uses the power of a song to escape from the lion.[1] This story, which I first heard as a child growing up in South Africa, is not peculiar to the African continent. According to the European ancient Greek myth of Orpheus, lynxes and lions were soothed by the melodious sounds of the lyre, bequeathed to Orpheus by Apollo to calm the "passions of the natural world" (Hicks, 1984, 48). While these tales of centuries ago are both charming and wondrous, the use of music in contemporary society does more than tame savage beasts. Music is a creative expression that lends itself to intercultural exchange, enhances mutual understanding, and generates respect and cooperation. Music is a form of "soft power" for cultural diplomacy, but how does music also serve as a vehicle for activism? How does music transform beliefs and attitudes among people from diverse backgrounds and viewpoints within societies and beyond?

This chapter examines the musical activism of four South African artists who have been selected based on their national and international activism. Miriam Makeba (1932–2008), known as "Mama Africa," was a United Nations goodwill ambassador and civil rights activist. Hugh Masekela (1939–2018) was recognized as an international proponent of African jazz and a fierce advocate for restoring African heritage in the arts. Johnny Clegg (1953–2019), popularly called the "White Zulu," was a South African academic, anthropologist, and antiapartheid activist. He mastered and incorporated indigenous African musical styles into his music, bringing social justice messages to Europe and the United Kingdom. Finally, Sharon Katz (1955–present) is a music therapist and musical activist. Her humanitarian work and peace initiatives through community engagement (with its vital educational component) in musical performances in South Africa in the 1990s have been replicated in the United States, Cuba, and Mexico. Although the discussion of each artist's musical activism and cultural diplomacy are addressed chronologically, there are several points of intersection and collaboration between the first two artists, Miriam Makeba and Hugh Masekela.

At this juncture, it is essential to unpack the existing notions of public diplomacy, cultural diplomacy, and soft power and how music connects to politics and social change. While public diplomacy is directly associated with a political system for a political purpose, cultural diplomacy is "the deployment of a state's culture in support of its foreign policy goals or diplomacy" (Mark, 2010, 43). As the global reach of cultures has expanded over the years, cultural diplomacy has become more inclusive. It also applies to practices "related to purposeful cultural cooperation between nations or groups of nations" (Ang, Isar, and Mar, 2015, 366). These ideas of cultural diplomacy are all pertinent, but they neglect the presentation of cultural products abroad that include interpersonal relationships and collaborations among musicians and artists. Fosler-Lussier addresses the role of musicians in creating cultural connections:

> Attention to the particular situations in which music crossed boundaries thus helps us to see globalization in the making, not as an abstract "flow" but as a result of specific and reasoned choices to push or pull music across borders. By observing musicians' visits closely, we recognize global cultural connections as the product of political and personal desires: the desire of state officials [and musical activists] to win political allegiances abroad, the desire of individual citizens for new musical pleasures, and the desire to understand one's place as a person and as a citizen of a nation-state in a volatile world situation. (2012, 63–64)

The author, in this passage, refers to the promotion of music from the United States during the Cold War. However, this analysis also speaks to the musical activism of artists from South Africa. This chapter highlights the efforts of South African musicians who used their musical platform to cross boundaries, create global connections, win political allegiances in other countries, expand and enrich their musical experiences abroad, and use the "soft power" of their music to realize a social and political change in apartheid South Africa. Nyedescribes soft power as "the ability to affect others to obtain the outcomes one wants through attraction rather than coercion or payment" (2008, 94). He adds that "a country;s soft power rests on its resources of culture, values, and policies [where] a smart power strategy combines hard and soft power resources" (94).

Clarke (2016) explains the conundrum of many scholars (Mark, 2010; Holden, 2013; Bayles, 2014) who examine the exercise of "soft power" within the broad subject of cultural diplomacy. Clarke asserts that one of the critical considerations in determining the efficacy of cultural diplomacy is to gauge how cultural products are received abroad. He states that "this process of reception can be better understood with reference to the theoretical approaches of Cultural Studies" (2016, 147). This approach encourages one to recognize the extent to which audiences are implicated in processes of meaning-making that are closely associated with the articulation of identity. Clarke adds that "by applying these approaches to cultural diplomacy, policymakers and researchers could shift their focus to an exploration of realities of the reception of cultural products abroad, which would better inform their assumptions about how to achieve successful cultural diplomacy" (147). In India, according to Ramabadran (2020), the impact of the Chennai Music Season, which brings international artists to India every year, is being assessed through extensive interviews. The Center for Soft Power has implemented a project called "Chennai Soft Power 30" to document the experiences of Indian artists while touring abroad and their success in proliferating Indian culture through their art (2020, 32). Similarly, an assessment of the soft power of South African musicians within the country and overseas in the years leading up to the dismantling of apartheid is possible through an understanding of their personal journeys.

These journeys are examined through a more complex prism. On the one hand, there is the soft power of music that has long been used as a vehicle for cultural diplomacy. On the other hand, musical activism has played a significant role in the political and social landscape of many countries over the years (see Yudkoff, 2021). This chapter explores the contributions of selected South African musicians, whose multifaceted musical experiences within South Africa and in exile have integrated both the ideas of cultural diplomacy and musical activism. These insights acknowledge the remarkable survival of musical endeavors that not only exposed the world to the unique beauty of South African music but also draw attention to the atrocities of the apartheid regime. Many South African musicians made a difference to the status quo during this dark period through their music, impacting the hearts and minds of people within South Africa and abroad.

Not all musicians survived the interference of the South African apartheid government. A poignant documentary film, *Stopping the Music* (Drewett et al., 2009 and Drewett and Mitchell, 2002), for example, reveals the story of a South African protest singer, Roger Lucey, and the systematic demise of his music career through the actions of the security branch of the apartheid regime. It highlights the dangers of censorship and the social and political consequences when musical activism is stymied.

MIRIAM MAKEBA AND HUGH MASEKELA

In the 1950s, the political, social, and cultural sensibilities of both Makeba and Masekela were influenced by their musical experiences in Sophiatown. This area was a vibrant cultural and political hub near Johannesburg and one of the few places in South Africa where people from different races mixed freely. Both Makeba and Masekela (seven years younger) performed and toured with the Manhattan Brothers as professional musicians. When Makeba landed a leading role in the jazz opera *King Kong* in 1959, Masekela was a musician in the orchestra. Together with another musician, Jonas Gwangwa, Masekela also had the daunting task of copying the orchestral part from sketches they completed diligently. In the same year, a four-minute cameo role, singing two songs in *Come Back, Africa*, catapulted Makeba to international stardom. Makeba's role in *King Kong* made her a more recognizable face among White South Africans as this was one of the few productions open to separate white and Black audiences.

The antiapartheid semidocumentary film *Come Back Africa*, by the American independent filmmaker Lionel Rogosin, reached international audiences. The film was shot covertly in Sophiatown because of its subject matter, highlighting the South African government's injustices. First, Makeba attended the Venice Film Festival in Italy, where the film won the Critic's Choice Award. Then, at the behest of the American celebrity Steve Allen and singer and activist Harry Belafonte, Makeba went from Italy to London and New York. There she forged a meaningful relationship with Harry Belafonte, a strong advocate of the antiapartheid movement. Belafonte profoundly impacted Makeba's life, becoming her sponsor and mentor in the United States. Meanwhile, in South Africa, several activists, including Nelson Mandela, were in the throes of the infamous Treason Trial in South Africa (1956–1961).

Despite Makeba's musical success in the 1960s, this was also a period of intense angst. Makeba arrived in the United States in the wake of two momentous events: the first civil rights sit-in of February 1960 in the United States and the Sharpeville massacre of March 1960 in South Africa. That same year, Makeba tried to return to South Africa to attend her mother's funeral. Instead, she discovered that the South African government had banned her from returning because of her role in *Come Back Africa*. This unfortunate turn of events brought the South African policy of apartheid into focus with negative media attention. Unable to renew her South African passport, Makeba went into exile. Makeba's grief is palpable in *Makeba: My Story*: "They have exiled me. I am not permitted to go home, not now, and maybe not ever. My family. My home. Everything that has ever gone into the making of myself, gone!" (1988, 98).

In 1960, while Makeba tried to return to South Africa, the political stranglehold on activists intensified. Masekela was desperate to leave South Africa. His self-exile from South Africa resulted from being framed as a subversive, "which caused the Special Branch to keep me under surveillance" (Masekela and Cheers, 2004, 87). Under pressure, Masekela implored Father Huddleston,[2] a British antiapartheid chaplain, to arrange his departure from South Africa. Masekela headed to London and then to New York with Huddleston's help. Harry Belafonte, Dizzy Gillespie, and Miriam Makeba helped Masekela enroll at the Manhattan School of Music in New York. Belafonte nurtured Masekela at many levels. Masekela affirms the influence of Belafonte when he says, "He has been a father to me, the strongest influence on my stage presentation, my community activism, and my commitment to the fight for human rights" (146).

While Masekela honed his skills and assimilated the American jazz culture, Makeba became increasingly popular in the United States. White Americans were drawn to her "exotic" African persona, while Black Americans identified with the South African struggle against racial segregation. Such was the popularity of Makeba that she performed for President John F. Kennedy's birthday celebration in 1962 at Madison Square Garden. In the same year, Makeba sang at a concert in Kenya when that country gained its independence from British colonial rule. As other African countries such as Zambia, Mozambique, and Angola gained their independence, Makeba's performances at those celebrations established her presence as "Mama Africa." Makeba's musical activism included fundraising activities for civil rights groups. Martin Luther King Jr. referred to a benefit concert for the 1962 Southern Christian Leadership Conference as the event of the year. Despite her popularity, Makeba's experience of racism in the United States was no different from her African American counterparts' experiences. In one notable incident after a concert and rally for Dr. King, Makeba and other Black people were denied entry to a restaurant due to Jim Crow laws. This incident led to a televised protest in front of the establishment.

During this period, Makeba married the South African trumpeter, Hugh Masekela. Both artists were protégés of Harry Belafonte. Although their marriage was short-lived (1964–1966), they remained lifelong friends collaborating on many songs and projects over the years. Makeba found herself among other artists such as Dizzy Gillespie, Louis Armstrong, and Ray Charles and the activist and singer Nina Simone with whom Makeba performed at Carnegie Hall. Makeba and Masekela were thrust into an environment of exciting performances and passionate activism among entertainers and intellectuals such as Maya Angelou and actors such as Sidney Poitier in New York. They firmly believed in the power of popular culture as a vehicle for social and political change.

The civil rights movement in the United States was at its height during this time. The Civil Rights Act was passed in 1964. Makeba recognized the similarities in racial inequities between South Africa and the United States. While she had previously been cautious in expressing her political views, Makeba began to use her platform as an international artist to speak to the atrocities of apartheid. In 1963 and 1964, she had the opportunity to address the General Assembly of the United Nations, presenting an insider view of White minority rule injustices and cruelty in South Africa. Makeba, a young woman in her early thirties at that time, made this appeal to the United Nations Special Committee on Apartheid in March 1964:

> I ask you and all the leaders of the world; would you act differently? Would you keep silent and do nothing if you were in our place? Would you not resist if you were allowed no rights in your own country because the color of your skin is different from that of the rulers, and if you were punished for even asking for equality. [. . .] I appeal to you, and to all the countries of the world to do everything you can to stop the coming tragedy. I appeal to you to save the lives of our leaders, to empty the prisons of all those who should never have been there.[3]

Makeba suffered the consequences of her act of courage. The South African apartheid government revoked Makeba's South African citizenship and banned her records even if she sang a love song. Makeba became a stateless person, but other countries such as Algeria, Guinea, Belgium, and Ghana welcomed her—all issued passports to her. She held nine passports during her lifetime, and she was granted honorary citizenship in ten different countries. The South African government's punitive measures increased Makeba's celebrity status, which "bolstered transnational perspectives on race and a transnational circulation of culture, in particular, because she made television an important part of her life as a performer and reached mass audiences through that medium" (Feldstein, 2013, 14).

One of the consequences of South Africa's apartheid policy was that cultural diplomacy through musical activism, for the most part, played out on an international stage. Miriam Makeba is a powerful example of a singer, actress, songwriter, United Nations goodwill ambassador, and human rights activist. Her most crucial advocacy for South Africa's liberation came through her diplomacy and performances abroad. However, in 1968, Makeba suffered a backlash in the United States when she married Stokely Carmichael, an American Black activist.

Conservatives in the United States saw Carmichael as a militant and an extremist. Makeba suffered professionally from this union with Carmichael. Some promoters canceled her concerts and she lost a recording contract in the United States. The United States refused to renew Makeba's visa while away in the Bahamas with Carmichael. As a result, Makeba was forced to relocate with Carmichael to Guinea, West Africa, where she remained after her divorce from Carmichael in 1979. She continued performing in Europe and Africa and as an honorary citizen of Guinea. As a measure of her ongoing activism, Makeba served as the Guinean ambassador to the United Nations. Her commitment to the advocacy for peace and justice in Africa earned Makeba the Dag Hammarskjold Peace Prize in 1986.

In 1990, the South African government finally succumbed to political pressure from the antiapartheid movement from within the country and abroad. The apartheid government lifted the ban on organizations such as the African National Congress. President de Klerk announced that Nelson Mandela, who had served twenty-seven years in prison, would be released. After his release in February 1990, Mandela encouraged Makeba to return to South Africa, which she did on her French passport in June 1990. After more than thirty years in exile, her physical and spiritual homecoming was long overdue (Allen, 2008).

Makeba's success as a musical artist and activist abroad spanned more than thirty years. Despite her notable performances in other countries over the years, it was only in 1991 that she was finally allowed to perform in South Africa since her exile. Filled with renewed enthusiasm and hope for South Africa's future, Makeba collaborated with her ex-husband, Hugh Masekela, Dizzy Gillespie, and Nina Simone on a 1991 studio album, *Eyes on Tomorrow*. It was stylistically an eclectic album with music that ranged from rhythm and blues to pop to jazz and traditional African music. It captured the diversity of the moment that found broad appeal throughout the continent and across the world. Makeba resuscitated her remarkable acting skills playing the lead character's mother in the film *Sarafina* in 1992. This film was based on Mbongeni Ngema's 1987 musical of the same name. Ironically, the movie with the title *Come Back, Africa* led to Makeba's exile. It was poetic justice that *Sarafina* would be the film (through its antiapartheid subject matter) that would help solidify the return of this consummate performer to her native South Africa.

Nelson Mandela's election as the first democratically elected president of South Africa in 1994 prompted Makeba to immerse herself in artistically fulfilling and culturally and socially uplifting projects. The South African government appointed Makeba as goodwill ambassador of the Food and Agriculture Organization of the United Nations in October 1999. Meanwhile, her album, *Homeland*, produced by Putumayo World Music (based in New York), was nominated in 2000 for a Grammy Award in the Best World Music Album category. In addition, Makeba worked with Graça Machel-Mandela, the South African first lady, for the special care of children who have HIV/

AIDS, children recruited as soldiers, and the physically disabled. She also established the Makeba Centre for Girls, a home for orphans. Makeba's philanthropy paralleled her commitment to cultural diplomacy and peace. She was honored in 2001when she was awarded the Otto Hahn Peace Medal in Gold by the United Nations Association of Germany in Berlin "for outstanding services to peace and international understanding."

Makeba also participated in the documentary *Amandla! A Revolution in Four-Part Harmony* (Hirsch 2002), directed by American filmmaker Lee Hirsch. It is a "powerful film that looks at the centrality of music during the anti-apartheid struggle" (Yudkoff, 2018, 54). As a lifelong musician and activist, Makeba addressed various social and political issues through song and diplomacy. Therefore, it was not surprising that during a visit to the Democratic Republic of Congo in March 2008, she addressed sexual violence against women.

Makeba died as she had lived—in the spotlight. The circumstances of Makeba's death could not have been more Shakespearean. Her concert on November 9, 2008—as were so many concerts since the early 1960s—was in support of the writer Roberto Saviano who was against the Camorra, a criminal organization in the Campania region in Italy. This performance was her last act of musical activism. Makeba suffered a heart attack and could not be revived after performing her most famous Xhosa song, "Pata, Pata." This song had become a worldwide hit in 1967 after being released—ten years after its original recording—in the United States. As a musical activist and a cultural diplomat, the impact of Makeba's work spanned more than six decades over many countries. She was a citizen of the world, but her most tremendous pride came from being "a native South African." For, as she declares in *Makeba: My Story*, "My life, my career, every song I sing and every appearance I make are bound up with the plight of my people" (Makeba with Hall, 1988, 1). Makeba's musical journey and opportunities for activism demonstrate the "soft power" of music. Her music was her message.

Masekela's activism also stemmed directly from his musical compositions and musical performances. "[Masekela's] remarks about his ambitions to be an all-American musician resulted in the failure of his first album, *Trumpet Africaine* [in 1962], and made him work hard at losing his stupid fascination with all things American" (Raditlhalo, 2009, 44). Belafonte encouraged Masekela to stay in the United States. Belafonte reminded him that he would have access to the media as a platform for activism if he became successful. Masekela's message would resonate throughout the world. Harry Belafonte also created musical opportunities for Masekela. During the recording of Miriam Makeba's album *The Many Voices of Miriam Makeba*, he had Masekela play his trumpet on three of her tracks: "Love Tastes Like

Strawberries," "Umqokozo," and "Ntyilo." Masekela's work on these tracks received high praise with extensive radio coverage. This exposure was the break that Masekela needed. Through his music and interviews, he developed a platform to strengthen the antiapartheid campaign against the South African government.

Through Dizzy Gillespie and Miles Davis's advice, Masekela discovered that imitating American jazz was not enough to become a breakthrough artist. He needed to infuse his music with his own South African musical heritage. In doing so, Masekela unlocked the formula for his future success. Over the next ten years, he focused on the heartbreak, corruption, and cruelty of apartheid policies of South Africa in his highly acclaimed music. As predicted by Belafonte, he had direct access to the media to protest the brutality of the apartheid system. In 1968, his first hit song, "Grazing in the Grass," a unique blend of jazz and African pop, sold more than four million copies. His highest compliment was the many artists who performed covers of his song, including Stevie Wonder. Masekela's collaborations with high-profile musicians flourished. Despite his early success in the United States, Raditlhalo (2009, 1) described Masekela as having a "skollie impishness" that translates (in South African terms) to a rascal mentality. This sensibility, combined with the proverbial "wine, women and song," resulted in the highs and lows of Masekela's life. He only found his equilibrium as he transitioned into his midlife and edged closer, geographically speaking, to his native South Africa.

Activism and diplomacy were organic outgrowths of Masekela's music. Although Masekela, Makeba, Clegg, and Katz fiercely opposed apartheid, they conveyed their resistance, protest, hope, and optimism through their music. Makeba echoed the sentiments of many South African musicians in a 2004 interview with Roy Hearst, the news and notes producer of National Public Radio. Makeba stated categorically:

> I am not a politician, but I am a South African who feels and who knows where I come from and what we are going through. And I said I don't sing politics; I sing—I merely sing the truth.[4]

This approach to singing coheres with a tradition of indigenous African music that captures its people's lived experiences where musical traditions are "the depth of their integration into the various patterns of social, economic and political life. [. . .] The aesthetic principles of African music are, to an extent, dependent on how the music can be socially relevant" (Chernoff, 1979, 35). Within this framework of an honest expression of the truth, Masekela brought unambiguous songs to the attention of international audiences to raise awareness of the predicament of South Africans.

Legendary composer Vuyisile Mini's[5] lyrics of an antiapartheid song, "Ndodemnyama we Verwoerd," meaning "Watch Out, Verwoerd," reveals a clear message. Masekela coproduced a recording of this song with Makeba. The up-tempo, playful quality of the music belies their powerful message to Verwoerd—the prime minister at that time in South Africa and a strong proponent of apartheid laws—that segregation was not sustainable. Masekela consciously addressed many issues that plagued South Africa through his music. His album, *Masekela*, was released in 1969 and included a track titled "Gold" that laid bare the inhumane conditions endured by mineworkers in South Africa. In his 1974 album, *I Am Not Afraid*, Masekela uses "Stimela" as the title of one of his songs. The significance of "Stimela" or the "Train" in South Africa is well documented (Yudkoff, 2021; Bethlehem, 2017; Smith and Ginzberg, in *When Voices Meet*, 2015; Coplan, 2014).

An excerpt from the song speaks to the horrendous conditions under which migrant workers are forced to live. Masekela decries this atrocity when he describes how "they sit in their stinky, filthy, funky, flea-ridden barracks and hostels" and explores the themes of dislocation and loss when he writes that "they think about the loved ones who they may never see again." The laws of apartheid were swift moving "because they have already been forcibly removed from where they last left them."[6]

As a child of color growing up in apartheid South Africa, this policy of forcible relocation resonates with me. My parents and extended family were forced to leave their family home on Bentley Street in Durban, which was declared a "White" area. The apartheid nationalist government relocated my family to a remote area designated for "Indians." This loss of prime real estate close to the Durban beachfront and forcible removal was based solely on race. The issue of dislocation and relocation was only one of the many painful issues of the apartheid system. The South African political landscape was the fertile ground that sprouted many deeply emotional songs related to atrocities as they occurred.

Masekela's musical journey was also an experience in cultural exchange as he ventured from one country to the next. In the mid-1970s, Masekela went to Africa, where he stayed in Guinea, Ghana, Nigeria, and Zaire, immersed in those countries' languages, music, and customs. This experience was also an opportunity for Masekela to help fellow Africans by performing concerts for charity and collaborating with other musicians.

Masekela wrote one of the most poignant songs of his career after the 1976 Soweto Uprising. A decree from the South African apartheid government announced Afrikaans (the language of the White minority government of South Africa), alongside English, was compulsory for instruction in all schools. This proclamation immediately caused an uprising in Soweto

Figure 11.1. Hector Pieterson carried by Mbuyisa Makhubo. Pieterson's sister, Antoinette Sithole, runs alongside. Photo by Sam Nzima

(designated an African township during the apartheid era). However, many discriminatory policies of the apartheid government, such as the Bantu Education Act in 1953, contributed to the 1976 student unrest.

During the peaceful march of thousands of African students, pandemonium broke loose when the students were brutally attacked by the South African police and army in armored vehicles. According to McKenna (2021), "It is estimated that when the police and the army responded to the demonstrators by firing tear gas and then bullets, between 400 and 700 people, many of them children, were killed." Two students, fifteen-year-old Hastings Ndlovu and twelve-year-old Hector Pieterson, were among the first two students shot. An iconic newspaper photograph by Sam Nzima of the dying Hector carried by a fellow student was published in South Africa and worldwide. This image had a visceral impact on people everywhere.

Masekela's 1977 song, "Soweto Blues," captures the melancholy and pathos of the events of June 16, 1976, with a strong opening descending melodic line interspersed with the plaintive strains of an electric guitar. Recorded in Ghana with the rich and resonant voice of Miriam Makeba on vocals, Masekela laments the pain of that massacre in a musical style that is reminiscent of the American blues. Besides the rapidly repeating notes of the trumpet that replicated the sound of bullets that killed children that day, the lyrics of a recurring line that runs through the chorus searches for answers: "Where were the men when the children were being shot." Masekela and Makeba's joint performances reverberated through international audiences. Their commitment to raising political awareness through their artistic collaborations sustained many decades despite their short-lived marriage in the mid-1960s.

Increasingly, Masekela used his concerts, tours, and events to raise awareness of apartheid and improve the conditions of Africans discriminated against by colonialism and apartheid. In 1982, Masekela moved to Botswana (a country bordering South Africa). Besides reconnecting and performing with Makeba at a "Going Home" concert attended by thirty-five thousand people, Masekela founded the Botswana International School of Music to inspire and mentor aspiring musicians from Africa.

Masekela highlighted the international issue of dictatorships throughout many parts of the world. He released one of his most successful albums, *Tomorrow*, which includes a song titled "Everybody's Standing Up." This song celebrates the fall of dictatorships throughout the world when Masekela declares that "every dictator has to step aside and make way for freedom." Masekela's activism was recognized when Nelson Mandela smuggled a birthday card to him from Pollsmoor Prison. Masekela was overwhelmed by this act of kindness, which prompted him to write the iconic song "Bring Him Home" (Masekela and Cheers, 2004, 338). This song served to protest the South African government's imprisonment of Nelson Mandela and demand his release. Although the song was banned in South Africa, it became a powerful anthem for activists as it captured their determination to overcome oppression and establish a country founded on democracy.

One of the most potent and controversial collaborations leading up to Nelson Mandela's release was Paul Simon and Ladysmith Black Mambazo (see

Yudkoff, 2021; Muller, 2004; Meintjies, 1990). When Simon decided to tour after the release of his album *Graceland*, he invited Masekela and Makeba to join him. This tour included shows in Zimbabwe, Europe, the United Kingdom, the United States, and Japan. Joyce (1988) captures the impact of Masekela and Makeba after they performed on that tour:

> Masekela's riveting "Stimela," a song about displaced workers set to the chugging rhythm of a coal train, quickly silenced the house, just as surely as his version of "Bring Back Nelson Mandela" later turned into a rousing audience sing-along. By contrast, Makeba made Masekela's "Soweto Blues" into a graceful, poignant, deeply moving elegy. If there was a common thread running throughout the show, it was Makeba and Masekela's concern for South Africa's youth.

After the release of Mandela from prison in 1990, Hugh Masekela returned to South Africa. He had released more than thirty albums at that point in his career and had established himself internationally as a musical activist.

The institutionalized racism of apartheid South Africa (1948–1994) had the unintended advantage of providing exiled musicians an international platform for activism and diplomacy through their music. The musical output of two of the most prominent activists in exile, Miriam Makeba and Hugh Masekela, provides ample evidence of their reach within the international community. However, the development of musical styles and musicians' social and political impact within South Africa was also noteworthy. Martin (1992, 195) states that "South African musics, despite the UNESCO cultural boycott, have thus been 'discovered' by the outside world while simultaneously undergoing profound changes within."

JOHNNY CLEGG

Almost a generation after Makeba and Masekela made their debut in Sophiatown, Johnny Clegg (1953–2019) came onto the South African music scene. A British-born South African, Clegg lived in Israel, Zimbabwe, and Zambia before his mother, Muriel (Braudo) Pienaar and stepfather Dan Pienaar (an international newspaper correspondent), settled in Johannesburg. His early excursions into African music began when he went with his stepfather to meet migrant Zulu workers in segregated Black townships rarely visited by White people. Although Clegg's early influences playing acoustic guitar included Jethro Tull and Irish folk bands, he was fascinated by Zulu songs played on the radio. Clegg's musical repertoire took on a whole new meaning when he met Charlie Mzila, a Zulu street guitarist, in 1967. Clegg explains that

Mzila "took me under his wing and opened this world to me. Johannesburg was filled with street music played on guitar, concertina, and violin in those days, and I managed to get quite a collection of songs down on tape" (Poet, 2010). He visited migrant hostels with Mzila, where more than a thousand men lived. Despite being arrested at fifteen yeard old (and many times later) for being in areas designated for African people, it was among migrant Zulu workers that Clegg learned Zulu songs and dance. In a interview on National Public Radio, Clegg describes the impact of this experience:

> The body was coded and wired—hard-wired—to carry messages about masculinity which were pretty powerful for a young, 16-year-old adolescent boy. [. . .] They knew something about being a man, which they could communicate physically in the way that they danced and carried themselves. And I wanted to be able to do the same thing. I fell in love with it. Basically, I wanted to become a Zulu warrior. And in a very deep sense, it offered me an African identity. (Clegg, 2017)

Clegg's fascination with African culture led to his study of anthropology at the University of Witwatersrand, where he eventually became a lecturer focusing on Zulu music and dance. Inspired by his passion for African music and his collaborations with Sipho Mchunu, an accomplished *maskandi* guitarist at seventeen, Clegg created a racially mixed band called Juluka (meaning "Sweat" in the isiZulu language). *Maskanda* is a neo-traditional musical style developed by Zulu migrant workers. This venture in the early 1970s defied the South African policies of racial segregation. Known as "The White Zulu," Clegg's music was a fusion of folk, rock, and maskanda that captured the imagination of White and Black audiences alike.

Although they could not play in public, Juluka avoided confrontations with the apartheid government by performing at private schools, churches, and private university halls. They also played at embassies and consulates (Clegg, 2017). These performances led to growing audiences at a time when the effects of apartheid were deeply entrenched. Baines describes Juluka's resistance to the South African regime as being coded from how the band members dressed, how they moved, and the lyrics that they sang (2008, 107). Clegg's "adoption of traditional Zulu attire in combination with Western dress, and the appropriation of Zulu dance routines amounted to a politicized cross-cultural collaboration." Baines asserts that "Clegg's performances suggest that whiteness (and also Zuluness) is a matter much less of race than of style, and that style itself is a cross-cultural phenomenon, working against the grain of racial essentialism" (2008, 108).

The racial harmony projected through the music of Clegg and Mchunu gave South Africans hope and optimism that positive race relations could dismantle apartheid. Apartheid was a system of institutionalized racial segregation. Therefore, an analysis of the concept of "cultural diplomacy" applied to the unique circumstances of South Africa is relevant to this discussion. Cultural diplomacy entails a course of action that has intercultural exchange at its core. It includes a sharing of ideas, traditions, values, and aspects of identity and culture. Intercultural dialogue strengthens relationships among people from different cultures, enhances sociocultural cooperation, and promotes national interests. The physical segregation of South Africans into homogenous enclaves based on racial identity due to the policies of apartheid meant that traditions and values of one race group did not naturally intermingle with those of another. The creative hybridization of music was one way to encourage intercultural exchange within South Africa and abroad. Clegg harnessed the power of Western folk and rock music with the vitality of Zulu songs and dance. His fluency in Zulu and Clegg's mastery of the highly energetic Zulu dances impressed African audiences in South Africa. International audiences were fascinated by Clegg's African-inspired music—with solid folk and rock elements—and the spectacular choreography of his performances.

Juluka released its debut album, *Universal Men*, in 1979. By 1982, Clegg and Mchunu enjoyed success in South Africa and abroad, with one of the songs, "Scatterlings of Africa," (from the album *Scatterlings*) becoming a Top-50 singles chart hit in the United Kingdom and reached number one in France. In this song, Clegg explores the theme of "dislocation" (previously discussed in the music of Masekela), "They are the scatterlings of Africa / Each uprooted one." Other songs such as "Work for All" echoed the South African trade unions slogan in the mid-1980s. The band's racial makeup and the more overt political messaging of their songs resulted in the disruption of concerts by the South African police and sometimes arrests of the band members. Regardless, the combination of Zulu and English lyrics and the eclectic mix of African culture, music, dance, and highly energetic choreography appealed to international audiences. Clegg and Mchunu had tapped into a performance niche, creating a platform for their musical activism. After a few years of touring internationally, Mchunu decided (while the band was in New York City in 1985) that it was time to return to cattle farming with his family in KwaZulu-Natal.

Clegg's new band, Savuka (meaning "We Have Awakened" in isiZulu), was launched during a declared state of emergency in South Africa in 1986. In an NPR (National Public Radio) Clegg remembrance compiled by Tsioulcas (2019), Clegg explains in an audio clip that "you could not ignore what was going on. The entire Savuka project was based (on) the South African experience and the fight for a better quality of life and freedom for all." While teaching anthropology at the University of Witwatersrand in Johannesburg,

Clegg recognized that this was a pivotal moment in South Africa. The liberation movement in South Africa was gaining momentum, and South Africa was on the brink of change.

In Clegg's 1987 album, *Third World Child*, he crafted a focused political statement. His hit song, "Asimbonanga" (meaning "We have not seen him" in isiZulu), was an antiapartheid call for Nelson Mandela's release, who had already been imprisoned for more than two decades. The song also references other activists such as Steve Biko and Neil Aggett (who died in detention) and Victoria Mxenge (a murdered Black civil rights lawyer). Coplan (2005) called "Asimbonanga" a "haunting tribute." At a concert in Frankfurt in 1999, after Mandela stepped down as president, he joined Clegg on stage as the song was being performed. Denselow (2019) describes this scene as one of "the most emotional scenes in political pop history." The video of this concert captured international media attention during the illness and death of Nelson Mandela in 2013. *Third World Child* included a few love songs such as "Dela," but there was no mistaking the political activism inherent in "One (Hu)Man, One Vote" and "Warsaw 1943 (I Never Betrayed the Revolution)."

The release of this album coincided with the release of Paul Simon's *Graceland* album of 1986. There was controversy regarding Paul Simon's recordings with Ladysmith Black Mambazo and other talented Black South African musicians (see Yudkoff, 2021; Muller, 2004; Martin, 1992; Meintjies, 1990). This debate was related to the cultural boycott of the time. Simon's collaboration with South African artists defied the United Nations-sanctioned cultural boycott, intended to pressure the apartheid government to end racial segregation policies. However, Paul Simon appeared to be tone-deaf to his actions' political and social ramifications. He did not heed the advice of Harry Belafonte, who wanted Simon to consult with both the ANC (African National Congress) and the organization Artists Against Apartheid. One of their initiatives was to encourage international artists to respect the cultural boycott of South Africa. Paul Simon went ahead with his recordings, the album sold worldwide, but antiapartheid protests followed at his concerts with outrage expressed in the media. Clegg, like Simon, believed that the world needed to hear the music of South Africa. He wanted the international community to witness the interracial collaboration of South African musicians. It represented harmony and cooperation among people irrespective of their racial backgrounds. The image of Clegg and Mchunu performing together was powerful. Like Makeba and Masekela, Clegg did not see himself as an activist. In an interview with Poet (2010), Clegg affirmed that while he did not consider himself a political activist, he believed that people have fundamental rights worth the fight. Clegg described the ugly subjects of his songs from "the murder squads and people who have been killed in prison."

Throughout Savuka's performances, Clegg maintained that they "tried to remain hopeful, to present a vision of a better future." Clegg's humility in this interview is striking when he says, "I don't think music can make a change in the political situation, but it can help make people more aware, and in that way, perhaps, we did make some small difference."

Clegg's popularity was particularly evident in France, corroborated by Lancombe (2019), who describes two concerts in 1988. Lancombe notes that Michael Jackson had to cancel a show in Lyon during his *Bad* world tour because of low ticket sales while Clegg's concert in the same city (scheduled for the same day) sold forty thousand tickets. In 1996, Clegg received the Medal of Honor from the City of Besançon. In 2004, he received the Mayoral Medal of Honor from the mayor of Lyon for fostering outstanding relations between the people of Lyon and South Africa. Finally, he received Medals of Honor from the Consul General of the Province of Nievre and the Consul General of the Province of L'Aisne.

In the United States, Clegg received the Mayor's Office of Los Angeles Award in 1988 for the promotion of racial harmony and the 1990 Humanitarian Award conferred by the secretary of state of Ohio. In 2015, Queen Elizabeth II honored Johnny Clegg with the Officer of the Order of the British Empire Award. Judith Macgregor, the British high commissioner to South Africa stated, according to SA People (2015), that the award was a "recognition of Johnny's unique services to the Arts, vulnerable people and children and to democracy in South Africa."

It is noteworthy that Clegg received significant awards from South Africa during the apartheid era. These include his 1987 Communication Contribution Award, a 1988 CCP Record Special Award that recognized his exceptional achievement in promoting South African music internationally, and the 1989 Radio 5 Loud & Proud Award for being the South African music ambassador of the year. In addition, Clegg received several honorary doctorate degrees from various academic institutions in South Africa and the United States. However, his highest honor in South Africa was conferred in 2012 by President Jacob Zuma when he received the Order of Ikhamanga, the highest honor a citizen can receive in South Africa.

With his multiracial bands Juluka and Savuka, Johnny Clegg created a crossover musical style that spoke to a "rainbow" moment. From the South African government's perspective, "Juluka's very existence was perceived as a threat by the apartheid regime with its notions of the absolute separation of strictly bounded cultures" (Coplan, 2005, 3). Clegg rejected the tribalism of apartheid ideologies by creating a unique fusion of Western musical styles with *maskanda*. He approached music from the opposite perspective of Paul Simon's *Graceland*.

Clegg's album, *Human*, released postapartheid in 2010, delves once again into social injustice issues, demonstrating his ongoing musical activism through his words and music. Clegg's songs exude energy and vitality that denotes a euphoric essence that often transcends his songs' sociopolitical issues. The first song, "Love in the Time of Gaza," is couched in the rhythms of Africa and elements of rock to address the struggle between Israel and Palestine. In addition to the profound messages of Clegg's songs, *Human* celebrates the sounds of South Africa. The rich harmonies of the backing vocals of "Congo" and "Asilazi," the township-jive riffs and rhythms of "All I Got Is You," and the two Zulu tracks, "Nyembezi" and "Magumede," speak to the heart, the identity, and the optimism of "The White Zulu." Until his death in 2019, Johnny Clegg lived his best life: recording, touring, performing, and sharing his messages of hope for South Africa's future.

SHARON KATZ

In another province of South Africa in the 1950s, a contemporary of Johnny Clegg was navigating her place in apartheid South Africa. Just two years younger than Clegg, Sharon Katz grew up in Cape Province in Port Elizabeth (now Mandela Bay). Like Clegg, Katz was negotiating her "whiteness" in a country where the differences between the lives of Africans and Whites were stark. Katz came from a Jewish background—Clegg's mother was Jewish—from whom she learned of the holocaust in Europe. However, Katz describes her angst and sadness when her family took holidays, and they drove through an area called Transkei. The poverty and abysmal conditions of life among Black people there reminded her of the holocaust.

Like Clegg, Katz felt the appeal of African music. Although her early musical influences were folk artists such as Joan Baez, Bob Dylan, Simon and Garfunkel, and Pete Seeger, Katz combined her love of folk music with the African-infused *maskanda* guitar style. She describes her "awakening" as the moment when she heard the song "Nkosi Sikelele iAfrica" sung at the end of a powerful dramatization of the play *The Just Assassins* by Athol Fugard (Smith and Ginzberg, *When Voices Meet*, 2015). At this closed audience performance, she met and eventually forged a lifelong friendship with the actor and activist John Kani. With the help of Kani, Katz (only fifteen years old at the time) was able to sneak into Black townships and participate in the music and culture of African people.

Katz was not a commercial artist. After her undergraduate studies in Cape Town, Katz chose to follow her music therapy interests after graduating from Temple University in the United States in 1981. Since 1983, Katz has practiced as a music therapist, educator, social activist, performer, and conflict resolution consultant. She has worked in prisons, schools, universities, mental health facilities, drug and rehabilitation centers, youth empowerment projects, HIV/AIDS orphanages, and community development programs. Her music's "soft power" is evident in how she has used her music therapy techniques to heal individuals and communities. Her work in prisons and a boys reform school in Philadelphia, Pennsylvania, earned her a reputation for converting "gang members into band members."

Nelson Mandela's release from Robben Island in 1990 created a sense of urgency among activists. Katz wanted to return to South Africa to support the inevitable tide of change as she knew that democratic elections were imminent (Katz, Personal Communication, 2016). In 1992, Katz, accompanied by her American-born partner, Marilyn Cohen, returned to South Africa, where she conducted workshops for children and youth at the Playhouse Theatre in Durban. Based on her experience with young people, Katz applied for an opportunity to create a multicultural production.

Through negotiation with schools, arduous rehearsals, and cultural sensitivity, Katz realized her vision of creating a five hundred-voice choir with children (African, White, Indian, and Colored [a race classification meaning "of mixed race" in South Africa]) from the four segregated population groups. Nonhlanhla Wanda, a talented Black teacher, performer, and activist, mediated Katz's entry into the African rural areas of KwaZulu-Natal. This multiracial and multilingual production, *When Voices Meet*, included original compositions by Katz in English, Zulu, and Xhosa. The enthusiasm for a multiracial and multicultural showcase of artistic unity was apparent as they played to sold-out performances at the Durban City Hall in 1993—at a time when special permission was required from the authorities to perform before a racially integrated audience. *When Voices Meet* demonstrated the "soft power" of musical activism intended to promote a peaceful transition to democracy in South Africa, incorporating music, songs, and dance.

Empowered by these concerts' success and encouraged by sponsorships, Katz auditioned students (ranging in age from nine to seventeen) from the five hundred-voice choir to tour the country. She wanted to bring a message of unity and peace to South Africans who were on the cusp of meaningful change. The policies of apartheid implemented in 1948 by the Nationalist Party were on the brink. So, boarding a train at the Durban station in 1993, 130 bright-eyed singers with chaperones (teachers and parents), a band, and the a cappella group Ladysmith Black Mambazo (famous for their collaboration with Paul Simon on his *Graceland* album) began an unforgettable journey through South Africa. With television and radio crews documenting the trip, Sharon Katz brought her choir to towns and cities along the way. The performers' ostensible mission on this journey was to create an environment of trust, joy, and sharing through music while breaking down the artificially imposed barriers of a racially segregated society. At each stop along the route, the performers encouraged people of all races, cultures, ages, and political affiliations to embrace the demise of apartheid, end hostilities, and prepare for South Africa's transition to a peaceful democracy. As a result, the performing group's name was solidified as The Peace Train (see Yudkoff, 2021, chapter 3).

Katz's work with The Peace Train drew the attention of the Independent Electoral Commission, which had recently set a date for South Africa's first democratic election. The commission's goal was to educate the previously disenfranchised majority in South Africa about the process of voting. For the African (Black) communities in the rural areas, who had never been allowed to vote during the apartheid era, bringing this knowledge of voting to them was critical. The provincial authorities in KwaZulu-Natal commissioned Sharon Katz to write songs in some of South Africa's African languages as a tool to teach people to vote. Worldwide audiences saw Katz for the first time when she appeared on the American television station CNN in April 1994. CNN captured Katz emerging from a helicopter to perform songs in remote and rural parts of KwaZulu-Natal because Chief Buthelezi[7] had agreed to let his people vote. Sharing this knowledge of voting with people through music was culturally sensitive, and it was empowering for the African people. CNN's coverage garnered international enthusiasm. Sharon Katz & The Peace Train subsequently recorded their music in CD compilations alongside international artists such as Sting, Tina Turner, Madonna, Paul Simon, and Pete Seeger.

In the same year (1994), Katz received a letter from the Consulate General of the United States endorsing a South African Peace Train tour to the United States. The letter states in part that the Peace Train is a "group that is representative of the myriad races and cultures," and that "they have been invited to the United States as well as to Israel to spread their music and methodology for peaceful co-existence" (Yudkoff, 2018, 138). In 1995, this tour took twenty-nine young singers with a full band on a five-week, eight-city tour that included the New Orleans Jazz Festival. Joni Mitchell, the iconic Canadian singer-songwriter, heard Katz and her choir during a chance encounter. She described the group as "a heavenly choir [who are] just great ambassadors for Africa" (*When Voices Meet*, 2015).

Over the next ten years, Katz taught in Ghana (invited by Dr. Nketia) and created the nonprofit Friends of The Peace Train—inspired by her encounter with the actress and performer Dolly Rathebe (see Yudkoff, 2021, chapter 3). This meeting led to an extensive building project in KwaZulu-Natal supported by Friends of The Peace Train. These were predominantly donors from the United States. In addition, Katz is deeply invested in her humanitarian work in South Africa, especially the Good Shepherd Community Organization (an orphanage in Mabopane) with Mama Mary at its helm. Fast forward to 2015, and Katz released a documentary film of her work with the Peace Train. The phenomenal success of this documentary, *When Voices Meet*—achieving several South African and international awards—precipitated a renewed interest in the grassroots activism of Sharon Katz & The Peace Train (see Yudkoff, 2021, chapter 4).

Across the Atlantic, in the United States, Katz replicated the South African Peace Train's original concept in 2016. The American Peace Train tour directly responded to racial tensions exacerbated by the shooting deaths of young, unarmed African American youth and men in various parts of the country. The Peace Train brought together young people from the United States to travel together, perform together, and bring a message of peace and harmony to audiences in different cities. The singing of African-inspired songs on the American Peace Train established its founder's identity and played well with American audiences who sympathized with the South African fight for freedom and acknowledged race and prejudice issues in American society. This form of outreach is the "soft power" of musical activism, lowering the temperature around heated rhetoric. Although her South African repertoire forms the basis of Katz's performances, she demonstrates a cultural awareness by including rap and the Spanish language, both of which resonate among Americans. The 2016 tour culminated in Washington, DC, on Sunday, July 17, 2016, with a Washington Monument's Sylvan Center performance. This performance with the UNESCO Centre for Peace was a celebration of Nelson Mandela Day. As part of her commitment to cultural exchange, Katz visited the South African embassy the following day, with her American performers in tow.

In response to the Trump-era policies against immigrants in 2017, Katz created a Peace Train project in Northern California. This grassroots effort focused on all children's human rights, especially children of color and migrant and immigrant families. This effort included more than one hundred youth and musicians performing at schools, train stations, and public parks with students, teachers, and families from Sacramento, San Pablo, Oakland, and Berkeley, raising their voices in song. With hope and optimism at the heart of their performances, La Pena Community Chorus singers and musicians joined the Peace Train's band for this special event.

Sharon Katz & The Peace Train have engaged in ongoing workshops and performances, including a binational Transcending Barriers Project of 2018 between the United States and Mexico. In 2019, the Peace Train went to Cuba with one hundred singers from the United States, South Africa, and Mexico to perform at the International Festival of Choirs in Santiago de Cuba. Throughout, Katz's activism through music fosters intercultural exchange with the broader goal of promoting understanding and tolerance among people.

CONCLUDING REMARKS

From an ethnomusicological perspective, these South African musicians embody South Africa's essence, where indigenous musical forms combine with contemporary Western music styles. This hybridization is not unusual in a digital age where there is a convergence of local and international ("glocal") influences in music. The selected artists have maintained their relevance within societies through their music by creating awareness of political and social injustices through a peaceful and conciliatory medium. In terms of cultural diplomacy, Western and African countries have provided South African musicians platforms to address human rights and peace issues through music unique to South Africa. In some instances, South African artists have enjoyed formal invitations from institutions in other countries. There have also been less formalized receptions through organizations that promote the arts within South Africa and abroad. Whatever the circumstances, these musical activists have highlighted the political and social injustices of their time. They have conveyed their messages of peace and skillfully demonstrated their mastery of South African music's rich cultural heritage through their music's "soft power." In doing so, artists hope to broaden the sociopolitical understanding and musical horizons of their audiences. The successful outcomes of soft power for cultural diplomacy are dependent on several factors. According to Nye:

> The soft power of a country rests primarily on three resources: its culture (in places where it is attractive to others), its political values (when it lives up to them at home and abroad), and its foreign policies (when they are seen as legitimate and having moral authority). (2008, 97)

Miriam Makeba, Hugh Masekela, Johnny Clegg, and Sharon Katz have demonstrated their musical and cultural appeal to both national and international audiences. Through their musical activism, they have espoused the ideals of freedom and peace for all South Africans. Moreover, all four artists have been acknowledged for their cultural contributions by the most iconic moral authority of South Africa, Nelson Mandela. These South African artists exemplify the soft power of cultural diplomacy.

NOTES

1. There are many variants of African folktales since these stories were repeated from generation to generation through oral transmission. See Adzenyah, Maraire, and Tucker (1997) for a variation of this folktale.

2. Masekela attended St. Peter's, an outstanding secondary school for Black children in Johannesburg. Father Trevor Huddleston, the antiapartheid chaplain at the school, took an interest in Masekela, purchased his first trumpet, and arranged music lessons. Soon enough, other students wanted instruments, and the Huddleston Jazz Band was born. Unfortunately, the school closed when the South African government tried to impose new restrictions on education. Although Huddleston went back to England, his interest in Masekela never waned. Huddleston also sent Masekela a trumpet from Louis Armstrong.

3. Ambigay Yudkoff, Transcription of speech by Miriam Makeba at the United Nations in 1963. Available at: https://www.youtube.com/watch?v=WlIM3msOJcc. Accessed February 16, 2021.

4. Farai Chideya, "Remembering the Activism of Miriam Makeba." In this 2008 obituary for Makeba, Chidaya, an American novelist, multimedia journalist and radio host, airs snippets of music and conversations with Makeba, and a conversation with the musician/activist, Harry Belafonte, who helped launch Makeba's career. Chidaya also speaks to Roxanne Lawson, the TransAfrica Forum's director of Africa Policy, for her insights. https://www.npr.org/transcripts/96869377. Accessed February 23, 2021.

5. Mini was actively involved with the ANC and was recruited into its military inception in 1961. He was arrested in 1963 for "political crimes," including sabotage and complicity in the death of an alleged police informer; when he refused to give evidence against his comrades, he was sentenced to death. Fellow prisoner Ben Turok describes him as walking defiantly to the gallows while singing Ndodemnyama. Available at: http://www.inquiriesjournal.com/articles/265/the-sounds-of-resistance-the-role-of-music-in-south-africas-anti-apartheid-movement. Accessed February 21, 2021.

6. Lyrics of "Stimela." Available at: https://genius.com/Hugh-masekela-stimela-the-coal-train-lyrics. Accessed June 14, 2021.

7. Mangosuthu Buthelezi was a South African politician and Zulu tribal leader who founded the Inkatha Freedom Party in 1975.

REFERENCES

Adzenyah, Abraham K., Dumisani Maraire, and Judith C. Tucker. 1997. *Let Your Voice Be Heard! Songs from Ghana and Zimbabwe*. Milwaukee, WI: World Music Press.

Allen, Lara. 2008. "Remembering Miriam Makeba: March 4, 1932–November 10, 2008." *Journal of the Musical Arts in Africa* 5, no. 1: 89–90.

Ang, Ien, Yudhishthir Raj Isar, and Phillip Mar. 2015. "Cultural Diplomacy: Beyond the National Interest?" *International Journal of Cultural Policy* 21, no. 4: 365–81.

Baines, Gary. 2008. "Popular Music and Negotiating Whiteness in Apartheid South Africa." In *Composing Apartheid: Music For and Against Apartheid*, edited by Grant Olwage, 99–113. Johannesburg, South Africa: Wits University Press.

Bayles, Martha. 2014. *Through a Screen Darkly: Popular Culture, Public Diplomacy, and America's Image Abroad.* New Haven, CT: Yale University Press.

Bethlehem, Louise. 2017. "'Miriam's Place': South African Jazz, Conviviality and Exile." *Social Dynamics* 43, no. 2: 243–58.

Chernoff, John Miller. 1979. *African Rhythm and African Sensibility: Aesthetics and Social action in African Musician Idioms.* Chicago and London: The University of Chicago Press.

Clarke, David. 2016. "Theorising the Role of Cultural Products in Cultural Diplomacy from a Cultural Studies Perspective." *International Journal of Cultural Policy* 22, no. 2: 147–63.

Clegg, Johnny. 2017. "A South African Superstar Says Farewell." Report by Anastacia Tsioulcas. NPR (National Public Radio), October 29, 2017. Audio: 5 minutes. https://www.npr.org/transcripts/558571470. Accessed February 27, 2021.

Coplan, David B. 2005. "God Rock Africa: Thoughts on Politics in Popular Black Performance in South Africa." *African Studies* 64, no. 1: 9–27.

———. 2014. "Verwoerd's Oxen: Performing Labour Migrancy in Southern Africa." In *A Long Way Home: Migrant Worker Worlds 1800–2014*, edited by Peter Delius, Laura Phillips, and Fiona Rankin-Smith, 169–85. Johannesburg, SA: Wits University Press.

Denselow, Robin. 2019. "Johnny Clegg Obituary." *The Guardian*. Guardian News and Media, July 19. https://www.theguardian.com/music/2019/jul/19/johnny-clegg-obituary.

Drewett, Michael, Douglas Mitchell, Roger Lucey, Paul Erasmus and Brendan Jury. 2009. *Stopping the Music*. South Africa: Freemuse. Accessed September 2, 2021. https://freemuse.org/resources/south-africa-film-documentary-stopping-the-music-2/.

Drewett, Michael and Douglas Mitchell. 2002. *Stopping the music: Music censorship in South Africa.* Cutting Grooves and Freemuse. 54 minutes. https://www.youtube.com/watch?v=btyYT9IPrig. Accessed September 1, 2021.

Feldstein, Ruth. 2013. "Screening Antiapartheid: Miriam Makeba, 'Come Back, Africa,' and the Transnational Circulation of Black Culture and Politics." *Feminist Studies* 39, no. 1: 12–39. Gale Academic OneFile, link.gale.com/apps/doc/A334380756/AONE?u=hvcc&sid=AONE&xid=296778cc. Accessed February 16, 2021.

Fosler-Lussier, D. 2012. "Music Pushed, Music Pulled: Cultural Diplomacy, Globalization, and Imperialism: Music Pushed, Music Pulled." *Diplomatic History* 36, no. 1: 53–64.

Hicks, Michael. 1984. "Soothing the Savage Beast: A Note on Animals and Music." *Journal of Aesthetic Education* 18, no. 4: 47–55.

Hirsch, Lee. 2002. *Amandla! A Revolution in Four-Part Harmony*. ATO Pictures.

Holden, John. 2013. *Influence and Attraction: Culture and the Race for Soft Power in the 21st Century*. London: British Council.
Joyce, Mike. 1988. "Miriam Makeba and Hugh Masekela," *Washington Post*, April 19, 1988. https://www.washingtonpost.com/archive/lifestyle/1988/04/19/miriam-makeba-and-hugh-masekela/a2ba9d51-70af-4e0d-a1d3-73998cc6c8c6/. Accessed March 3, 2021.
Lancombe, Bruno. 2019. "White Zulu was loved in France." *The Connextion*. July 17, 2019. https://www.connexionfrance.com/French-news/White-Zulu-was-loved-in-France. Accessed March 1, 2021.
Makeba, Miriam and James Hall. 1988. *Makeba: My Story*. London, UK: Bloomsbury.
McKenna, Amy. 2021. "The Soweto Uprising." Encyclopedia Britannica. https://www.britannica.com/story/the-soweto-uprising. Accessed February 25, 2021.
Mark, Simon L. 2010. "Rethinking Cultural Diplomacy: The Cultural Diplomacy of New Zealand, the Canadian Federation and Quebec." *Political Science* 62, no. 1: 62–83.
Martin, Denis-Constant. 1992. "Music Beyond Apartheid?" In *Rockin' the Boat: Mass Music and Mass Movements*, edited by Reebee Garofalo, 195–208, Cambridge, MA: South End Press.
Masekela, Hugh and D. Michael Cheers. 2004. *Still Grazing: The Musical Journey of Hugh Masekela*. New York: Crown Archetype.
Meintjes, Louise. 1990. "Paul Simon's Graceland, South Africa, and the Mediation of Musical Meaning." *Ethnomusicology* 34, no. 1: 37–73.
Muller, Carol A. 2004. *South African Music: A Century of Traditions in Transformation* (World Music Series). Santa Barbara, CA: ABC-CLIO.
Nye, Joseph S. 2008. "Public Diplomacy and Soft Power." *The Annals of the American Academy of Political and Social Science* 616, no. 1: 94–109. Accessed June 20, 2021. http://www.jstor.org/stable/25097996.
Poet, J. 2010. "Johnny Clegg: Breaking Down Boundaries." *Sing Out!* November 2010, 33+. Gale Academic OneFile. Accessed February 24, 2021. https://link.gale.com/apps/doc/A246534732/AONE?u=hvcc&sid=AONE&xid=7a097dd.
Raditlhalo, Sam. 2009. "The Self-Invention of Hugh Masekela." *Journal of Literary Studies* 25, no. 1: 34–52.
Ramabadran, Sudarshan. 2020. "Music as an Expression of Soft Power." *Hinduism Today* 42, no. 3: 30–33.
SA People. 2015. "Johnny Clegg Receives OBE for Services to South African Democracy." https://www.sapeople.com/2015/11/26/johnny-clegg-receives-obe-for-services-to-south-african-democracy/. Accessed February 28, 2021.
Smith, Nancy Sutton and Abby Ginzberg. 2015. *When Voices Meet: One Divided Country; One United Choir; One Courageous Journey*. Crystal Journey Productions.
Tsioulcas, Anastacia. 2019. "Johnny Clegg, A Uniting Voice Against Apartheid, Dies At 66." Remembrance on *Morning Edition*. NPR (National Public Radio), July 16, 2019. Audio: 5 minutes. https://www.npr.org/2019/07/16/738065415/johnny-clegg-a-uniting-voice-against-apartheid-dies-at-66. Accessed February 27, 2021.

Yudkoff, Ambigay. 2018. "When Voices Meet: Sharon Katz as Musical Activist during the Apartheid Era and Beyond." PhD Diss. Pretoria: University of South Africa.

———. 2021. *Activism through Music during the Apartheid Era and Beyond: When Voices Meet*. Lexington Series in Historical Ethnomusicology: Deep Soundings. Lanham, Maryland: Rowman & Littlefield.

Chapter Twelve

Intercultural Relations in Church Music of Nigeria and South Africa

Rhoda Abiolu

Music shapes the values and identities of people worldwide, with a power that is both culturally and cross-culturally visible (Corrigall and Schellenberg, 2015, 265; White, 2008, 35). This chapter focuses on the use of Christian music—a socioreligious cultural phenomenon common across South African and Nigerian societies—to both reaffirm identities and facilitate intercultural exchanges. Language, in both its verbal and visual constructs, is vital to the preservation of one's culture, defining how context and experiences are represented within a culture, and in the awareness and appreciation of otherness. Consequently, the overarching aim of this chapter highlights how Christian music, and the various languages and musical elements therein, serve as mediums to uphold the cultural and national identities of those who identify with it. However, music performances, instrument use, dance, and clothing, as well as accommodative cultural practices often appeal to a wider audience apart from those who share similar interpretative frameworks. To this end, the chapter considers the Soweto Gospel Choir in South Africa and the Lagos City Chorale in Nigeria as communities, and reflects on their impact both inter- and cross-culturally.

CASE STUDIES

I selected the Soweto Gospel Choir in South Africa and Lagos City Chorale in Nigeria because of their importance within the cultural and musical landscapes of their countries of origin. Specifically, the Soweto Gospel Choir, a group of choristers from Soweto, is one of the most successful gospel choirs in South Africa (Mojapelo, 2008, 339). This group is heavily invested in the promotion of African gospel music, especially South African styles. The

Lagos City Chorale, which has been in existence for more than thirty years, is a similarly prominent singing group in Nigeria, led by Senator Lere Adesina and directed by Sir Emeka Nwokedi (Choral hub, 2017; Sadoh, 2011, 41). The Lagos City Chorale is widely known both within and outside Nigeria for its musical feats and prowess (Otufodunrin, 2013). These groups have developed cultural programs and projects that not only engage locals with their indigenous cultural practices, but present those practices to an international audience. These projects have drawn media attention, which have highlighted the importance of Christian music to the local people and their communities (Haskell, 2015, 464).

To illustrate the relevance of Christian music within the context of Africa—particularly in South Africa and Nigeria—to cultural identity, I analyze how both verbal and nonverbal languages used in the performance of Christian music represent and support rhythmic and cultural competencies. In addition, I reflect on how these performances serve to enhance multiculturalism, particularly considering that Christian religious contents have become "glocalized," entailing a globally shaped localization (Robertson, 2012, 1995). I argue that these performances forestall cultural homogenization, promote cultural heterogenization, and function as forms of cultural diplomacy.

CONTEXTUALIZING WITHIN SOFT POWER TUSSLE AND CULTURAL DIPLOMACY

Ogunnubi and Isike (2015) point to the ever-present and ongoing soft power relations between Nigeria and South Africa. Their relationships hinge on each state's capacity to find subtle nonviolent means to influence the behavior of the other. Using cultural displays, they indirectly promote their national interests. Although each country assumes a dominant position/view to exert their power and influence, performance becomes a bridge that represents notions of a "collective good." Cultural displays such as religious music performances are widely popular, socially acceptable, and transcend borders. Ogunnubi and Isike (2015) suggest that the postapartheid international acceptance of South Africa largely rests on South Africa's careful and aggressive strategy to maintain a favorable public image. In short, the country uses soft power as leverage for foreign policy to make the country more endearing and commanding of respect. In the same vein, Nigeria's entertainment industry ("Nollywood"[1] and popular music industry[2]) and performances of African Christian music through groups such as Lagos City Chorale, reflect Nigeria's intentional use of soft power to promote its international status. Thus, the use of the media to influence international narratives and political imaging is a common practice among nations of the world (see Roselle, Miskimmon, and O'Loughlin, 2014, 71).

Cultural diplomacy in itself "is on the soft power side of the hard power–soft power equation since it functions by attraction and not coercion (and) rests on the assumption that art, language, and education are among the most significant entry points into a culture" by which it bridges differences and opens new avenues of communication (Goff, 2013, 420–21). Through music, a more favorable position can be attained. Consequently, music performance, as an intentional form of soft power, becomes a practical tool to positively impact perceptions and the development of human character, serving as a conduit for image building and international rapport (Meyer, 2019, 97).

HOMOGENIZING OR HETEROGENIZING IMPACT OF RELIGION?

Christian music is a medium through which Christian communities express and reinforce their religious identities and beliefs. In addition, although there are many forms of Christian worship and various denominations throughout the world, as a religion, it cuts across ethnic and national identities (Adedeji, 2007, 85). Traditional African genres and contemporary genres of music have deeply influenced African Christian music and its subgenres. For African Christians, its hybridity mirrors an undifferentiated universal culture that has culminated into a new African religious heritage and musical taste, much in line with the consequences of globalization (Mbaegbu, 2015, 177; Castells, 2010, 89; Garfias, 2004, 2). However, does a unifying religious identity necessarily indicate religious and cultural homogenization or heterogenization, especially considering the diversity of the South African and Nigerian milieus?

Because of the nature of Christianity, which has a long history of missionary practice and European colonial discourse, its links to globalization and cultural homogenization are well documented (Taylor, 2016, 81; Scott, 2013). This concern focuses on the continuous struggle between the globalization process, the reaffirmation of identities, and its adaptation within different cultures (Castells, 2010, 89). Because music cuts across boundaries and barriers, it embodies "a profoundly meaningful and emblematic aspect of cultural heritage" (Hebert and Hauge, 2019, 248). Therefore, there is a growing concern as to actual policy implementation in the preservation of the musical cultural heritage of indigenous communities through music education (273).

Several authors have outlined the homogenizing impact of religion on the cultural identities of western and southern Africa, after the introduction of

Christianity to these regions. As a result, missionary practices transposed their modes of worship. Converted Christian Africans combined the aesthetics and worship styles of their previous belief systems with that of their newly found faith (Mugambi, 2005, 521). These new African converts reckoned that maintaining their historical cultural identity in the contexts of shifting religious expression would be a challenge, especially if they did not wish to get lost in a foreign culture (Muyingi, 2014, 539).[3] The act of consciously infusing local traditions, translating some of the liturgical and lyrical features of Protestantism, and approaching Christian music as a form of glocal (global localization; Robertson, 2012, 194) in the African context, led to a wider acceptance of Christianity and Christian music (Pawlikova-Vilhanova, 2007, 254).

Within our more globalized world, Christian music among Africans, both within and beyond the continent, has been drawn upon to address concerns relating to identity through the recognition of the potency of cultural songs for the preservation of ethnic and cultural identities (Taylor, 2016, 83). These create avenues for more transnational, cultural, and musical exchanges without the subordination of indigenous identities. Lucas (2016), in a similar project situated among selected Brazilians who had roots from Black slaves from Africa, underscored and alluded to the significance and symbolism of music and drums in cultural resistance and power, and in preserving and reinforcing their identities and values (163). This became a deliberate attempt to break away from unpleasant reminders of racial issues entrenched in traditions that encouraged a White colonizer versus Black slave mentality. It is of little surprise that such terminology as "Black Catholicism" was introduced by this group to serve as differentiation (164). In a similar encounter, but on a global front, Palackal's (2016,) project among a group of Indian Christians concluded that these people only "accepted selectively what was thrust upon or presented to them and made it their own" (358). This revealed the power of musical adaptation into local contexts and how such compositions gained more acceptability as the locals sought to protect their culture against external forces. By selectively accommodating liturgical, musical, and theological practices, they conserved their identities and simultaneously provided local alternatives and variants to the "new" or somewhat hybridized and heterogenous ways of worship.

The glocalization process reinforces the connection between what happens outside a national boundary (globalization), and what happens within the local boundary (localization) (Robertson, 2012, 194 and 1995, 28). It upholds local identities as well as the relationships that may exist between such local and global entities (Hebert, 2018, 2). In other words, glocalization impedes the superimposition of globalization, which may result in homogenized practices. Hence, global practices situate themselves within local terrains to make outside forces suitable and relatable.

Shyllon's (2020) recent investigation into the legislative protection of cultural property (tangible and intangible) illustrates attempts to forestall homogenization in Nigeria and South Africa. The review showed that the Nigerian legislative acts for the protection of cultural heritage are obsolete. However, it revealed that Nigeria is one of the countries in Africa that acceded to the Bangui Agreement of the African Intellectual Property Organization of 1977 for the protection and safeguarding of traditional music heritage. For South Africa, cultural properties are protected by the National Heritage Resources Act of 1999. With the involvement of the South African Heritage Resources Agency, its council, and the participation of national, provincial, and local authorities. This cultural legislation reflects a bottom-up approach reckoning the people to be custodians of their heritage.

A CONCISE CROSS-CULTURAL ANALYSIS OF CULTURAL DIVERSITY IN NIGERIA AND SOUTH AFRICA

A cross-cultural analysis reveals both similar and unique traits in the representation of "South Africanness" and "Nigerianness" in Christian music performances. This cross-cultural perspective not only underscores common and uncommon cultural features within and outside the physical boundaries of South Africa and Nigeria, but illustrates the fluidity of cultural practices, especially in instances where there is a unifying feature, such as religion. In as much as religious communities present the chances for intercultural fellowship and relations through a shared bond (King, 2003, 199), common religious practices among these communities potentially foster intercultural connections. Multicultural settings as South Africa and Nigeria, where cultural diversity and awareness thrive, allow for interactions among different cultures resulting in mutually agreed-upon adjustments to cultural practices. These conditions give rise to heterogeneous practices that are inherently unique to such contexts (Andersen and Taylor, 2008, 68). Hebert and Hauge (2019) assert that to foster a more diverse world, musical and cultural practices should be tailored to be more inclusive and representative of groups and identities. And one of the tools that can be used to accomplish this is music, which is culturally, linguistically, and globally borderless (Hoene, 2015, 5).

South Africa is a multicultural nation with a variety of religious expressions, languages, and ethnicities (Statistics South Africa, 2017). Its religious diversity includes, but is not limited to African Traditional Religion, Islam,

Judaism, Hinduism, and Christianity (Mbaegbu, 2015). Eighty-six percent of the South African populace practice Christianity (Statistics South Africa, 2015, 30). South Africa also enjoys the linguistic diversity of eleven official languages (English, Zulu, Afrikaans, Southern Sotho, Northern Sotho, Xhosa, Tswana, Venda, Swati, Tsonga, and Ndebele) (Rosmarin and Rissik, 2004). Speakers of Nguni (Zulu, Swati, Xhosa, and Ndebele), who share some linguistic similarities, constitute two-thirds of the Black population of South Africa and dominate the indigenous language of the country (Afolayan, 2004; Rosmarin and Rissik, 2004).

Similarly, Nigeria enjoys rich cultural, religious, and linguistic diversity. Although there are more than five hundred indigenous languages and 370 ethnic groups in Nigeria, the official languages are English, Yorùbá, Igbo, and Hausa (Sowunmi, 2017; Amfani, 2012). Apart from English, these indigenous languages are what most ethnic groups speak thereby giving them prominence and coverage on a national scale (Falola, 2001, 5). The most practiced religions include Christianity, Islam, and African Traditional Religion, respectively.

Unlike the South African Nguni speakers, who share linguistic similarities, most Nigerian indigenous languages do not share similar phonetic structures.[4] Suffice it to say, even among Yorùbá speakers, some Yorùbá dialects may not be understood by general speakers of the Yorùbá language due to linguistic technicalities unique to those dialects (Falola, 2001, 5).

Though people appreciate music in unique ways because of differences in cultural backgrounds, contrarily, there may be some shared similarities based on religion. Hence, the connections shared in the two contexts, Nigeria and South Africa, are mainly religious (Christianity) and linguistic (English language), although both are culturally diverse. By recognizing music as a cultural norm in the two contexts, it ties in with the contribution of culture to sustainable development. These are in terms of celebrating religious and cultural diversity while creating an awareness of global citizenship, and still not losing touch with one's cultural roots[5] (United Nations, n.d.; United Cities and Local Governments, 2018).

According to Hall (1990), cultural and/or national identity rest with one's experiences that necessarily transform throughout time, space, and history (225). This is what is referred to as "South Africanness" and "Nigerianness" in the context of this chapter. For example, '"South Africanness" becomes recognized within an associated system of cultural representation unique to South Africa, which includes food culture, language culture, music and dance cultures, and clothing culture, among many other factors. These factors speak to the "cultural" and "national" identity of being South African. Therefore, the national identity of an individual is one of the fundamental sources of their cultural identity because of affiliated cultural representations and vice versa (Hall, 1992, 291–92).

LANGUAGE IN MUSIC REPRESENTATION

Through language, people reinforce their identities, identify with their cultural heritage, and interact with others outside of their societies. Through careful analysis of verbal and objectified/visual language use in music performance, I consider cultural markers that indicate notions of "South Africanness" and "Nigerianness" in live performances of the Soweto Gospel Choir and the Lagos City Chorale. Language use is a dominant feature of vocal music representation, and it can influence how meanings are interpreted and understood (Hall, 1997, 4–11 and 2013, 1). Such influences on exposure are "embedded in the 24-hour saturated media stream and establish(ed) norms and common sense about people, groups and institutions in contemporary society (. . . These are) constitutive of culture, meaning and knowledge about ourselves and the world around us" (Fursich, 2010, 115). Therefore, the uniqueness of a particular culture can be adequately emphasized in how they are represented.

Linguistic Diversity

Not only did the Soweto Gospel Choir highlight linguistic diversity in the selected analyzed performances, but they also celebrated African cultural diversity. Their first performance at their Blessed Live in Concert as part of their Australian tour in 2005 was titled *Oluwa* (the Yorùbá word for God) (CTPannell Traditional Gospel Music, 2011a). This performance in Yorùbá reflects how African Christian music potentially enables cross-cultural exchange based on a variety of linguistic representation (Koichiro Matsuura, former director-general of UNESCO in UNESCO, 2002, 3).

Linguistic diversity continued with the second song, *Thina Simnqobile* (CTPannell Traditional Gospel Music, 2011b), in Zulu and the third, *Joko ya hao* (CTPannell Traditional Gospel Music, 2011c), in Sotho (the tune was like the hymn *O Jesus I Have Promised*). The fourth song *Noyana* (CTPannell Traditional Gospel Music, 2011d), was sung in Zulu and the fifth, *Tshepa Thapelo* (CTPannell Traditional Gospel Music, 2011e), was an a cappella song in Tswana. These performances stressed the need to celebrate multicultural practices like linguistic diversity, instead of accentuating points of dissimilarities. Due to linguistic similarities, particularly among Nguni speakers and other linguistic similar groups (Afolayan, 2004), music specific to a particular tribe may be easily understood by other ethnic groups.

Similarly, Nigeria's Lagos City Chorale performed in multiple languages at the 2016 Musica Sacra International. Three of their renditions titled *Jehova Emewo*, *Amuworo Ayi Otu Nwa*, and *Agidigba* were sung in the Igbo language (Modfestivals Marktoberdorf, 2016a, 2016b, 2016c). The fourth and fifth performances, *Messiah Baba Mi* and *Polongo Jesu*, were sung in Yorùbá (Modfestivals Marktoberdorf, 2016d, 2016e).

It is of little wonder that Nigerian artists like Joe Praize (with the song titled *Mighty God*) and Darey Alade (with the song titled *Pray for Me*), have collaborated with the Soweto Gospel Choir on songs that have enjoyed millions of views on YouTube. Other cross-cultural collaborations include Davido (a Nigerian artist) and Mafikizolo's (a South African singing sensation group) *Tchelete (Goodlife)*, Wizkid (Nigerian artist) and Bucie's (a South African artist) *All for love*, and Master KG (a South African artist), Nomcebo (a South African artist) and Burna Boy's (Nigerian artist) *Jerusalema*, which became a global hit during the COVID-19 pandemic. These songs are all available on YouTube and are but a few of the South African and Nigerian musical associations. And interestingly, they infused bits and pieces of the cultures of the various countries represented, for example, through spoken language, musical instruments, and clothing (Kpade, 2018).

One major challenge with cross-cultural collaborative practices is in the interpretation and understanding of differences in the cultural background and nuances of the artists, as identified by Merriam as far back as 1964. However, though he acknowledged this obstacle, Merriam still indicated that music is a useful medium to unravel insights into other cultures (1964, 13). Some of these musical and cultural considerations are giving rise to the popularity of African music[6] as a useful resource to unite Africans and provide common characteristics (Mbaegbu, 2015, 117). Without a doubt, these musical practices and cross-cultural partnerships can prove advantageous in fostering cohesion. So, there is the need for these to be properly utilized for intercultural relations and musical as well as cultural education.

Traditional Garments

The language of clothing is an illustrative method of nonverbal communication, making it a vital aspect of visual and objectified representations (Tijana, Tomaž, and Čuden, 2014, 322). Consequently, the traditional clothing associated with any context is their unspoken language of representation. For instance, the use of language—in speech or clothing, music performance, or dance—says much about one's cultural background. Therefore, "representation is an essential part of the process by which meaning is produced and exchanged between members of a culture. It (involves) the use of language, of signs and images which stand for or represent things" (Hall, 2013, 1).

African fashion or clothing culture epitomizes both cultural variety and individual uniqueness. For example, in countries around the world, people may generally recognize traditional African fabrics as being representative of the African continent, although they may not understand how specific patterns and fabric choices reflect the many cultures found on the continent. For Africans, types of clothing material, styles, and accompanying fashion accessories help one identify and interpret cultures. Some specific examples include the Ghanaian kente, the Nigerian àdìrẹ (tie and dye), the Kenyan kanga, the South African bead culture, and Zulu leopard skin. In other words, the designs and patterns of clothing are linked to specific cultures and locations by a variety of visual and textual means (Rovine, 2015, 3). What is vital to an African is to be well-represented and that the cultural traditions represented in clothing are fit for the occasion (Macleod, 2002, 32). As Rovine (2015) observes, African fashion is poised to tell stories, a narrative for the exploration of an African's fashion sense and interpretation of non-verbal communication from others (3).

As a result of Christian missionary practice, African worship incorporated Western clothing styles (choir robes, for example) along with European musical traditions. When performing, Africans wear both Western and traditional African styles that represent their specific cultural identities and patriotism (Sadoh, 2015, 30). This glocal practice (i.e., global localization of musical practices and trends) allows performers to preserve and represent their cultures. For example, the Soweto Gospel Choir's Afrocentric approach to performance is in how their attire displays a rare blend of different cultural costumes, including brightly colored headpieces, black stripes, animal prints, and beads to celebrate Zulu and Xhosa designs. The vibrant fabrics of Venda, Ndebele, and Zulu interweave the members' various cultural backgrounds (CTPannell Traditional Gospel Music Traditional Gospel Music, 2011a, 2011b, and 2011c).

As with the Soweto Gospel Choir, the Nigerian Lagos City Chorale communicates the power of intercultural exchange with their costumes. For example, during the performance of *Jehova Emewo*, they wore Yorùbá outfits, even though they sang in the Igbo language. Their celebration of cultural diversity was also reflected in their performances of the songs *Amuworo Ayi Otu Nwa* and *Agidigba*. Women's Yorùbá outfits include ìró (wrapper), bùbá (blouse), gèlè (head-tie), and ìpèlé (shoulder piece), while men wore bùbá (men's top) and ṣọ́ọ́rọ́ (trousers) with *fìlà abetí ajá* (cap) (Modfestivals Marktoberdorf, 2016a, 2016b, and 2016c). As a contrast, the choirmaster, Sir Emeka Nwokedi, wore an Igbo outfit during the performance of *Agidigba*.

What made the choir's outfits more significant, specifically during the performance of *Agidigba*, were the green and white color representations of these outfits. These colors are the official colors of Nigeria, reflected on the country's national flag and coat of arms. Additionally, although the performances of *Messiah Baba Mi* and *Polongo Jesu* were in the Yorùbá language, their outfits were Igbo, a blend of two distinct cultures. Men wore the *isi agu*, while the women wore blouses and *akwa* (Modfestivals Marktoberdorf, 2016d).

Clothing reflects one's culture and self-regard; an indirect form of advertisement, a cultural indicator, and the most noticeable way other people judge an individual (Macleod, 2002, 4). Through performance, South Africans and Nigerians have endeavored to protect their cultural traditions through clothing choice and inspire a sense of intercultural awareness about the diversity in both countries and on the continent. Protection of the cultural heritage and traditions of societies around the world is as much the duty and responsibility of the government and authority in power as it is of the people (Shyllon, 2020, 815). Deeply embedded in these traditions are aspects of what makes people who they are, as a reflection of a true sense of community of people and an overarching expression of their identities, values, and norms. These aspects of culture and identity are fundamentally distinctive for individual communities because clothing's universality and acceptability transcend and neutralize polarizing and divisive political elements. Both choral groups use clothing to represent their cultural diversities without verbal utterances. The popular adage "you will be addressed the way you are dressed" is an expression that further illuminates how people can understand other people they encounter, even without a proper or formal introduction. It consequently stresses the need to pay attention to the way we present ourselves nonverbally.

LANGUAGE IN RHYTHM

Although language appears to be an obvious marker of a group of people, other visual and object markers such as musical accompaniments of clapping, dancing, and musical instrumentation—that make up a constellation of performing arts or the language in rhythm—are equally significant identifiers (Stone, 2010, 7, 13; Hall, 1997, 1990). These are channeled through the medium of live performance during church services or Christian music concerts. Live performance is mostly an interactive medium whereby performers occupy center stage in the bid to entertain their audience. It is often characterized by a lead singer (or singers) and an audience who may be the immediate recipients of those performances (either present at the venues or streaming online in real time), or later consumers (those who access media content in delayed time or at a much later time, devoid of real-time live performances). In this case, the analysis of the selected performances in this chapter was done in the capacity of "a later consumer."

On the part of the performers, church music in Africa necessitates participatory strategies to keep the performance lively and inclusive. There is the awareness that the basis of their performances may be hinged on the strategies of the constellation of performing arts and language in rhythm (Stone, 2010, 7). This may include rhythmic claps that complement the music, a sing-along aided by projecting the lyrics of songs performed, dance steps, and other visual arts and effects. All these strategies enhance interactions between the audience and the performers. Moreover, they constitute the rhythmic nature of music and how music depicts the uniqueness of identities in different cultures.

Music and Dance

Typically, within most South African traditions, music and dance go hand in glove to reaffirm and reinforce cultural and national identities (Levine, 2005, 41). Songs can be high or low tempo, but what is more important is the celebration of cultural and religious values exuded by music and dance. South African music, particularly music with a more traditional outlook, should be culturally consistent, be they protest songs or songs of everyday use, thereby acting as a force of support and cohesion (Muller, 2008, 37). The idea of a culturally consistent musical orientation is an indication of the reinforcement of represented traditions. The aim of a culturally consistent representation is often to articulate and reinforce the cultural identities of that framework (Hebert and Hauge, 2019; Muller, 2008), which are quite evident in the song choices and linguistic representations of the Soweto Gospel Choir.

Another distinctive characteristic of South African church music tradition is how people use their voices as instruments of expression with rich harmonies, chants, and ululations (Levine, 2005, 88). Even without modern musical instruments, through language expressed in rhythm, the performances of the Soweto Gospel Choir shone. For instance, the performance of *Thina Simnqobile* heralded and sustained the Zulu dance of a momentous dancer with his leg high above his head, stamped on the ground and accompanied by whistling, ululations, and chants (CTPannell Traditional Gospel Music Traditional Gospel Music, 2011a).

Another interesting fact was how their voices and hums complimented the beats of the *djembe* drums to provide musical accompaniments without the need for any other musical instrument. The djembe drum is culturally adapted because it originated from West Africa (Mattioli, 2008; Modfestivals Marktoberdorf, 2016d).

On the Nigerian terrain, because of the size of its population and diversity of its cultures, the country's musical heritage has been prominent within the African music market (Servant, 2003, 5; Graham, 1999, 588). As noted in the South African tradition, music and dance are also two faces of the same coin within the Nigerian musical and cultural landscape; though there might be occasions where singing is done without dance as an accompaniment (Falola, 2001). Furthermore, some Nigerian music and dance traditions are difficult to classify because of the multiethnic nature of the country. An attempt to delineate the Nigerian music tradition was established on approach to production (either as traditional or modern genres), origin (local or foreign formats), and means of production (as an instrumental—identified by traditional or more modern instruments) (160). At the inception of choral singing in Nigeria, performances were accompanied by Western instruments like the organ and piano, but the inculcation of traditional instruments in recent times has provided danceable rhythmic patterns that have made performances more endearing (Sadoh, 2015). This is no different from the modes of representation of the Lagos City Chorale. The piano was supported by indigenous musical instruments like the *ekwe* (slab and stick of the Igbo people) and the *gangan* (of the Yorùbá people—the talking drum) (Modfestivals Marktoberdorf, 2016b and 2016c).

It is interesting to note how traditional and modern instruments were combined to create heterogeneous instances, a shift from the homogeneous tendency of which globalization, and indeed religion, have been characterized. Translations of these Western norms birth new practices within the African context. The use of the gangan, or "talking drum," was particularly unique because it enunciated Igbo words. What makes this special is that the drum is poised to pronounce Yorùbá words with its various distinctive tones and inflections. For instance, "*ilu*" and "*ilu*" can be confused as the same word without proper intonations. In order to get the exact meaning, the use of the tonal inflections dò (\), re ( ), mí (/) distinguish both words to mean ìlù (drum) and ìlú (town), which can be correctly enunciated by the drum. The inculcation of the drum to pronounce Igbo words draws attention to an intercultural and linguistic dimension to the talking drum's beats where there is the superimposition of indigenous Yorùbá rhythms on the Igbo language. A result of this intermix is the heterogeneous instance of cultural flows produced to add richness to traditions of both cultures in adaptive and collaborative situations (Sotunsa, 2012, 404). Additionally, other musical instruments incorporated into most of their performances were the *ṣẹ̀kẹ̀rẹ̀* (beaded dry gourd), and the *udu* (Igbo drum) (Modfestivals Marktoberdorf, 2016b). From these discussions, both contexts displayed indigenous practices through dance and instrumental accompaniment, including cases where modern and traditional instruments were combined, as in the use of the piano with the ṣèkèrè, the ekwe, the gangan, as well as the udu, and the adapted instance of the djembe drum.

Language is an essential index in any cultural system because it is through language that the codes and symbols of that culture are communicated (Ekeh, 2005, 1). Accurately, language is the repository of culture, vital in creating mental representations through spoken words and representations (Obiegbu, 2016, 70). But within these South African and Nigerian musical and dance representations, language was not only limited to abstract constructs, but also visible representations of cultures. This acknowledges Hall's (2013, 1997) viewpoint on the use of language to signify images, as well as objects and other visual or audio-visual entities.

CONCLUDING THOUGHTS

The traditions of Christian music, musical performances/expressions, and representations are entrenched within specific African contexts. Religious music ensembles function as social actors who use their agency and music as vehicles for social change. Meyer (2019) considered this to be an actor-oriented approach, which is believed to facilitate a deeper understanding of social complexities and the social construction of music-making and performance. These chorale groups similarly serve multiple roles of cultural diplomacy and as cultural projects in postconflict situations. Through this strategy, (that is engaging musical projects that involve those within a postconflict environment), practitioners "ease social upheaval, create economic opportunities for musicians (and cultural groups), and strengthen existing cultural venues and institutions, as well as establish new ones" (Haskell, 2015, 454). The South African and Nigerian governments must buffer the effect of the economic side of music, performance, and cultural education on the basis that the "emotion, functionality and everyday experience of music is a value that may translate to economic value if properly harnessed" (Abiodun, 2018, 41). Because of its socioeconomic benefit to generate funds for individuals and the nation, music education and production should be effectively nurtured by government policies.

In the musical, linguistic, and visual (e.g., clothing) representations of each chorale group, they reaffirmed both cultural and national identities and brought about some level of their cultural awareness. For instance, the choice of the Lagos City Chorale, to showcase the national colors of Nigeria, and the traditional clothing of major cultural tribes in Nigeria, were indications of the celebration of national identity. Similarly, for the Soweto Gospel Choir, their beaded outfits, and multilayered patterns brought together bits and pieces of the South African clothing tradition of the different ethnicities within the country. The use of indigenous musical instruments, by the Lagos City Chorale, reiterated a national identity, while the cross-cultural adaptation of the djembe drum and the rendition of the Yorùbá song by the Soweto Gospel Choir captured the essence of, and awareness of, cultural exchanges and diversity. Enabling dialogues and intercultural exchanges across cultures and transcending national borders are attributive to the cultural diplomatic relations that can be established through musical arts across Africa. Even if there are "no official relations between two governments, artists can communicate with each other and forge meaningful ties" thereby creating fertile grounds for traditional diplomacy (Goff, 2013, 422).

As contained in the United Nations' SDG 4 (United Nations, undated), these groups have:

- fostered active participation in cultural life (sociocultural and religious);
- aided the development of both individual and collective liberties;
- preserved the tangible and intangible cultural heritages of their countries (ranging from music, dance, clothing, and jewelry and;
- protected and promoted diverse cultural expressions through (religious) musical contents which reaffirm the universal role of music and musical representations. Here, universal may be understood as relative, in respect to the context of one of the world's major religions, as seen in the case of Christian music in this chapter.

Although commonalities were traceable based on religion, the distinctive qualities that differentiated these groups, and countries, became the expression of their traditional clothing, dance, linguistic, and musical practices. These representations emphasize how important music is, how it stretches into diverse cultural aspects, and the need for the furtherance and preservation of the cultural heritages of people to avoid the domination of cultural traditions in this globalized world. Music serves to affirm that society is possible (Abiolu, 2020), in as much as unified attempts are targeted at fostering social cohesion and the preservation of the entire well-being of the humans who make up societies.

NOTES

1. See Nwankwo (2018) who made the case for the proper utilization and harnessing of the abundant potential of the Nigerian creative industry that comprises Nollywood, and the vibrant music sector among others. He emphasized the significance of Nollywood's soft power and cultural policies in creating favorable rebranding for the plummeting image of Nigeria and Nigerians (home and abroad). He concludes that through clearly articulated and implemented policies, Nollywood is set to make the creative industry in Nigeria more viable and visible both locally and globally. With the full support of relevant actors, especially the Nigerian government, this creative industry is set to create employment opportunities, economic growth, and an advanced entertainment sector that will attain more global relevance.

2. Similarly, Adedeji (2016) provides compelling arguments on the historicity of the Nigerian popular music industry as well as obstacles faced in the industry, the ensuing prospects, and how advantageous this sector can grow for the Nigerian state. In a way, the propensity of the soft power within the Nigerian music industry and local/international collaborative practices evident within the industry can be leveraged upon for socioeconomic advancement. Nwankwo (2018) and Adedeji (2016) agree on the importance of Nigeria's creative industry as a feasible source of revenue for Nigeria thereby promoting less dependence on crude oil.

3. Events that led to this adoption indicated a growing discontent and skepticism toward the introduction of Christian music and accompanied practices that were foreign (Axelsson, 1974, 93). In some cases, only churches that presented the Christian message in local terms were acceptable. For instance, this was the case in some churches in the Democratic Republic of Congo (Wild-Wood, 2008, 2), South Africa (Haecker, 2012, 9; Gerstner, 1997, 20), and Nigeria (Osigwe, 2016, 68–69). Therefore, to be more tolerable, the infusion of local cultural practices such as language and musical instrumentation, became essential (Pawlikova-Vilhanova, 2007, 254). All these suggest the glocalization of Christian musical practices and traditions.

4. Some do, such as the Urhobo and Benin dialects because of geographical proximity (Ekeh, 2005, 31), but a more significant number do not share understandable codes due to dispersion of the Nigerian geographic and ethnic landscape.

5. These encapsulate Goal 4, target 4.7 of the United Nations' sustainable development goals.

6. This concept has been argued to be more of a blend of music genres emanating from the abundant diversity on the African continent, and not as a singular or analogous genre (Agordoh, 2005, 1). Therefore, African music comprises more varieties of music genres or types (Mensah 2008, 45).

REFERENCES

Abiodun, Femi. 2018. "What Matters and How it Matters: The Economic Framework of Music Pedagogy in Nigeria." *Journal of Nigerian Music Education (JONMED)* 10, no. 1: 32–44.
Abiolu, Rhoda T. I. 2020. "Understanding Christian Music as a Catalyst for Social Cohesion within Sociocultural and Religious Settings in South Africa." In *Social Cohesion in the Last Decade: Taking Stock to Inform the New Decade*, edited by Kariuki Paul, Maria L. J. Goyayi, and Sphamandla Mhlongo, 268–311. Durban: Democratic Development Program.
Adedeji, Adewale. 2016. "The Nigerian Music Industry: Challenges, Prospects, and Possibilities." *International Journal of Recent Research in Social Sciences and Humanities (IJRRSSH)* 3, no. 1: 261–71.
Adedeji, Femi. 2007. "Christian Music in Contemporary Africa: A Re-examination of its Essentials." *Koers* 72, no. 1: 85–100.
Afolayan, Funso. 2004. *Culture and Customs of South Africa*. Westport, CT: Greenwood Press.
Agordoh, Alexander. A. 2005. *African Music: Traditional and Contemporary*. New York: Nova Science Publishers, Inc.
Amfani, Ahmed H. 2012. *Indigenous Languages and Development in Nigeria*. Paper presented at the Professor A Bamgbose Annual Personality Lecture organized by Linguistics Students Association, University of Ibadan.
Andersen, Margaret. L. and Howard, Taylor F. 2008. *Sociology: Understanding a Diverse Society.* Fourth edition. California: Thomson Learning, Inc.
Aning, Ben A. 1973. "Varieties of African Music and Musical Types." *The Black Perspective in Music* 1, no. 1: 16–23.
Axelsson, Olof E. 1974. "Historical Notes on Neo-African Church Music." *Zambezia* 3, no. 2: 89–102.
Castells, Manuel. 2010. "Globalisation and Identity." *Quaderns de la Mediterrània* 14: 89–98.
Choral hub. 2017. "10 Nigerian Choral Groups You Should Get Yourself Acquainted With. Accessed October 11, 2018. https://www.choralhub.com/2017/09/19/10-nigerian-choral-groups-you-should-get-yourself-acquainted-with/.
Corrigall, Kathleen A. and E. Glenn Schellenberg. 2015. "Liking Music: Genres, Contextual Factors and Individual Differences." In *Art, Aesthetics and the Brain*, edited by Huston Joseph, Marcos Nadal, Francisco Mora, Luigi F. Agnati, and Camilo José Cela Conde, 263–84. Oxford: Oxford University Press.
CTPannell Traditional Gospel Music Traditional Gospel Music. 2011a. "Soweto Gospel Choir—Oluwa." Accessed June 01, 2021. https://www.youtube.com/watch?v=9lsx1Ypm6l8.
———. 2011b. "Soweto Gospel Choir—Thina Simnqobile." Accessed June 01, 2021. https://www.youtube.com/watch?v=38-NQvhgIwY.
———. 2011c. "Soweto Gospel Choir – Joko Yahao." Accessed June 01, 2021. https://www.youtube.com/watch?v=8jXUJ3fJ4Ug.

———. 2011d. "Soweto gospel choir—Noyana." Accessed June 01, 2021. https://www.youtube.com/watch?v=xtqNhCfRO30.
———. 2011e. "Soweto gospel choir—Tshepa Thapelo." Accessed June 01, 2021. https://www.youtube.com/watch?v=ry9BPUqjjms.
Ekeh, Peter. 2005. "A Profile of Urhobo Culture." In *Studies in Urhobo Culture*, edited by Peter Ekeh, 1–51. New York: Urhobo Historical Society UHS.
Falola, Toyin. 2001. *Culture and Customs of Nigeria*. Westport, CT: Greenwood Press.
Fursich, Elfriede. 2010. "Media and the Representation of Others." *International Social Science Journal* 61, no. 199: 113–30.
Garfias, Robert. 2004. *Music: The Cultural Context*. Senri Ethnological Reports 47. Osaka: National Museum of Ethnology.
Gerstner, Jonathan. N. 1997. "A Christian Monopoly: The Reformed Church and Colonial Society under Dutch Rule." In *Christianity in South Africa: A Political, Social, and Cultural History*, edited by Richard Elphick and Rodney Davenport, 16–30. Los Angeles: University of California Press.
Goff, Patricia M. 2013. "Cultural Diplomacy." In *The Oxford Handbook of Modern Diplomacy*, edited by Andrew F. Cooper, Jorge Heine, and Ramesh Thakur, 419–35. Oxford: Oxford University Press.
Graham, Ronnie. 1999. "Nigeria: from Hausa Music to Highlife." In *World Music: The Rough Guide*, edited by Simon Broughton,, Mark Ellingham, and Richard Trillo, 588–600. Volume one. London: Rough Guides Ltd.
Haecker, Allyss A. 2012. "Post-Apartheid South African Choral Music: An Analysis of Integrated Musical Styles with Specific Examples by Contemporary South African Composers." PhD diss. University of Iowa.
Hall, Stuart. 1990. "Cultural Identity and Diaspora." In *Identity: Community, Culture, Difference*, edited by Rutherford, Jonathan, 222–37. London: Lawrence & Wishart.
———. 1992. "The Question of Cultural Identity." In *Modernity and its Futures: Understanding Modern Societies*, edited by Anthony McGrew, Stuart Hall, and David Held, 274–316. Cambridge: Polity Press in association with the Open University.
———. 1997. *Representation: Cultural Representations and Signifying Practices*. London: Sage.
———. 2013. "The Work of Representation." In *Representation*, edited by Stuart Hall, Jessica Evans, and Sean Nixon, 1–38. London: Sage.
Haskell, Erica. 2015. "The Role of Applied Ethnomusicology in Post-conflict and Post-catastrophe Communities." In *The Oxford Handbook of Applied Ethnomusicology*, edited by Svanibor Pettan and Jeff T. Titon, 453–80. Oxford: Oxford University Press.
Hebert, David. G. 2018. "Music in the Conditions of Glocalization." In *Music Glocalization: Heritage and Innovation in a Digital Age*, edited by David G. Hebert and Mikolaj Rykowski, 2–19. Newcastle upon Tyne: Cambridge Scholars Publishing.
Hebert, David G. and Torunn Bakken Hauge. 2019. "Conclusion: Learning from Two Decades of Music Education Leadership." In *Advancing Music Education in*

Northern Europe, edited by David G. Hebert and Torunn Baken Hauge, 247–76. New York: Routledge.

Hoene, Christin. 2015. *Music and Identity in Postcolonial British South-Asian Literature*. New York: Routledge.

King, Pamela E. 2003. "Religion and Identity: The Role of Ideological, Social, and Spiritual Contexts." *Applied Developmental Science* 7, no. 3: 197–204.

Kpade, Sabo. 2018. "The 15 Best Nigerian-South African Collaborations." Accessed June 1, 2021. https://www.okayafrica.com/nigerian-south-african-music-collaborations-best/.

Levine, Laurie. 2005. *The Drumcafés: Traditional Music of South Africa*. Johannesburg: Jacana Media Pty Ltd.

Lucas, Glaura. 2016. "Drums in the Experience of Black Catholicism in Minas Gerais, Brazil." In *The Oxford Handbook of Music and World Christianities*, edited by Suzel A. Reily and Jonathan M. Dueck, 163–88. New York: Oxford University Press.

Macleod, Guy. 2002. *Cultural Considerations: A Guide to Understanding Culture, Courtesy and Etiquette in South African Business*. Claremont: Spearhead.

Mattioli, Paulo. 2008. *First Lessons Djembe*. Fenton, MO: Mel Bay Publications, Inc.

Mbaegbu, Celestine C. 2015. "The Effective Power of Music in Africa." *Open Journal of Philosophy* 5: 176–83.

Mensah, Joseph. 2008. "Cultural Dimensions of Globalization in Africa: A Dialectical Interpretation of the Local and the Global." In *Neoliberalism and Globalization in Africa: Contestations from the Embattled Continent*, edited by Joseph Mensah, 33–54. New York: Palgrave MacMillan.

Merriam, Alan P. 1964. *The Anthropology of Music*. Evanston, IL: Northwestern University Press.

Meyer, Marcel. 2019. "The Power of Music: Can Music at Work Help to Create More Ethical Organizations?" *Humanistic Management Journal* 4, no. 1: 95–99.

Modfestivals Marktoberdorf. 2016a. "Lagos City Chorale Nigeria: Jehova emewo, MUSICA SACRA INTERNATIONAL 2016." Accessed May 18, 2018. https://www.youtube.com/watch?v=dhs0Le_F3SE.

———. 2016b. "Lagos City Chorale Nigeria: Amuworo Ayi Otu Nwa, MUSICA SACRA INTERNATIONAL 2016." Accessed May 18, 2018. https://www.youtube.com/watch?v=agBgM3B2mOY.

———. 2016c. "Lagos City Chorale Nigeria: Agidigha, MUSICA SACRA INTERNATIONAL 2016." Accessed May 18, 2018. https://www.youtube.com/watch?v=mqIld1OkVPw.

———. 2016d. "Lagos City Chorale Nigeria: Messiah Baba Mi,

———. 2016e. "Lagos City Chorale Nigeria: Polongo Jesu,

Mojapelo, Max. 2008. *Beyond Memory: Recording the History, Moments and Memories of South African Music*. Somerset West: African Minds.

Mugambi, Jesse N. K. 2005. "Christianity and the African Cultural Heritage." In *African Christianity. An African Story*, edited by Kalu, Ogbu, 516–42. Pretoria: Department of Church History, University of Pretoria.

Muller, Carol A. 2008. *Focus: Music of South Africa*. Second Edition. New York: Routledge.
Muyingi, Mbangu A. 2014. "The Place of African Traditional Religion in the Democratic Republic of the Congo since the advent of Christianity." *Mediterranean Journal of Social Sciences* 5, no. 14: 539–45.
Nwankwo, Allwell Okechukwu. 2018. "Harnessing the Potential of Nigeria's Creative Industries: Issues, Prospects and Policy Implications." *Africa Journal of Management* 4, no. 4: 469–87.
Obiegbu, Ifeyinwa. 2016. "Language and Culture: Nigerian Perspective." *African Research Review* 104: 69–82.
Ogunnubi, Olusola and Christopher Isike. 2015. "Regional Hegemonic Contention and the Asymmetry of Soft Power: A Comparative Analysis of South Africa and Nigeria." *Strategic Review for Southern Africa* 37, no. 1: 152–77.
Osigwe, Chinedum N. 2016. "Contemporary Nigeria Church Music: A Search for True Identity and Cultural Relevance." *International Journal of Music and Performing Arts* 4, no. 2: 65–71.
Otufodunrin, Lekan. 2013. "Nigeria's Global Gold-Winning Choir." Accessed October 11, 2018. http://thenationonlineng.net/nigerias-global-gold-winning-choir/.
Palackal, Joseph J. 2016. "The Survival Story of Syriac Chants among the St. Thomas Christians in South India." In *The Oxford Handbook of Music and World Christianities*, edited by Suzel A. Reily and Jonathan M. Dueck, 340–63. New York: Oxford University Press.
Pawlikova-Vilhanova, Viera. 2007. "Christian Missions in Africa and Their Role in the Transformation of African Societies." *Asian and African Studies* 16, no. 2: 249–60.
Robertson, Roland. 1995. "Glocalization: Time-Space and Homogeneity-Heterogeneity." In *Global Modernities*, edited by Mike Featherstone, Scott Lash, and Roland Robertson, 25–44. London: Sage.
Robertson, Roland. 2012. "Globalisation or Glocalisation?" *The Journal of International Communication* 18, no. 2: 191–208.
Roselle, Laura, Alister Miskimmon, and Ben O'loughlin. 2014. "Strategic Narrative: A New Means to Understand Soft Power." *Media, War & Conflict* 7, no. 1: 70–84.
Rosmarin, Ike and Dee Rissik. 2004. *Cultures of the World: South Africa*. Westport, CT: Greenwood Press.
Rovine, Victoria L. 2015. *African Fashion GlobalSstyle: Histories, Innovations, and Ideas You Can Wear*. Bloomington: Indiana University Press.
Sadoh, Godwin. 2011. *Christopher Oyesiku: Preeminent Nigerian Choral Conductor*. Bloomington, IN: Universe, Inc.
Sadoh, Godwin. 2015. *Five Decades of Music Transmutation in Nigeria and the Diaspora*. Ohio: GSS Publications.
Scott, Jillian. 2013. *Post-Westphalianism Versus Homogenization Theories of Globalization and Religion*. Religious Studies Project. Accessed October 26, 2018. https://www.religiousstudiesproject.com/response/post-westphalianism-versus-homogenization-theories-of-globalization-and-religion-by-jillian-scott/.

Servant, Jean-Christophe. 2003. *Which Way Nigeria?: Music under Threat: A Question of Money, Morality, Self-Censorship and the Sharia*. Copenhagen: Freemuse.

Shyllon, Folarin. 2020. "Grasping the Nettle of Illicit Export, Import, and Transfer of Ownership of Cultural Objects." In *The Oxford Handbook of International Cultural Heritage Law*, edited by Francesco Francioni and Ana. F. Vrdoljak, 227–49. Oxford: Oxford University Press.

Sotunsa, Mobolanle E. 2012. "Exploiting Resources of Yorùbá Drum Poetry for Contemporary Global Relevance." In *Focus on Nigeria: Literature and Culture*, edited by Gordon Collier, 401–10. Amsterdam: Rodopi.

Sowunmi, Zents K. 2017. "Full List of all 371 Tribes in Nigeria, States Where They Originate." Accessed June 12, 2018. https://www.vanguardngr.com/2017/05/full-list-of-all-371-tribes-in-nigeria-states-where-they-originate/.

Statistics South Africa. 2015. "General Household Survey." Accessed March 16, 2017. http://www.statssa.gov.za/publications/P0318/P03182015.pdf.

———. 2017. "Statistical Release P0318 General Household Survey." Accessed September 20, 2018. http://www.statssa.gov.za/publications/P0318/P03182017.pdf.

Stone, Ruth M. 2010. "African Music in a Constellation of Arts." In *The Garland Handbook of African Music*, edited by Ruth M. Stone, 7–12. New York: Garland Publishing Inc.

Taylor, Julie. 2016. "Coexistence of Causal and Cultural Expressions of Musical Values among the Sabaot of Kenya." In *The Oxford Handbook of Music and World Christianities*, edited by Suzel A. Reily and Jonathan M. Dueck, 78–97. New York: Oxford University Press.

Tijana, Todorovič, Toporišič Tomaž, and Alenka P. Čuden. 2014. "Clothes and Costumes as Form of Nonverbal Communication." *Tekstilec* 57, no. 4: 321–33.

UNESCO. 2002. "Unesco Universal Declaration on Cultural Diversity: A Vision, a Conceptual Platform, a Pool of Ideas for Implementation, a New Paradigm." Series No. 1. A document for the world summit on sustainable development, Johannesburg, August 26–September 4.

United Cities and Local Governments. 2018. "Culture in the Sustainable Development Goals: A Guide for Local Action." Accessed October 31, 2019. http://www.agenda21culture.net/sites/default/files/culturesdgs_web_en.pdf.

United Nations. Undated. "Sustainable Development Goal 4: Ensure Inclusive and Equitable Quality Education and Promote Lifelong Learning." Accessed October 31, 2019. https://sustainabledevelopment.un.org/sdg4#.

White, Bob W. 2008. *Rumba Rules: The Politics of Dance Music in Mobutu's Zaire*. Durham, NC: Duke University Press.

Wild-Wood, Emma. 2008. *Migration and Christian Identity in Congo [DRC]*. Leiden: Koninklijke Brill, NV.

5

LEGAL PERSPECTIVES FROM ASIA

Chapter Thirteen

Cultural Heritage and Music Diplomacy

The Legal Framework in India

Karan Choudhary

Management of cultural diversity is a solemn affair. Nation-states have developed various strategies for the conservation and protection of their cultural heritage in all its varied expressions. With the recognition of culture as a strategic dimension of sustainable development, there is an urgent need to assess and fully comprehend national responses in terms of law and policy designs—whether such designs construct a sustainable, informed, transparent, and participative system of governance for culture. In this chapter, I trace the historical roots of music in the Indian subcontinent and analyze it with respect to the fields of cultural heritage and diplomacy, specifically examining the legal framework of Indian cultural policies. Policy design and national responses to the conservation and protection of culture have a direct nexus with cultural diplomacy, and this discussion draws linkages between cultural policy and diplomacy in India.

The annals of humankind demonstrate that our innate and insatiable curiosity for knowledge has often propelled us into uncharted territories. This quest for the unknown has aided us in discovering and unraveling the world around us. In the Indian context, the documented history, such as *Indica* by Megasthenes, indicates that especially during the Vedic period (1500–600 BCE), there was significant progress in the developmental understandings of mathematics, astronomy, Indian philosophy, drama, music, town planning, economics, science, yoga, Ayurveda, and others.

The Vedic period can be categorized into the early Vedic period (1500–1000 BCE) and later Vedic period (1000–600 BCE), an era that witnessed the composition of Vedas, ancient Sanskrit texts that mark the origins of Hinduism. Vedas comprise a uniquely rich body of ancient knowledge that arose over the course of centuries, transmitted from generation to generation through oral traditions. Shruti (hearing) is understood in this tradition as eternal, self-evident, and divinely revealed. Vedic oral traditions, including mantras, are examples of shruti. Some scholars, such as Professor S. K. Prasoon, John Grimes, Sushil Mittal, and Gene Thursby, conclude that shruti penultimately crystalized into Smriti (recollection), constituting what can be remembered of the oral traditions. In other words, Smriti elaborate, interpret, and clarify the primary revelations of Hinduism. The Ramayana, the Mahabharata, and the Upanishads are examples of Smriti, and they have deeply influenced song traditions across South and Southeast Asia. The four Vedas are Rig Veda (containing hymns), Sama Veda (which Indian classical music is usually traced to), Yajur Veda, and Atharva Veda. In this way, music is profoundly connected to the most ancient knowledge on which Indian culture is based.

Since antiquity, great Indian minds such as Sri Mataṅga Muni and Bharat Muni, have explored music as a serious field of study and research. Sound has long been part of Indian philosophical systems. Sound itself is considered to be key to both the inner world and the outer world. For instance, Vedic literature describes—and the Upanishads further elaborate upon—the chakras (energy centers) and various sounds that assist in activating the chakras, and thereby the Kundalini awakening (The Sanskrit Channel, 2019, YouTube video). Similarly, because of the powerful effects that ragas have on the moods and circadian rhythm of both singer and listener, the *raag* systems prescribe which raga must be sung/heard during what time of the day. In the king's court (durbar), trained singers captured these "powers" and channeled them through a melodic framework to awaken the king at dawn or to put him to sleep at dusk.[1] These examples indicate the depth of the exploration of music and sounds by Indian ancestors who understood the interconnectedness between sound and the human body (including physical, mental, and spiritual dimensions). Put elegantly, in the Indian historical context, sounds are God, or as close as we can get to the Divine.

It is interesting to note that even in intimate and sacred spaces, musical instruments themselves have been worshipped and also used for Divine liberation. In other words, Indian instruments are used to aid devotees in channeling the human mind and thought toward their ultimate spiritual goal. For example, it is worth noticing the semiotics in the *Shiva Purana* (Ramesh, n.d.) wherein the graphic portrayal of Lord Shiva mentions *Damroo/Damaru* (a percussion instrument) as part and parcel of himself. The concept of "justice" in Vedic literature may be interpreted as suggesting musical connotations: *Justice is melodious and sweet. It is a timeless soothing piece. Whereas anything short of justice is noise.*[2] Having now offered a glimpse of music's central role in Indian antiquity, we now move to examine the conception of Indian culture, cultural heritage, and cultural diplomacy by considering the impact of cultural policies laid out in the Indian constitution.

In common understanding, culture can be defined as our interactions within a community that shares common social space and history, a common imagination (Anderson, 2006) as a basis for "perceiving, believing and evaluating" (Kramsch and Hua, 2016, 39). When juxtaposed with *nature*, which stands for what is born and grows organically, *culture* finds its roots in what has been grown and groomed. Cultural *heritage* is an expression of the ways of living developed by a society and passed on from generation to generation, including customs, practices, places, objects, artistic expressions, and values (Donders, 2020). Tangible cultural heritage refers to physical artifacts, such as monuments, buildings, and handicrafts, while intangible cultural heritage refers to immaterial elements (as opposed to the material) and includes ritual practices, knowledge, and oral traditions (UNESCO, 2003).[3]

Until recently, the main focus of "heritage preservation" has been on tangible cultural heritage (e.g., monuments and buildings); thereby cultural heritage was synonymous with cultural property. However, in recent years, appreciation of intangible culture has increased, along with the appreciation of its role in cultural identity and one's sense of belonging to a community (Jakubowski, 2020). An interesting question arises, that is, whether in a given geopolitically demarcated territory can there be space for many cultures? This question leads us to interrogate other concepts. Specifically, *multiculturalism* means policies and practices that recognize and respond to cultural diversity—in a given society at a given point of time—enabling diverse groups to live together harmoniously, while maintaining their distinct cultural heritage. Multiculturalism can take various forms, and Kymlicka, for example, has delineated *neo-liberal* multiculturalism and *inclusive* multiculturalism (Vitikainen, 2015, 20–24; see also Young, 2002).

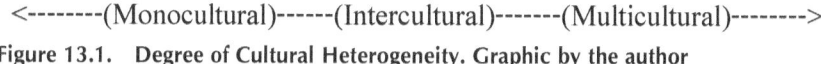

Figure 13.1. Degree of Cultural Heterogeneity. Graphic by the author

From figure 13.1, it can be seen that any given society can be

1. Monocultural, that is, consisting of only one cultural group. For example, the whole society is consisting of only Muslims. It is at the left end of the spectrum, which represents the least cultural heterogeneity.
2. Intercultural, that is, there is more than one cultural group and they interact with each other. For example, intercultural communication is an important field of communication in an increasingly globalized world.
3. Multicultural—the presence of two or more cultural groups. For example, present-day nation-states are de facto multicultural.

Such notions are based on perceptions of the nexus between culture, race, and ethnicity. Race is usually linked with physical/biological properties (e.g., skin/hair/eye color) while ethnicity is linked with cultural factors (e.g., language or dialect), and is an always evolving identity negotiation. Indeed, ethnicity is contextual because individuals may prefer different aspects of their ethnic belonging in different situations and it is multidimensional since ethnic self-identification and ethnicity as observed by others can be different. The question of whether cultures coexisting in a given society may flourish together or are merely tolerated and accommodated raises another new set of difficult questions. It takes us to the issue of dominant and minority cultures since people who identify themselves as members of a particular social group tend to acquire common ways of viewing the world. They acquire common ways of imagination (both fulfilled and unfulfilled). Do they also acquire common dreams? Should influential figures be allowed to dictate whose and what values and beliefs are deemed worth adopting by the group, which historical events are worth commemorating, and which futures are worth imagining? National culture resonates with the voices of the powerful and is covertly filled with silences of the powerless (Freire, 2000, 25). Edward Said observed how the French constructed for themselves a view of the culture of the Orient" (in the writings of Chateaubriand, Nerval, and Flaubert, for instance)," to reinforce a sense of superiority of European culture ([1978] 2016, 3438).

HERITAGE AND CULTURAL RIGHTS

A brief look at the nature of rights generally enables us to better appreciate the specific rights associated with culture. First, a legal right must be distinguished from a moral or natural right. A legal right is an interest recognized and protected by the rule of law: an interest, the violation of which would be a legal wrong. Moral right means an interest recognized and protected by a rule of natural justice: an interest that if breached would constitute a moral wrong, and respect for which is a moral duty." The difference between the two also lies in the threat of punishment behind them (Lazarev, 2005). Violations of legal rights are addressed by the state while violations of moral rights are addressed with societal disapprobation. A duty, on the other hand, is an obligatory act. In order to clarify "legal right," legal theorist Wesley Hohfeld (1879–1918) observed that a right is a jural correlative of duty. Hence, if a person has a legal right they also have a duty. Therefore, if a legal right is infringed, there is always a duty that is violated. An understanding of rights enables apprehension of the nature of claims to the heritage that various cultural groups make and the consequences this entails for the state. Various categorizations of rights are used.

First Categorization

Rights seen in terms of consequences/obligations:

1. Positive Rights—these rights are considered to be entailing action on the part of the State. For example, the right to health or the right to food.
2. Negative Rights—they are considered to be those rights that do not entail positive obligations. For example, the right not to be killed.

This categorization of rights is not immune to criticism. What is considered a negative right might not be solely a negative right but might also entail positive actions. For example, the right to life, if viewed as a negative right, would mean that a person should not be killed. However, the right to life also means a dignified existence and not mere animal existence. This would entail positive action on the part of the state. Thus, the categorization of positive and negative rights is not absolute.

Second Categorization

Rights are seen in terms of their source/origin:

1. Natural rights—these are rights that are bestowed by nature and hence are considered universal and inalienable. For example, John Locke terms life, liberty, and estate (property) as natural rights.
2. Legal rights—these are bestowed by the legal system. Examples include the right to contract as permitted by the extant laws in a legal system.

Among the few lines of criticism relevant here are that the term "natural" is vague and what is considered universal and inalienable might turn out to not be true in every conceivable situation. However, there are important instruments that are based on this conception, for example, The Universal Declaration of Human Rights (1945). There are various criticisms of this categorization; however, they will not be dealt with here, as they have little relevance to cultural heritage.

Third Categorization

Rights can be categorized in terms of the *user* of the right in question:

1. Individual rights—these are rights which individuals use, for example, the right to freedom of speech and expression. These rights are held by members collectively but in an individual capacity.

2. Group rights—these are also known as collective rights. They are held by a collective rather than in an individual capacity. For example, the right of Indigenous people to preserve their culture.

With regards to human rights generally, rights can be categorized into the following categories:

1. Civil and political rights—these are rights that enable the security of the individual's freedom and liberty.
2. Economic and social rights—these are rights that are necessary to enable individual well-being. For example, the right to education, and the right to health.
3. Collective rights—these rights are held by specified groups.

This classification of human rights aligns with Karel Vašák's conception of three generations of rights (Domaradzki Khvostova and Pupovac, 2019). However, it is pertinent to note that these forms of rights are not sequential. Further, despite the pragmatic utility of such conceptions, Vašák's generations of rights suffer from some logical incoherency (Fredman, 2008).

There are various permutations and combinations into which rights can be categorized, and in the cultural sphere rights may be claimed by either individuals or communities. Therefore, cultural rights are part of human rights, which relies upon notions of equality, human dignity, and nondiscrimination.

THE LEGAL FRAMEWORK IN INDIA

The Constitution of India guides law and policy in India. The Indian constitution commences with a Preamble:

> WE, THE PEOPLE OF INDIA, having solemnly resolved to constitute India into a SOVEREIGN SOCIALIST SECULAR DEMOCRATIC REPUBLIC and to secure to all its citizens: JUSTICE, social, economic and political; LIBERTY of thought, expression, belief, faith and worship; EQUALITY of status and of opportunity; and to promote among them all; FRATERNITY assuring the dignity of the individual and the unity and integrity of the Nation; IN OUR CONSTITUENT ASSEMBLY this twenty-sixth day of November, 1949, do HEREBY, ADOPT, ENACT AND GIVE TO OURSELVES THIS CONSTITUTION.

The constitution should always be read and interpreted in the light of the noble vision stated in the Preamble.[4] Despite efforts to argue that the Preamble is not part of the constitution (see the Berubari Union case),[5] it was upheld (see the Keshavananda Bharati case) that the Preamble is a living embodiment of the values, objectives, ideals, and basic principles of the constitution. It is the key to the entire constitution, indicating both its foundations[6] and basic structure (Gaur, 2012). The Preamble protects cultural diversity, stating "liberty of (. . .) expression" and ensuring "dignity" of "the individual." The interests of minorities are thereby meticulously safeguarded by the framers of the Indian constitution. Their intentions were to offer a sense of security, protection against discrimination, and to help all the citizenry to partake in the mainstream of national life.[7]

The spirit of the Preamble was poignantly expressed by Justice Leila Seth (2010) in the poem "We the Children of India":

> Free to love and free to care
> Let's be equal, just and free –
> Strong in our diversity.

Every person—irrespective of caste, creed, religion, gender, ethnicity, race—shares equally with dignity as an Indian, according to the constitution of India. Inclusion of key terms in the Preamble like "justice," "liberty of expression," "equality," and "dignity" of the individual are all testament to that vision. One need not sacrifice one's cultural identity (including religious, linguistic, or other features) in order to be Indian. This vision was further articulated by Jawaharlal Nehru on August 15, 1947, by giving a clarion call "to bring freedom and opportunity to the common man, to the peasant . . . to build up a prosperous, democratic and progressive nation and to create social, economic and political institutions which will ensure justice and fullness of life to every man and woman" (Nehru, 1947). Culture is understood in the field of Indian law as one of the key components of the fullness of life, social justice, and human dignity.

ARTICLES 29–30 OF THE CONSTITUTION OF INDIA AND JUDICIAL INTERPRETATION

Part III of the Constitution of India pertains to fundamental rights. In part III of the constitution, under cultural and educational rights, there are two relevant articles.

Article 29 (1) concerns the protection of the interests of minorities:

1. Any section of the citizens residing in the territory of India or any part thereof having a distinct language, script, or culture of its own shall have the right to conserve the same.

2. No citizen shall be denied admission into any educational institution maintained by the State receiving aid out of State funds on grounds only of religion, race, caste, language or any of them."

Similarly, Article 30 ensures Rights of Minority to Establish and Administer Educational Institutions:

1. All minorities, whether based on religion or language, shall have the right to establish and administer educational institutions of their choice.

    (1-A) In making any law providing for the compulsory acquisition of any property of an educational institution establish and administered by a minority, referred to in clause (1), the State shall ensure that the amount fixed by or determined under such law for the acquisition of such property is such as would not restrict or abrogate the right guaranteed under that clause."
2. "The State shall not, in granting aid to educational institutions, discriminate against any educational institution on the ground that it is under the management of a minority, whether based on religion or language."

It is important to note that the right conferred upon the citizens to conserve their culture, language, etc. is made absolute by the constitution (note here that unlike 19(1), Article 30(1) is not subject to any reasonable restrictions). Still, it has been judicially understood that the right to administer cannot encompass the right to mal-administer. Thus, although Article 30(1) is couched in absolute terms, it has to be interpreted as subject to the regulatory power of the State (Pal, 2014, 1275).

Protection is given to every minority group having a distinct language, written script, or culture by guaranteeing their right to conserve the same. If such a group desires to preserve their language and culture, the State would not stand in their way. Moreover, it is a fundamental duty under Art 51-A (f) as stated in Part IV A of the Indian constitution "to value and preserve the rich heritage of our composite culture." The Preamble, along with other parts of the constitution, affirms this objective, whereby diversity emerges as an imperative (Choudhary, 2017). Simply put, it can be stated that the Indian model is attuned to "unity in diversity," that is, a salad bowl ideology as opposed to a melting pot ideology (May, 2003). As a whole, India, in fact, arguably takes pride in and celebrates its diversity as its crowning glory.

Still, respect for human dignity and preservation of culture requires decisive and concrete positive steps on the part of the State. The Ministry of Culture,[8] a division of the national government of India, oversees and undertakes such efforts. Various schemes—for instance, a scheme for safeguarding intangible cultural heritage, a scheme for the creation of cultural infrastructure, a scheme for promotion of international cultural relations, and projects like National Mission on Cultural Mapping—are routinely undertaken to preserve the rich Indian cultural fabric. Additionally, the Indian Council for Cultural Relations was established in 1950 to revive and strengthen India's cultural relations with the rest of the world.

However, despite all of these efforts on the ground, reality has not changed much.[9] More needs to be done to translate the principles enshrined in the constitution into policies that bring about real change at the grassroots level. For instance, Ragni, which is a traditional performative cum musical art practice in the northern region of India (popular especially in the State of Haryana)[10] needs incentives from the State to ensure its preservation. It is a welcome step that the government of India has taken note of the erosion of cultural heritage and is taking steps including promoting research and development to conserve and preserve cultural heritage.

INTELLECTUAL PROPERTY RIGHTS QUA MUSIC IN INDIA

Intellectual property rights (IPR) with respect to music have been rapidly changing in India, so much so that some say the *once-sleepy realm of music copyright law has turned into a minefield.* But what exactly are the rights usually associated with a piece of music, and who is involved in its creation? Generally, a piece of music requires the following contributions:

1. Lyricist–one who writes the words for the song.
2. Music composer—one who provides the melodic framework/tunes. It can be created on piano, guitar, harmonium, etc. The creation process of a song can also happen in the reverse order, that is, a composer can provide the melodic framework and ask the lyricist to write words.
3. Music director—discharges their musical duties by enhancing the musical score. It includes guiding, that is, which part is to be played where and selecting the musical arrangement.
4. Music arranger—designs a supporting structure for the basic tune, for example, what beats of which percussion instruments need to be included in the song.
5. Music producer—controls the ideas and essentially oversees all aspects of the creation of a sound recording. This includes the choice of vocalists or instruments as well as technical matters.
6. Sound engineers—also known as audio engineers, they provide balance and clarity to the sound recording. Their duties may include mixing, equalizing, audio effects, mastering, etc.

7. Musicians/Artists—this commonly includes singers and instrumentalists on various musical instruments.
8. Music publisher—record label or music companies that distribute the product.

It must be noted that there may be either more or less people than described above involved in the creation of a song. Additionally, these categories are fluid, meaning a person can be a singer-songwriter and also a producer, for instance. Consider the song "Liggi" (Ritviz, 2019, YouTube video) by Ritviz Srivastava, which was written, composed, produced, and performed by the artist.[11] Original musical pieces require a myriad of creative input before they reach their final shape. This final creation constitutes intellectual property, and the creator/owner[12] enjoys a bundle of rights[13] associated with it. These rights include:

1. Right to reproduce, that is, mechanical reproduction of the musical work
2. Right to distribute
3. Right to prepare derivates
4. Right to publicly perform the musical work
5. Right to assignment[14]
6. Special rights also known as Moral rights[15]

The Indian Copyright Act of 1957 is the law currently governing music copyright in India.[16] Until recently, it had remained ambiguous on the definition of what will constitute a "musical work." The earlier definition completely excluded the presence of the lyrics and voice as part of a musical work and completely ignored the rights of the singer and that of the lyricist.[17] Even after the an amendment in 1994, ambiguity persists concerning the protection of the lyrics (for instance, songs with the same lyrics but different music or composition—would it be copyright infringement?).

It is important to understand the underlying philosophy of copyright to stimulate artistic creativity for the general public good. Further, one must note that musical language cannot be copyrighted: basic building blocks of music, common motivic patterns, should be available to everyone.[18] Hence, it becomes a legal imperative to delineate unprotectable ideas in the public sphere of common practice and other such elements from protected original creative expressions, because not every element of a work is protectable, although the work itself as a whole may be. Doctrines like de minimis, scène à faire further augment creativity by preserving and expanding the common stock expression of ideas. Importantly, copyright protects the expression of an idea rather than the idea itself. Further, melodic monopolies cannot be permitted since to do so would hinder artistic creativity. For example, an eight-note ostinato cannot qualify for copyright infringement.[19] This raises questions about remixes, version songs, sound sampling, mash-ups, etc. and whether they can amount to copyright infringement. However, these questions are beyond the scope of this chapter. The main point of such legislation is that we should aim to foster and protect creativity but at the same time not end up creating an environment of stifled creativity.

This brings us to parsing the interface between IPRs concerning music and cultural rights: Do they share a symbiotic relationship or are they antagonistic to each other? Let us try to answer this by addressing a recent controversy in India. YouTuber and singer Maithili Thakur posted a video singing *Ramcharitramanas*[20] and *Chaupai*[21] on her YouTube channel. Indian music record label T-Series lodged copyright claims against Maithili Thakur (Parekh, 2001). Can a record label claim copyright over something that is found invariably in every Hindu household and sung routinely in prayer as a traditional devotional song? The matter had not yet entered the court of law and hence no authoritative answer can be given. However, it raises an interesting question about the contours of copyright and whether traditional songs and hymns fall under these guidelines. Traditional cultural expressions, including folklore and common musical traditions (such as hymns or folk songs), are artistic heritages preserved and maintained by a community. It is helpful to examine the positions of the World Intellectual Property Organization (WIPO) to throw some light on these issues. The WIPO handbook (*WIPO Intellectual Property Handbook*, 2008) on intellectual property states:

> 2.273: Pre-existing traditional culture is generally trans-generational (that is, old), collectively "owned" by one or more groups or communities and is likely to be of anonymous origin, to the extent that the notion of authorship is relevant at all. Pre-existing traditional culture as such and particular expressions thereof are generally not protected by current copyright laws and are treated, from the perspective of the intellectual property system, as part of the "public domain."[22]

> 2.274: On the other hand, a contemporary literary and artistic production based upon, derived from or inspired by traditional culture that incorporates new elements or expression is a "new" work in respect of which there is generally a living and identifiable creator or creators. Such a contemporary production may include a new interpretation, arrangement, adaptation or collection of pre-existing cultural heritage and expressions in the public domain, or even their "re-packaging" in the form of digital enhancement, colorization and the like. Contemporary, tradition-based expressions and representations of traditional cultures are generally protected by existing copyright for which they are sufficiently "original." The law makes no distinction based on "authenticity" or the identity of the author—that is, the originality requirement of copyright could be

met by an author who is not a member of the relevant cultural community in which the tradition originated.

Therefore, if a song builds on folk songs or other traditional musical expressions in a way that entails originality and involves substantial skill and judgment, it might qualify for protection under extant IPR law. However, one must not lose sight of the fact that authorship as a construct has shaky foundations. Deconstruction of the assumptions of originality and individualism reveals the collaborative nature of cultural production. This holds true especially for traditional musical expressions including folk music, for example Jugni, a poetic narrative device used in Punjabi folk music. While it is true that "there are no virgin births in Music, music comes out of other music," to what extent this argument can be stretched in the realm of traditional music is open to debate (Wang, 2020). Hence, in a way, musical and legal tango need to learn newer steps when it moves on the dance floor of traditional musical expression. Having dealt with IPR, music, and cultural rights, let us now look at diplomacy and culture.

DIPLOMACY AND CULTURE

When thinking about the term "diplomacy," is it common to invoke Joseph Nye's theoretical framework concerning "soft power."[23] Is the summum bonum of cultural diplomacy solely to advance the state's interest and burnish its global image? Cultural diplomacy, a component of soft power, is not easy to define:

> There is no general agreement among scholars about cultural diplomacy's relationship to the practice of diplomacy, its objective, practitioners, activities, timeframe or whether the practice is reciprocal or not. Some regard cultural diplomacy as a synonym for public diplomacy, others for international cultural relations or a state's foreign cultural mission, and others regard these as a distinct practises. (Mark, 2008, 39)

As reported in Haigh (1974, 28) and Mark (2008, 43), another question that arises is whether the state is part and parcel of cultural diplomacy (see also Asgard, 2010). Few scholars have cautioned us about the dangers of the association of government in cultural diplomacy and consequently its effectiveness (Kennedy, 2003, 318; see also Feigenbaum, 2001). For instance, when a famous photography exhibition after the September 11, 2001, terrorist attacks in the United States was selected by the US State Department and various embassies for cultural diplomacy, most exhibitions were held in the

Middle East and North Africa, with fewer in Europe and South America. The exhibition was intended to show the emotional side of the American experience of September 11, but also to transcend this particular case to touch on a more universal empathy toward human suffering (Goff, 2013, 10–11). Some responses to the exhibition were quite negative precisely because it was received as a calculated attempt on the part of the US government to elicit sympathy for itself (10–11).

In my estimation, cultural diplomacy has deeper potential for humanity than merely serving as a soft power instrument used to exert power to entice, influence, and attract other governments and populations globally (Mullen, 2015, 1–2). Rather, it can be a way of sharing profound meanings and beneficial ways of life with the larger global family, much like the concept of global common goods.[24] For instance, if a nation has something to offer that could benefit the whole world, then it should be shared irrespective of whether it garners praise or burnishes the nation-state image on the global platform. The latter may happen as a consequence but it should not be the sole objective of cultural diplomacy. For instance, since Vedic times, even much before the advent of the Magna Carta, Vedic culture advocated *Vasudhaiva Kutumbakam*, meaning the world is one family. This is in direct conflict with the concept of "barbarians" (i.e., those who were from distant lands or who did not speak Greek). Edward W. Said in his seminal work entitled *Culture and Imperialism* (1993), notes that the West needed to bring civilization to "primitive" people or to destroy it where it existed, an approach which later led to the great movement of decolonization in Asia, Africa, and the Arab world. Said notes that the notion of inferior races helped fuel the imperial acquisition of territory during the colonial period. The culture of imperialism, which entails venerating one's own culture at the expense of other cultures, is completely antithetical to the Indian approach. Rather, imperialism is linked to the "white man's burden," a concept first introduced by Rudyard Kipling (and immediately rejected by Mark Twain) that signifies justification of attempts to "civilize the uncivilized" and unabashedly carry out the global project of colonialism (Collins, 2018, 95).

Musical expressions have immense potential in cultural diplomacy including in international relations. A recent example comes from both India and Pakistan. Despite being poltical adversaries, music has helped in building the bridges of communication between these two nations, through shared traditions with mutually-respected artists, even when other channels of communication are broken (see Pundziūtė-Gallois, 2018).

Another example is how the Indian tradition of yoga has spread globally. The UN General Assembly recognized June 21 as the International Day of Yoga, which began in 2015. The Indian prime minister, Narendra Modi said,

> Yoga is an invaluable gift of India's ancient tradition. It embodies unity of mind and body; thought and action; restraint and fulfillment; harmony between man and nature; a holistic approach to health and well-being. It is not about exercise but to discover the sense of oneness with yourself, the world, and nature. By changing our lifestyle and creating consciousness, it can help us deal with climate change. (Fit India, 2021)

During the recent global pandemic (COVID-19), some in the global community adopted the Indian way of greeting, "namaste." For instance, in a 2020 news segment, it was reported that Germany's vice-chancellor Angela Merkel and France president Emmanuel Macron greeted each other with namaste (Sarkar, 2020), while other news media have reported this greeting was also at least briefly adopted by Donald Trump and Prince Charles.

CONCLUSION

We see that both internationally and within India there is growing awareness about the need for conservation and preservation of cultural heritage. The focus has expanded from tangible to intangible heritage in such discussions. The Indian legal framework envisages and adumbrates a place where various cultures can flourish together. However, these principles enshrined in the Constitution of India must be translated into effective policy to bring about change at the grassroots level. In the global setting, cultural diplomacy needs to be viewed as a mechanism to share the best of global practices. Contrary to some views of cultural diplomacy, in my perspective, global appeal and popularity should not be the primary objective of such initiatives, but rather mere consequences. There is an urgent need for developing policy designs that are not only sustainable but also incorporate newer conceptions of cultural heritage to ensure that individuals, irrespective of background, are able to participate fully in the public sphere. Caution is also needed to ensure that such policies are not culturally tokenistic in nature, but rather emanate from genuinely collaborative efforts between the state and the communities concerned.

NOTES

1. A crude, modern example of this phenomenon can be seen in the movie *Titanic*, wherein in a scene when the ship starts to sink, musicians were asked to play their instruments in order to calm the frightened passengers (which actually happened).

2. These are the author's interpretations. For further commentary, see Alfred John Hiltebeitel (2011) and Jamison and Brereton (2014).

3. However, it must be noted that the distinction between tangible and intangible, as scholars argue is arbitrary as they are not binaries or polar opposites, rather interwoven concepts. For further information, see Iacono and Brown (2016) and Isar, Anheier, and Viejo-Rose (2011). They note that "all monuments, sites and artifacts embody intangible components such as spiritual values, symbols, and meanings, together with the knowledge and the know-how of craftsmanship and construction" (49).

4. Kesavananda Bharti v. State of Kerala, AIR 1973 SC 1461 at 1505: (1973) 4 SCC 225.

5. AIR 1960 SC 845.

6. S. R. Bommai v. Union of India, (1994) 3 SCC 1.

7. For discussion in the Constituent Assembly, see III CAD, 211–314.

8. The official website of the Ministry of Culture, Government of India, can be accessed at https://www.indiaculture.nic.in.

9. For instance, India tops the chart in UNESCO's *Atlas of The World's Languages in Danger* (UNESCO, 2021; Moseley 2010; see also Choudhary 2020).

10. A few of the iconic names associated with *ragni* are Pt Lakhmi Chand, Rajkishan Agwanpuriya, and others. Ragni in simple terms involves the performance component coupled with musical instruments and singing.

11. Though there are other credits such as cinematography etc. they are not relevant to be mentioned here.

12. As per Section 17 of the The Indian Copyright Act, 1957, the author is the first owner of copyright in music. However, Section 17 proviso (c) states that in the case of a work made in the course of the author's employment under a contract of service or apprenticeship . . . the employer shall, in the absence of any agreement to the contrary, be the first owner. Section 2(d) (ii) states composer is author in relation to musical work and Section 2(d) (v) states producer shall be the author in regards to sound recording. Section 2(d) (vi)—In relation to musical work which is computer generated, person who causes work to be created is the author.

13. Section 14 (a) (i)—(vii) of the The Indian Copyright Act, 1957 elaborates these exclusive rights w.r.t musical work.

14. Section 18 of the The Indian Copyright Act, 1957 states that the owner of copyright can assign copyright either wholly or partially to any person. Furthermore, the second and third Proviso states, "Shall not assign or waive the right to receive royalties to be shared on an equal basis with the assignee of copyright for any utilisation of such work except to the legal heirs of the authors or to a collecting society for collection and distribution and any assignment to the contrary shall be void."

15. These are set of inalienable rights that the author of the musical work has, for example, the right to claim authorship; right to restrain or claim damages in respect of any distortion, mutilation, modification or other act in relation to the said work . . . if such distortion, mutilation, modification or other act would be prejudicial to his honour or reputation. For more see, Section 57 of the The Indian Copyright Act, 1957. See *Amar Nath Singh v. Union of India*, 117 (2005) DLT 717 wherein in paragraph 24, Justice Pradeep Nadrajog observes that, "Moral Rights of the author are the soul of his works. The author has a right to preserve, protect and nurture his creations through his moral rights."

16. There are a a host of international IPR treaties and conventions that protects a country's copyrighted work outside its boundaries.

17. Earlier Section 2(p) of the Copyright Act, 1957, reads, "Musical work means any combination of melody and harmony or either of them printed, reduced to writing or otherwise graphically produced or reproduced." Post amendment, it currently reads as "'Musical work' means a work consisting of music and includes any graphical notation of such work but does not include any words or any action intended to be sung, spoken or performed with the music."

18. Ronald S. Rosen (2008) writes: "Likewise, musical ideas and commonplace building blocks and motifs should be found unprotectable upon analytic dissection of the composition involved. In other words, we must isolate the musical equivalents of 'once upon a time' and 'I travelled to' and remove them from consideration in order to properly analyze infringement claims involving musical compositions. Once again, to do so requires an understanding of musical ideas and of the language embodying those ideas" (3).

19. Judge Christina A. Snyder observes that the individual elements of the Christian rap song "Joyful Noise" were the kinds of commonplace elements that courts have routinely denied copyright protection. Further, the signature elements of the eight-note ostinato in the rap song "is not a particularly unique or rare combination." See also Johannes Hoffman (2020).

20. Composed by Goswami Tulsidas, it is considered to be part and parcel of the hindu devotional literature.

21. The English equivalent of the term "chaupai" is "quatrain."

22. The concept of public domain is highly contentious in musical practice. Anthony McCann (2001) observes that in musical practice "'public domain' is inadequate . . . it is synonymous with uninhibited exploitation of the music or song, and it reinforces the anonymous/authored dichotomy. Not only is a piece that sounds traditional often assumed to be of unknown origin, but it is therefore assumed to be open to all for free and unbridled exploitation" (99).

23. Cultural diplomacy is soft power device used by nation-states to serve their interest (Nye, 2004).

24. It is based on the revitalised understanding of common good in an increasingly globalised world.

REFERENCES

Anderson, Benedict. 2006. *Imagined Communities: Reflections on the Origin and Spread of Nationalism.* London: Verso.

Asgard, Ramin. 2010. "U.S.-Iran Cultural Diplomacy: A Historical Perspective." *Al Nakhlah.* Fletcher School Online Journal for issues related to Southwest Asia and Islamic Civilization: 1–12.

Choudhary, Karan. 2017. "Moving Away from Weak Pluralism and Closer to Linguistic Justice: Educating Nation with Multiple Voices," presented in Tri-National Winter Univeristy on theme of Culture and Law in Europe and India held at National Law University Delhi. 20 February to 26 February.

———. 2020. "An In-depth Look at Endangered Languages and Related Issues of Social Justice and Law." PhD diss., Université Paris Nanterre, France and National Law University Delhi.

Collins, Deborah. 2018. "Mark Twain at Home in India." *Mark Twain Journal* 56, no. 2: 85–104.

Domaradzki, Spasimir, Margaryta Khvostova, and David Pupovac. 2019. "Karel Vasak's Generations of Rights and the Contemporary Human Rights Discourse." *Hum Rights Rev* 20: 423–43.

Donders, Yvonne. 2020. "Cultural Heritage and Human Rights." In *The Oxford Handbook of International Cultural Heritage Law*, edited by Francesco Francioni and Ana Filipa Vrdoljak, 379–406. Oxford University Press.

Feigenbaum, Harvey B. 2001. *Globalization and Cultural Diplomacy.* Art, Culture, and the National Agenda Series. Washington, DC: Americans for the Arts.

"Fit India." 2021. Accessed November 12, 2021. https://fitindia.gov.in/event-archives.

Fredman, Sandra. 2008. *Human Rights Transformed: Positive Duties and Positive Rights.* New York: Oxford University Press. DOI:10.1093/acprof:oso/9780199272761.001.0001

Freire, Paulo. 2000. *Pedagogy of the Oppressed.* New York: Continuum.

Gaur, Abhinav. 2012. "Is Preamble a Part of the Constitution of India." April 21. http://dx.doi.org/10.2139/ssrn.2043496.

Goff, Patricia M. 2013. "Cultural Diplomacy." *The Oxford Handbook of Modern Diplomacy*, edited by Andrew F. Cooper, Jorge Heine, and Ramesh Thakur. New York: Oxford University Press.

Haigh, Anthony. 1974. *Cultural Diplomacy in Europe.* Council for Cultural Cooperation, Strasbourg (France). Scarsdale, NY: Manhattan Publishing Company, 1974.

Hiltebeitel, Alfred. 2011. *Dharma: Its Early History in Law, Religion, and Narrative.* Oxford, New York: Oxford University Press.

Hoffman, Johannes. 2020. "Breaking Up Melodic Monopolies: A New Approach to Originality, Substantial Similarity, and Fair Use for Melodies in Pop Music." *Journal of Law and Policy* 28, no. 2: 762–96.

Iacono, Valeria Lo, and David H. K. Brown. 2016. "Beyond Binarism: Exploring a Model of Living Cultural Heritage for Dance." *Dance Research* 34, no. 1: 84–105.

Isar, Y. R., H. K. Anheier, and D. Viejo-Rose. 2011. "Introduction." In *Heritage, Memory & Identity:The Cultures and Globalization*, edited by Helmut

Anheier and Yudhishthir R. Isar, 1–20. London: SAGE Publications. http://dx.doi.org/10.4135/9781446250839.

Jakubowski, Andrzej. 2020. "Cultural Rights and Cultural Heritage as A Global Concern." In *The Oxford Handbook of Law and Anthropology*, edited by Marie-Claire Foblets, Mark Goodale, Maria Sapignoli, and Olaf Zenker. United Kingdom: Oxford University Press. DOI: 10.1093/oxfordhb/9780198840534.001.0001

Jamison, Stephanie W. and Joel P. Brereton, trans. 2014. *The Rigveda: The Earliest Religious Poetry of India*. 3 volumes. South Asia Research. Oxford, New York: Oxford University Press.

Kennedy, Liam. 2003. "Remembering September 11: Photography as Cultural Diplomacy," *International Affairs* 79, no. 2: 315–26.

Kramsch, Claire, and Zhu Hua. 2016. "Language, Culture and Language Teaching." In *Routledge Handbook of English Language Teaching*, edited by Graham Hall, 38–50. London: Routledge, Taylor & Francis Group.

Lazarev, Nikolai. 2005. "Hohfeld's Analysis of Rights: An Essential Approach to a Conceptual and Practical Understanding of the Nature of Rights." 2005 *Murdoch University Electronic Journal of Law* 9. http://www.austlii.edu.au/au/journals/MurUEJL/2005/9.html.

Mark, Simon. 2008. "A Comparative Study of the Cultural Diplomacy of Canada, New Zealand and India." PhD diss. University of Auckland.

May, Stephen. 2003. "Misconceiving Minority Language Rights: Implications for Liberal Political Theory." In *Language Rights and Political Theory*, edited by Will Kymlicka and Alan Patten, 123–52. Oxford: Oxford University Press.

McCann, Anthony. 2001. "All That Is Not Given Is Lost: Irish Traditional Music, Copyright, and Common Property." *Ethnomusicology* 45, no. 1: 89–106.

Moseley, Christopher, ed. 2010. "Atlas of the World's Languages in Danger." 3rd ed. Paris, UNESCO Publishing. http://www.unesco.org/culture/en/endangeredlanguages/atlas.

Mullen, Rani D. 2015. "India's Soft Power." *The Oxford Handbook of Indian Foreign Policy*, edited by David M. Malone, C. Raja Mohan, and Srinath Raghavan. New York: Oxford University Press.

Nehru, Jawaharlal. 1947. "A Tryst with Destiny." August 24. Accessed November 12, 2021. https://www.files.ethz.ch/isn/125396/1154_trystnehru.pdf.

Nye, Joseph. 2004. "The Decline of America's Soft Power." *Foreign Affairs* 83, no. 3 (May–June), 16–20.

Pal, R. 2014. *M. P. Jain's Indian Constitutional Law*, 7th edition. New York: LexisNexis.

Parekh, Bhikhu. 2001. "Rethinking Multiculturalism: Cultural Diversity and Political Theory." *Ethnicities* 1, no. 1 (March): 109–15.

Pundziūtė-Gallois, Emilija. 2018. "Music that Divides: The Case of Russian Musical Diplomacy in the Baltic States." In *International Relations, Music and Diplomacy: Sounds and Voices on the International Stage*. The Sciences Po Series in International Relations and Political Economy, edited by Frédéric Ramel and Cécile Prévost-Thomas, 235–56. London: Palgrave Macmillan.

Ramesh, B. M. n.d. "Shiva Purana." *The Vyasa Online Blog*. http://www.vyasaonline.com/shiva-purana/.
Rosen, Ronald S. 2008. *Music and Copyright*. Oxford, New York: Oxford University Press.
Ritviz. 2019. "Liggi." Youtube Video. 3:11. December 23. https://www.youtube.com/watch?v=6BYIKEH0RCQ
Said, Edward W. 1993. *Culture and Imperialism*. London: Chatto & Windus.
———. (1978) 2016. *Orientalism: Western Conceptions of the Orient*. Imprint India, Penguin Books.
Sarkar, Shankhyaneel, ed. 2020. "Macron, Merkel Greet Each Other with Namaste before Meet at French Presidential Palace." *Hindustan Times*, August 21. https://www.hindustantimes.com/world-news/macron-merkel-greet-each-other-with-namaste-before-meet-at-french-presidential-palace/story-EtQNyNh1EMuNRNsGeCNCFO.html.
Seth, Leila. 2010. *We the Children of India: The Preamble to Our Constitution*. Imprint India Puffin.
The Sanskrit Channel. 2019. "Complete Description & Activation of Muladhara from Shat Chakra Nirupanam." Youtube Video. 18:14. March 27. https://www.youtube.com/watch?v=hbU3lfsiPm8&list=PLAPrVB8wngPlHHryHcNjrncd624CI2r7m&index=6.
UNESCO. 2003. "What Is Intangible Cultural Heritage?" Accessed November 12, 2021. https://ich.unesco.org/en/what-is-intangible-heritage-00003.
———. 2021. UNESCO Atlas of the World's languages in Danger. Accessed November 12, 2021. http://www.unesco.org/languages-atlas/.
Vitikainen, Annamari. 2015. *The Limits of Liberal Multiculturalism: Towards an Individuated Approach to Cultural Diversity*. Series: Palgrave Studies in Ethics and Public Policy. First edition, Palgrave Macmillan UK.
Wang, Amy X. 2020. "How Music Copyright Lawsuits Are Scaring Away New Hits." Rolling Stone. *Rolling Stone*, January 9. https://www.rollingstone.com/pro/features/music-copyright-lawsuits-chilling-effect-935310/.
WIPO Intellectual Property Handbook. 2008 (2004). WIPO Publication No. 489 (E). https://www.wipo.int/publications/en/details.jsp?id=275&plang=EN.
Young, Iris Marion. 2002. *Inclusion and Democracy*. Oxford University Press.

Chapter Fourteen

China's Legal Framework Supporting Protection and Sustainability of Artistic Heritage

Juqian Li

Standing in front of a colorfully decorated painting, a memorial to poet and musician Amannisaha in Shache County, Xinjiang, I am in awe of the legendary contributions and splendid music culture of the Twelve Muqam that Amannisaha helped compile in the sixteenth century. This monument to the Twelve Muqam illustrates the diversity of musical traditions preserved and passed on in China. Artistic heritage is a prominent component of cultural heritage, and in China it is protected by law in various ways. The "Chinese Music Heritage Map" by the Central Conservatory of Music describes the music heritage and the locations of fifty-six ethnic groups living within China's vast borders (Gao, 2021, 159). The diversity of ethnic groups and their geographic locations across this vast nation-state make the protection and sustainability of cultural heritage a complex, if not unwieldy, endeavor. The legal framework that supports this objective requires interplay between negotiating international treaties, with oversight by Chinese national and local laws. This chapter examines this multifaceted legal structure with respect to examples of musical and artistic heritage.

China comprises various ethnic groups and has a rich documented history. Researchers have access to a staggering array of artistic resources compared to many other nations. For example, although the *guqin* and *guzheng* are perhaps the most recognizable examples of the Han people's traditional musical instruments, there are a plethora of examples of Chinese traditional music represented by minority cultures such as the previously mentioned Twelve Muqams still performed today by culture-bearer musicians in Xinjiang and the ancient Morin Khuur, celebrated for its historical importance by people living in Inner Mongolia. Not only can we observe living musical instrument traditions from thousands of years ago, but scholars also have access to a vast array of historical musical treatises and artifacts. For example, written more than two thousand years ago during the Han Dynasty, *Yue Ji* (*Book of Music*), the nineteenth chapter of *Li Ji* (*Book of Rites*, 2019), is the earliest fully-developed treatise on music that discusses the basic functions and forms of classical Chinese music, underscoring the cultural impact of Confucian thought that persisted until the early twentieth century. Dating back to 6000 BCE, more than thirty *Jiahu Gudi*, (Jiahu bone-flutes) were discovered in Henan Province in 1986 (see Zhang, Xiao, and Lee, 2004; Wang, 2012). While these artifacts are relatively simple compared to, for instance, chime bells from the Zeng-Hou-Yi Tomb, they remain a testament to the immense importance of musical expression across many centuries of Chinese culture.

This chapter differs from others in that it argues that the Chinese legal framework's support of the protection and sustainability of artistic heritage, specifically in terms of minority groups within China, serves as a form of cultural policy and diplomacy that highlights their important historical and present-day contributions. As such, I discuss this theme in four sections. The first section describes the hierarchy of the Chinese legal system, specifically as it pertains to the making and enforcement of laws. The second section discusses how China applies international treaties to the protection of cultural heritage. The third section reflects on national law, specifically as it relates to the preservation of artistic heritage. Finally, the fourth section considers the general landscape of local decrees and rules and the current policies and practices that encourage international communication and diplomacy in art and culture.

It is important for readers to bear in mind that this chapter focuses on the *lex lata*, that is, the "current law" applied in China. The lex lata analyzed in this chapter includes the basic rules for how judicial courts apply law. With more than twenty million cases per year, the sheer volume of legislative impact is impressive. Indeed, the Supreme People's Court presides over thirty thousand cases per year. Therefore, the examples discussed in this chapter relate directly to artistic heritage to illustrate how the general landscape of the current law actively supports the protection and sustainability of artistic heritage in China.[1]

HIERARCHY OF LEGAL RULES

Before considering the nuances of the legal frameworks that specifically relate to artistic heritage, it is necessary to briefly clarify the hierarchical Chinese legislative process. According to the 1982 constitution and the legislation law enacted in 2000,[2] China's legal framework is divided into four distinct levels. The constitution rests at the top, which is followed by national law, administrative regulations, and finally local regulations, local rules, and ministerial rules. To make matters more complex, international law, including international treaties and international customs, are not regulated in Chinese legislation law, so the legal status of international law within the national legislation is relatively unclear. However, the constitution provides the procedural requirements for concluding international treaties.

THE SUPREMACY OF THE CHINESE CONSTITUTION

In China, the National People's Congress (hereafter referred to as the NPC) makes and amends the constitution. According to Article 87 of legislation law, "The Constitution shall have the supreme legal effect, and no laws, administrative regulations, local regulations, autonomous regulations, separate regulations, or rules may contravene the Constitution."[3] The preface of constitution (中华人民共和国宪法) indicates the following:

> This Constitution, in legal form, affirms the achievements of the struggles of the Chinese people of all nationalities and defines the basic system and basic tasks of the state; it is the fundamental law of the state and has supreme legal authority. The people of all nationalities, all state organs, the armed forces, all political parties, and public organizations, and all enterprises and institutions in the country must take the Constitution as the basic standard of conduct, and they have the duty to uphold the dignity of the Constitution and ensure its implementation.[4]

In addition, articles within the constitution uphold its legal supremacy:

> No laws or administrative or local rules and regulations may contravene the Constitution.[5] The people's congresses of provinces and municipalities directly under the Central Government and their standing committees may adopt local regulations, which must not contravene the Constitution and the law and administrative rules and regulations, and they shall report such local regulations to the Standing Committee of the NPC for the record.[6]

National Laws under the Constitution

National laws can be made and amended by the NPC and its Standing Committee according to specific rules relating to the legislation. Specialized subfields of law, such as criminal law, civil law, laws on state authorities, and other laws with the same importance can only be developed and amended by the NPC.[7] The Standing Committee of the NPC develops and amends other laws,[8] and therefore exercises a significantly more important legislative power compared to its Standing Committee. Still, the Standing Committee of the NPC has some flexibility such as being allowed to partially supplement and amend laws developed by the NPC when it is not in session, provided, of course, that the basic principles of such laws are not violated.[9]

Administrative Regulations

The legislative authority for administrative regulations is the State Council, that is, the central government of China. The State Council develops administrative regulations per the constitution and laws apply to all of mainland China.[10]

Local Regulations, Local Rules, and Ministerial Rules

Local regulations and local rules are both applied in a local area. The difference is that the former is made by the local People's Congress and standing committee, and recognized as higher than the latter, which are made by a local government. Ministerial rules, on the other hand, are created by ministries of the State Council and apply throughout China. Any conflicts that ensue between local regulations and ministerial rules, or between local rules and ministerial rules, are decided by the State Council or the Standing Committee of NPC according to the procedure of legislation law.

The constitution, at the top of the hierarchy, contains a provision that specifically relates to cultural heritage at both the national and local levels. Article 22 of the constitution states that "the state protects sites of scenic and historical interest, valuable cultural monuments and relics and other significant items of China's historical and cultural heritage." At local levels, the local congresses and local governments endeavor to protect cultural heritage. The constitution also protects the cultural heritage of autonomous areas as well as different ethnic groups. Article 119 of the constitution states:

> The organs of self-government of the national autonomous areas independently administer educational, scientific, cultural, public health, and physical culture affairs in their respective areas, protect and sift through the cultural heritage of the nationalities and work for a vigorous development of their cultures.

INTERNATIONAL TREATIES

According to the Ministry of Foreign Affairs, as of 2021, China has negotiated and entered 7,224 specific international treaties (People's Republic of China-Treaty Database, 2021), a dynamic number that alters from time to time as new treaties are negotiated. In addition, some treaties become invalid for various reasons, and some are renegotiated and replaced. All the valid treaties shall be applied in China based on pact sunt servenda (i.e., agreements must be kept), the legal principle universally accepted by the international community. Every treaty in force is binding upon the parties to it and must be performed by them in good faith.[11] The judgment of the International Court of Justice on interpretations of treaty application has a profound influence on every state, although the judgment legally binds only the states that are parties to the dispute in each case. The term "cultural heritage" has appeared in three cases decided by the International Court of Justice.[12]

Cultural Treaties and their Application in China

Cultural treaties can be categorized into two types, depending on the number of state parties: multilateral treaties and bilateral treaties. Bilateral treaties are treaties where both China and another country have a common interest in the specific cultural heritage or cultural performance. As of 2021, there were currently 643 bilateral treaties on cultural matters between China and another country (People's Republic of China-Treaty Database, 2021). Multilateral cultural treaties are necessarily more complex and include treaties that directly relate to cultural heritage within the framework of UNESCO. Other treaties indirectly related to cultural heritage, such as copyright and neighboring rights, impact the rights that performers and record companies have to performances and sound recordings.

UNESCO Treaties

The results of the 1972 World Heritage Convention, which sought "to adopt new provisions in the form of a convention establishing an effective system of collective protection of the cultural and natural heritage of outstanding universal value," went into force on December 17, 1975. China joined on December 12, 1985 (UNESCO, 2021). This convention has served as the most influential legal instrument for the recognition and protection of the world's natural and cultural heritage. The convention now recognizes 1,121 cultural properties: 869 cultural heritage properties, 213 natural heritage properties, and 39 mixed cultural heritage properties and natural heritage properties worldwide. China has 37 cultural heritage properties, 14 natural heritage properties, and 4 mixed heritage properties. China currently also has 60 heritage properties on the tentative list waiting to be recognized by the World Heritage Committee (UNESCO, 2021).

The application of this convention in China is complicated. Presently, no national law on "world heritage" has been passed, but there is a national law on "cultural heritage" protection. In addition, in April 2002, the Opinions on Strengthening and Enhancing the Administering of the World Heritage Protection was jointly announced by nine ministries.[13] In November 2006, the Ministry of Culture passed the Administering Methods on Protection of World Cultural Heritage, as announced in the No.41 Ministerial Order. It is interesting to point out that there are also provincial legal rules on "world heritage" protection, such as The World Heritage Protection Rules of Sichuan Province, which was adopted by the Standing Committee of Sichuan Province People's Congress in 2002 and revised in 2015.

The 2003 ICH Convention and Its Application in China

The ICH Convention was adopted at the UNESCO 32nd General Conference on October 17, 2003, which expanded the types of cultural heritage that qualify for protection to include *intangible* cultural heritage, such as oral traditions, performing arts, social practices, rituals, festive events, traditional knowledge, practices concerning nature and the universe (cosmology), and the knowledge and skills to produce traditional crafts. According to the current director-general of UNESCO Madam Audrey Azoulay, "Cultural heritage is not only about the buildings and monuments of the past—it is also about the rich traditions that have been passed down the generations."[14] Before the 2003 ICH Convention, there was no binding multilateral legal force in the international community, except for UNESCO's Proclamation of Masterpieces of the Oral and Intangible Heritage of Humanity program, which in 2001, 2003, and 2005 designated a total of ninety forms of intangible heritage around the world as Masterpieces. China ratified this convention on December 2, 2004, and then the NPC accordingly passed the Intangible Cultural Heritage Law on February 25, 2011.

World Intellectual Property Organization

China is a contracting party among five of the eight World Intellectual Property Organization (WIPO) administered copyright treaties and has signed one treaty.

The 1886 Berne Convention was the first multilateral treaty on the protection of copyright. China approved the 1971 version of the Paris Act on July 10, 1992, and it entered into effect on October 10, 1992. This treaty was approved a year after China enacted a specific copyright law in 1991. Prior to this, the protection of copyright was under the 1986 General Principles of Civil Law. The fact that China joined WIPO in 1980 affirms that these laws were affected to some extent by WIPO-administered treaties including the 1997 criminal law code.

Table 14.1. WIPO-Administered Copyright Treaties China Signed, Ratified, or Accessed[1]

Treaty	Signature	Instrument	In Force
Beijing Treaty on Audiovisual Performances	June 26, 2012	Ratification: July 9, 2014	April 28, 2020
Berne Convention for the Protection of Literary and Artistic Works		Accession: July 10, 1992	October 15, 1992
Geneva Convention for the Protection of Producers of Phonograms Against Unauthorized Duplication of Their Phonograms		Accession: January 5, 1993	April 30, 1993
Marrakesh Treaty to Facilitate Access to Published Works for Persons Who Are Blind, Visually Impaired, or Otherwise Print Disabled	June 28, 2013		
WIPO Copyright Treaty (WCT)		Accession: March 9, 2007	June 9, 2007
WIPO Performance and Phonograms Treaty (WPPT)		Accession: March 9, 2007	June 9, 2007

1. Data accessed from the WIPO official website,(WIPO Administered Treaties, 2021)

According to the Supreme Court's judicial case database, there have been four judgments applied to the 1886 Berne Convention after January 1, 2014 (Judgment Document; The Supreme People's Court of the People's Republic of China, 2021). These cases involved different Chinese and foreign parties' rights granted in China, Japan, and the United States. As a caveat, these are likely not all of the cases involving the application of the convention because the online database of the Supreme Court only goes as far back as 2014.

Beijing Treaty on Audiovisual Performances

The 2012 Beijing Treaty on Audiovisual Performances supports the moral and economic rights of performers including: the right of reproduction, the right of distribution, the right of rental, and the right to make accessible. For those performers whose performances are unfixed,[15] three types of economic rights are protected: the right of broadcasting (except in the case of rebroadcasting), the right of communication to the public (except where the performance is a broadcast performance), and the right of fixation. The term of protection is at least fifty years, and all the above-mentioned rights were regulated by the 2010 amended copyright law and maintained in the 2020 amended copyright law.[16]

Trade-Related Aspects of Intellectual Property Rights

The Trade-Related Aspects of Intellectual Property Rights (TRIPS) agreement entered into effect on January 1, 1995. Considering the fact that the World Trade Organization (WTO) has 164 members, TRIPS profoundly influences the regulation of intellectual property rights protection and enforcement throughout the world. To date, forty-two TRIPS cases have been "complained" in the WTO, of which China was the target of a "complaint" in four of those cases (World Trade Organization, 2010). In comparison, the United States faced complaints in four cases, while the European Union has seen five complaint cases. Of the four cases in which a complaint was lodged against China, one remains in consultation procedure, one is in panel procedure, one was withdrawn, and only one was ruled upon, the DS362 case, China – Intellectual Property Rights.

The DS362 case was brought by the United States for alleged violations of trademark and copyright protection rules on April 10, 2007 (World Trade Organization, 2021). The panel concluded on January 26, 2009, "To the extent that the Copyright Law and the Customs measures as such are inconsistent with the TRIPS Agreement, they nullify or impair benefits accruing to the United States under that Agreement, and recommended that China bring the Copyright Law and the Customs measures into conformity with its obligations under the TRIPS Agreement" (World Trade Organization, 2021). On the copyright law issue, the panel concluded the following:

> (1) the Copyright Law, specifically the first sentence of Article 4, is inconsistent with China's obligations under:
> (i) Article 5(1) of the Berne Convention (1971), as incorporated by Article 9.1 of the TRIPS Agreement; and
> (ii) Article 41.1 of the TRIPS Agreement.[17]

China was asked to change "the first sentence of Article 4," which led to this result in the WTO implementation procedure:

> On 19 March 2010, China reported that on February 26, 2010, the Standing Committee of the 11th National People's Congress had approved the amendments of the Chinese Copyright Law and that on March 17, 2010, the State Council had adopted the decision to revise the Regulations for Customs Protection of Intellectual Property Rights ("China—Measures Affecting the Protection and Enforcement of Intellectual Property Rights," 2010).

This case and other WTO cases are good examples where international law arguably worked as intended.

NATIONAL LAW

The 2011 Intangible Cultural Heritage Law of the People's Republic of China

The Standing Committee of the NPC adopted the Intangible Cultural Heritage Law of the People's Republic of China in 2011. Prior to this law, the Regulations on Protection of Traditional Arts and Crafts, which was approved by the State Council in 1997 and revised in 2013, was the only regulation that dealt with cultural heritage protection. While the regulation underscored the need for the protection of cultural heritage, its subject matter was limited to handcrafts and their techniques.[18] According to the Legislative Explanation on the Draft of ICH law presented to the Standing Committee of the NPC on August 23, 2010, this law was needed to meet the necessary obligations of the 2003 ICH Convention and resulted in six types of protected heritage: 1) traditional oral literature and the language as a vehicle thereof; 2) traditional fine arts, calligraphy, music, dance, drama, quyi, and acrobatics; 3) traditional techniques, medicine, and calendar; 4) traditional rituals, festivals, and other folk customs; 5) traditional sports and entertainment; 6) other intangible cultural heritages. The law endows the state, the State Council, and local governments with different obligations to protect intangible cultural heritage, and establishes national and local lists for heritage preservation. Among the 1,372 items on the national list, 401 fall into the traditional music catalog, comprising up to 29.2 percent of the ten total catalogs, which indicates the importance of *music* as a form of cultural heritage in China ("List of Representative Items of National Intangible Cultural Heritage," 2021). Recently it has also been proposed that digital technologies should be applied in the archiving and categorization of musical heritage (Zhan and Zhou, 2014).

Copyright Law Relating to Intangible Cultural Heritage

Copyright is protected by the Civil Law Code enacted from January 1, 2021, which replaced the General Principles of Civil Law enacted on January 1, 1987. The current copyright law (from 1991) has been amended three times, in 2001, 2010, and 2020.

Intangible Music Cultural Heritage Protection

Copyright protection is applicable in some cases to intangible cultural heritage, which includes musical heritage. One case concerned with folk music protection ended in 2003, setting an important precedent for distinctions between expressions of folklore and adapted works. The case concerned Mr.

Guo Song, a musician who was sued by Sipai Hezhezu Township People's Government of Raohe County, Heilongjiang Province, and appealed and lost again on the plaintiff's main claims.[19] The Hezhezu are an ethnic group with a total population of only around five thousand people.[20] They are well-known for their distinctive traditional life of fishing and hunting, as well as rich folk songs that describe their lifestyle. Specifically, this case involved a folk song melody titled "Xiang Qinglang" and another song with a similar melody "Shouliede Gege Huilaile" from the 1950s.[21] When Guo Song visited and investigated folk music in the Hezhezu in 1962, he found different popular melodies such as "Xiang Qinglang." Based on that melody, he composed the song "Wusuli Chuange."[22] According to the file in the Central Radio Station, where the song was first recorded in 1963, the creator of this song was labeled "Northeast Hezhezu Folk Song," and the performer was indicated as "Guo Song of Heilongjiang Chorus."[23] When this song was published in 1964, similar credits were indicated, "recomposed by Wang Yuncai, Guo Song." The dispute arose in 1999 when Guo Song attended a performance and the TV presenter declared that the song was produced and composed by Guo Song, despite it having long been regarded as a Hezhezu folk song. Both parties recognized the conclusion from the Music Copyright Society of China, even though the introductory part and the coda were composed. Therefore, the song is regarded as "adapted" music instead of a newly composed work.[24]

There are two key legal issues in this case. First, is the local town government entitled to initiate the case for the protection of Hezhezu intangible music heritage? Second, is the melody of "Wusuli Chuange" adapted from the Hezhezu melody? As for the first issue, the judgment in the first case recognized that the local government is entitled to sue in its name against those who infringe on the copyright of works of folk literature and art connected with local heritage. The main reasons for this judgment are: (1) works of folk literature and art are jointly owned by all the individuals of the Hezhezu ethnic group and do not belong to any individual; and (2) the local town government is both the political representative and the public interest representative of the ethnic group. As for the second issue, the judgment in the first case ruled that the song is adapted from the Hezhezu folk song, according to the Music Copyright Society of China. The judgment was reaffirmed by the appeals court and the case ended.

This case is typical for folk music under intangible cultural heritage protection since there are various forms of folk music and adaptations (or arrangements). Hence, it is fair to recognize both the folk songs and the creative contribution of the adapted work. The adapted work author's copyright is protected under the law. For example, Mr. Wang Luobin was famous for his collection, "King of Western China Songs," in which he adapted western

Chinese folk songs. After his death, his son, Mr. Wang Haicheng, entrusted the right of performance, the right of broadcasting, and the rights to recording and distribution to the Music Copyright Society of China. When a company distributed the recorded work of his music without paying royalties, he successfully sued.[25]

Local Opera and Traditional Image Intangible Cultural Heritage Protection

Besides folk music cases, there are other relevant types of disputes concerning copyright protection of intangible cultural heritage. This includes, for example, local opera as intangible cultural heritage, and local workmanship as intangible cultural heritage. In a case in 2011, the court ruled that the name of an opera is not protected in fiction work according to copyright law, even if the opera itself is protected as intangible cultural heritage. Movie director Mr. Zhang Yimou distributed his movie *Riding Alone for Thousands of Miles* in 2005 and used "Anshun Dixi," from an Anshun local opera, but instead called it "Mask Opera of Yunnan China." Anshun Dixi was put on the list of national intangible cultural heritage in June 2006. So, Mr. Zhang Yimou and the movie company were sued for infringement of the right of authorship. After two instances of procedure, both courts ruled the right of authorship of the Anshun Dixi was not infringed upon, since the Anshun Dixi itself is neither the subject nor the object of the right of authorship.[26]

In 2017, the Supreme Court took up the "No. 80 leading case" recognizing that derivative works based on folk literature and art are protected by copyright law.[27] Mr. Hong Fuyuan had designed batik (cloth dying) for many years and was formally designated a "Top Ten Folk Artist and Outstanding Individual on Intangible Cultural Heritage Protection" by the Ministry of Culture. He produced a work "Hexie Gongsheng Shier," ("Twelve Harmonious Coexistence") published in Fuyuan Batik Arts. The Wufufang Company later modified and used this image, without permission, on their packaged booklet of commercial products. The court ruled that the derivative works of Mr. Hong Fuyuan are protected by copyright law and as a result, Mr. Hong Fuyuan was compensated. Similarly, *Huangmei Tiaohua* is also a kind of workmanship listed on National Intangible Cultural Heritage since 2006. When a company infringed the copyright of fourteen kinds of images of the intangible cultural heritage, it was sanctioned and fined by Hubei Province Copyright Administration.[28] These cases set precedents that may prove relevant to future cases of music heritage including traditional musical instruments.

Neighboring Right Protection

Neighboring Right Protection ensures that performers, record producers, or broadcasting institutions are protected. The performer's right and the right of performance are treated differently. The latter refers to the right enjoyed by the author of a work. In the intangible cultural heritage area, many performers are not the original authors of folk songs, dances, opera, rituals, but rather are skillful performers of these genres. For example, there is a famous traditional dance called *Nuo Wu*, a ghost dance to pray for fortunes and drive away plagues. Since this is a historic dance, the exact time of its origination is untraceable. However, an early written record can be found in the *Lunyu Xiangdang, Analects of Confucius* (2004), which is more than 2,500 years old. The different forms of Nuo Wu can be found in many provinces. As a result, Nuo Wu has been listed in the national intangible cultural heritage protection index since 2006. The protection extends to sixty-seven items of Nuo Wu and is combined with other rituals on the national list ("List of Representative Items of National Intangible Cultural Heritage," 2021).

Local Regulations and Rules, Ministerial Rules, and Policy

At the lowest level in the hierarchy of the legal system in China are the local regulations and rules and ministerial rules. Although there are several notifications on the national list announced by the State Council on intangible cultural heritage protection, the State does not specifically regulate them. As mentioned above, local regulations and rules, and the ministerial rules are coequal in their legal authority in the Chinese legislative system. Local regulations and rules relate to specific situations in the provinces and focus on the protection of intangible cultural heritage within their specific jurisdictions. Ministerial rules, on the other hand, extend to broader geographical areas and are more specific in terms of provisions compared to national law. As of 2021, there were sixty-six local regulations and rules for intangible cultural protection in mainland China. Among these sixty-six local regulations and rules, twenty-nine were at the provincial level and others were at the city or autonomous county level. In some areas, (e.g., Tibet), local regulations seek to ensure cultural eco-protection.[29] The Ministry of Culture and Tourism is tasked with enforcing ministerial rules on intangible cultural heritage protection, and three ministerial rules in this area have been promulgated since 2006.[30] In other countries, Chinese embassies often use folk music to promote cross-cultural communication between China and other nations as a form of cultural diplomacy.

CONCLUSION

The basic elements of cultural protection and development in China are chiefly defined by the legal framework of the Chinese constitution and the legislation law, the judgment of the international court or domestic courts, and the practice of government policy. China's long historical record, its numerous ethnic groups, and vast geographic differences reflect its cultural diversity. The constitution, international treaties, national laws, and local laws provide an interactive framework to support both tangible and intangible cultural heritage, which may function as a foundation for cultural diplomacy.

NOTES

1. For general information on legal cases, please see the Supreme People's Court Work Report, Zui Gao Ren Min Fa Yuan Gong Zuo Bao Gao, made by the Chief Justice to the National People's Congress in the 2021 report on the official website of the Supreme People's Court (Chief Justice Zhou, 2020).
2. Legislation law establishes rules surrounding how law itself is developed and interpreted, particularly at different levels of jurisdiction (e.g., national vs. local).
3. Article 87, Legislation Law of the People's Republic of China (中华人民共和国立法法), 2015 Amendment.
4. The last paragraph of the preface of Constitution of the People's Republic of China (中华人民共和国宪法), 2018 Amendment.
5. Article 5, Constitution of the People's Republic of China, 2018 Amendment.
6. Article 100, Constitution of the People's Republic of China, 2018 Amendment.
7. Article 7, Legislation Law of the People's Republic of China, 2015 Amendment.
8. Ibid.
9. Ibid.
10. Article 65, Legislation Law of the People's Republic of China, 2015 Amendment.
11. Article 26, Vienna Convention on the Law of Treaties, 1969.
12. The case of Application of the Convention on the Prevention and Punishment of the Crime of Genocide, 1993 and 1999; the case of Temple of Preah Vihear, 2011.
13. The nine ministries were Ministry of Culture, Administration of Cultural Heritages, National Planning Committee, Ministry of Finance, Ministry of Education, Ministry of Construction, Ministry of Land and Resources, Administration of Environment Protection, and Administration of Forestry.
14. See the foreword of "Basic Texts of the 2003 Convention for the Safeguarding of the Intangible Cultural Heritage" (Azoulay, 2020).
15. The term "unfixed" here refers to performances that are at least semi-improvisatory, or not fully transcribed as a definitive version.
16. See Judgment Document, 2021.

17. See the WTO panel report, WT/DS362/R, para. 8.1.

18. According to Article 2 of the regulation, "Traditional arts and crafts used in these Regulations refer to a variety of handicrafts and techniques that have existed for over one hundred years and marked by a long history, exquisite skills, have been passed on from generation to generation, have a complete technical process, have been made of natural materials, have a distinct national style and local features, and are renowned both at home and abroad."

19. Guo Song, et al. v. Sipai Hezhezu Township People's Government of Raohe County, Heilongjiang Province (case of copyright infringement).

20. See the population numbers on the State Council's official website, which may be altered according to updated statistics (Cao, 2021).

21. "Xiang Qinglang" translates as "Missing My Beau," "Shouliede Gege Huilaile" translates as "My Brother Came Back after Hunting."

22. "Wusuli Chuange" translates as "Wusuli River Chanty."

23. *Guo Song, et al.* (case of copyright infringement).

24. *Guo Song, et al.* (case of copyright infringement).

25. Wang Haicheng, et al. v. Three Gorges Co., Dasheng Co., Guangdong Audio-visual Communication Co., Liansheng Co., and Nanchang Department Store (copyright infringement).

26. An Shun Culture and Sports Bureau v. New Picture Company and Mr. Yimou Zhang (copyright infringement).

27. Leading Case No.80: Fuyuan Hong v. Guizhou Wufufang Food Company Ltd and Guizhou Jincai Ethnic Cultural Research and Development (copyright infringement).

28. See https://www.ip1840.com/case/nonphysical/11625.html, accessed June 15, 2021.

29. See Xizang Autonomous Region's Methods on Enactment of Intangible Cultural Heritage Protection Law.

30. The Temporal Methods on Protection and Administering of National Intangible Cultural Heritage 2006, the Recognition and Ademinstering Methods on the National Representative Bearers of Intangible Cultural Heritage 2008, and the Administering Methods on National Eco-Cultural Protection Area 2019.

REFERENCES

Azoulay, Audrey. 2020. "Foreword." In *Basic Texts of the 2003 Convention for the Safeguarding of the Intangible Cultural Heritage*. Accessed March 20, 2022. https://ich.unesco.org/doc/src/2003_Convention_Basic_Texts-_2020_version-EN.pdf.

Cao, Xiaoxuan. 2021. "He Zhe Zu. Official webpage of Chinese Central Government. Accessed September 29. http://www.gov.cn/guoqing/2015-09/24/content_2938147.htm.

Chief Justice Zhou, Qiang. 2020. "The Supreme People's Court Work Report" [Zui Gao Ren Min Fa Yuan Gong Zuo Bao Gao (最高人民法院工作报告)]. http://www.court.gov.cn/zixun-xiangqing-290831.html.

———. 2010. "China—Measures Affecting the Protection and Enforcement of Intellectual Property Rights." Accessed November 12, 2021. https://www.wto.org/english/tratop_e/dispu_e/cases_e/ds362_e.htm.

Gao, Xinran. 2021. "Report on the Meeting of 'Chinese Music Heritage Map.'" *Journal of Central Conservatory of Music*: 159.

Judgment Document-The Supreme People's Court of the People's Republic of China. 2021. Accessed November 12, 2021. http://www.court.gov.cn/paper/default/index/page/2.html.

Li Ji (*Book of Rites*) (礼记). 2019. Changsha, China: Yue Lu Shu She Press (岳麓书社).

"List of Representative Items of National Intangible Cultural Heritage." 2021. China Intangible Cultural Heritage Network · China Intangible Cultural Heritage Digital Museum [Zhōngguó fēi wùzhí wénhuà yíchǎn wǎng· shùzì bówùguǎn (中国非物质文化遗产网·字博物馆)]. Accessed November 12. http://www.ihchina.cn/project#target1.

Lunyu (The Analects)(论语). 2004. Changsha, China: Yue Lu Shu She Press (岳麓书社).

People's Republic of China-Treaty Database. 2021. Accessed June 15. http://treaty.mfa.gov.cn/web/index.jsp.

"The Supreme People's Court of the People's Republic of China." 2021. The Supreme People's Court Of The People's Republic Of China. Accessed November 12. http://english.court.gov.cn/.

UNESCO World Heritage Centre. 2021. "China." UNESCO World Heritage Centre. Accessed September 29. http://whc.unesco.org/en/statesparties/cn.

Wang, Zichu. 2012. "Ten Discoveries in Music Archaeology in China," *Journal of Xinghai Conservatory of Music* 2: 34–49.

WIPO Administered Treaties. 2021. Accessed September 29. https://wipolex.wipo.int/en/treaties/ShowResults?country_id=38C.

"World Trade Organization." 2021. WTO. Accessed September 29. https://www.wto.org/english/tratop_e/dispu_e/cases_e/ds362_e.htm.

Zhan, Yihong and Yucheng Zhou. 2014. "Zhong Guo Min Jian Yin Yue Lei Fei Wu Zhi Wen Hua Yi Chan Fen Lei Yan Jiu" ("Research on the Categorizing of Chinese Folk Music Intangible Cultural Heritage"). *Journal of Hubei University for Nationalities* (Philosophy and Social Sciences) 32, no. 3: 24–27, 57.

Zhang, Juzhong, Xinghua Xiao, and Yun Kuen Lee. 2004. "The Early Development of Music. Analysis of the Jiahu Bone Flutes." *Antiquity* 78, no. 302: 769–78.

6

CONCLUSION: RETHINKING MUSIC HERITAGE AND CULTURAL DIPLOMACY

Chapter Fifteen

Toward Global Models and Benchmarks for Music Diplomacy

David G. Hebert and Jonathan McCollum

At present, the field of ethnomusicology, and by extension related disciplines such as musicology, music education, cultural anthropology, etc. sits at a crossroads, where scholars today are rethinking the field's historical role in the perpetuation of Western-centric power and privilege. Indeed, the 2020 Society for Ethnomusicology annual conference began with a preconference symposium, "Decolonizing strategies in ethnomusicology, teaching, and performance: Perspectives from the U.S. Southwest and Latin America," which underscored that "Decolonization is an ongoing project, with the complexities and tensions of the word, and the different epistemologies produced when used in different languages." But what does it really mean to decolonize knowledge in a globalized world where information has never before been so quite literally at our fingertips?

This book is concerned with music's role in cultural diplomacy, but it simultaneously offers an illuminating angle from which we may consider cultural diplomacy's aims and prospective role for decolonizing knowledge in the field of ethnomusicology. Recognition of an immediate need to decolonize ethnomusicological knowledge requires that we share the intellectual landscape with the communities we study not as subjects, but as collaborators, and become activists in the support of marginalized communities and for those scholars who teach and research in universities outside of Western Europe and North America. Maurits Berger (2008) underscores this complex, but necessary goal, stating that "cultural policy demands that one enters a relationship on the basis of equality and reciprocity" and "demands a genuine interest in the other: where does it stand, what does it think, and why does it think that way?" (6). The present volume, which purposefully includes voices of scholars from around the globe, including China, Ethiopia, India, Iran, Japan, Nigeria, Norway, South Africa, Sweden, Syria, the United

States, Uzbekistan, and Vietnam hopes to play a small part in demonstrating how ethnomusicology may prioritize indigenous voices, reconsider and reshape musical canons in more equitable and thoughtful ways, and illustrate how musical expressions break down walls, build bridges, and create diverse opportunities for the creation of collectively-just communities.

Given the examples presented in this volume, it is evident that both historical and present-day modes of cultural diplomacy worldwide have, and continue to make, expedient use of performative genres for a variety of political aims. Although one argument we make in this chapter is that the term "music diplomacy" merits broad acceptance as an appropriate way for explaining this phenomenon, we also seek to offer deeper descriptions of its components and mechanisms through cross-cultural analysis and synthesis of essential features from diverse cases of music diplomacy. Finally, we offer recommendations for the various stakeholders in this and related fields.

TYPOLOGY OF MUSIC DIPLOMACY CONTEXTS

Music diplomacy occurs in diverse forms and among diverse actors, but some of the major categories include ensembles and artists, and intercultural music institutions, which are shaped by forms of governance and individual activism, as we explain below.

Music Ensembles and Artists

Music diplomacy can take place within the artistry between musicians in intercultural music ensembles—such as the Six Tones Vietnamese-Swedish ensemble—who sensitively respond as they deeply "listen to the Other" to develop shared creative expressions across a substantial cultural and musical divide (Östersjö, 2020). Specifically, the ensemble reports that "we understand cultural diplomacy in music as a matter of musicians tuning their ears to the Other, seeking intersubjective understanding, also across culturally defined ways of listening." Furthermore, they argue that the Six Tones negotiate a shared understanding through the listening process with an "inversed ear" with respect to intercultural practice. Therefore, they hope to use intercultural musicianship to "create change, both in individuals, in institutions, and eventually, potentially also in nations" (chapter 9). In Afghanistan, Zohra's performances develop "a unique sound which is achieved by blending traditional Afghan and Hindustani Classical instruments—the *rubāb*, *tanbur*, *dutar*, *tabla*, and *sitar*—with Western classical orchestral instruments," mostly with music "arranged and orchestrated by the school's international faculty" (chapter 3). In its many international tours, the ensemble "always extends a musical olive branch to their audiences by playing a specially arranged piece of music from their host country: in Sweden, a medley of ABBA songs; in the United Kingdom, *Greensleeves*; and in India, the Bollywood classic *Meera Joota Hai Japani*." Indeed, within this diverse platform, music performance affirms and represents identities, while at the same time creating unity through diverse collaborations (chapter 3). The Music Confucius Institute was founded in 2012 in Copenhagen, and prior to its closure in 2020, which resulted from a proposal from The Royal Danish Academy of Music, it regularly developed "many projects with composers for contemporary music creation" (chapter 7). According to their mission, one of its most important activities was the promotion of intercultural artistic collaboration between China and Denmark, which enabled European composers to access professional-level players of Chinese instruments. Political tensions between Western powers and China, combined with conservative political organizations, have promulgated negative media attention on Confucius Institutes. Despite this, Marianne Løkke Jakobsen and David G. Hebert conclude that negative perceptions of Confucius Institutes "are related to the Western world having a rather fixed focus on general power relations between East and West rather than the actual quality of CI activities." This situation may be recognized as part of a broader phenomenon whereby China's approach to public diplomacy increasingly promotes the notion that its major international projects are to be recognized as Chinese "gifts" to the world" (d'Hooghe, 2021), while diverging interpretations are promoted by a range of sceptics (2015). Matsunobu also reports on a Cultural Envoy program administered by Japan's Ministry of Culture that led to the "co-creation of cultural hybrid" music projects featuring Japanese traditional instruments outside of Japan, while acknowledging that "teachers of traditional Japanese music often experience a gap between the Japanese teaching methods" and a "more "understanding-oriented" pedagogy requested by non-Japanese students" (chapter 8).

On the other hand, complicated approaches to fusion between disparate musical and cultural sources can also be seen in the work of Iranian music ensemble, Safir-e Eshgh, as described in chapter 6, which combines a Western power-pop anthem style offering praise for the supreme leader on their homepage with a quote: "Deeply understanding cultural concepts, both for the people and authorities, while increasing their awareness can prevent from cultural cracks and this is one of the most important characteristics of a right cultural activity" [*sic*]. Futhermore, they offer praise of Khomeini in their song, *Qalb-e Ārām* (Calm Heart). While music and other cultural activities used in cultural diplomacy potentially cultivate positive transnational and intercultural domestic relationships, the example above reminds us that the use of cultural expressions as propaganda remains a component of many of these diplomatic efforts. However, creative fusions can ultimately lead to the establishment of entirely new genres, as seen with the Haile Selassie I Theatre Orchestra, which combined global jazz with Ethiopian sounds that heavily influenced Ethiopian popular music. This set the stage that would lead to the development of the rich art of Ethio-Jazz by the contributions of Mulatu Astatke and others (described in chapter 10). We see similar trends in various South African genres such as Afro-Pop, which was promoted by Johnny Clegg and, to some extent, the multilinguistic, pan-African gospel a cappella performed by the Soweto Gospel Choir and Lagos City Chorale in Nigeria, as discussed in chapters 11 and 12, respectively. Ambigay Yudkoff writes that "Clegg harnessed the power of western folk and rock music with the vitality of Zulu songs and dance" and "his fluency in Zulu and Clegg's mastery of the highly energetic Zulu dances impressed African audiences in South Africa. International audiences were drawn to Clegg's African-inspired music—with strong folk and rock elements— and the spectacular choreography of his performances" (chapter 11). In chapter 12, Rhoda Abiolu provides a potent example of how cross-cultural performance may unite by describing how the use of costumes informs cultural diversity in the performance of the song "Jehova Emewo." Here, performers wore Yorùbá outfits while singing in the Igbo language (chapter 12).

Intercultural Music Institutions

Entire institutions have been established for music diplomacy, such as the Music Confucius Institute in Copenhagen described above (chapter 7). Other types of institutions have also given rise to music ensembles devoted to cultural diplomacy. Indeed, from the 1950s and 1960s jazz ambassadors, who toured the world perpetuating American popular culture, to the Live Aid concert to raise funds for the 1980s famine in Ethiopia, the practice of creating large-scale diplomatic performances attained prominence in the twentieth century. In the case of the Zohra Orchestra, which was established in Kabul in 2015 within the sphere of the Afghanistan National Institute of Music, the ensemble was created to highlight women's abilities and potential in Afghan society. Having performed at the World Economic Forum and toured the United Kingdom and Australia, its members work as ambassadors to change global perceptions of their homeland (chapter 3). Sadly, given the fall of Afghanistan to the Taliban in the summer of 2021, one can only guess what public activities, if any, this orchestra may enjoy in the future. Music festivals, such as Uzbekistan's spectacular international event Sharq Taronalari, can also function as another kind of "soft power" institution. Held every two years in Samarkand, the festival's goals and objectives are to "popularize, preserve, and develop the best achievements of national musical art; to educate of the younger generation about national traditions; and further expand international creative ties," which certainly qualify as music diplomacy, with powerful effects that linger despite their fleeting seasonal existence (chapter 4). Music is also interculturally disseminated through lifelong learning, outside formal educational institutions, as seen in the case of North Americans learning traditional *shakuhachi* flute from Japan through special tours tailored to fit their interests (chapter 8). Finally, it is plausible that even small efforts to broaden Western music curriculum, to include such topics as the influence of Arab-Islamic culture on Western art music, can positively impact attitudes, contributing in a modest way to improved relations between Western nations and the Middle East. Citing historical sources such as *La Escatologia Musulmana en la Divina Comedia*, which was inspired by "the Islamic night journey (Levitation) [*al-'Isra wal-Mi'rag*] of Prophet Muhammad to the seven heavens" and *Ḥayy ibn Yaqẓān* [*The Improvement of Human Reason: Exhibited in the Life of Hai Ebn Yokdhan*] by Sufi Ibn Tufail (1110–1185), which was widely read during the Age of Enlightenment, Chaden Yafi calls for a rethinking of the Western music history narrative (chapter 5).

Forms of Governance

Some governments actively promote the use of music in cultural diplomacy through programs with targeted aims for either internal social cohesion or external international relations. For Karan Choudhary, in India (chapter 13), music has traditionally been perceived as inseparable from spirituality, and with such a view it is less likely to be reduced to a tool within a deliberate governance strategy: "Sounds are god . . . they are as close as we get to the god." On the other hand, music diplomacy can ebb and flow with different historical eras and political regimes, as seen in the case of Ethiopia, where the authors claim that the previous governments of Haile Selassie and the Derg used cultural expressions as tools for political gains through cultural policy. Although they conclude that the federal parliamentary government has placed a priority on multiculturalism "by incorporating the rights of all ethnic groups in its Constitution," they contend that although "cultural rights, equality, and sustainable development have become widespread within cultural policy documents in recent times, the actual conceptual and operational implications often remain vague" (chapter 10). Among the cases discussed in this book, it is especially clear that Uzbekistan and China fully recognize the value of music as a tool for international diplomacy and invest relatively well in this area. Uzbekistan's state-sponsored music festivals, described by *Global Times* (2019) as among "the most significant music events in Central Asia," are unusually impressive and attract much international attention, while China has in recent years especially expanded knowledge of its cultural traditions through its Confucius Institute related programs that have been the subject of much critical discussion. Although Japan has also deeply invested into arts diplomacy since the early 1980s, even referred to as a "soft power superpower" in the early 2000s (see Watanabe and McConnell, 2008), in recent times, its prominence seems to have become eclipsed by China (see Blanchard and Lu, 2012; Zhang, 2012; and Nye, 2013). Some countries, such as Iran, Afghanistan, and Ethiopia have recognized music as potentially so culturally and politically threatening as to require severe restrictions at various points in their history (see, for example, Baily, 1994; Semati, 2017). As Yafi explained, "Both culture and politics are powers: The first aims to connect, the second to control" (chapter 5). Still, sometimes music manages to transcend politics, even in places where it was repressed such as during the Derg, for in Ethiopia today popular music mostly serves to unify diverse peoples within a single state.

Individual Activism

Entire individual careers, as seen in the work of Sharon Katz (b. 1955), leader of the "Peace Train," which promoted reconciliation in post-Apartheid South Africa (Yudkoff, 2021), is also discussed in chapter 11 alongside other visionaries including Miriam Makeba (1932–2008), Hugh Masekela (1939–2018), and Johnny Clegg (1953–2019), all of whom may be understood as devoted to using music as a means for cultural diplomacy. The same may be said of the visionary founders and leaders of some of the institutions and ensembles highlighted in this book as notable examples of music diplomacy, who have successfully maneuvered between complex political forces, including leaders of the Zohra Orchestra in Afghanistan, the Sharq Taronalari festival in Uzbekistan, the Music Confucius Institute in Copenhagen, and others. We hope that readers of this book may ultimately be inspired to forge new forms of music diplomacy that meet new challenges in various communities worldwide, and to that end it is helpful to consider the social institutions that serve as a foundation to music diplomacy possible.

Law and Cultural Policy as Foundations of Music Diplomacy

Legal Foundations of Artistry

Many important questions concerning the legal bases for cultural policy and diplomacy have arisen throughout this volume and three chapters explicitly discuss the legal frameworks relevant to music sustainability and intercultural exchange. Differing legal foundations are a concern of great importance from the perspective of decolonization, since "respect for the needs and beliefs of non-Western communities continues to lag behind and non-Western music remains unprotected and exploitable under the intellectual property laws of most Western nations" (Mills, 1996, 58). Chapter 2 considers relevant forms of international "soft law" that shape global relations in the cultural sphere, while chapters 13 and 14 examine the status of specific Asian legal traditions in relation to music. Specifically, Heimonen and Hebert ground our understanding of the important role of "soft law" initiatives in the formation of international agreements: "Understanding of music in cultural diplomacy requires recognition of diplomacy in multiple directions, not only how European and North American states use music to relate with other parts of the world, but also vice versa, how other countries use music as part of their outreach to 'the west' as well as in international relations that do not directly involve western countries" (chapter 2). They identify five pressing issues that reflect the complexity involved in analyzing the relationships between "soft law," music rights, and the rights of cultural bearers: (1) the cultural appropriation versus cultural approbation debate, (2) finding a middle ground between legal traditions, (3) acknowledging the evolution and sustainability of musical practices, (4) participatory rights in relation to music, and (5) interpretations of law versus cultural rights (chapter 2).

Choudhary (chapter 13) examines the legal framework of cultural policy in India, thoughtfully illustrating how it intersects with universal principles as a basis for international law and the constitution of India, and how the legal system ultimately impacts arts diplomacy. Specifically, Choudhary shows how the 1994 amendment of the Indian Copyright Act (originally from 1957) changes some of the conditions for music as intellectual property, including improved rights for singers and lyricists, and he explores the question of whether creative arrangements of traditional music, such as sixteenth-century *Ramcharitmanas*, can be protected by copyright. He notes the challenges of imperialism and postcolonialism while describing how music has played an important role in recent cultural diplomacy to help reduce tensions between the nuclear states of India and Pakistan.

Li (chapter 14) analyzes the legal framework in China for supporting the protection and sustainability of artistic heritage in relation to the hierarchy of the Chinese legal system, application of international treaties for the protection of cultural heritage, and the impact of national law on the protection of artistic heritage. Perceptive readers will likely understand why this kind of discussion matters, but we feel it should be made especially explicit, since, as evidenced from this volume, systems of governance may either enhance or restrict the impact of artistic diplomacy.

Music as Intellectual Property

Law and policies determine whether copyright systems are balanced so that artists receive proper credit and compensation for their work, but, at the same time, are sufficiently free to experiment with derivative forms. An imbalance in either direction hinders the work of artists by either constricting their creativity or inhibiting their opportunities to obtain sufficient financial rewards from their creative work. Ethnomusicologists have identified the Right to Access, Right to Steward, and Right to Control as essential cultural rights with particular relevance to music traditions (Trimillos, 2009, 34). Such concerns impact "ownership" to a corpus of shared cultural heritage associated with specific groups, including Indigenous and minority peoples.

Figure 15.1 illustrates the delicate situation for music as intellectual property today, contrasting how the development of creative processes is controlled by different approaches to copyright.

As we see in figure 15.1, on the one hand are concerns associated with artistic freedom, namely that the creative work of musicians needs sufficient

Artistic Freedom   **Ownership and Attribution**

Figure 15.1. Balance of Copyright Law. Developed by David Hebert and Zhengcui Guo.

space so they may develop arrangements and derivative works inspired by preexisting material, enjoying a range of artistic practices that fall under "fair use" for limited purposes. Such values have led to advocacy for the Creative Commons approach to intellectual property, as signified by "cc" to the left of the figure, by which artistic creation is treated rather "lightly" and relatively freely shared. On the other hand, the right side of the figure represents how musicians need to be sufficiently protected by copyright, depicted by artistic creation being "heavily" shielded behind a traditional copyright symbol. Through copyright, musicians control the right to copy and distribute their works and the right to monetize them, with values advocated by such entities as the International Federation of the Phonographic Industry. Here we should also acknowledge prominent international organizations like Freemuse, that are dedicated to ensuring that the human rights of musicians are respected, and their creative work faces minimal restrictions from political censorship.

Mechanisms of Music Diplomacy

Because music diplomacy appears in such diverse forms and contexts, it is difficult, if not impossible, to develop a robust theory to account for all its manifestations. Still, there are certain mechanisms associated with many forms of music diplomacy that are worth recognition and discussion. First, relevant legal foundations and policy frameworks, as previously described, establish the background from which one may envision music diplomacy projects. Effective laws and legislative policies ensure that there are realistic opportunities for musicians to devise cultural diplomacy projects to foster "enhanced mutual understanding, respect, and reconciliation" (chapter 1). If nation-states put into place suitable legal and policy frameworks, institutional stakeholders, including not only formal educational institutions but also relevant organizations, music festivals, NGOs and other entities will be able to work together under a unified goal. At the next level, there is a need for sources of funding, which are often facilitated directly through institutions, but in other cases may come from separate public or private individuals or organizations, often in combination. To be effective, music diplomacy can rarely succeed as a one-sided endeavor. In other words, it requires support from multiple parties with genuine and sustained efforts to minimize the challenges inherently associated with unequal power relations by ensuring disadvantaged partners are meaningfully represented in strategy development and decision making. This approach is relevant not only to the framework but to the artistry itself, which ideally is also collaborative in its approach to "cocreation."

Figure 15.2. Components of Music Diplomacy Initiatives. Developed by David Hebert and Zhengcui Guo.

Figure 15.2 illustrates the various entities that visionaries seeking to establish effective cultural diplomacy projects would do well to keep in mind.

International norms, policies, and laws comprise the bedrock for collaboration within any international cultural diplomacy projects. Prospective collaborators in two (or more) locations are likely situated within different systems of local and national laws that shape the relevant cultural policies in their respective locales. These differing policy systems inform how relevant cultural institutions operate, whether schools, museums, performance halls, or other organizations. The funders and managers of cultural institutions then directly contribute to the development of specific frameworks for the music diplomacy projects in which musicians operate. In order to be lasting and effective, music diplomacy is established with recognition of each of these key components, aligning with institutional values that may differ between the different partners.

Benchmarks for Music Diplomacy

Various institutions, ensembles, and government bodies might in some circumstances be prompted to reflect on their efficacy and impact in terms of music diplomacy initiatives. What reasonable basis for comparison might enable such entities to determine how well they are performing in this area relative to peers or self-determined objectives? In other words, if a municipality or school sought to reflect on its efficacy in terms of music diplomacy, how might they know where to begin the process? This is a complicated matter since there is such extreme diversity to consider vis-à-vis the kinds of entities that might seek to explore such a question, as well as the array of diverse activities that may qualify as music diplomacy. Still, certain variables may be worth systematic consideration relative to the context in question, and that call here for careful consideration.

To begin, it is essential to clarify stakeholders and objectives for the institution or specific project. Identification of relevant stakeholders requires a breadth of creative, interdisciplinary thinking, since there may be potentially viable entities in both public and private sectors that have long been dismissed as irrelevant to the institution or its projects (e.g., museums, music industry, NGOs, etc.). Many artists and institutions fail to recognize prospective stakeholders and thereby neglect to benefit from relevant resources, and some identify objectives that are either vague and mundane or too lofty, ill-defined, and unrealistic. For projects connected with the objective of peace and conflict alleviation, for instance, it is important to specify manageable yet significant steps that can realistically be attained (O'Connell and Castelo-Branco, 2010; Urbain, 2015). SMART, which stands for objectives that are *specific* (and/or strategic), *measurable* (and/or motivating), *achievable* (and/or agreed, ambitious, aligned), *relevant* (and/or realistic, resourced), and *testable* (and/or time-bound, trackable) represent one of the most widely used approaches in the field of project management (Doran, 1981). Similar leadership models based on mnemonic acronyms have also been proposed for PURE objectives and CLEAR objectives (Whitmore, 2017, 105). The point here is that if carefully designed, goals enable a project or institution to establish a clear sense of what it intends to achieve, and which actions are necessary to obtain that outcome. Artists and scholars who are engrossed in creative and theoretical work often find that their most brilliant visions remain unrealized due to practical impediments, so it can be worthwhile to explore project management strategies even if they may strike artists as oversimplistic or uninteresting compared to their creative work.

When it comes to diplomacy projects, the practical challenges are two-fold since they typically require not only the full support of one institution and its milieu but often also the equivalent in a very different cultural context. Diplomacy projects that are perceived as merely one-sided are unlikely to succeed across time since they may lead to indifference, subtle resistance, and even resentment from the less powerful (or less engaged) partner. Institutions with very different values may discover that a shared project might align for entirely different reasons than originally conceived. Therefore, careful diplomacy is needed to effectively explain to one partner why a project is useful for them while using a completely different explanation for the other partners. Of course, it is unethical to be deceptive in such a situation, but appealing for support based on the project's alliances with different institutional values may almost be understood as a form of translation relative to each unique context.

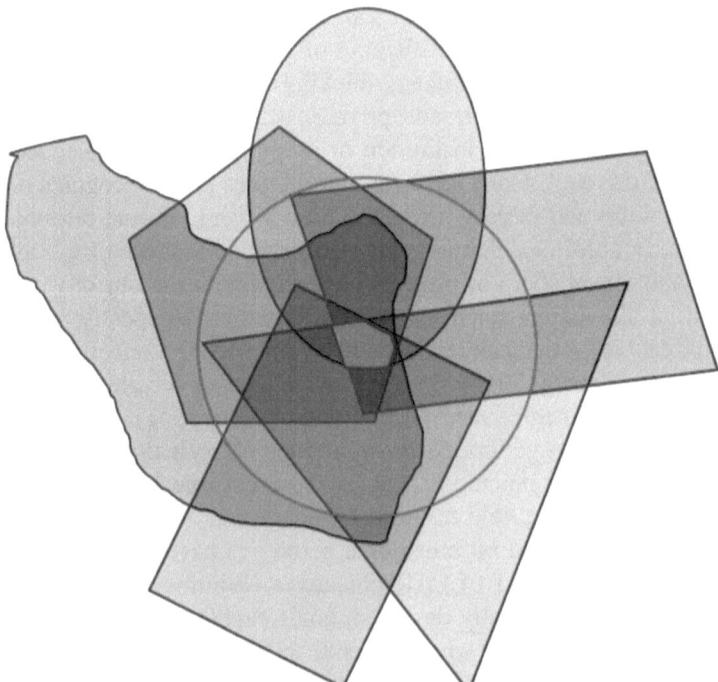

Figure 15.3. Core Project Values in Shifting Stakeholder Alignments. Developed by David Hebert and Zhengcui Guo.

As figure 15.3 illustrates, despite changing conditions, if planned well, the music diplomacy project's identity (round central shape) ideally remains relatively stable even while its core identity seeks to align with diverse institutional values.

Music diplomacy projects are impacted by how stakeholder involvement intersects in various situations (diverse rotating shapes). Such dynamic tensions between diverse actors inevitably make the management of music diplomacy an especially challenging endeavor, hence the need for more studies to firmly establish research-based practices in the field of music diplomacy.

Music Diplomacy in Research and Education

If we are to regard music diplomacy as a unified field—something akin to musical activism (Hess, 2019; Yudkoff, 2021) but absent any specific provocation or "cause"—what kinds of specialized skills are collectively needed to advance this field of study? Might future leaders in music diplomacy benefit from studies in project management and music law, for instance, as well as performance and pedagogy? Furthermore, how might indigenous modes of knowledge thereby gain legitimacy in higher education?

Decolonizing Knowledge in Ethnomusicological Discourse

Epistemological thought, scholarly endeavors, and pedagogical methodologies center around the concept of knowledge and how one shares it. But this very notion of "knowledge" as a cultural construct is complicated to unravel because one can safely argue that knowledge has, over the past six hundred years, been the purview of Europe and the last two hundred years, North America, and all at the expense and suppression of indigenous forms of knowledge and theoretical orientations. Perhaps the most important scholar in recent times to lay the groundwork for a rethinking of Colonial-centric orientations to knowledge was Palestinian American scholar Edward W. Said (1935–2003). His *Orientalism* (1978) was groundbreaking and made many necessarily uncomfortable because it laid bare the long-lasting hegemonic impact of Western explorers, travelers, missionaries, and scientists on Indigenous peoples, with particular emphasis on the imposition of Western modes of thinking, production, and the singular "truth" of knowledge, as defined by the West. Frantz Fanon (1925–1961), whose contributions to the Algerian revolution are well-known and his writings focusing on antiracism and anticolonialism, such as *Black Skin, White Masks* (*Peau noire, masques blancs*) in 1952 and *The Wretched of the Earth* (*Les damnés de la terre*) in 1961 also challenged the bedrock of colonial power.

Still, it is unfortunate that despite decades of efforts to uplift and bring to the fore marginalized people's voices, Indigenous forms of knowledge remain largely unknown or considered illegitimate in many academic disciplines because they do not necessarily conform to modes of inquiry perpetuated by Western universities and research institutes (Hunt, 2014, 29). We find that ethnomusicology, as an interdisciplinary field that involves performance, scholarship, and teaching, is in a unique position to contribute to recentering indigenous and marginalized people's epistemologies as part of the broader theoretical corpus of musical knowledge.

Therefore, ethnomusicologists must consider the relative strengths of indigenous epistemologies and modes of knowledge in the contexts of the histories and cultures where they formed, while at the same time, consider how the discipline of ethnomusicology might incorporate them into both preexisting and newly created theoretical orientations. Music diplomacy may entail the sincerest approach to decolonization that musicians and ethnomusicologists can offer in our globalized world, and we should be wary of overly theorizing the decolonization of knowledge. As Chávez and Skelchy (2019) note, "Part of the issue is that the impulse to theorize in ethnomusicology has contributed to the abstraction of decolonization from practical applications in teaching, research methodology, and ethnographic representation" (116). Ethnomusicology has the potential to "help marginalized groups reclaim their identities, even while more privileged European-heritage students develop cultural sensitivity, empathy, and humility through an attitude of open-mindedness and activism" (Coppola, Hebert, and Campbell, 2021, 10).

This volume represents a collaboration of scholars from around the world, some writing from war-torn countries, some writing as migrants or even former refugees. Collaborating on a scholarly volume such as this is not only a form of cultural diplomacy in its own right, but also represents a step toward decolonizing knowledge in the sense that the authors have challenged notions of how to listen, how to hear, how to perform, and importantly, how to think about music. Such work is not without its challenges, as the editors of such projects inevitably come to recognize, but in our view, the benefits compensate for the inconveniences. Here we outline our conclusions regarding how higher education might better accommodate future interests in developing the subfield of music diplomacy.

DECOLONIZED INTERCULTURAL RESEARCH METHODS

Future research in this area could proceed with the objective of deepening the understandings that we have begun to develop through the present book. This would require an approach that deliberately seeks to decolonize knowledge in this area while also aiming for the promotion of trustworthy foundations with the potential to contribute to research-based policy development and transparent and effective leadership. Decolonized research would ideally proceed with a collaborative orientation, placing as much value on objectives codetermined to be of immediate benefit to the peoples studied as on the desire to make a significant new contribution to global knowledge. From the cultural insider perspective, relevant concerns might include such questions as "How can we ensure this unique tradition, and its embodied knowledge, is appreciated and does not completely die away?" or "How can we explain cherished aspects of this heritage to the outside world in a way they will understand and that inspires their interest and support?" Keeping in mind that according to the UN Permanent Forum on Indigenous Issues, "It is estimated that there are more than 370 million indigenous people spread across 70 countries worldwide" (UN, 2015), we sense that Indigenous peoples, in particular, require empathetic recognition in this vision.

Decolonized Intercultural Music Education

What prospective role could, or should, music diplomacy play in *education*? Would it be sensible to develop courses or even programs in the field of music diplomacy, and if so, what might they entail? In *College Music Symposium*, American philosopher Kathleen Higgins (2018) produced arguments that seem especially illuminating and useful in relation to this theme. Based on recognition of music's "positive potential for promoting social harmony" Higgins proposed "four strategies for utilizing music to advance peace and other humanizing ends." These are described as follows:

> First, efforts should be made to promote engagement with music that helps develop receptivity, empathy, and other peacebuilding attitudes and skills. Second, music education should make efforts to pre-empt the tendency to identify music with "us" or with "them." Third, opportunities should be created for people to engage in "participatory performance," which can transform people from relative strangers into shared musical participants. Fourth, musical hybridization, in which elements of diverse kinds of music are utilized in new musical forms, should be fostered.

Higgins thereby illustrates how attention to these four objectives will enable music to be better connected to ethical foundations in the public sphere. One could certainly envision a curriculum that uses these points as its foundation, the first strand emphasizing project development and management, the second part fostering awareness of musical identities, the third concerned with developing skills for leadership of participatory music-making, and the fourth focusing on strategies for creative hybridity in music. Interestingly, what Higgins endorses here actually resembles what some in the field of music diplomacy have been striving to achieve in recent years, as well as those active in such education-related fields as world music pedagogy (Coppola, Hebert and Campbell, 2021). Various models have been proposed for how music studies might adopt a more global approach (Kertz-Welzel, 2018; Richerme, 2020), and in the field of music teacher education, there is growing recognition of the need for "music lessons that entail the promotion of *reconciliation* in the relationships between ethnic groups or nations that share a history of political tensions or even the hostility of armed conflict" (Hebert and Kertz-Welzel, 2016, 177). 31). Future developments should consider the growing importance of the internet and social media in music learning (Waldron, Horsley, and Veblen, 2020), as well as the altering trajectories of global influence that, for varying reasons, bring new nations and regions to the forefront of change (Ho, 2021). However, here it may also be useful to consider what Kim Boeskov calls "ambiguous musical practices" that run the risk of instilling "docile agency" through music diplomacy initiatives (2019, 116–19). In other words, a common paradox—one that requires careful attention from conscientious scholars and practitioners—is that music participation that contributes to desirable social transformation may nevertheless simultaneously sustain some unintended aspects of social reproduction. Since music diplomacy initiatives can be multifaceted and result in both intended and unintended consequences, leaders should ensure there is a critical approach to rigorous planning and robust evaluation.

CONCLUDING REMARKS

Using an ethnomusicological approach, we have endeavored through this book to demonstrate music in cultural diplomacy from an unprecedented orientation: music diplomacy in efforts taken by other nations to negotiate with Europe and North America. Our contributors have offered examples from many of the nations that in the West are most commonly regarded as problematic in terms of foreign relations, a number of which have experienced military conflict with Europe or the United States at some point over the past fifty years. Despite the diversity of examples discussed, unity can be found in the shared notion of music diplomacy as a potentially effective tool for peace and reconciliation. We have seen that music diplomacy projects today are situated within a sphere shaped not only by local and national laws but also international law (including that pertaining to intellectual property and copyright), and that cultural policies influence the form and trajectory of these projects through such institutions as NGOs, schools, and festivals. Music diplomacy, regardless of its source, can be seen as a kind of "soft power" and it often plays an important role in what has come to be known as "nation branding," or the image a nation presents to the outside world in order to attract positive attention and tourism.

In the introduction we noted that music diplomacy of various kinds has occurred in many locations across the vast expanse of human history. When one considers the ancient origins of music, diplomacy might very well have been a significant factor in its evolution, as a creative way of communicating—with either amiability or aggression—across linguistic boundaries (Mehr et al., 2020). The weight of many unknown generations of human lives implores us to reflect on how humanity has been shaped equally by the nurturing tenderness of lullabies and the unrelenting drumbeat and bugle calls of war. Ethnomusicologists may contribute in some valuable ways to seeing that music is used for the admirable purpose of inspiring empathy and reconciliation between contentious groups for a more just and peaceful world.

REFERENCES

Berger, Maurits, et al. 2008. "Introduction." In *Bridge the Gap, or Mind the Gap? Culture in Western-Arab Relations*. The Hague: Netherlands Institute of International Relations 'Clingendael' Diplomacy Papers 15, 3–7. Available at https://www.clingendael.org/sites/default/files/2016-02/20080100_cdsp_paper_berger.pdf.

Baily, John. 1994. "The Role of Music in the Creation of an Afghan National Identity, 1923–73." In *Ethnicity, Identity and Music*, edited by Martin Stokes, 45–60. Oxford: Berg.

Blanchard, Jean-Marc F., and Fujia Lu. 2012. "Thinking Hard About China's Soft Power." *Asian Perspective* 36, no. 4 (October-November): 565–89.

Boeskov, Kim. 2019. *Music and Social Transformation: Exploring Ambiguous Musical Practice in a Palestinian Refugee Camp*. Doctoral dissertation. Oslo: Norwegian Academy of Music.

Chávez, Luis and Russell Skelchy. 2019. "Decolonization for Ethnomusicology and Music Studies in Higher Education." *Action, Criticism, and Theory for Music Education* 18, no. 3:115–43.

Coppola, William J., David G. Hebert, and Patricia Shehan Campbell. 2021. *World Music Pedagogy, VII: Teaching World Music in Higher Education*. New York: Routledge.

d'Hooghe, Ingrid. 2021. "China's Public Diplomacy Goes Political." *The Hague Journal of Diplomacy* 16, nos. 2–3: 299–322.

———. 2015. *China's Public Diplomacy*. Leiden: Brill.

Doran, George T. 1981. "There's a S.M.A.R.T. Way to Write Management's Goals and Objectives." *Management Review* 70, no. 11: 35–36.
Fanon, Frantz. 1952. *Peau noire, masques blancs*. Paris: Éditions du Seuil.
———. 1961. *Les damnès de la terre*. Paris: François Maspero.
Global Times. 2019. *Oriental Melodies Fill Ancient City in Uzbekistan*. https://www.globaltimes.cn/content/1164177.shtml.
Hebert, David G. and Alexandra Kertz-Welzel, eds. 2016. *Patriotism and Nationalism in Music Education*. New York: Routledge.
Hess, Juliet. 2019. *Music Education for Social Change: Constructing an Activist Music Education*. New York: Routledge.
Higgins, Kathleen M. 2018. "Connecting Music to Ethics." *College Music Symposium* 58, no. 3. https://doi.org/10.18177/sym.2018.58.sr.11411.
Ho, Wai-Chung. 2021. *Globalization, Nationalism, and Music Education in the Twenty-First Century in Greater China*. Amsterdam: Amsterdam University Press.
Hunt, Sarah. 2014. "Ontologies of Indigeneity: The Politics of Embodying a Concept." *Cultural Geographies* 21, no. 1: 27–32.
Kertz-Welzel, Alexandra. 2018. *Globalizing Music Education: A Framework*. Bloomington: Indiana University Press.
Mehr, Samuel A., Max M. Krasnow, Gregory A. Bryant, and Edward H. Hagen. 2020. "Origins of Music in Credible Signaling." *Behavioral and Brain Sciences*, 1–41. doi:10.1017/S0140525X20000345.
Mills, Sherylle. 1996. "Indigenous Music and the Law: An Analysis of National and International Legislation." *Yearbook for Traditional Music* 28, 57–86. doi:10.2307/767807.
Nye, Joseph S. 2013. "What Russia and China Don't Get About Soft Power." *Foreign Policy* (April 29). http://www.foreignpolicy.com/articles/2013/04/29/what_china_and_russia_don_t_get_about_soft_power.
O'Connell, John M. and Salwa E. Castelo-Branco, eds. 2010. *Music and Conflict*. Urbana: University of Illinois Press.
Östersjö, Stefan. 2020. *Listening to the Other*. Ghent: Orpheus Institute.
Richerme, Lauren K. 2020. *Complicating, Considering, and Connecting Music Education*. Bloomington: Indiana University Press.
Said, Edward. 1978. *Orientalism*. New York: Pantheon Books.
Semati, Mehdi. 2017. "Sounds Like Iran: On Popular Music of Iran." *Popular Communication* 15, no. 3: 155–62.
Trimillos, Ricardo. 2009. "Agency and Voice: The Philippines at the 1998 Smithsonian Folklife Festival." In *Music and Cultural Rights*, edited by Andrew N. Weintraub and Bell Yung, 19-41. Urbana: University of Illinois Press.
UN. 2015. United Nations Permanent Forum on Indigenous Issues, 5th Session. Fact Sheet. https://www.un.org/esa/socdev/unpfii/documents/5session_factsheet1.pdf.
Urbain, Oliver, ed. 2015. *Music and Conflict Transformation: Harmonies and Dissonances in Geopolitics*. London: I. B. Tauris.
Waldron, Janice L., Stephanie Horsley, and Kari K. Veblen, eds. 2020. *Oxford Handbook of Social Media and Music Learning*. New York: Oxford University Press.

Watanabe, Yasushi and David L. McConnell. 2008. *Soft Power Superpowers: Cultural and National Assets of Japan and the United States*. Armonk, NY: M. E. Sharpe.

Whitmore, John. 2017. *Coaching for Performance: The Principles and Practice of High-Performance Leadership* (5th edition). Boston, MA: Nicholas Brealey Publishing.

Yudkoff, Ambigay. 2021. *Activism through Music during the Apartheid Era and Beyond: When Voices Meet.* Lanham, MD: Lexington Books.

Zhang, Wanfa. 2012. "Has Beijing Started to Bare Its Teeth? China's Tapping of Soft Power Revisited." *Asian Perspective* 36, no. 4 (October–December): 615–39.

Index

Page references for figures are italicized.

academia: cultural diplomacy and, x; mutual understanding and, 151–52
activism. *See* Clegg, Johnny; Katz, Sharon; Makeba, Miriam; Masekela, Hugh
Adesina, Lere, 256
Adiba, Zarifa, 62
Administering Methods on Protection of World Cultural Heritage, 302
Adorno, Theodor W., 111–12
Aduonum, Ama Oforiwaa, 10
Afghanistan, xv; ArtLords and, 55, *56*, 70n16; attacks on women in, 65, 71n22; Elphinstone on, 57; Free Women Writers and, 61; Golden Age and, 51, 69n5; Hazara *dambura* music, 51, 70n7; identity construction and, 50; music and cultural diplomacy in, 53; negative perceptions of, 56–57; Orientalist narratives of, 56–60; positive images and, 60–65; Saur Revolution, 51, 69n6; Taliban taking, 69n4; topics addressed, 13; US geopolitical agendas and, 66–68; US military expenditures in, 67, 71n23; Western media and, 57–59; women and, 52, 55, 58, 61, 64, 65, 71n22. *See also* Zohra Orchestra
Afghanistan National Institute of Music (ANIM), 50; Australia and, 54; cultural diplomacy at, 53–56; cultural relations and, 53–54; films about, 70n9; Pakistan and, 54, 70n13; technology and, 54–55; US geopolitical agendas and, 66–68. *See also* Zohra Orchestra
Afran Qallo, 215, 223n25
Africa: *Come Back, Africa*, 232, 235; garments and, 262–64; jazz/African fusion of, 237; music genres, 262, 269n6; rhythm and, 264–65; "Scatterlings of Africa," 243; *Trumpet Africaine* and, 236. *See also specific countries*
African folk tale, 229, 251n1
Afro, Teddy, 220
Afwerki, Isaias, 224n37
Agency for Cultural Affairs. *See* Bunkacho
agreements must be kept. *See pact sunt servanda*
Ahmadinejad, Mahmoud, 124
Ahmed, Abiy, 221, 224n37

Ahrendt, Rebekah, 7
Alade, Darey, 262
Alizadeh, Hossein, 121
Alpharabius, 96
Amannisaha, 297
Amhara-speaking people, 222n5; *Ethiopia Hoy* and, 212; scholarship on, 209–10
Andrew (pseudonym), 166–68, 169
ANIM. *See* Afghanistan National Institute of Music
Ansari, 102
Antigone Viêt Nam (Destandau), 182
apartheid: Belafonte and, 232; Clegg and, 242–43; *Come Back, Africa* and, 232; end of, 235; Juluka and, 245; Lucey and, 231; Masekela and, 237–41; Soweto Uprising, 238–40, *239*
appropriation/approbation debate, 36
Arab-Islamic culture. *See* Muslim medieval philosophers
Argerich, Martha, 110
arranger, 285
Art Amongst War exhibition, 56–57
artistic freedom, 28–29
artistic research, 181, 198n1
artists. *See specific artists*
ArtLords (art collective), 55, *56*, 70n16
"The Art of Maqom and its Role in World Civilization" conference, 86–87
"Asimbonanga," 244
Astatke, Mulatu, 214
al Attar, Farid al Din, 105–6, *107*
Australia: ANIM and, 54; Soweto Gospel Choir in, 261
Avicenna, 97, 98. *See also* Ibn Sina
Aweke, Aster, 217
Al Azem Palace, 95
El 'Azifet, 51
Azoulay, Audrey, 302

Bach, J. S., 112
Bachelard, Gaston, 93–94

Bacon, Roger, 96, 97
Baily, John, 70n9
Baizai, Siavash, 121
Bajoghli, Narges, 120, 128–29, 131, 134n5
Baker, Geoffrey, 70n10
Bastaninezhad, Arya, 122
Baumann, Max Peter, 222n2
Beethoven, 49, 95
Beijing Treaty on Audiovisual Performances, 303, *303*, 309n15
Belafonte, Harry: Makeba and, 232; Masekela and, 233, 236; Simon, Paul, and, 244
Belder, Lucky, 26
Bell, Gertrude Lowthian, 70n8
Bennoune, Karima, 27, 29
Bergen Summer Research School (BSRS), xi
Bergh, Arild, 10–11
Berne Convention, 1886, 302, 303, *303*
Bernstein, Leonard, 200n6
Betreyohannes, Simeneh, 210
Betty G. (pop star), 221
Al Biruni, 102
Blends (NHK World-Japan), 158, 175n4
Bloom, Benjamin, 199n3
Blout, Emily L., 126–28
Blue Nile Group. *See* Orchestra Ethiopia
Boeskov, Kim, 330
Boethius, 95
bone-flutes. *See Jiahu Gudi*
Book of Music. *See Yue Ji*
Book of Rites. *See Li Ji*
Booth, Greg, 35
Boulanger, Nadia, 110
"The Bowl-Lyre of Northeast Africa" (Kebede), 211
Braithwaite, Lauren, xv
Brazil, xii
The Breadwinner (Ellis), 58
Breitscheidplatz, Berlin, 49
"Bring Him Home," 240
British Forum for Ethnomusicology, xiii
Brown, Danielle, 9–10

BSRS. *See* Bergen Summer Research School
Build (Katz, Mark), 8
Bunkacho, 175n10; *iemoto* system, 159, 175n9; living national treasures criteria, 159, 175n7; role of, 158, 175n5; traditional artistry transmission and, 159, 175n6
Bush, George W., 127
al Bustami, 102, 103
Buthelezi, Mangosuthu, 248, 251n7
Butler, Mervin L., 197

Cải Lương: discussion, 197–98; guitar and, 186–87; *Hát Bội* theater and, 185, 200n12; hybrid forms and, 185–86; Linh interview and, 188; in Sài Gòn, 185, 200n13; transculturation between tradition and modernity, 184–87; *Vọng Cổ* and, 186
Campbell, Patricia Shehan, ix
Cao Văn Lầu, 186, 201n
capabilities approach, 30–32
Ca Ra Bộ (singing with gestures), 185, 200n11
Carmichael, Stokely, 234–35
Carr, Nicholas, 115
Castelo-Branco, Salwa El-Shawan, 11
Castiglione, Baldassare, 182
CCOM. *See* Central Conservatory of Music
censorship: internet and, 34; by Selassie, 215
Center for Constitutional and Human Rights (ECCHR), 24
Center for Language Education and Cooperation (CLEC). *See* Hanban
Center for Soft Power, 231
Central Conservatory of Music (CCOM), 141–42, 297
Channick, Jan, 173, 178n24
Charles (prince), 290
chaupai (quatrain), 287, 292n21
Cheetham, Tom, 112, 113

"Chennai Soft Power 30" project, 231
Chideya, Farai, 251n4
China: Amannisaha and, 297; background, 139–41; conclusions, 153–54; copyright and, 35–36; Hanban/CLEC agreement and, 149; music institutions in, 139; mutual understanding and, 151–53; overseas population of Chinese, 139–40; Paris Act and, 302; shakuhachi music in, 162; soft power concept implications and, 146–47; topics addressed, 14, 16–17, 139; treaties, international, and, 300–304, *303*; TRIPS and, 304. *See also* Confucius Institute; Hanban; Music Confucius Institute; National People's Congress
China, artistic heritage legal framework: administrative regulation and, 300; CCOM, 297; conclusions, 309, 321–22; constitution supremacy, 299–300; copyright law, 305; cultural treaties and, 301; current law and, 298; Guo Song case, 306; ICH and, 302; image cases, 307; Intangible Cultural Heritage Law, 305–7; international treaties and, 300–304, *303*; introduction, 297–98; local regulations, local rules, ministerial rules, 300, 308; minority groups and, 298; national law, 299–300, 305–8; Neighboring Right Protection, 308; opera case, 307; rules hierarchy, 298–99; UNESCO treaties and, 301–2; WIPO and, 302–3, *303*; World Heritage Convention and, 301–2
China University of Political Science and Law, Beijing, xi
"Chinese Music Heritage Map," 297
Chittick, William, 102
Chopin, 101
Choudhary, Karan, xiv
Christian music: conclusions, 267–68; cultural diversity and, 259–61;

garments and, 263; homogenizing impact of, 257–59, 269n3; rhythm and, 264–65
CI. *See* Confucius Institute
civil rights, 282
Clarke, David, 64, 231
CLEC. *See* Hanban
Clegg, Johnny, 229; apartheid and, 242–43; awards conferred on, 245; conclusions about, 318; dislocation and, 243; France and, 245; Mzila and, 241–42; racial harmony projected by, 242–46; Simon, Paul, and, 244. *See also specific works*
Coe, John, 223n10
Cold War, 200n6
collaboration, intercultural: CI and, 148–49; cultural diplomacy and, 181–84; discussion, 197–98; injustice and, 182; Lagos City Chorale and Soweto Gospel Choir, 262; listening habits and, 197, 202n36; long-term change and, 183; Spangler and, 182–83; transculturation through, 189–97
College Music Symposium (Higgins), 329–30
Colonial Expo, Marseille, 1906, 185
colonialism, 184. *See also* decolonization
Come Back, Africa, 232, 235
common good, 289, 292n24
composer, 285
compound. *See tarkib*
The Conference of the Birds. *See Manteq al-Tayr*
Confucius Institute (CI): administrative challenges, 147–50; collaboration and, 148–49; conclusions about, 320; Erasmus program and, 149–50; foreign side of, 147; local director challenges, 147–48; local staff resources and, 150; MCI, 140; middle ground for, 151–53; negative images attributed to, 150; recommendations for, 150–51; research on, 146; soft power concept and, 146–47; solutions for, 151–53; unbalanced incentives and, 148; US and, 147. *See also* Music Confucius Institute
Cool Japan, 157–58, 175n3
Copenhagen, 141–42
copyright: law, 305; music rights and, 35–36; WCT, *303*. *See also* Indian Copyright Act; intellectual property rights
"Copyright Policy and the Right to Science and Culture" (Shaheed), 29
Corbin, Henry, 102, 112, 113
Cordova, Spain, 101
Covid-19 pandemic, xiv–xv, 290
creative incorporation, 214
Crusader coalition, 49, 69n1
Cuba, 249–50
Cull, Nick, 5
cultural diplomacy. *See* diplomacy, cultural
cultural rights: appropriation versus approbation debate, 36; capabilities and, 30–32; conclusions, 36–39; cultural imports and, 34–35; cultural policies and, 33–36; evolution for sustainability and, 37–38; heritage and, 35, 280–82; invention of tradition theory and, 37; IPR and, 287–88, 292n22; law interpretations versus, 38; legal traditions compromise and, 36–37; *Negotiating Cultural Rights*, 26; participatory rights and, 38; "Report of the Special Rapporteur in the Field of Cultural Rights," 29; soft law, international, and, 24–26; *The Transforming Power of Cultural Rights*, 22; UN Human Rights Council and, 26–27; UN special rapporteur and, 26–30
"Cultural Rights" (Shaheed), 28
"Cultural Rights Defenders" (Bennoune), 29
Culture and Imperialism (Said), 289

El-Dabh, Halim, 210–11, 222n9, 223nn10–11
Dạ Cổ Hoài Lang, 186, 201n15
Dale, Katrine Ørnehaug, 58
Damascus University, 93
dance, 265–67, 308
đàn gáo and đàn cò (two-stringed fiddles), 188, 201n18
đàn kìm (lute), 187, 201n16
Dante, 105–6, 107
David (king), 3
Davis, Miles, 237
Al-Dawla, Saif, 100
Debalke, Tsegaye, 211
decolonization: ethnomusicology and, 9–10, 12, 327–28; of intercultural music education, 329–30; of intercultural research methods, 328–30; knowledge, 315
Defoe, Daniel, 106, 107
Denmark. *See* Copenhagen; Royal Danish Academy of Music
Denning, Michael, 183
DeNora (pseudonym), 170
De philosophia peripatetica apud Syros (Renan), 96–97
Derg socialist government: conclusions, 319; cultural production/policy under, 215–19; cultural revolution of, 217; departments of culture, 218–19; equality and, 216–17; *Etyopiya Tiqdem* and, 216; *Hager Feqer Tiyater* and, 213–14, 218; Medhin and, 217; migration away from, 217, 218
Destandau, Alain, 182
DeWald, Erich, 185
diplomacy, cultural: background and rationale, 6–11; concluding remarks, 330–31; government and, 289–90; history and, 3–4; key concepts, 4–6; notions of, 230–31. *See also specific topics*
director, 285
Dissanayake, Ellen, 170

Divine Comedy (Dante), 105–6, 107
Đờn Ca Tài Tử, 200n9; Ca Ra Bộ and, 185, 200n11; as chamber music revival, 184, 200n10; colonialism and, 184; đàn kìm and, 187, 201n16; guitar and, 186–87; *Hát Bội* theater and, 185, 200n12; Linh interview, 187–88; in Sài Gòn, 185, 200n13; violin and, 187–88; *Vọng Cổ* and, 186, 201n15
Donders, Yvonne, 30
doubling. *See Tad'if*
Dr Sarmast's Music School (Watkins), 70n9
Dunkel, Mario, 7–8

ECCHR. *See* Center for Constitutional and Human Rights
economic/social rights, 282
Elham, Zahra, 65
Ellis, Deborah, 58
Elphinstone, Mountstuart, 57
Emerson, Ralph Waldo, 97
engineers, 285
Enheduanna (Akkadian princess), 3
Entezami, Majid, 70n21
EPRDF. *See* Ethiopian People Revolutionary Democratic Front
Erasmus program, 149–50
Eritrean music, 214–15
La Escatologia Musulmana en la Divina Comedia (Palasios), 105, 319
Eshete, Alem, 217
Ethiopia, xiv; Amhara-speaking people, 209–10, 212, 222n5; creative incorporation in, 214; El-Dabh and, 210–11, 222n9, 223nn10–11; derogatory terminologies related to, 210, 222nn5–7; Eritrean music and, 214–15; *Etyopiya Tiqdem*, 216; *galla* and, 210, 222nn5–6; *Hager Feqer Tiyater* and, 213–14, 218; Harar people, 210, 222n8; highland traditions, 211; Imperial Bodyguard Orchestra, 212; Italian occupation

aftermath, 213–15; Jenkins and, 211, 223n15; *Kaffichos* people, 210, 222n4; language groups, 209, 222n1; as multicultural, 209–10; musicians as low caste in, 211–12; "The Music of Ethiopia," 210; NDR, 216–17; Orchestra Ethiopia, 211, 223nn10–12; patriotic songs, 213; Russia and, 223n20; "The Sacred Chant of Ethiopian Monotheistic Churches," 211; St. Yared Music School, 214; scholarship on, 209–12; theater as propaganda in, 212–13; theatrical traditions, 212; topics addressed, 15, 209; Yehager Fikir Mahber in, 213. *See also* Derg socialist government; Selassie, Haile
Ethiopia Hoy (Nalbandian), 212
Ethiopian Music (Powne), 210, 222n3
Ethiopian People Revolutionary Democratic Front (EPRDF): constitution, 219; cultural policies/creative industries under, 219–21; ethnic groups, marginalized, and, 220–21; Ministry of Culture and Tourism of, 220; peace performances and, 221, 224n37
Ethio Stars, 217
ethnomusicology: background and rationale, 6–11; key concepts, 6; scholarship on, 6–9; shortcomings, xiii–xiv. *See also specific topics*
Ethnomusicology Forum, 9–10
Ethnomusicology journal, 10
Etyopiya Tiqdem (Ethiopia First), 216
Eurasian Music Science Journal, 87
Europe: Chinese traditional music education in, 140; Muslim medieval philosophers and, 96–97; topics addressed, 139. *See also* Music Confucius Institute; *specific countries*
"Everybody's Standing Up," 240
Eyes on Tomorrow, 235

Fabula (Mariam), 212
Falasha people, 211, 223n16
Al-Farabi: axioms of, 99–100; Greek philosophers and, 99, 101; human voice and, 100–101; as Muslim medieval philosopher, 98, 99–101; as practical and theoretical, 100
Farhat, Hormoz, 121
Farmer, George, 97
Far Right Alternative für Deutschland, 69n2
Ferraguto, Mark, 7
al-Fihri, Fatima, 108
Finland: artistic research and, 198n1; Sibelius Academy in, xi
Finnish Music Council (FMC), 32–33
Firkunsy, Rudolf, 112
flutes: *Jiahu Gudi*, 298; *ji-ari* shakuhachi, *163*, 163–66; *ji-nashi* shakuhachi, *163*, 163–66, 176nn16–17; shakuhachi music and, 162–64, *163*, 176nn16–17
FMC. *See* Finnish Music Council
Fosler-Lussier, Danielle, 8, 62, 230
France: Clegg and, 245; Colonial Expo, Marseille, 185; Paris exposition, 1900, 184–85
Free Women Writers, 61
Friends of The Peace Train, 248–49
From Apology to Utopia (Koskenniemi), 25
Fugard, Athol, 246
al-Futūḥāt al-Makkiyya (Ibn Arabi), 113–14

galla (derogatory term), 210, 222nn5–6
gangan (talking drum), 266
garments, traditional African, 262–64
gatherings of intellectuals. *See majales*
Gebremariam, Aleqa Taye, 210
Gedächtniskirche Church, 49
General Principles of Civil Law, 1986, 302

Geneva Convention for the Protection of Producers of Phonograms Against Unauthorized Duplication of Their Phonograms, *303*
Geoffroy, Eric, 114
Germany: Far Right nationalism in, 49, 69n2; Gedächtniskirche, 49
Gessese, Télahun, 213–14
Gessesse, Tesfaye, 217
Al Ghazali, Sufi, 103, 105, 110
Ghost of Tsushima (video game), 172
Gibbs, Jason, 186
Gilbert of Aurillac, 96
Gillespie, Dizzy, 235, 237
glocalization, 8, 258–59
Goethe, 97, 107
Goff, Patricia M., 132, 133n1
Goldmann, Matthias, 24
Graceland, 241, 244
Grand Book on Music (Alpharabius), 96
"Grazing in the Grass," 237
Great Britain, 198n1
Green Zone, 67, 71n24
Grosseteste, Robert, 96
group rights, 282
Gubegna, Abbe, 217
Guinea, 235
guitar, 186–87
Guo, Song, 306
Gwangwa, Jonas, 232

Habtewold, Mekonnen, 213
Hadith, 108
Hager Feqer Tiyater, 213–14, 218
Haile Selassie I Theatre Orchestra, 214, 318
Hall, James, 232, 236
Al-Hallaj, 103
Hamann, Johann Georg, 112–13
Hamuyah, Sa'd al-Din, 105
Hanban: administrative challenges, 147–50; recommendations for, 150–51; soft power concept and, 146–47; solutions for, 151–53. *See also* Confucius Institute; Music Confucius Institute
Hanban/CLEC agreement, 149
Hanoi New Music Festival, 192–93
Harar people, 210, 222n8
Harris, Rachel, 36
Hassani, Shamsia, 61
Hát Bội theater, 185, 200n12
Ḥayy ibn Yaqẓān (Ibn Tufail), *106*, 106–7, 319
Hazara *dambura* music, 51, 70n7
hearing. *See shruti*
Hebert, David G., 8, 67
Heimonen, Marja, xi
Hemmasi, Farzaneh, 121
hermeneutics, 111–13
Herzfeld, Michael, 120, 129, 132–33
Higgins, Kathleen, 329–30
Histoire de la médicine arabe (Leclerc), 96
Histoire d'un voyage faict en la terre du Bresil (Léry), 3
Historical Facts for the Arabian Musical Influence (Farmer), 97
hogaku (traditional Japanese music), 157
"The Holy Longing" (Goethe), 107
Homeland, 235
Hong Fuyuan, 307
Honjo Hidejiro, 173, 174
honkyoku (solo pieces, 18th century): biological perspectives on, 169–70; culture as hindrance to spirituality and, 164–68; Liam on, 164–66; shakuhachi music and, 159–60, 162, 164–68; as universal, 164–66; universal perspectives on, 169–70
Horowitz, Vladimir, 110
Hosseini, Khalid, 58
Howard, Keith, 8
Howell, Gillian, 65
Hrncirikova, Miluše, 23
Huddleston, Trevor, 233, 251n2
Human, 246

human rights: categories of, 282; Koskenniemi and, 25–26; Logan on, 22; music conferences and, xiii; UN Human Rights Council, 26–27
Huỳnh Tuấn, 188; collaborative experimentation with, 190–94; Hanoi New Music Festival and, 192–93; solo recordings of, 189–90, 194–95

I Am Not Afraid, 238
Ibn Arabi, 113–14
Ibn Sina, 101
Ibn Tufail, *106*, 106–7
ICH. *See* Intangible Cultural Heritage Convention
identity: alternative construction of, 50; religion and, 257
iemoto system, 159, 175n9
IMC. *See* International Music Council
Imperial Bodyguard Orchestra, Ethiopia, 212
imperialism, 289
India: Articles 29-30 of constitution, 283–85; common good and, 289, 292n24; conclusions, 290, 321; cultural heritage and, 279, 291n3; imperialism and, 289; instruments of, 278; legal framework in, 282–83; multiculturalism and, *279*, 279–80; *namaste* and, 290; Pakistan and, 289; *ragni* and, 285, 291n10; sound and, 278, 291n1; topics addressed, 16, 277; Vedic periods, 277–78; "We the Children of India," 283; Yoga and, 289–90. *See also* intellectual property rights
Indian Copyright Act: ambiguity of, 286, 292n17; conclusions, 321; Section 14, 291n13; Section 17, 291n12; Section 18, 291n14; Section 57, 292n15
Indian greeting. *See namaste*
Indigenous peoples, 38
individual rights, 281
inspiration, 113–14

Intangible Cultural Heritage Convention (ICH), 302
Intangible Cultural Heritage Law, 305–7
intangible heritage rights, 35
intellectual property rights (IPR): commonplace elements and, 286–87, 292n19; contributors and, 285–86; creator/owner and, 286, 291nn12–14, 292n15; cultural rights and, 287–88, 292n22; international, 292n16; musical language and, 292n18; music as, *322*, 322–23; public domain and, 287, 292n22; Section 14, Indian Copyright Act, 291n13; Section 17, Indian Copyright Act, 291n12; Section 18, Indian Copyright Act, 291n14; Section 57, Indian Copyright Act, 292n15; TRIPS and, 304; WIPO and, 287–88
interactive participants, 62–63
intercultural collaboration. *See* collaboration, intercultural
intercultural society, 279, *279*
International Council for Traditional Music, xiii
International Court of Justice, 301
International House. *See Kokusai Kaikan*
International Maqom Festival, 77–78, 85–88
International Music Council (IMC), 23, 32–33
International Relations, Music and Diplomacy (Ramel and Prevost-Thomas), 7
International Shakuhachi Festival, 161
International Shakuhachi Society, 176n14
International Society for Music Education, xiii
internet: censorship and, 34; Iran and, 123
interpretation, 111–13
Introduction to the History of Science (Sarton), 96
invention of tradition theory, 37

IPR. *See* intellectual property rights
Iran: conclusions, 132–33; dress codes and, 134n5; internet and, 123; Peace and Friendship Symphony from, 70n21; Permanent Bureau for Soft War and, 128; Safir-e Eshgh and, 129–30; soft war and, 126–32; survey of music/music education, 120–25; topics addressed, 14, 119–20; Trump and, 124–25, 133n1; Western influence and, 126, 133n4
Israel, xiii
Italy, 213–15

Jalata, Asafa, 218
Jankelevitch, Vladimir, 114
Japan: *Kokusai Kaikan* in, ix–x; topics addressed, 14; Western music in, ix, x
Japanese cultural policy: Cool Japan, 157–58, 175n3; NHK World-Japan, 158, 175n4; topics addressed, 157–58; traditional music priorities of, 158–61. *See also* Bunkacho
Japanese music: cultural policy priorities for, 158–61; *hogaku*, 157; non-Japanese cultural gap and, 157–58; *taiko*, 157. *See also* shakuhachi music
Japanology Plus (NHK World-Japan), 158, 175n4
Jenkins, Jean, 211, 223n15
Jiahu Gudi (bone-flutes), 298
ji-ari shakuhachi (flute): Liam on, 164–66; as modern, 163, *163*
ji-nashi shakuhachi (flute): Liam on, 164–66; making, *163*, 163–64, 176nn16–17; Pamela on, 168–69
John of the Cross (Saint), 97
Juluka, 242, 243, 245
The Just Assassins (Fugard), 246

Kaffichos people, 210, 222n4
Kaiser Wilhelm Memorial Church. *See* Gedächtniskirche Church
Kaizan, John Neptune, 172

Kani, John, 246
von Karajan, Herbert, 111
Karimov, Islam, 81, 89
Al Kashani, 103–4
Katz, Mark, 8
Katz, Sharon: background, 229–30, 246–47; choir of, 247–48; in Cuba, 249–50; elections and, 248; Friends of The Peace Train and, 248–49; in US, 248, 249; *When Voices Meet* and, 247, 249
Kebede, Ashenafi, 211
Keyhati Embaba (Red Flowers), 214
Khatami, Mohammad, 121, 123
Kimberlin, Cynthia Tse, 210, 211
Al-Kindi, 98–99, 100
King, Martin Luther, Jr., 233
King Kong (jazz opera), 232
King Raam (musician), 126
kinko ryū (shakuhachi school), 159, *160*, 161
Kipling, Rudyard, 289
Kitab al Musiqi al Kabir (Al-Farabi), 99
Kitab al Najat (Ibn Sina), 101
knowledge decolonization, 315
Kokusai Kaikan (International House), ix–x
Kontrowicz, Alexander, 214
Koskenniemi, Martti, 21, 25–26
Kress, Gunther, 62–63
Kurosawa, Kinko, 159

Lagos City Chorale: as case study, 255–56; conclusions, 267–68; dance and, 266; garments of, 263–64; linguistic diversity and, 261–62; Soweto Gospel Choir collaborations with, 262
language: dance and, 265–67; diversity, 261–62; Ethiopian language groups, 209, 222n1; garments and, 262–64; IPR and musical language, 292n18; in music representation, 261–64; in rhythm, 264–67. *See also* linguistics

law: artistry and, 320–22; as foundation of music diplomacy, 320–27, *322*; national and international interests and, 22; topics addressed, 16–17. *See also* China, artistic heritage legal framework; Indian Copyright Act; intellectual property rights; rights; soft law, international
Lebanon, 33
Leclerc, Lucien, 96
legal right, 280
Lemma, Mengistu, 217
Lemma, Tesfaye, 223n10
Léry, Jean de, 3
Li, Juqian, xiv–xv
Liam (pseudonym), 164–66, 169
"Liggi," 286
Li Ji (Book of Rites), 298
linguistics: diversity, linguistic, 261–62; Nigeria and, 260, 269n4; South Africa and, 259–60
Linh (Vietnamese musician), 187–88
local regulations/rules, 300, 308
Logan, William, 22
Lomonosov Moscow State University, Russia, x
Long Distance Call project, 25
Lotfi, Sharif, 121
"Love in the Time of Gaza," 246
"Love Tastes Like Strawberries," 236–37
Lucey, Roger, 231
lute. *See đàn kìm*
lyricist, 285

Macgregor, Judith, 245
Machel-Mandela, Graça, 235
Macron, Emmanuel, 290
Mahiet, Damien, 7
Maimonides, 97
majales (gatherings of intellectuals), 97
Makeba, Miriam, 229–30; accomplishments, 233–36; backlash in US, 234–35; Belafonte and, 232; Carmichael and, 234–35; citizenship revoked, 234; death and legacy of, 236, 251n4; in exile, 232–35; Guinea and, 235; homecoming of, 235; *The Many Voices of Miriam Makeba*, 236–37; Masekela and, 232–41; "Ndodemnyama we Verwoerd" and, 238; political activism of, 234; popularity of, 233; in South Africa, 232, 235–36; on truth, 237; in US, 232–35. *See also specific works*
Makeba Centre for Girls, 236
Makeba: My Story (Makeba and Hall), 232, 236
Mamadjanova, Elnora, xiv
Mamdani, Mahmood, 61
Al-Ma'mun, Abdullah, 98
Mandela, Nelson, 235, 240–41, 244
Manteq al-Tayr (al Attar), 105–6, 107
The Many Voices of Miriam Makeba, 236–37
Maori: Dutch explorers and, 3; Te Wananga O Aotearoa and, x; Thai-Maori Musical Exchange Project, xi
maqamat (scales), 98
Maqam-based music: "The Art of Maqom and its Role in World Civilization" and, 86–87; background about, 78–79, 91n2; International Maqom Festival, 77–78, 85–88; self-accompaniment and, 79, 91n3; tradition and, 87–88
Mariam, Tekle Hawaryat Tekle, 212
Marrakesh Treaty to Facilitate Access to Published Works for Persons Who Are Blind, Visually Impaired, or Otherwise Print Disabled, *303*
Martin (Saint), 103
Maryam, Tekle, 213
Masekela, 238
Masekela, Hugh, 229–30; apartheid and, 237–41; Belafonte and, 233, 236; cultural exchange and, 238; dictatorships and, 240; *Eyes on Tomorrow* and, 235; Huddleston and, 233, 251n2; jazz/African fusion of,

237; Makeba and, 232–41; Mandela and, 240–41; *The Many Voices of Miriam Makeba* and, 236–37; "Ndodemnyama we Verwoerd" and, 238; Soweto Uprising and, 238–40; truth and, 237. *See also specific works*
Mashayekhi, Alireza, 121
"Masinqo and the Nature of Qenet" (Kimberlin), 211
Massignon, Louis, 93–94
Matsumoto, Naomi, 8
Matsunobu, Koji, xiv
al Mausili, Ishaq, 101
Mawlawi, Sabri, 93, *94*
McCollum, Jonathan, xii
Mchunu, Sipho, 242, 243
MCI. *See* Music Confucius Institute
Medhin, Tseggaye Gebre, 217
Mekonen, Dawite, 220
Mekong Delta, 184, 187
Mekong plain, 187–88
Merkel, Angela, 290
Mérode, Cléo de, 185
Michon, Jean-Louis, 103
Mini, Vuyisile, 238, 251n5
ministerial rules, 300, 308
Ministry of Culture and Tourism, of EPRDF, 220
Mirzaev, Shavkat, 79
Mirziyoyev, Shavkat, 77, 83, 84–85, 89–90, 91n6
Mitchell, Joni, 248
Mittwoch, Eugen, 210
Miyata Mayumi, 174
Modi, Narendra, 290
Mohammad, 108–9
Mohanty, Chandra, 59
Mondon-Vidailhet, Casimir, 210
monocultural, 279, *279*
moral right, 280, 286
Morin Khuur, 297
Movahed, Azin, 121
Mulcahy, Kevin, 4, 21–22
multiculturalism, *279*, 279–80

music: artistic research in, 181, 198n1; borders transcended by, ix; as IPR, *322*, 322–23; peace studies and, 10–11; prohibition of, 109; savage beasts tamed by, 229; universality of, 50. *See also specific topics*
musical art practice, northern India. *See ragni*
Musical Transformations project: insider/outsider perspectives and, 181, 198n2; Linh interview and, 187–88; methodology and, 181; repository, 199n5; stimulated recall and, 181, 199n3; transculturation through collaboration and, 189–97
Music and Diplomacy (Ahrendt, Ferraguto, and Mahiet), 7
Music as Heritage (Norton and Matsumoto), 8
Music as Intangible Cultural Heritage (Howard), 8
Music Confucius Institute (MCI), 139; case studies, 143–45; CCOM and RDAM, 141–42; challenges faced by, 142; CI and, 140; collaboration partners, 142, 145; conclusions about, 317; in Copenhagen, 141–42; diplomatic impact of, 145–46; high school collaboration with, 142
music diplomacy: benchmarks for, 325–27, *326*; history, 3–4; mechanisms of, 323–25, *324*; in research and education, 327–28. *See also specific projects*
Music Glocalization (Hebert and Rykowski), 8
Music in America's Cold War Diplomacy (Fosler-Lussier), 8
"The Music of Ethiopia" (Kimberlin), 210
"The Music of Ethiopian Peoples" (Sárosi), 210
music rights: conclusions, 36–39; copyright and, 35–36; cultural policies and, 33–36; current issues

in, 23–24; IMC and, 32; intangible heritage and, 35; participatory rights and, 38; rethinking, 36–38; soft law, international, and, 23–24, 32–33; topics, 13
Al Musiqi al Kabir (Al-Farabi), 99–100
La Musique éthiopienne (Mondon-Vidailhet), 210
Muslim medieval philosophers: conclusions, 114–16; dark ages and, 101–2; European thinkers embracing, 96–97; Al-Farabi, 98, 99–101; Ibn Sina, 101; Al-Kindi, 98–99, 100; music theorists, 98–102; rationale for studying, 96–98; scale used by, 98
myoan ryū (shakuhachi school), 159–60, 176n11
mystical experience, 109–10
Mzila, Charlie, 241–42

Nagatani Kengyo Memorial Hogaku Music contest, 157, 175n1
Nakao Tozan, 159
namaste (Indian greeting), 290
National People's Congress (NPC): administrative regulation and, 300; constitution supremacy and, 299–300; Intangible Cultural Heritage Law, 302, 305; local regulations, local rules, ministerial rules, 300; national laws under constitution, 299–300
nation branding: diplomacy, cultural, and, 4–17; key concepts, 5
natural rights, 281
Ndlovu, Hastings, *239*, 240
"Ndodemnyama we Verwoerd," 238
NDR. *See* New Democratic Revolution Programme
negative rights, 281
Negotiating Cultural Rights (Belder), 26
Nehru, Jawaharlal, 283
Neighboring Right Protection, 308
Nettl, Bruno, ix
New Democratic Revolution Programme (NDR), 216–17

New Zealand: Te Wananga O Aotearoa in, x; Tongan youth band and, x–xi
Nguyễn, Thanh Thủy, xi
Nhạc Tài Tử (*Tài Tử* music), 200n9
NHK World-Japan, 158, 175n4
Nietzsche, Friedrich, 116
Nigeria: cultural diversity in, 259–61; linguistics and, 260, 269n4; Nollywood in, 269n1; popular music industry, 269n2; soft power used by, 256, 269nn1–2; topics addressed, 15–16. *See also* Lagos City Chorale
9/11. *See* September 11, 2001
Nitzsche, Sina A., 7–8
Nollywood, 269n1
Nooshin, Laudan, 122, 123–24
Nordic Network for Music Education, xi
Norton, Barley, 8
Norway, xi
Norwegian Ministry of International Affairs, xii
NPC. *See* National People's Congress
"Ntyilo," 237
Nuclear Energy (Tataloo), 131
Nun, Dhu'l, 104–5
Nuo Wu (dance), 308
Nussbaum, Martha C., 30–32
Nwokedi, Emeka, 256, 263
Nye, Joseph, 5, 126, 230, 250
Nzima, Sam, *239*, 240

O'Connell, John Morgan, 11
O'Connor, Eileen, 66
"Ode to Joy" (Beethoven), 49
Ohashi Taizan, 177n21
Oluwa, 261
opera case, 307
Opinions on Strengthening and Enhancing the Administering of the World Heritage Protection, 302, 309n13
Orchestra Ethiopia, 211, 223nn10–12
organum, 101
Orientalism (Said), 327

Orientalist narratives, of Afghanistan, 56–60
Östersjö, Stefan, xi
Otto Hahn Peace Medal, 236
Ozawa, Seiji, 111

pact sunt servenda (agreements must be kept), 301
Pahlavi, Mohammad Reza, 120
Pakistan: ANIM and, 54, 70n13; India and, 289
Palasios, Asin, 105
Pamela (pseudonym), 168–69
Paris Act, 1971, 302
Paris exposition, 1900, 184–85
Pascale, Louise, 53
"Pata, Pata," 236
"Patent Policy and the Right to Science and Culture" (Shaheed), 29–30
Peace and Friendship Symphony, 70n21
peace studies, 10–11
The Peace Train, 248–49
Permanent Bureau for Soft War, Iran, 128
Phạm Công Ty, 188; collaborative experimentation with, 190–94; Hanoi New Music Festival and, 192–93; on mutual understanding, 195–96; solo recording of, 189–90
Phạm Văn Môn, 188; collaborative experimentation with, 190–94; Hanoi New Music Festival and, 192–93; on listening, 196; solo recording of, 189–90
Phoasavadi, Pornprapit, xi
Piano Concerto No. 4 in G Major Op. 58 (Beethoven), 95
Pieterson, Hector, *239*, 240
Pirmatova, Nadira, 79
Poland, xi
policy, cultural, 4
popular culture, 172–73
Popular Music and Public Diplomacy (Dunkel and Nitzsche), 7–8
Porsdam, Helle, 22

positive rights, 281
Powne, Michael, 210, 222n3
Praize, Joe, 262
Prevost-Thomas, Cécil, 7
producer, 285
"Prospects for the development of traditional music of the peoples of the East" conference, 85
public diplomacy: cultural diplomacy contrasted with, 5–6; *Popular Music and Public Diplomacy*, 7–8
public domain, 287, 292n22
publisher, 286

Qalb-e Ārām, 130–31
Qanun fil tibb (Ibn Sina), 101
quatrain. *See chaupai*

Rachmaninoff, Sergei, 110
racism, 9–10
Raditlhalo, Sam, 237
ragas (Vedic classical music), 278
ragni (musical practice, northern India), 285, 291n10
Ramel, Frédéric, 7
RDAM. *See* Royal Danish Academy of Music
recollection. *See smriti*
Red Flowers. *See* Keyhati Embaba
Rees, Helen, 35–36
Registan Square, *82*, 82–83
Regulations on Protection of Traditional Arts and Crafts, 305–7, 310n18
religion: culture protection and, 259; glocalization and, 258–59; homogenizing impact of, 257–59, 269n3; identity and, 257. *See also* Christian music
"Remembering the Activism of Miriam Makeba" (Chideya), 251n4
Renan, Ernest, 96–97
"Report of the Special Rapporteur in the Field of Cultural Rights" (Bennoune), 29
represented participants, 62–63

Return of the Nightingales (Baily), 70n9
revelation, 113–14
rhythm, 171, 177n20, 264–67
rhythm instrument ensemble. *See taiko*
Riding Alone for Thousands of Miles, 307
rights: Articles 29-30 of Indian Constitution, 283–85; categorizations of, 281–82, 286; heritage and, 280; intangible heritage, 35. *See also* cultural rights; human rights; intellectual property rights; music rights
"The Right to Freedom of Artistic Expression and Creation" (Shaheed), 29
Risala fi Khubr ta'lif al alhan (Al-Kindi), 98
Robinson Crusoe (Defoe), 106, 107
Rogosin, Lionel, 232
Roha Band, 217
Rosen, Ronald S., 292n18
Rossini, Conti, 209
Rouhani, Hassan, 124–25, 133n3
Royal Danish Academy of Music (RDAM), 141–42, 145
Rumi, 104, 116–17
Russia: Ethiopia and, 223n20; Lomonosov Moscow State University in, x; objections to conferences held in, xiii
Rykowski, Mikolaj, xi, 8

Sabet, Farzan, 126–28, 132
"The Sacred Chant of Ethiopian Monotheistic Churches" (Kebede), 211
Safir-e Eshgh (boy band), 129–31, 317–18
Safshekan, Roozbeh, 126–28, 132
Said, Edward, 57, 289, 327
Sài Gòn, Vietnam, 185, 200n13
St. Yared Music School, 214
Sama (spiritual listening or concert): al-Ghazzali and, 103, 105; Hamuyah and, 105; Al Kashani and, 103–4; Nun and, 104–5; Rumi and, 104
Samuelsson, Torbjörn, 194, 202n31
Sarafina, 235
Sarmast, Ahmad, 52, 66
Sárosi, Bálint, 210
Sarton, George, 96–97
Saur Revolution, Afghanistan, 51, 69n6
Saviano, Roberto, 236
Savuka, 243, 245
Sayfullaev, Bakhtiyor, 85
scales. *See maqamat*
"Scatterlings of Africa," 243
Schaeffer, Pierre, 196, 202n35
Scot, Michael, 96
Sekiro (video game), 172
Selassie, Haile: Afran Qallo and, 215, 223n25; brass band and, 212, 223n20; censorship by, 215; conclusions about, 319; cultural production/policy under, 212–15; Haile Selassie I Theatre Orchestra, 214, 318; patriotic songs and, 213; propaganda of, 212–13; theater and, 212
SEM. *See* Society for Ethnomusicology
Semati, Mehdi, 120
Sen, Amartya, 31
September 11, 2001, 94–95, 289–90
Seth, Leila, 283
Shabboo, Ali, 215
Shaheed, Faridah: reports by, 28–30; as special rapporteur, 26–27
shakuhachi music: Andrew on, 166–68; authenticity and, 170–71, 177n19; in China, 162; conclusions, 174; cultural ambassadors and, 161–62; cultural diplomacy and, 171–74; cultural hybrids and, 173–74; definitions related to, 176n13; DeNora on, 170; discussion, 170–74; Dissanayake and, 170; earth energy and, 168–69; flutes and, 162–66, *163*, 176nn16–17; *honkyoku* and, 159–60, 162, 164–68; International Shakuhachi Festival,

161; International Shakuhachi Society, 176n14; Liam on, 164–66; misunderstandings and, 174; national living treasure rank and, 159; non-Japanese practitioners, 171, 177n21; outside Japan, 161–62, 176n14; Pamela on, 168–69; popular culture and, 172–73; popularity factors, 162; as primitive, 177n18; spiritual and secular orientations, 158–61; spirituality of, 162–64, 176n15; *taiko* and, 171, 177n20; teachers of, 161–62, 176n12; topics addressed, 157, 158
shakuhachi schools. *See kinko ryū*; *myoan ryū*; *tozan ryū*
The Shallows (Carr), 115
Sharifi, Omaid, 61
Sharq Taronalari music festival: conclusions about, 318–19; diversity and, xiv; International Musicology Conference within, 84–85; Karimov on, 89; management of, 89–91; objectives of, 83, 84; organization of, 83–84; overview of, 77; Registan Square and, *82*, 82–83; Samarkand and, 81–83, *82*
Al Sheikh al rais. *See* Ibn Sina
Shelemay, Kay Kaufmann, 211
Shibabaw, Ejigayehu, 217
Shifa (Ibn Sina), 101
Shilan, Dawit, 221
Shimura, Satoshi, 176n17
Shirazi, Hafez, 107
"Shouliede Gege Huilaile," 306, 310n21
shruti (hearing), 277–78
Sibelius Academy, Finland, xi
Silk Road, 80–82, 89
Simon, Abbey, 111
Simon, Paul, 240–41, 244
Simone, Nina, 233, 235
singing with gestures. *See Ca Ra Bộ*
El Sistema orchestra, 52, 70n10
The Six Tones: conclusions about, 316; injustice and, 182; Musical Transformations project and, 187–88; overview about, 199n4; transculturation through collaboration, 189–97
Smith, Laurajane, 26
smriti (recollection), 278
Snyder, Christina A., 292n19
Society for Ethnomusicology (SEM), xii, xiii, 9–10
soft law, international: appropriation versus approbation debate, 36; conclusions, 36–39, 321; copyright and, 35–36; cultural imports and, 34–35; cultural policies and, 33–36; cultural rights and, 24–26; evolution for sustainability and, 37–38; IMC and, 32–33; intangible heritage and, 35; interpretations of, 38; Koskenniemi and, 25–26; legal traditions compromise and, 36–37; Mulcahy and, 21–22; music rights and, 23–24, 32–33, 36–38; participatory rights and, 38; topics addressed, 13, 21–23; tradition theory and, 37; understanding, 24–26
soft power: "Chennai Soft Power 30" project, 231; concept implications, 146–47; movies as, 24–25; nation branding and, 4–17; Nigeria using, 256, 269nn1–2; Nollywood, 269n1; Nye and, 5, 230; South Africa using, 256; unbalanced incentives and, 148
soft war: Blout and, 126–28; Iran and, 126–32; musical implementations of, 128–32; Permanent Bureau for Soft War, 128; rhetoric surrounding, 126–28; topics addressed, 14, 119–20
solo pieces, 18th century. *See honkyoku*
South Africa: activists, overview of, 229–30; cultural diversity in, 259–61; linguistics and, 259–60; soft power used by, 256; topics addressed, 15. *See also* apartheid; Clegg, Johnny; Katz, Sharon; Makeba, Miriam;

Masekela, Hugh; Soweto Gospel Choir
Soviet Union (USSR), 200n6
"Soweto Blues," 240
Soweto Gospel Choir: Australian tour, 261; as case study, 255; conclusions, 267–68; dance and, 265–66; garments and, 263, 264, 318; Lagos City Chorale collaborations with, 262; linguistic diversity and, 261–62
Soweto Uprising, 1976, 238–40, *239*
Spangler, Matthew, 182–83
Sperber, Dan, 116
spiritual listening or concert. *See Sama*
Sreberny, Annabelle, 126
Srivastava, Ritviz, 286
"Stimela," 238, 251n6
stimulated recall: Musical Transformations project and, 181, 199n3; as qualitative research method, 199n3; rationale for using, 201n17
Stopping the Music, 231
Sufism: conclusions, 114–16; condemnation of, 103; European thinkers embracing, 97; inspiration and revelation, 113–14; interpretation and hermeneutics, 111–13; musical and mystical experience and, 109–10; music prohibition and, 109; music writings of, 98; origins of, 102; philosophy, 102–3; *Sama* and, 103–5; themes related to, 96; topics addressed, 14; Western world influenced by, 105–8; whirling dervishes and, 104
Sutton, Charles, 211, 223n10
Syria, xii
Syrian National Orchestra, 95

Tad'if (doubling), 101
Tafari, Ras. *See* Selassie, Haile
taiko (rhythm instrument ensemble), 157, 171, 177n20

Tài Tử music: Colonial Expo, Marseille, and, 185; Paris exposition and, 184–85. *See also Đờn Ca Tài Tử; Nhạc Tài Tử*
Taliban, 52, 57, 61, 69n4, 71n22, 318
talking drum. *See gangan*
Tan, Shzr Ee, 10
tarkib (compound), 101
Taruskin, Richard, 112
Tasman, Abel, 3
Tataloo, Amir, 131
Tatsumi Manjiro, 173
Ta'wil (hermeneutic), 112, 113
Taylor, Keith Weller, 184
Taylor, Philip, 184, 188
Taylor, Timothy, 177n19
technology: ANIM using, 54–55; heritage documentation and, 37–38
Teresa of Avila (Saint), 110
terrorism, at Gedächtniskirche, 49
Te Wananga O Aotearoa, New Zealand (Maori college), x
Thailand, xi
Thakur, Maithili, 287
theater: *Hager Feqer Tiyater*, 213–14, 218; Haile Selassie I Theatre Orchestra, 214; *Hát Bội*, 185, 200n12; as propaganda in Ethiopia, 212–13
Theory and Method in Historical Ethnomusicology (McCollum and Hebert), xii–xiii
Third World Child, 244
Tholuck, August, 97
A Thousand Splendid Suns (Hosseini), 58
Tigray, Ethiopia, xiv
Tojibayev, Mahmud, 79–80
Tomorrow, 240
Tonga youth band, x–xi
tozan ryū (shakuhachi school), 159, *160*, 161
Trade-Related Aspects of Intellectual Property Rights (TRIPS), 304
traditional Japanese music. *See hogaku*

transculturation: cultural diplomacy and, 181–84; hybridization and, 200n8; through intercultural collaboration, 189–97; Kartomi on, 183; between tradition and modernity, 184–87; transmission and, 200n6
The Transforming Power of Cultural Rights (Porsdam), 22
transmission, 200n6
treaties, international: Beijing Treaty on Audiovisual Performances, 303, *303*, 309n15; Berne Convention, 302, 303, *303*; China and, 300–304, *303*; cultural treaties, 301; ICH, 302; Paris Act, 302; UNESCO, 301–2; WIPO-administered, *303*
TRIPS. See Trade-Related Aspects of Intellectual Property Rights
Trump, Donald, 124–25, 133n1, 290
Trumpet Africaine, 236
Tulsidas, Goswami, 292n20
Turkey, xiii
Twelve Muqam, 297
two-stringed fiddles. See *đàn gáo* and *đàn cò*
typology, of music diplomacy contexts: activism, individual, 320; ensembles and artists, 316–18; governance forms, 319–20; intercultural music institutions, 318–19

Underhill, Evelyn, 110
UNESCO. See United Nations Educational, Scientific and Cultural Organization
UN Human Rights Council, 26–27
United Nations Educational, Scientific and Cultural Organization (UNESCO), 77; ICH and, 302; treaties, 301–2; Uzbekistan recognition and, 80–81
UN special rapporteur: cultural rights and, 26–30; initiatives of, 28–30; mandate of, 27; Shaheed, 26–27

United States (US): Afghanistan and, 66–68, 71n23; CI and, 147; civil rights movement in, 234; Cold War and, 200n6; geopolitical agendas and, 66–68; Katz, Sharon, in, 248, 249; Makeba in, 232–35; military expenditures in Afghanistan, 67, 71n23; school music militarized in, 67; TRIPS and, 304
Universal Men, 243
University of Colorado, Denver, x
Urbain, Olivier, 10
US. See United States
Uses of Heritage (Smith), 26
USSR. See Soviet Union
Uzbekistan: conclusions about, 319–20; music-based culture, since independence, 78–80; renaissances of, 83, 91n6; Samarkand in, 81–83, *82*; scholars and, 79, 91n4; Silk Road and, 80–82, 89; topics addressed, 13; traditions from, 81; UNESCO recognition, 80–81. See also Maqam-based music; Sharq Taronalari music festival

van Leeuwen, Theo, 62–63
Vasudhaiva Kutumbakam (world is one family), 289
Vaziri, Ali Naqi, 121
Vedic classical music. See ragas
Vietnam, xi; *Antigone Việt Nam*, 182; Mekong Delta, 184, 187; Sài Gòn, 185, 200n13; topics addressed, 15
violin, 187–88
Vọng Cổ: *Cải Lương* and, 186; discussion, 197–98; *Đờn Ca Tài Tử* and, 186, 201n15; emergence of, 186; guitar and, 186–87; hybridization and, 181, 184, 198n2; insider/outsider perspectives and, 181, 198n2; Linh interview, 187–88; methodology surrounding, 181; Musical Transformations project and, 187–88; stimulated recall and, 181, 199n3;

topics addressed, 15; transculturation between tradition and modernity, 184–87; transculturation through collaboration, 189–97

Wanda, Nonhlanhla, 247
Wang, Haicheng, 307
Wang, Luobin, 306–7
Watkins, Polly, 70n9
WCT. *See* WIPO Copyright Treaty
WEF. *See* World Economic Forum
Weldu, Abraha, xiv
West-Eastern Divan (Goethe), 107
"We the Children of India," 283
Wheeler, David, 162
When Voices Meet, 247, 249
whirling dervishes, 104
white man's burden, 289
White Zulu. *See* Clegg, Johnny
Whitlock, Gillian, 58
Williams, Raymond, 119
WIPO. *See* World Intellectual Property Organization
WIPO Copyright Treaty (WCT), *303*
WIPO Performances and Phonograms Treaty (WPPT), *303*
women: Afghanistan and, 52, 55, 58, 61, 64, 65, 71n22; attacks on, 65, 71n22; Free Women Writers and, 61; gender equality/rights and, 52, 55, 64. *See also* Zohra Orchestra
World Economic Forum (WEF), 65
World Heritage Convention, 1972, 301–2
World Heritage Protection Rules, Sichuan Province, 302
World Intellectual Property Organization (WIPO), 287–88, 302–3, *303*
world is one family. *See Vasudhaiva Kutumbakam*
World Trade Organization (WTO), 304
WPPT. *See* WIPO Performances and Phonograms Treaty
WTO. *See* World Trade Organization

"Wusuli Chuange," 306, 310n22

"Xiang Qinglang," 306, 310n21

Yafi, Abdul Karim: culture versus politics and, 94–95; at Damascus University, 93; education of, 93–94; as influential intellectual, 95
Yafi, Chaden, xii
al Yafi, Omar, 93
Yakima Indian Reservation, ix
Yamaguchi Goro, 161
Yamaji Miho, 173
Yehager Fikir Mahber (Ethiopian Patriotic Association), 213
Yoga, 289–90
Yohannés, Iyoýel, 213
Yohannes, Welde Giorgis Welde, 213
Yokoyama, Katsuya, 161
Yousafzai, Malala, 108
Youssefzadeh, Ameneh, 122
Yue Ji (Book of Music), 298
Yulchieva, Munojat, 79

Zhang, Yimou, 307
Zohra Orchestra: as all-female ensemble, 50–51; ArtLords and, 55, *56*, 70n16; conclusions about, 316–17, 318; coproduction of meaning and, 64–65; female agency and, 59–60; frame of references shifted by, 60; Gedächtniskirche and, 49; gender equality/women rights and, 52, 55, 64; local impact of, 65; multimodal communicative acts of, 63; nationalism and, 55; participation model related to, 62–63, 64; Persian goddess of music and, 52, 70n8; positivity promoted by, 55, 60–65; sonic experience created by, 63; stereotypes and, 55–56; touring of, 62, 70n19; Western media and, 58–59; Western music and, 63–64

About the Editors and Contributors

EDITORS

David G. Hebert, PhD, is professor of music at Western Norway University of Applied Sciences (Bergen). He is also manager of the Nordic Network for Music Education, a Nordplus multinational state-funded organization that coordinates Masterclasses and exchange of teachers and students across eight northern European nations. Additionally, he is Professor II (visiting professor) in Sweden with the Malmo Academy of Music, Lund University, and honorary professor in China with the Education University of Hong Kong. He is a widely published and cited researcher (h-index: 17), whose background features employment with universities on five continents. Since accepting the position in Norway, he has authored (or edited) several books. He serves on several editorial boards and has contributed articles to thirty-five different professional journals. Reviews of his books are published in fifteen scholarly journals in the fields of musicology, education, and Asian studies, and he authors a professional blog. He has taught courses on cultural heritage policy for international PhD students at Bergen Summer Research School and for law students at China's leading law school, CUPL-Beijing.

Jonathan McCollum, PhD, is professor of music at Washington College in Chestertown, Maryland, and founding chair of the Historical Ethnomusicology Section of the Society for Ethnomusicology. He is known for his widely published contributions to the historiography of global music and music traditions in Armenia and Japan. McCollum is the author of *Armenian Music: A Comprehensive Bibliography and Discography*. His most recent book, *Theory and Method in Historical Ethnomusicology* (with David G. Hebert) was published in 2014. He is co-editor of the Lexington series Historical

Ethnomusicology: Deep Soundings, has contributed to many other edited volumes and journals, and has contributed multiple entries to the *Bloomsbury Encyclopedia of Popular Music*, the *Sage International Encyclopedia of Music and Culture*, and the *New Grove Dictionary of Musical Instruments*. He has also worked as a consultant for the Armenian Library and Museum of America, the Smithsonian Institution, and Folkways Alive! of the Canadian Centre for Ethnomusicology at the University of Alberta. He holds a Shihan 師範 (master's) license in shakuhachi performance.

CONTRIBUTORS

Rhoda Abiolu is a postdoctoral fellow with the Durban University of Technology and holds a PhD from the University of KwaZulu-Natal. Her research interests are in media and cultural studies, with emphasis on media representations, ethnomusicology, participatory culture, and political economy. She was a participant in Bergen Summer Research School.

Lauren Braithwaite is a PhD candidate in music at Oxford University. She has lived and worked in Afghanistan in recent years, where she researched music education in the "post-Taliban" era. Her study focuses on Zohra, Afghanistan's first all-female orchestra.

Karan Choudhary holds a PhD from National Law University Delhi, India and Université Paris Nanterre, France. Presently, he is a judge in Delhi, India. He was recipient of an Erasmus Scholarship from the European Union. His research interests include culture, law, Indigenous rights, and policy designs, with publications in *Interactions between Culture and Law in India and Europe*, and *Language, Law and Community*.

Marja Heimonen, DMus, docent in music education, is a university lecturer at the University of the Arts Helsinki. She also has a master-level law degree from the University of Helsinki. In addition to her doctoral dissertation on music education and law, she has published chapters in books and anthologies, and articles in several different scholarly journals. She is the managing editor of the *Finnish Journal of Music Education*.

Marianne Løkke Jakobsen is director of international affairs with the Royal Danish Academy of Music, Copenhagen, where she also has served as founding director of the Music Confucius Institute. She has led several projects that advance music collaborations between China and Europe.

Juqian Li, PhD, is the Qian Duan-sheng chair professor of international law with China University of Political Science and Law, Beijing, where he has directed the Public International Law Research Institute. He has authored fifteen books and twenty articles on international law and international economic law, including in *Introduction of Space Law*, *WTO Dispute Settlement Mechanism*, *International Law*, and *International Law Commentary*.

Elnora Mamadjanova, PhD, is a professor in the Department of Music History and Criticism with the State Conservatory of Uzbekistan, Tashkent. She has coordinated several international musicology symposia affiliated with international music festivals in Uzbekistan. Her publications include the book *Traditional Music of the Uzbeks*.

Koji Matsunobu is associate head of the Department of Cultural and Creative Arts at the Education University of Hong Kong. An accomplished player of the Japanese shakuhachi flute, he holds PhD degrees from both Tokyo Gakugei University and the University of Illinois and is widely published on such topics as music education, spirituality, mindfulness, Indigenous knowledge, and creativity.

Nasim Niknafs, PhD, is an associate professor of music education at the Faculty of Music, University of Toronto. Nasim's research concerning social justice, activism, and politics of contemporary music education is widely published. Concluding her longitudinal research on the music education of rock musicians in Iran, Nasim has recently begun research on migratory and diasporic practices in music education. Nasim holds degrees from Northwestern University, New York University, Kingston University, London, and University of Art, Tehran.

Thanh Thủy Nguyễn, PhD, is a leading master performer of the Vietnamese traditional instrument *dan tranh* who recently completed a PhD at the Malmo Academy Music, Lund University, Sweden, and is now a Swedish Research Council funded postdoctoral researcher at Western Norway University of Applied Sciences.

Stefan Östersjö, PhD, a professional guitarist and widely published pioneer of intercultural studies in the field of artistic research, is now a full professor and coordinator of doctoral studies in music at Lulea University of Technology, Sweden.

Jan Magne Steinhovden is a lecturer at NLA University College and a PhD candidate with the University of Bergen, Norway. He spent much of his childhood in Ethiopia and holds a master of world music studies from the University of Sheffield. His dissertation concerns music and identity among Ethiopian and Eritrean refugees in Norway.

Abraha Weldu holds a PhD in history and cultural studies from Mekelle University, Ethiopia, where he currently works as lecturer. His doctoral dissertation is an intellectual biography of one of the most prominent diplomats and cultural attachés of twentieth-century Ethiopia. For more than seven years he has taught courses in history and heritage studies at Bule Hora University. He was also a participant in the Bergen Summer Research School.

Chaden Yafi is a professionally trained pianist and music educator with a doctorate in music from Boston University. Born in Syria, she has published on musical aesthetics and held a full-time position as a recitalist with the National Opera House in Damascus before moving to the United States. She now teaches many piano students in Houston, Texas.

Ambigay Yudkoff holds a PhD in musicology from the University of South Africa. She has served as guest conductor of the Sai Movement's youth choir of Isipingo in South Africa and the Battenkill Chorale of Vermont in the United States, each boasting notable performances for Nelson Mandela. Her monograph on Sharon Katz was volume 1 of the Deep Soundings series, *Activism through Music during the Apartheid Era and Beyond: When Voices Meet*.

www.ingramcontent.com/pod-product-compliance
Lightning Source LLC
Chambersburg PA
CBHW021339300426
44114CB00012B/1004